REDEEMING THE BROKEN BODY

THEOPOLITICAL VISIONS

SERIES EDITORS:

Thomas Heilke
D. Stephen Long
and C. C. Pecknold

Theopolitical Visions seeks to open up new vistas on public life, hosting fresh conversations between theology and political theory. This series assembles writers who wish to revive theopolitical imagination for the sake of our common good.

Theopolitical Visions hopes to re-source modern imaginations with those ancient traditions in which political theorists were often also theologians. Whether it was Jeremiah's prophetic vision of exiles "seeking the peace of the city," Plato's illuminations on piety and the civic virtues in the Republic, St. Paul's call to "a common life worthy of the Gospel," St. Augustine's beatific vision of the City of God, or the gothic heights of medieval political theology, much of Western thought has found it necessary to think theologically about politics, and to think politically about theology. This series is founded in the hope that the renewal of such mutual illumination might make a genuine contribution to the peace of our cities.

PUBLISHED VOLUMES:

Stanley Hauerwas and Romand Coles
Christianity, Democracy, and the Radical Ordinary: Conversations Between a Radical Democrat and a Christian

Bryan C. Hollon
Everything Is Sacred: Spiritual Exegesis in the Political Theology of Henri de Lubac

Nathan R. Kerr
Christ, History and Apocalyptic: The Politics of Christian Mission

Redeeming the
BROKEN BODY

Church and State

after Disaster

GABRIEL A. SANTOS

CASCADE *Books* • Eugene, Oregon

REDEEMING THE BROKEN BODY
Church and State after Disaster

Theopolitical Visions 2

Cascade Books
A Division of Wipf and Stock Publishers
199 W. 8th Ave., Suite 3
Eugene, OR 97401

www.wipfandstock.com

ISBN 13: 978-1-55635-725-1

Cataloging-in-Publication data:

Santos, Gabriel A.

Redeeming the broken body : church and state after disaster / Gabriel A. Santos.

xxiv + 302 p. ; 23 cm. —Includes bibliographical references.

Theopolitical Visions 2

ISBN 13: 978-1-55635-725-1

1. Church and state. 2. Oklahoma City Federal Building Bombing, Oklahoma City, Okla., 1995. 3. September 11 Terrorist Attacks, 2001. 4. Hurricane Katrina, 2005. 5. Terrorism—Religious aspects—Christianity. I. Title. II. Series.

BR115. W6 S25 2009

For Betsy

. . . you are beautiful, my beloved,

truly lovely.

Song of Solomon 1:16

Our government makes no sense unless it is founded in a deeply felt religious faith—and I don't care what it is.

Dwight D. Eisenhower

Contents

List of Figures

Acknowledgements

This book would not have been possible without the unceasing support of many friends, both in the academy and without, and many family members. My mother, Arnalda Capiato, and my father, Vidal Santos, provided the foundation for my life as a learner—they taught me to love the process of discovery. I would like to extend many thanks to each member of the dissertation committee that oversaw the initial version of this work: Benigno Aguirre served as both a wonderful advisor on all matters, academic and otherwise, and as a motivator when progress was slow. I would also like to extend my deepest gratitude to Gerald Turkel and Russell Dynes for their poignant comments and input on very important topics relating to the research process and the implications of what was being uncovered. Bill Cavanaugh devoted much time over the course of about three years, through long-distance phone calls and e-mail messages, assisting me through many difficulties and initiating me into (at the time) the awkward attempts at gleaning theological insight from sociological material. I also owe many thanks to Anne Bowler for her adept instruction in all things "theoretical."

I am deeply indebted to the editors of the Theopolitical Visions series, Chad Pecknold, Steve Long, and Thomas Heilke, for showing steadfast support for this project. I am especially, immensely, grateful for Chad's desire to initiate the process of bringing this project to publication and providing seemingly endless words of encouragement and advice throughout. Many thanks to Steve Fowl for telling Chad about my research—I never would have thought that a brief talk in the salad line at the Ekklesia Project annual gathering would have had such impact.

I am also thoroughly indebted to Joseph Trainor, William Donner, Lauren Barsky, and Brian Monahan of the University of Delaware for the friendship, support, motivation, and intellectual stimulation they provided during my time at the University of Delaware. Our experiences designing and conducting research represent some of my most cherished memories as a student of sociology.

The faculty of sociology at Lynchburg College provided perpetual support during my first few years as a faculty member. Kim McCabe, Chip Walton, and Charles Shull have always made sure that my confidence and determination were at an optimal level; Professor Shull showed a tireless interest in my research and furnished many helpful perspectives on the work. I owe him and Dr. Walton a great deal in terms of personal and academic support during trying times. The fieldwork for this research was almost entirely funded by a grant from the Lynchburg College Faculty Development Fund. Many thanks are due to the Faculty Development Committee of the college for approving trips to Oklahoma City and New York City in order to carry out qualitative interviews.

I cannot list all of the members of two congregations that offered their bodies and souls to me while I completed my graduate education at the University of Delaware. To each member of the Northern Delaware Church of Christ and of Blue Ridge Church of Christ: this work belongs to you. I offer the most sincere appreciation for your love and strength. I would like to specifically express gratitude for the support my wife and I received from Mark and Elena Rushing, Mike and Terrie Fontenot, Forest and Amanda Versele, Paul and Jennifer Hutchins, Phil and Ayhanna Booker, and Corey and Angela Stuck.

It is my honor to dedicate this book to my wife, Betsy, without whom it would not have been possible to complete it. Her incessant and amazing encouragement, friendship, and love provided all I needed to forge ahead with the work and learn much about myself in the process. I put her through much more anxiety and confusion than she ever deserved. She is the crown of my life. My three terrific daughters, Isabella, Lilianna, and Cecilia, are the gems that stand at her sides. I am forever mesmerized in the light of their vibrant smiles and jubilant hearts—things that I cannot muster for myself. It is my greatest aspiration that this work honors and upholds their sacrifices on my behalf—and that of God, the primary character whom many human actors in this research project seemed to want to know, manipulate, honor, summon, construct, and explain. Perhaps through this work we may learn in some small measure how to listen and understand him, or approach him, more closely and humbly.

Gabriel A. Santos
June 21, 2008

Abbreviations

ARIS	American Religious Identification Survey
EOC	emergency-operations command
FEMA	Federal Emergency Management Agency
NVOAD	National Voluntary Organizations Active in Disaster
NYSE	New York Stock Exchange
ODCEM	Oklahoma Department of Civil and Emergency Management

Introduction

This book is primarily concerned with ecclesiological reflections on the cultural politics of disaster. In taking up the question of cultural politics, I share Graham Ward's concern with the importance of power relations positioned within the broader production of public accounts of truth, or of what is believable[1] and credible with regard to human nature and human destiny after disaster. More specifically, this study is an extended exercise in descriptive theology with a concern for political and social organization after disasters. Viewed from the perspective of the ecclesial body, it is inextricably linked with considerations of the identity and self-understanding of the congregation in relation to other social bodies, including other states and nations, in a world that is both passing away and invaded by divine newness. For the study at hand, I take disasters to be occasions of cultural and material trauma whereby continued life in landed community cannot be restored without the implementation of resources often considered to be external to the community that has suffered harm. That which is "external" to the threatened community is often a matter of the typical and sufficient use of public resources or works: in other words, if the technology and persons that usually serve the harmed community cannot handle the problem without using the resources internal or sufficient to another community, then a disaster is likely at hand. There is also an important imaginative and communal component to disasters. This understanding applies equally to disasters that stem from the deliberations and actions of humans against other humans (e.g., terrorism) and to those that result from severe weather patterns and natural hazards. Disasters signal the massive destabilization

1. Ward, *Cultural Transformation*, 8, 12.

or destruction of those material bodies that most crucially mediate the narratives of collective existence. When federal administrative buildings, skyscrapers housing global commercial firms, and homes are torn asunder or flooded, the stable "lifeworld" as it has been imagined and storied is severely undermined. It becomes clear in disaster that the making and remaking of the intertwined material and symbolic world and its narratives is something collectively achieved.

It is into an experience of this sort of collective trauma or marginal occasion that signals the entrance of the ecclesial body, itself a body that bears the marks of death among the broken bodies of the world, individual and corporate. The ecclesial body as both a physical and spiritual totality marks the redemption of concrete human beings and the fruit of their engagement among themselves and the world. This is what, as a whole, challenges the fall of *shalom*. The ecclesial body, composed of persons who at once mutually inhabit one another and make individual decisions of commitment and service, confronts the curse that characterizes all human relations and human *poiesis*, or human making. It accomplishes this through participation in the Trinitarian life of God. This is only possible from within the recognition that in living between curse and promise, unredeemed humans must reject the idea that they can be "like God" rather than be "in the image of God."[2] Specifically, my construal of disaster aims at emphasizing God's intentions for creation as the divine expression of abundantly and freely given love that constitutes life. Indeed, divine love thus understood actually composes others and hence the interrelationship between those that are from, but *other* than, God. These others include all manner of creatures and objects in creation: rocks, plants, rivers, air, and soil. The communal element is meant to emphasize a relational ontology of "creaturehood." It is the political ground upon which human and ecological relationships are based and maintained in the occasion of ecclesial response to disaster.

In a span of ten years, local, regional, and national governmental agencies and landed communities were forced to encounter a disheartening combination of disasters: the bombing of the Murrah Federal

2. See Bonhoeffer, *Creation and Fall/Temptation*. Bonhoeffer distinguishes between human beings *secut Deus* (like God) and human beings *imago Dei* (in the image of God). The former represents postlapsarian humanity, which, absent the intervention and acceptance of grace, must live out of its own resources and its own determinations of good and evil.

Building in Oklahoma City at the hands of American citizens, the mass-casualty assault in New York City involving extremist hijackers, and the mass flooding of New Orleans due to the combined effects of Hurricane Katrina and poor levee construction, among other things. The relationship between two institutions (understood as embodiments of differing disciplined imaginings of space and time), the church and the state, assumes a crucial position in these (and similar) events. It is more than unsettling that an adequate sociological and theological understanding of this relationship, especially at a concrete, individual-case level, has received little treatment. Deeper attention is necessary because the reverberations of deadly collective trauma cross many social boundaries, directly piercing the notion of solidarity. Most significantly, events of this sort ask how the institutional responses define the individual and the social body per se, as well as the individual's identity in the social body. As Mary Douglas posits in plain terms in *How Institutions Think*, "institutions confer identity," and "institutions make life-and-death decisions." It is vital, therefore, to develop some rigorous sociological approach that engages the institutions most familiar with the high-stakes cultural constitution of social bodies: local churches and various levels of governmental agency at the local level. In what follows, I briefly present the impetus for this study (hence, its main interests, which are to be found at the nexus of theology, disasters, and politics). This discussion then leads to an overview of the layout of the book.

This project was prompted by a desire to make sense of some observations, sporadically made over a period of three years, about politics, religion, and American response to disaster. These observations demanded reconciliation with many views concerning secularization (including the division of religion and politics), especially as presented first by Max Weber and then by others in the second half of the twentieth century and beyond. These scholars include Harvey Cox, Bryan Wilson, Jürgen Habermas, Richard Fenn, and many others. Here is a sample of some such observations:

- About two weeks after the September 11 attacks in New York City, Pope John Paul II led a worship service in Russian at a site in Kazakhstan. A prayer of peace and admonitions to the crowd punctuated the ceremony; Pope John Paul II declared: "work together to build a world without violence." The pope's pacifist prayer was said in

English, which, one reporter claimed, was done in order to reach a universal audience. This reporter also mentions that people went to see the "81-year-old spiritual globe-trotter," not to pray. In addition, the pope admonishes those present: "I urge you to work toward a more united world." However, near the end of that very ceremony, the president of Kazakhstan mentioned that the country was willing to join a "U.S. led alliance" in the fight against terrorism.

- A multitude of World Trade Center commemorative services employed the notion of peace and unity, emphasizing interfaith and interracial silent group prayer. Some churches, moreover, used red, white, and blue candles in lieu of the normal white altar candles. In one commemorative church service, an emergency service worker and military officer were asked to share some thoughts about the tragedy and then to dedicate a flag that was flown at a U.S. military base in Afghanistan devoted to combat missions of Operation Enduring Freedom (formerly Operation Infinite Justice).

- Following the Columbine High School shooting tragedy, a religious revival of sorts sprang up (as happens after many disasters) in Littleton and the surrounding area in Colorado, eventually catching on with many other Christian groups throughout the nation. When the school decided to memorialize the event by allowing the families of victims to post a small tile on a school wall containing a personalized, artistic or stylized message, several limitations were established. These limitations surrounded the use of religious expressions, as well as vulgar or violent expressions. The parameters were vehemently challenged, and eventually the tenth Federal Circuit Court of Appeals upheld the restrictions, essentially stating that "first, the tiles might serve as a reminder of the shooting, and second, their religious content might create 'divisiveness and disruption at school.'"[3] Similarly, in April 2001, the ninth Circuit Court of Appeals claimed that relational assertions such as "accept God's love," "God seeks a personal relationship," and the sectarian statement "Jesus wants to be our best friend," were elements of a "religious sermon" and could not be included within a high school covaledictorian's graduation speech.

---

3. *Donald F. Fleming, et al. v. Jefferson City School District.* No. 01-1512 (10th Cir. 2002).

- In September 2004, a combined conference and training session titled "Calling All Angels" was held in Albuquerque, New Mexico, sponsored by the National Institute for Urban Search and Rescue. Besides the bold sacralization of the task of first responders, the official poster image of the event featured typical first responders from government agencies (e.g., firefighters, paramedics, police officers, rescue specialists, and administrators) running out from the center of a dazzling, white light.

- Shortly after the tragedy of the space shuttle Columbia on February 1, 2003, government officials from the United States, Canada, and Europe declared that the deceased astronauts were "true American heroes," and "heroes" of their nations and "humanity," while an ABC network logo depicted their shuttle heading towards the heavens with a halo revolving around the spacecraft's nose.[4]

Note the particular instances in which a confessional or theological agenda is found in seeming apposition to political affirmations, while in others, political and theological affirmations are deliberately separated from each other. These disparate observations, which range from the legal sphere to international politics, did share at least one key characteristic: to be precise, they shared the patent appeals to theological symbols or narrative constructions that carry distinct and compelling ethical, epistemological, and even ontological assumptions.

This has not been lost to academics from various disciplines. In the past fifteen years, a seemingly ever-growing legion of scholars has attempted to collect and expound upon the evidence that speaks of the deprivatization of religion or the resurgence of publicly embraced religious affiliation and activity. José Casanova, Peter Berger, and Talal Asad have delivered perhaps the most influential studies in this regard. In light of the persistent confusions and uncertainties surrounding the actual nature of secularization and to what extent secularization has been curbed or does not exist, it is perhaps best to come to terms with just this condition: it is downright confusing.

From the perspective of sociology in general and disaster studies in particular, this condition is compelling for two reasons. First, these observations demand some sustained reflection in light of the seeming

---

4. See "Lost: Space Shuttle Columbia." The logo with the haloed shuttle appeared on *Nightline* from ABC News on February 1, 2003.

intractability of the conventional binaries, sometimes viewed as antitheses, of "faith and politics," "secular and sacred," and "church and state." Second, these and similar phenomena must deeply affect collective identity formation after a disaster—but how?

The chief aim of this project is to construct and analyze the elements consisting in the political imaginary of disasters pertaining to three cases of disaster. The "political imaginary" refers to the condition from which foundational commitments or basic understandings of such things as "rationality," "government," "unity," and "human beings" emanate and are (often precariously) combined within a supposedly accepted and hoped-for political ordering. Specifically, this study inquires about the social processes and cultural products that obtained within the relationship between congregations, the agents (and agencies) of the state, and local communities after two instances of violent attack (the bombing of the Alfred P. Murrah Building in Oklahoma City and the attack on World Trade Center on September 11, 2001) and, for comparative purposes, Hurricane Katrina. A study of this sort tackles the generation of idealizations, assumptions, and theological legitimacy (among other things) at the cultural intersection of church and nation-state (or, "theology and the secular") as these are embodied in the concrete social relationships and practices following the collective trauma in question. This study enables a critical comparison between the symbolic products that are created and disseminated through mass communications (primarily newspapers) and even retail consumer outlets, on the one hand, and the social practices and struggles that undergird such productions, on the other hand. Such social struggles encompass the spaces in and through which the proper ordering of relations takes place.

This research is thus important for various reasons. It tackles many provocative and admittedly popular questions about "church-and-state" matters, but through the prism of disaster, and more important, through a description of how actual persons and collectivities deal with such a binary. An analysis of this sort is necessary because if massive innovation and change are potential consequences of disruptive events, which were manifest in the case of the Civil War, the Great Depression, and World War II, then it can safely be assumed that the terrorist attacks of the past decade have introduced massive changes into many collectivities.[5]

---

5. See Neal, *National Trauma and Collective Memory*. Neal carries out case studies of nine instances of "national trauma" from a social-psychological perspective.

    The importance of this sort of approach also lies in its ability to address various lacunae in the theology and sociology of disaster literature surrounding the nature of the local church-and-state relations after disasters. The particular gap in need of filling pertains to the actual practices and narrative applications in which the church personnel, church members, and statist officials engage and, more important, to the cultural production—production incorporating poetics (the means of creative activity) and *poiesis* (the actual objects made)—stemming from their relationship. This relationship between agents of varying social and political locations or statuses challenges the presumed, conventional construal of the separation of "faith" from "politics." The cultural production arising from the mutual responses of clergy, citizens, and political officials defines a particular, preferable collective identity after a disaster, and does so by means of an account of the situation that joins theology and politics. In so joining theology and politics, this emergent collective identity, in the eyes of a state-making agenda that is wed to global corporate interests, legitimates disaster response and recovery from a theological standpoint. This has been virtually disregarded from most sociological treatments of disaster response (and preparedness), which have typically been directed toward generating accounts of the rational, political, and economic justifications for disaster response.

    This endeavor is thus centered on three main sociological questions, from which theological reflections pertaining to ecclesial response are developed: (1) After disasters, how did church personnel deal with the supposed boundary between theologically rooted discourse, convictions, and practices, on the one hand, and seemingly autonomous, secular political interests and practices? The structure and struggle linked to the relations between clergy and state officials, including what assumptions about human nature, violence, and politics were chosen, discussed, and ignored, are the crucial topics under study. (2) How did the hybrid cultural objects stemming from "church-and-state" poetics affect the social reorientation of the community following violent attack? Finally, (3), what picture could be drawn, taking account of the answers to questions (1) and (2), of the contested political imaginary following a disaster in question? Put differently, beyond what local churches and state agencies enacted about human nature and future harmony after the collective trauma—no doubt as supposedly distinct and exclusive sites of political action—how did the churches absorb, negotiate, or reject the discourse and practices of the state, and vice versa?

All the relevant data for this study are qualitative and were generated through a host of methods, including one-on-one interviews, content analyses of newspaper articles, speeches, video footage, and focus groups with local residents. The first question is primarily explored by means of content analyses, employing the constant comparative method, of newspapers, memorial ceremony footage, and focus groups. The second question, concerning the nature of sociocultural relations between clergy and government officials, is explored by means of responses to questions in an interview instrument.[6] The themes that were translated into the questions that compose the interview instrument draw on the notion of the political imaginary as a basis for exploring the following: theologically driven praxis and role performance during the disaster response and recovery period, interpretation of violence and its consequences, symbolic dedifferentiation (e.g., using "national" colors or icons inside church buildings), and evaluation of governmental leadership in the postdisaster period. These social elements, which are interrelated in several ways, are all integral components of the ecclesial and theological response to disasters.

Finally, this study says much about the ambiguity that attends to defining "religion." It uses this ambiguity as a theoretical point of departure. What the analysis shows of the recovery periods after the disasters under consideration is that the actual defining of certain activities as "religious" or "sacred" served to reconstitute the world of space and time in a manner that fit some perhaps emergent criteria of communality and social organization. To claim, as President Clinton did after the Oklahoma City bombing, that "this sin against humanity will not go unpunished" was

6. Ministers, church employees, state officials, and all manner of local residents (whether church members or not) were considered potential interviewees to the degree that they met the aim of maximizing the range of experiences, collective or political responsibilities, class status, and denominational involvement during the disaster response and recovery phases. I also hoped to select persons with varying degrees of involvement in different aspects of postdisaster relief services. Hence, I did not employ a random sampling method, so that the probability of selecting a certain type of respondent was known in advance. Alternatively, I endeavored to gather a purposive, theoretical sample. As it turns out, each "case study" contains a set of respondents that assumes everything from persons with little-to-no involvement in church life to active church members with no connection to church leadership or government relief agencies, to disaster-response executives in both ecclesial and statist contexts.

to inject the language of theology into the public sphere in a manner that is not typical—that is, it challenged our usual "secular," liberalist and rational/legal mode of speaking in public matters. In such instances, the state seemed to "unveil" an inclination to theological grammar and modes of thought that betrays some inconsistency with many other statist forms of discourse. In these cases of disaster response and recovery, it was not simply a matter of rights, failed diplomatic maneuvers, or lack of legislation, but of a cosmological contest or eternal conflict. At the level of social interaction and experience, the influx of public theological statements and broader claims to the political imagination had to be handled in certain ways within the relationship between clergy and government personnel following the attacks in question. This is why Talal Asad has asked for scholars to research to what extent clergy must appeal to nationalist agendas in order to gain legitimacy.[7] However, the converse seems to be important too. It seems as if the state has had to appeal to theology in order to achieve legitimacy as well, but only (or especially) in certain periods of crisis or in response to unexpected attack. This "equalizing" conception of the political imaginaries of church and state, consequently, qualifies Robert Bellah's notion that American civil religion contains its own temples, rituals, discourse, and conceptual integrity.[8]

In light of these views, therefore, secularization appears more like a particular strategy of an institution vying for civic power and the diffused disciplines of governmentality that embody that power. It seeks leverage for regulating the attribution of "sacredness" (or profaneness) to time, space, and people. Why, then, would the church be used, during one period in English history, as the basis for unifying the people under a certain banner of identity, while in another period the church was used as the justification for separate spheres of identity and activity—one for "souls" and the other for politics and commerce?[9] Why, then, did some ritual events in New York City after the September 11, 2001 attacks identify the American citizen as possessing incontrovertibly internal "spiritual" qualities and global significance, whereas particularized, "thick" discus-

---

7. See Asad, *Formations of the Secular*, 3. Here Asad is specifically concerned with what would constitute political legitimacy in light of two key characteristics of modern democracies, the "horizontal, direct-access character of modern society" and "secular, homogeneous time."

8. Bellah, "Civil Religion in America."

9. Asad, *Formations of the Secular*, 3.

sion of God and well-known historical figures (such as Moses, Jesus, and even Mohammed) was marginalized?

With these considerations in mind, the format of the book may be set forth. The first chapter, which mainly draws on key research in sociology and anthropology, recasts the problem involving the church's and state's vision of social and political life in terms of the operations of disaster response and cultural production. It shows that the most glaring gaps in the academic literature occur precisely because of the lack of attention directed toward cultural processes in which both churches and statist agencies participate. These processes are matters of imaginative participation in a living narrative and highlight the importance of micro-level encounters—that is, face-to-face encounters that serve as the condition for innovation and for the alteration of long-standing (and perhaps destructive) assumptions about the course of social life and about human beings in general. This initial chapter, finally, should also sensitize readers to a certain sociological perspective and to how it may encourage or incite theological articulation in a manner consistent with that presented in the substantive chapters of the book. The second chapter is the first of three substantive explorations of disaster. Readers should be aware that these chapters carry out sociological analysis (the methodological details of which are relegated to footnotes in the first two chapters) that in turn serves as the basis for theological commentary. This theological commentary deals for the most part with ecclesial *poiesis* and *praxis*, that critical point at which what I take to be the orthodox doctrines of the church must be lived in a given political and social context, manifesting either wise and faithful action that participates in the work of God or capitulation to another political imaginary, thereby delaying, rejecting, or disregarding divine presence. Along the way, I invoke the resources of scriptural testimony, focal church practices or sacraments, and various conversation partners, including Søren Kierkegaard and Dietrich Bonhoeffer, in order to clarify the nature and tasks of the ecclesial body before, during, and after disasters. These theological reflections or recommendations emerge not out of a preestablished systematic agenda, but are thematic and emergent, or simply responsive to the social and political portrait of postdisaster life arising from the analysis of newspaper articles, speeches, and interview responses. Sometimes, the participants provide keen theological insights that propel the study into vital avenues of reflection.

The postdisaster relationship between statist organs and congregational agents in Oklahoma City, explored in chapter 2, offers a case in which localized forms of ecclesial practice (of which theology is fundamental) struggled to propose a viable politics of forgiveness and a united, cross-denominational theological affront against state-orchestrated public memory work (i.e., memorialization). Nonetheless many congregations played a central role in "housing" crucial emergency service functions, thereby restricting complete statist or expert co-optation of local places in the course of disaster response and recovery activities. The almost dialectical tension between the local theologies of church bodies and statist goals for rebinding the body politic was fully evident. The statist political imaginary remained formidable in its insistence upon using the disaster as the basis for delivering "wholeness" through economic revitalization and the imputation of "historic" status to certain places over against others. A significant number of churches, in the midst of this statist maneuvering, consciously presented themselves as a core component in the reconstruction of city culture and vision, while both "statist liturgies" and local citizens effectively spiritualized "the people" of Oklahoma, although for different ends. Chapter 3 is dedicated to the World Trade Center disaster of September 11, 2001. In this case, the statist political imaginary was mediated through large-scale nationalization of local spaces and identity, including ecclesial structures. Various ritual or liturgical performances of the state absorbed well-established congregations and their buildings. These incursions were carried out for the purpose of establishing a culturally uniform set of ritual performances that consequently embodied the positive theological endorsement of emergency response measures and strategies for entering a national body politic in need of loyalty, healing, and an enemy. Local congregations without public status remained focused on the needs of immediate community members without overt nationalization of ministerial service or church-member identity. Even so, no sustained theological criticism or counterliturgy was mounted, given considerable misgivings on the part of citizens with respect to the federal government's "global" response and the perceived need among local congregational members for integrity and ecclesial engagement with political matters in general. The fourth chapter, which is decidedly more theological in its perspective, advances a comparative case of disaster in which the friend/foe theme, as generally construed in armed or violent struggle, is absent. The instance of Hurricane Katrina signifies the promise of ecclesial "creativity" in numerous respects, in formulating imaginative solutions for community needs (that served as alternatives to an unresponsive or overwhelmingly slow bureaucratic response), in welcoming divine creative agency to establish new relationships among strangers and in criticizing profound neglect of the working poor in New Orleans, many of whom formed the backbone, so to speak, of the unique cultural practices of the city. The final two chapters are comparatively brief. Chapter 5 offers a short analysis of the role of postdisaster commodities as material bodies that feign compassionate participation in a suffering body. The last chapter proffers further theological, political, and sociological reflections on a select number of topics, including the trivialization of the poor and statist redevelopment plans, which emerged throughout the course of analysis, and which presents theological responses about faithful ecclesial practice with respect to these topics.

CHAPTER 1

The Modern State, Theology, and Disaster Response

Since this study addresses noteworthy topics in the literature of at least three separate disciplines, it is more sensible to review a selection of a few relevant studies in order to create conceptual boundaries for this endeavor. The first section of this chapter draws on various theoretical, historical, and sociological studies of the modern state, laying out some basic characteristics that apply to the present course of investigation focusing on disaster. This section includes a discussion of some of the more dynamic components involved with the state's self-designated functions and modes of "seeing" or of imagining the social world as victim of a violent attack or severe weather system. The second section presents a survey of relevant findings and arguments pertaining to the relationship between the church and state in historical and contemporary perspective. Although the Establishment Clause of the United States Constitution seems to govern many discussions of church-and-state relations, the involvement of various theological traditions in politics has had an incontrovertible influence on the course of American political history. The third section brings the issue of the relationship between the ecclesial and statist political imaginary, culture, and collective identity to the forefront. In taking up the centrality of emergent definitions of the collectivity, this section is buttressed by a fourth section that reviews the disaster-studies literature about postimpact consensus and solidarity. The fifth and final section brings together all the relevant arguments and findings of the chapter in order to underscore the need for a political-theological framework of analysis that adequately accounts for the cultural production of a body politic—which stems from church and state relations and is executed under a common imaginative project.

1

This literature, along with the substantive claims that will be made as the book progresses, point to a deeply controversial, provocative, and vital theme of contemporary social life in the United States. This aspect can most generally be labeled as the confused state of cultural and political relations between the nation-state and the church. This confused and conflicted situation is not obvious to the population at large, however, unless a significant degree of cultural trauma occurs. This is the main reason why disasters prove to be an effective window through which to view how the nation-state and the church define themselves and to what extent they actually operate under the lasting binaries of "faith and politics," "sacred and secular," "spiritual and material." The disasters under consideration in this study show that these binaries are not only highly questionable but downright misleading, when in fact it appears that the state requires theology (as a quasi-theology or antitheology) to reestablish social organization, and churches contain all the narratival, rhetorical, and social resources necessary to engage in the fundamental reordering of political, social, and economic structures in a manner on par with the state. The struggle between the way these two institutions (as embodiments of particular disciplined imaginings of space and time) conceive of life and see life is played out, I will argue, on who makes the more impressive case for a primordial or natural role in creating a social body, or a highly interdependent assemblage of humans who all need and belong to one another. The struggle is also played out on who mutually fulfills a crucial role in upholding a particular way of being. To achieve this, the state must work against an atomization of citizenry (which it has perpetuated) while upholding an ethos of pluralism in political, ethnic, and economic life and a particular rights tradition that privileges the accumulation of private property and other forms of wealth (in unregulated markets) over against the needs of landed communities. In order for the church to achieve the same goal, it must come to grips with how it has promoted the said actions of the state and work with a different ensemble of resources, a lack of technoexpert system credibility, and a narrow "sphere" of legitimate activity in the realm of American politics. The *ekklesia* of God draws on its faith-driven resources to live, authentically, in hope, because it is not called to control other groups and agencies in order to secure safety.

The primary witness of the church also rests in its initiative to identify weakness as a locus of strength. That is, it receives strength because it knows it is constituted by weak people. To the extent that any agency responsible for the "common good" (often a vaguely defined concept) cannot view itself as in need and impoverished in numerous ways, the link it forms with the actual, concrete lives of the humans it serves will be precarious. The church realizes that it first must receive gifts from God before it can ever give anything. It lives in self-giving love if its discipleship is one that requires promise and risk, Scripture and prayer—and all these within the context of dedicated relational bonds for the sake of holiness. A congregation that does not listen to God in Scripture and speak to God in prayer in its collective life (that is, as something to which all are devoted) is fragmented. It is going in a variety of directions in the negative sense; indeed, it does not act as a body and hence has no *leitourgia* for the sake of the world.

THE MODERN STATE

Many scholars from varying disciplines, from Joseph Gusfield to (more recently) William Cavanaugh, have propounded the central role of the state during periods of moral and cultural challenge.[1] Gusfield's dramatistic theory of status politics posits the state as the only institution that attempts to speak for all of society while other institutions assume a more secondary or supportive position. Cavanaugh, writing from a political-theological perspective, maintains that the state is "not a product of society, but creates society."[2] Cavanaugh is instructive in his historical analysis relating how the modern state quelled complex, overlapping societies typical of medieval social forms in an attempt to create a unitary space, *a society*, which is "legible" and amenable to administrative tactics.[3] Given the increased pluriformity of contemporary American cultural life, the state has often been likened to a juggler of interests, in that it cannot affirm any single cultural, moral, or confessional agenda;[4] it must devise a series of compromises and deals that protect individual rights and, more recently, identities. Because a liberal state cannot arrange political life in such a way that normally or justifiably demands

---

1. See Gusfield, *Symbolic Crusade*, 5–15; Cavanaugh, "Killing for the Telephone Company."

2. Cavanaugh, "Killing for the Telephone Company," 250.

3. Ibid., 251; cf. Scott, *Seeing Like a State*.

4. Unger, *Law in Modern Society*, 63–70.

allegiance from all members in a direct and physically coercive manner, it is always attempting to salvage or refine modes of unification.[5] Despite such challenges, the liberal nation-state takes on a deliberately aggressive role in response to large terrorist-related disasters, especially with regard to collective identity formation. This role is perhaps best described by the German ideologist Carl Schmitt, who considered it the most important responsibility of the business of politics.[6] Schmitt assumed a more contentious existence between human groupings so that orderly relations centered on value allocation was considered exceptional and merely secondary to a more pressing concern: the identification of friends and foe. Clearly the view of human social life upon which this stance is conceived is one of disorder and menace. The only manner in which persons may engage in value-allocation transactions is if the integrity of the territorial boundaries is established and protected.

According to this line of reasoning, the province of political reflection lies outside legal scrutiny: politics does not handle decisions that are or can be standardized. Decisions concerning friend and foe are the result of confrontations between two self-serving collectivities that are not answerable to a larger body of rule. These confrontations, Schmitt contended, are too momentous, unpredictable, and open ended to be subject to standardization. Juridical, moral, and economic criteria are secondary to the political decision, which is solely focused on an existential (non-normative) reflection—what are we to do about what this "other" has imposed upon "us"? Schmitt's work, despite the adversarial ontology on which it rests, rightly indicates that the realm of "the political" necessarily names those qualities, privileges, and other characteristics that a people enjoy jointly and not singly.

Schmitt's view and operation of "the political" is not too distant, experientially or conceptually, from what seems to ensue after terrorist attacks that lead to significant casualties. The state must serve as the locus of expertise on identifying what is evil, on knowing what is going on with the potentially dangerous "others" and on drawing up the correct set of strategies for defense. The state is the manager and appraiser of risk, and the generator of "sure truth."[7] Martial-law proceedings and other immediate

---

5. Ibid.

6. See Poggi. *Development of the Modern State*, 7–10.

7. Brueggemann, *David's Truth*, 23.

military counterstrikes are actualized because a massive network of tech-nically skilled men and women are rigorously trained precisely to manage such risks using advanced communication and information-gathering technologies created explicitly for military action and swift response. All such devices are bound together under a unitary although contested plot or mythos of social and political life.[8] Oppositional cultures, especially during post-attack periods, are absorbed into the seemingly perennial public narrative. Indeed, as Fenn has stated, "the secular state *imagines a whole* that legitimates even its most recalcitrant individual parts."[9] So, the contemporary nation-state (especially in the United States) in some sense sustains the organs of administration, legitimation, and categorization (on the one hand) that serve as resources for the sustenance of disparate identities, yet also generates a "master" identity (on the other hand) that serves one of the quintessential aims of politics as statecraft—namely, the identification of friend and foe. This identity subsumes all others into a broader narrative.

Even so, it is important to refrain from conceiving the state as a monolithic apparatus administered by conspiratorial elites bent on con-quest. Rather, it is more intriguing to frame the state as a "structure of intelligibility," a set of propositions about what is true and what is not; hence the state is itself an actual strategy and approach, a diffuse reper-toire of disciplines, rife with narrative potentiality and assumptions of how human life ought to proceed.[10] This conception of the state lends itself to a more valid portrayal of social activities that distinguish it from government per se, or the actual provincial administrative bodies that formulate budgets, implement plans, and devise or enforce statutes. Local political administrations in the United States possess a flexibility and exclusive set of constitutional rights that constrain the direct coercive power of the state. It is this range of freedom that introduces the possibil-ity of localized relations between churches and local government that are not subject to total, direct, and formal control. In these local relations, a veritable struggle against or acquiescence to the state-idea can be poten-tially observed.

8. Bell, *Liberation Theology*, 25.
9. Fenn, *Liturgies and Trials*, xxvi (emphasis added).
10. Steinberger, *Idea of the State*, 19.

Given such observations about the liberal nation-state in relation to collective identity and (often scientifically) refined responsibilities and potentialities, what then could be said about its relationship to the brands of "terror" faced in Oklahoma City in 1995 and New York City in 2001, or to the tragic flooding of New Orleans, the three historical examples explored in this study? Anthropologist Michael Taussig designates our contemporary situation as a "chronic state of emergency, as a Nervous System."[11] He further argues that the state's definition of the abnormal or of terror and evil is of the variety that benefits the state, because it all occurs under its purview and organs of information gathering—nothing escapes the *cosmos* of the state, because a total universe of technology and other resources has been mobilized to make sure that responsibility is assumed, while other spheres of social life assume another, usually dependent, posture in relation to it. This is due to the overarching concern with the "ideal of order," a discourse that permeates statist, military, and media involvement, and therefore almost unquestionably includes all public response to disasters.

For present purposes, thus, the state appears to have assumed the position of institution *par excellence*. As Steinberger asserts, following Aristotle, the state is the "institution of institutions. It is the institution that directs all of the lesser institutions of society. Its distinctiveness is, thus, largely a matter of scope and authority."[12] The disasters of the present inquiry, however, allow us to ask the following question: in what ways do state disciplines make life intelligible by being enmeshed in the lifeworlds of other institutions? That is, after disasters, institutions need to repair the "coherence" of their descriptions of reality; they need another institution to vouchsafe its goals or ends. What is the nature and shape of such institutional relationships? The present study reads the nation-state as an institution that models social behavior and shapes the contours and content of public theology through the implementation of disciplines, discourses, and material bodies that build identities after disasters.

Public Theology in America

The status of public theological expression has a dizzying array of undulations and variations, depending on historical period and geographic

---

11. Taussig, *Nervous System*, 13.
12. Steinberger, *Idea of the State*, 20.

location. Mark Noll considers "the scandal of the evangelical mind," arguing that there is, quite frankly, not much of one.[13] Despite the apparent increase in output from evangelical thinkers and writers in the nineteenth century, the entire evangelical academic enterprise eventually succumbed to a large-scale movement toward dissociation, pitting "academic" and "theological" modes of thinking against one another. One result of this detachment was the proliferation of educational centers for biblical study and general social studies (seminaries and Christian colleges) that only rarely valued intensive interdisciplinary dialogue. The "secular" institutions of higher learning obliged this insular disposition toward academic work, hardening the chasm between separate spheres of inquiry through an elaboration of fact/value dichotomies and concerns over separating studies of "myth" from those of "reality."

Another important development in theological reflection that molded the prevailing framework for most expressions of "religious language" in the public sphere was the modern decoupling of views of God, sin, and even congregational life from cosmological perspectives.[14] The subordination of theological speech to the demands of cultural pluralism and universalized liberal-democratic discourse compelled publicly active theologians and pastors to translate explicitly theological language into "values" or generalized positions that adopted the discourse of the "public square." Evans argues that the alterations theologians and pastors are impelled to make, however, do not completely evacuate theological notions; rather, they sublimate and alter various forms of speech to create an "implicit" theology that combines, with often ambiguous or odd results, sacred and secular aims, or even theological and antitheological assumptions.[15] In this way, certain agents in church and governmental roles have grown accustomed to a way of expression that seems to involve religion, but is actually always answerable to the overarching intentions of liberal democratic regimes.[16]

13. Noll, *Scandal of the Evangelical Mind*, 1.

14. See Habermas, *Reason and the Rationalization of Society*; see also Schüssler Fiorenza, "Church as a Community of Interpretation," 66–74.

15. Evans, "Public Vocabularies of Religious Belief." John Milbank takes up this same topic, but in a much more theologically sophisticated manner, in *Theology and Social Theory*.

16. See Casanova, *Public Religions in the Modern World*; and Asad, *Genealogies of Religion*.

Theology, Church, and State

The literature within political science and cultural anthropology has engaged and studied various facets of the confused nature of church-and-state relations. Carlton Hayes considered nationalism a religion that had displaced the zealous sense of belonging and purpose that institutionalized religion once proffered.[17] Carolyn Marvin and David Ingle argue that American nationalism can be well understood as a civil religion of blood sacrifice, with the American flag as its crucial "totemic" symbol of group cohesion.[18] They further argue that the notion of civil religion in the popular sense, however, is problematic insofar as "Americans generally see their nation as a secular culture possessed of few myths, or weak myths everywhere, but none central and organizing." In an attempt to address the utility of "civil religion" as an analytical tool, the authors adopt a Durkheimian conception of totem myth as the theoretical basis for a study of the American civil religion of patriotism. The American flag is the "ritual instrument of group cohesion" that is most powerfully enacted in the publicly confirmed "blood sacrifice" that preserves the nation.[19] Death, either as a combatant or victim, interpreted as sacrifice, turns the individual body into a "social body" insofar as it represents the central expression of *national* faith. "The memory of the last sacrifice" is afforded a remarkably significant position during the staging and execution of ceremonies aimed at the remembrance of victims.[20] Even if the victims were not military personnel, the simple fact that they participated in a representative American institution assures "absorption" into the totem flag and its accompanying symbols of loyalty and duty.

Among scholars in religious studies and philosophy, Robert Jewett and John Shelton Lawrence argue that foreign policy has oscillated between a "prophetic realism" and "crusading zeal" since the very establishment of independent government.[21] The former orientation represents those periods of American political practice during which the emphasis was on the self-conscious criticism and condemnation of injustices, that is, deliberate multifaceted sanctioning without self-omission from the

17. Hayes, *Nationalism as Religion.*

18. Marvin and Ingle, *Blood Sacrifice and the Nation,* 7.

19. Ibid., 2.

20. Ibid., 10.

21. Jewett and Lawrence, *Captain America,* 3–12.

very same standard. This tradition is contrasted to zealous nationalism, which seeks to rid the earth of evil by means of the identification and wholesale elimination of enemies. The central pop symbol of this stance is Captain America: a figure that embodies aggressive crusading ideals, perfect moral qualities, and remarkable "extralegal" abilities to "right the wrongs." Jewett and Lawrence contend that both these traditions persist alongside each other and thus promote a "contradictory civil religion."[22] These authors also discount the importance of certain ceremonial events, such as the Fourth of July and presidential inaugurations, arguing that these are only marginal cultural "formative experiences," whereas the credible narratives to which most Americans subscribe require further analysis. My view is that both narratives and ritual must be taken into account because they are mutually constitutive of each other and of contexts of social interaction in that genre of social phenomena known as "cultural traumas," of which disasters (both "manmade" and "natural") are a part (along with presidential assassinations, mass murders, and the like). Even if routine holidays such as the Fourth of July or Presidents' Day lack such experiential strength, the memorial services following disasters do not. Whether the interests and disciplines of the state discussed above are to become relevant to such theologically rich narratives and ritual events depends upon the generation of some believable or intelligible public account of "the truth" of an event—an account that both endorses certain social boundaries between friend and foe and defines a social whole that will believe the implicit or explicit theological aspects of the account.[23]

THE PRODUCTION OF CULTURE:
THE STATE AND INSTITUTIONAL INTERRELATIONS

From a sociological perspective, the late Robin M. Williams was one of the first to devise a set of formulations about how institutions are interrelated—formulations that are amenable to empirical inquiry and even operationalization.[24] Williams claimed that institutional dominance could be discerned by observing what happens when "various sets of institutional norms conflict in particular situations." His approach employs the idea that a particular normative system of social action ought

22. Ibid., 6

23. The conceptualization of cultural politics employed here roughly matches that of Graham Ward in *Cultural Transformation and Religious Practice*.

24. Williams, *American Society*, 511.

to receive a preponderant degree of attention, not "institutions in general."[25] This move is roughly congruous with the premium that Oliver O'Donovan places on the concepts of created order, judgment, and the political act, with the latter concept reflecting a critique of the preeminence that Lockean political theory affords abstract political institutions. These concepts are in turn trussed to an idea of the individual moral subject as owner or controllers of their own acts and of their own moral and physical environments.[26] This moral responsibility is crucial, because social restorative projects of the postdisaster period in Oklahoma City, New York City, and New Orleans lay emphasis on more-or-less clear exhortations to action on the part of citizens. What is perhaps even more intriguing, however, is that average people do not seem to attempt to disentangle the origins of certain norms or values; on the contrary, average people appear to resolutely attempt to reconcile them into a total scheme for daily life and thereby reduce cognitive dissonance. Average people try to dissolve the incommensurability of certain sets of ideas, convictions and practices. This is quite applicable to postdisaster scenarios of every kind. For this reason, the production of a "total scheme," beyond the immediately functional and practical, demands investigation from the perspective of cultural politics.

In an essay titled *Producing the Sacred*, Robert Wuthnow urges that a proper sociocultural study of religious groups in the contemporary context must adequately conceptualize the interinstitutional alliances that wittingly or unwittingly produce visions and artifacts of "the sacred." Not surprisingly, the three main institutions mentioned are government, church, and economy (read: capitalism). Wuthnow, therefore, argues on behalf of a multi-institutional view of "sacred culture," whereby the church alone is not the purveyor of images, relics, or other symbols of the kind; on the contrary, a conglomeration of institutions seems to have some vested interest in what is conveyed under the terms "divine" or "sacred." That the nation-state would appear among this group is not unsettling or startling, because, as Benedict Anderson once stated, nationalistic thought shares

---

25. Ibid., 515.

26. There is a certain level of accord between the Frankfurt school's position on the import of individuality and that of Oliver O'Donovan on the individual subject's "bearing of reality . . . its presence to him as authority and his fulfillment within it as a free agent" (O'Donovan, *Resurrection and Moral Order*, 108).

a peculiar affinity with "religious thinking," a comparison that will be pursued in light of disaster response in subsequent sections.[27]

Along the same lines but from another disciplinary perspective, Eldon J. Eisenach has argued that the struggle over American identity and the meaning of American citizenship involves participants who "unwittingly" fill the role of a "national political theologian" even if they explicitly deny that their claims have any appreciable relation to such a "private" matter.[28] Writing before September 11, 2001, Eisenach also claimed that "it is commonly accepted" that a post-Protestant and postgeneric Judeo-Christian establishment subsided during the late twentieth century and, with few exceptions, gave way to a decidedly secular "post-religious" establishment. Eisenach further claims that "a new voluntary religious establishment is required as a precondition for reaching agreement on church-state/religion-politics issues."[29] If this is so, then, the United States Constitution cannot "authorize" a common national identity through provision of formal legal mandates and powers—that is, it cannot be used as an "autonomous ground of authority" by virtue of which a national project can be mobilized. Resembling Wuthnow, Eisenach claims that national identity is a voluntary "cultural achievement . . . the product of the institutions and practices of . . . educational, cultural, religious, and intellectual leaders."[30] What is more, the American national identity is shaped by a voluntary religious establishment that carries with it a corresponding theology. All "American political theologies" function as metanarratives that inculcate any happenings within specified borders with certain fundamental understandings, commitments, and operative beliefs. The formation and maintenance of a voluntary religious establishment and national political theology involves the exclusion and inclusion of certain groups. Those included groups are enabled to fully participate in national political life insofar as their ethnic or religious identities are mediated through and partially incorporate American national identity. This assimilative social process requires that the participant modify his or her ethnic and religious identity to "fit the national one."[31]

27. Anderson, *Imagined Communities*, 10.

28. Eisenach, *Next Religious Establishment*, 4.

29. Ibid., 5.

30. Ibid., 6.

31. Ibid., 7.

Several of Eisenach's assertions provide guidance for this study. His notion of a "culturally produced" national identity and the moral orientation furnished by means of theological thought forms and institutions is noteworthy and requires further analysis in contexts of response to violent attack and community restoration. That is, in the aftermath of violent attack, communities generate unitary symbols of great consequence to other communities and identities. The state, however, especially after the Oklahoma bombing and September 11, 2001, cannot be considered merely *one* institutional player among many that participate in the complex array of negotiations and appropriations that attempt to fashion a "religious" establishment and a corresponding political theology and metanarrative. The state itself can be viewed as a common imaginative project in which persons and institutions participate. William Gamson and David Meyer have rightly asserted, along these lines, that different political systems represent not simply varying accounts of efficient administrative and economic structures in service of resource distribution and a stable polity, but different public accounts of the proper magnitude and responsibilities of the state. This suggests that all citizens are enjoined to participate in a public and common imaginative enterprise whereby a particular vision of all social relations is advanced and that cultural production from different social groups follows or resists. By means of a constellation of social practices, relationships, and liturgical events the state serves as a clearinghouse of symbolic production. So if the notion of a common imaginative project is as significant as it seems in the absence of disasters, then, once again, drawing a proper conceptualization of the relations between churches and statist agencies after disasters is imperative. Meeting this conceptual need would address two core questions: (1) what social factors serve to link and mutually interpret church theologies and the state's interest in social order and social legibility? And (2) what cultural objects do such interrelations produce to mold a local citizen's understanding of the required identity and social vision for life after the disaster in question?

Solidarity, Consensus, and the "Social Body" in Disaster Response

After a disaster, human beings attempt to fashion solidarity at two different levels of social reality. First, major institutions and their players seek to unite under a common imaginative banner; the aggregate uniting often includes all the families, government workers, clergy, and economic leaders of an entire state or nation. The term "imaginative" here refers to the fact that the relation is vital and believable but may not ever involve actual contact with another person. Second, concrete, local groups of residents that engage in familiar and literal relations (e.g., involving tactile, physical, or sensate presence) and that live in the vicinity of the attack must engage processes of community identity formation.

With respect to the first level, the aftermath of terrorist-related disasters requires a rather socially rigorous and complex positioning of institutions in relation to one another in order to assure, in Jeffrey Alexander's language, an impressive and captivating "counterperformance" in response to the initial deadly "performance" of the terrorist group.[32] This underscores the centrality of claims making, which is a set of processes constitutive of the larger dramatic performance that must be staged in order to offset any harm to the "narrative order" stemming from the terrorist attack. The counterperformance thus demands a forceful alignment of broad yet absolutely crucial institutional symbolism that in turn serves as a model of allegiance between institutions at a more parochial level. Viewed from another perspective, institutional animosity or interinstitutional criticism must be diminished as much as possible in order to model social cohesion during a period of massive instability. Jeffrey Alexander et al. provide a working definition of the constitutive elements of a "social performance," including plot, script, audience, actors, directors, and access to the means of symbolic production. From this list, the element of *directors* will receive significant attention in the present study. Directors are "organizers . . . and leaders of collective action" who mold the motivations and patterns of actors.[33] Indeed, it is reasonable to label clergy in disaster-stricken areas and the federal officials who engage such localities as "directors," considering their significant leadership roles. Leadership in these contexts takes on an even more compelling function when the disaster demands a cogent, public response that carries serious repercussions for collective imaginings of human beings, of order, of time, and of security. From the viewpoint of local and national institutional leaders, what must be done when the development of a common

32. Alexander et al., *Cultural Trauma and Collective Identity*, 90.

33. Ibid., 91.

story with a common resolution requires articulation and presentation to other community members and to the larger "national community"? Who is involved in this process, and who is to be disqualified?

Various sociologists have addressed the problem of postdisaster community consensus and solidarity. This literature furnishes important guidelines for the present theoretical and methodological framework. In the anthropological literature, Anthony Oliver-Smith's case studies about community response to the 1970 earthquake in Peru raise questions about the nexus between crisis, ritual, and action.[34] Oliver-Smith first considers Durkheim's view that a substratum of mechanical solidarity (which requires an overarching spatial identity) persists in company with organic solidarity in highly differentiated modern societies. As people attend to the same issues surrounding individual and familial health, the typical division of labor is deferred, and each person bears the label of "victim."[35] Then, citing the work of Victor Turner, Oliver-Smith adds, "in disasters, modern societies may revert to that substratum of mechanical solidarity, *their common human identity at some fundamental level*, since the division of labor with all its differentiation and hierarchy has been rendered temporarily inoperative."[36] This statement implies that persons seek a common cultural identity or some "deep" sense of unity that defies mundane categorizations. Also, "ritualized interactional forms" mitigate the low-level stress occasioned by the constant changes in context and daily life."[37] Oliver-Smith contends that the emotionally charged, egalitarian vision of life among equals eventually succumbs to the more-structured, value-determining social interactions that typify differentiated modern social forms. More predictable, structured behavior is required for reconstructive purposes and extensive relief efforts. The "mechanical" response to the September 11, 2001 attacks makes a provocative demand on Oliver-Smith's empirical claims simply because of its prolonged duration. That is, why did it last as long as it did? Indeed, the *Gemeinschaft*-like solidarity of the postdisaster period met considerable challenge from the vicissitudes of legislative and capitalist practice. For instance, the United States Congress deemed that compensation for the families

34. Oliver-Smith, "Brotherhood of Pain," 164.

35. Ibid., 165.

36. Ibid. (emphasis added)

37. Ibid.

of the deceased should be gauged according to the occupational status of the victim. What is also intriguing (although not necessarily original) about the last two terrorist attacks within the borders of the United States is that in these instances, the notion of a robust national identity and "civilization" assumed a prominent yet contested place alongside articulations of good and evil so that all these concepts were elemental and basic in the communal and "mechanical" (Durkheimian) sense. This is not surprising, but the intensity of nationalist discursive constructions and material culture surrounding such articulations should be examined and compared among the three cases of disaster. Furthermore, the nature and length of mechanical solidarity may actually rely on a different scale of social organization in Oklahoma City than the scale of organization in either New York City or New Orleans.

The social-scientific literature concerning processes of group integration and solidarity, especially that of Victor Turner, Ralph Turner, and Randall Collins, also offers a few insights that interpret a key difference between the Murrah Building bombing and the September 11, 2001, attacks. In particular, Ralph Turner underscores the decisive role that attributions of internality or externality may have on group response (or accommodation) to a threat.[38] That is to say, is the source of the crisis internal to the community (e.g., a recognized faction) or external, to which the label "foreign" would not be highly controversial? In the former instance, an American citizen carried out the actual bombing. In the latter, non-American citizens, who enacted an agenda both distinct and similar to that of Timothy McVeigh, carried out the attack. Hence, how do the processes of threat discernment and symbolic attribution that serve community solidarity differ in these situations? Was McVeigh an "insider" who lost his way and so became a "traitor": once loyal but then somehow misguided and perverted in his sense of justice and necessity? Or, was he always an "outsider"? A positive answer to this question implies that it is impossible to consider someone who carries out such attacks to ever have been deemed an American. In other words, defining a threat as external or internal carries consequences with regard to what is assumed about the nature of the American polity and about human nature in general. In terms of field research, this concern would demand questions linked to what the discursive constructions of the respondents and the data

38. Turner, Ralph. "Integrative Beliefs in Group Crises."

sources say about where one finds terrorists: not only geographically but socially and symbolically. How can America harbor such individuals and detect these "sites"?

Randall Collins stresses the notion of the microreality of macro-social structures, specifically in terms of conversation ritual and emotional tone, thereby enriching our understanding of solidarity, order, and congregational fellowship with a more multidimensional view of social interaction.[39] As Joanne Nigg comments in her review of Collins's central theoretical claims, "the microreality of any social structure is due to the repetitive associations among people in relation to particular physical objects and places."[40] In extending Collins's insights more deeply into the disaster context, Nigg further posits the importance of how conversational rituals "at moments of extremely high social density (both physical and moral) . . . create a perception of 'common life,'" but only because "the interaction is sustained by a common emotional tone."[41] Emotional tone increases with the severity of the disruption: the disruption then inculcates even greater particularity and emotional arousal into the conversational rituals. Crucially, the road to the reemergence of stable or routine social interaction runs through such microlevel conversations, which although conducive to feelings of tremendous unity among disaster-affected victims, tend to eventually assimilate aspects of the general cultural community as more individuals and agencies from outside the victims' circle join the conversational ritual chains. This contributes in no insignificant manner to the reestablishment of status-group memberships and other aspects of the predisaster social order. These observations and claims enjoin an approach that opens up the possibility of exploring microinteractional exchanges during the postdisaster period—exchanges involving those actors who generate narratives and who introduce practices (practices that enact a form of solidarity that may or may not be unique to the participants) into a highly stressful and anxiety-laden social environment. In other words, disasters invite openness to novelty. Also worthy of investigation is the manner in which, during the response period and beyond, emergency-response workers and victims engage

---

39. Collins, "On the Micro-Foundations of Macro-Sociology."

40. Nigg, "Social Action and Social Order," 391.

41. Ibid., 392.

other actors from churches and response agencies in a culturally productive manner.

Viewing this entire chapter as a whole, we note that collective attributions about unity, victimization (e.g., "we are all [as Americans] victims"),
proper citizenship, God's will, and the role of government are not simply
or totally determined at the microlevel, and certainly do not occur in a
neutral civil space. As I have argued above, the church and the state both
promote accounts of truth and social disciplines, singly and jointly, which
make certain assumptions about human nature, and which sponsor certain actions. Attention to microlevel encounters, however, does introduce
the possibility of novel interpretations of public cultural products from
local churches and statist activities. In addition, attention to microlevel
encounters fosters resistance to prevailing institutional processes. In other
words, the microlevel analysis exposes agency amid an array of cultural
productions that seek to order social relations, to appropriate goods, and
to settle upon a vision of how things will be after a disaster.

THE THEOPOLITICAL CULTURE OF THE POSTDISASTER PERIOD

What follows combines the central themes of the previous sections and
situates them within the context of the postdisaster period. First, I present a brief consideration of the modern state's historic struggle with the
presumed theodicy of Christian churches and with the enduring power
of theological narratives in disaster planning. Second, institutional interrelations are recast in light of collective attributions of guilt, responsibility, and resilience and in light of the emerging theodrama centered
on responding to fatal attack and severe weather. Collective symbolic
attribution is best defined in terms of practice: it is what happens when
human beings begin to construct "deeper" narrative symbols in association with pragmatic and even technical emergency-response activities.
For example, the convergence and filial cooperation of persons from
different backgrounds during the postdisaster period is interpreted in
utopic ways, sometimes as "pure" unity. This process is part of the collective dramatic interpretation during the response and recovery periods
after a violent attack or a hurricane. In such an interpretation state and
church play major roles. These dramatic attributions, furthermore, can
be perceived as identity-building processes that must be activated during a period of substantial instability. This chapter now concludes with a

simplified delineation of empirical and theoretical concerns that account for the gaps in the sociological literature.

Disasters, Theology, and State

Russell Dynes and Susan Neiman have both highlighted the significance of the state's involvement in the response and recovery processes following the Lisbon earthquake.[42] Dynes claims that government responsibility over disaster response went far beyond simply providing financial or material support to affected citizens; governmental agencies and attendant programs eventually assumed control over the discourse through which the conditions and outcomes of disasters would be analyzed. This event, sometimes known as the first "modern disaster," arguably provided the impetus for the formulation of a social-scientific view of disaster; it likewise spelled the demise of the popular and traditional theodicy that had lost favor among a considerable number of intellectuals. Dynes further argues that "the evaluation of the consequences of disaster is more closely related to the development of the modern state" than is any other developmental factor.[43] This implies that the state's interests would serve as the model discourse and key interpretive scheme for dealing with disasters. However, this discourse has depended on many preexisting narratives and categories of thought; it assumes a thoroughgoing cultural syncretism.

The modern state possesses among its chief interests a desire to acquire and propound knowledge, which, in turn, can be used to "prevent" disasters. The corollary to construing disaster as knowledge dependent is that instances of disaster can be prevented through certain "cultural protections," or mores, beliefs, and customs that generate a shield, as it were, against the forces that pose a threat to a given society.[44] Although this particular view of disasters develops in light of "natural forces," it still enriches the present project's interest in the role of institutions. The notion of "cultural protections," as Stallings asserts in his review of various arguments in the sociology-of-disaster literature, is inextricably bound to the idea of and belief in social order.[45] Social order as such subsumes the creation of social routines. Who or what, therefore, will serve as the

---

42. See Dynes, "Dialogue"; see also Neiman, *Evil in Modern Thought*.
43. Ibid., 14.
44. Dombrowsky, "Social Dimensions of Warning," 246–50.
45. Stallings, "Disaster and the Theory of Social Order," 130.

font of regeneration; or what amalgam of institutions is held accountable for the disruption of the vast array of social routines that, according to Wolf Dombrowksy, constitute the social structure? Of course, it is the state and other supportive institutions to which it can serve as model. Hence the nation-state is singularly concerned to develop "legitimate" cultural protections that reestablish the very condition for social routines or, as Porfiriev maintains in different terms, for the reemergence of social stability.[46] Robert Stallings adeptly summarizes the vital point: "the potential for a crisis of legitimization calls attention to the need to understand the role of all institutions, including the state, in the process of (re-) legitimization following the disruption of social routines."[47] This assertion elicits yet another question linked to church-state relations following the disasters in Oklahoma City, New York City, and New Orleans. This question pertains to the manifold forms of legitimation employed during the postdisaster period, including technical, rational, and legal forms. As important as these approaches of legitimation may be, however, of equal importance is the need to theologically legitimize an instance of disaster and disaster response. The theological legitimacy of disaster response demands that institutional interrelations, cultural production, and narrative become highly significant objects for analysis and reflection. These topics yield a corollary emphasis on the nearly synonymous concepts mentioned various times in the disaster-related literature just cited: concepts including "structure," "routines," "stability," "habit," and "order." All these can be suitably complemented (and critiqued) with the concepts of "discipline" and "liturgy." "Discipline" refers to thought forms (primarily imaginative) and bodily actions, including "social disciplines," whereas "liturgy" takes up rhythmic collective offerings, including the work of celebration and lamentation, of a people that on the one hand acknowledges receiving life from God and that on the other hand allows such a truth to mold daily interaction. The primacy of "social disciplines," then, privileges a consideration of practices and further calls readers to acknowledge the importance of considering beliefs and practices in a dialectical manner. Ecclesial habits, in both their predisaster and postdisaster modes, must also be trussed to this set of considerations, because, as Chris Shilling asserts in his review of the early pragmatist philosophers,

---

46. Porfiriev, "Issues," 60.
47. Stallings, "Disaster and the Theory of Social Order," 130.

> Habits seep into the furthest recesses of the body. They have a
> structural basis in the nervous system, shape the selections our
> senses make, condition our preferences, predate and provide a ba-
> sis for our deliberative orientations to the environment, direct our
> muscular responses, and structure our identities.[48]

The church as a faithful body concerned with the state of larger social
structures must grasp, through its understanding of liturgy and politics,
the primacy of ecclesial habits, because we are in large part our habits.
Habits, especially those growing out of the virtue of love, are ordered
toward expanding fields of action that may otherwise appear closed.

This conceptualization of disciplined imaginings in particular affects
views of culture and cultural production in that neither could be considered separate from "society" or "political structures." On the contrary,
structures take on a meaning that William Sewell describes aptly as "cultural schemas" that carry and sustain resources that reproduce unevenly
distributed power."[49] The scope of such schemas not only transcends but
also enforces certain basic interests and views of the human body and
intellectual faculties, including the "spirit," God, or anything else that
animates the lives of men and women as a collectivity. It is no surprise,
therefore, why theological legitimation would play such a crucial role in
postdisaster institutional interrelations. Any attempt at addressing social
order or socius as a whole touches upon how any one citizen imagines social relations, human beings in general, material goods, time, leadership,
and a host of other anthropological matters that may not receive explicit
attention in a public manner but that carry grave social consequences.

This combination of interests in disciplined imagining as it relates
to social order and resource distribution, however, has received scant attention in the fields of the sociology and politics of disaster. Nonetheless,
several studies provide a helpful precedent because they shed light on the
need for institutions to link their operations and practices with a larger
cosmological system. As Mary Douglas argues, any institution that is going to keep its shape needs to gain legitimacy by appealing to nature and
reason: "then it affords to its members a set of analogies with which to
explore the world and with which to justify the naturalness and reason-
ableness of the instituted rules, and it can keep its identifiable continu-

---

48. Shilling, *Changing Bodies*, 13.
49. Sewell, "Theory of Structure," 35.

ing form."[50] Of considerable interest, of course, is Douglas's omission of theology or deity in this specific discussion. Whatever the reasons behind the absence, it is worth remembering the predominant approach toward conceiving of deity in the liberal-democratic tradition—chiefly, as a god that institutes the natural laws and ideals that govern the behavior of matter and morals. This conception of God, in turn, is linked with a contractual theology that dovetails with the view of the state, with its supportive organs of technical expertise and with its underlying assumptions about disaster-related behavior. This contractual theology advances a foundational construct that creates a sense of "orderliness and coherence in life, the interconnectedness of acts and their results . . . There are orders, limits, and boundaries within which humanness is possible and beyond which there can be only trouble."[51] Anything that questions this order is perceived as a disturbance that must be eradicated.

At the intersection of theology and disaster planning, Russell Dynes stresses the centrality of the biblical flood story as a frame for our imagination and understanding of present-day disasters in the West. Specifically, he advances two claims. First, he underscores the enduring influence of the assumption within Western culture that chaotic and even violent behavior typically follows natural disasters, a type of conduct that demands authoritative intervention from the outside. Second, Dynes points to the social and cultural assumptions that condition disaster planning in the United States.[52] When local emergency officials and citizens prepare emergency- response plans, they work with assumptions about what will most likely occur and hence about what circumstances they must be prepared to face. Dynes induces, on the basis of an analysis of numerous disaster-response plans, a set of common themes that could be grouped into different model-types of disaster-response strategies. The three main models identified all stress (1) the need for government to reestablish continuity in social life, (2) the expectation of irrational and unstable behavior among victims that requires the actions of heroes to assure efficacious response, and (3) the overwhelming need for command-and-control methods to restore "control" over disorganized and overwhelmed local institutions. This analysis indicates that command-and-control

50. Douglas, *How Institutions Think*, 112.

51. Brueggemann, *Theology of the Old Testament*, 15.

52. For insightful analysis on this matter, see Drabek, "Alternative Patterns," 280–82, and *Emergency Management*. See also Dynes, "Structure of Disaster Research."

approaches undermine volunteer or civilian involvement and "spontaneous" behavior, seek to establish unidimensional authority, and justify official instructions to assist a passive and uninformed population.[53] In view of these criticisms of emergency-planning strategies, Dynes goes on to challenge the basic upshot of these views: they paint a picture of inert victims that presumably require the intervention of a comprehensive state program. When such interventions become the object of analysis, as they are in this project, it is imperative to explore what is transmitted culturally in the interactions between the federal, state, and local governments on the one hand, and local church members and clergy on the other hand.

Having reviewed some crucial insights from a variety of scholarly sources pertaining to the workings of the state and local communities, and having resituated them within a wider set of questions pertaining to ecclesial cultural practices in response to disasters, I now turn to a more in-depth study of three separate disasters.

53. See Clarke, *Mission Improbable*. Clarke argues for "symbolic" rather than actual practical efficacy of disaster-response protocol.

CHAPTER 2

The Oklahoma City Bombing:
"This Sin Against Humanity Will Not Go Unpunished"

The Churches of Oklahoma City

The state of Oklahoma is home to a very large body of Baptists, representing 42.8 percent of all confessional adherents (not including African Americans) and 29.8 percent of the total population.[1] Southern Baptists compose the largest proportion of Baptist denominational representation, claiming 967,223 members. Between 1930 and 1990, the Oklahoma Baptist Convention grew 48 percent faster than the population of Oklahoma.[2] As Bill Leonard notes in his survey of religion and public life in the Southern Crossroads (Texas, Oklahoma, Missouri, Louisiana, and Arkansas), although the Southern Baptist Convention only grew by 0.3 percent between 1990 and 2000, the American Baptist Churches USA grew 108 percent, an increase of 2,609 members over the same decade.[3] Comprising Forming over a quarter of the population, Baptists of one stripe or another have exerted considerable influence over the course of politics and public theological expression in the South (and in the United States as a whole if one considers the influence of Independent Baptist Jerry Falwell). Oran Smith's account of "Baptist Republicanism" in particular emphasizes the thoroughgoing and dynamic inculcation of Baptist views into a plethora of political agendas throughout the latter half of the

1. Leonard, "Southern Crossroads," 37.
2. Ibid., 37.
3. Ibid., 46.

23

twentieth century, notwithstanding the relative decrease in membership growth between 1990 and 1995, the year of the bombing.[4]

Roman Catholic churches experienced a membership increase of 17.4 percent between 1990 and 2000, composing 7 percent of all church members and 4.9 percent of the state population. In Oklahoma City in particular, Roman Catholics grew by 24.1 percent during the same period. St. Joseph's Old Cathedral was the closest church to the west of the Murrah Building on the day of the bombing and consequently incurred heavy damage to its rectory and main cathedral building. As a result, Roman Catholics received an unprecedented level of attention during the bombing aftermath, even if, of those killed in the blast, the relative proportion that belonged to the church was quite minimal. Various newspaper articles that publicized church recovery activities emphasized just this point; moreover, church leadership seemed especially inclined to mention the number of active members that a congregation lost to the bombing, or the extent to which St. Joseph's Old Cathedral could share, albeit indirectly, in the loss of any church member in the city.

United Methodists make up about 13.5 percent of all confessional adherents in the state and 9.4 percent of the total population. Interesting is that United Methodists in Oklahoma as a whole decreased by 1.1 percent between 1990 and 2000. In Oklahoma City, to the contrary, the church grew by 4.6 percent between 1990 and 2000. The First Methodist Church of Oklahoma City sustained heavy structural damage due to the attack and yet still served as a venue for emergency mortuary and family-counseling services.

Besides such mainline or long-standing denominations, Pentecostal-charismatic churches have experienced extraordinary growth: for example, the Church of God grew by 38.6 percent, Independent charismatics grew by 25.7 percent, and the International Church of the Foursquare Gospel increased 173.4 percent to 2,791 adherents. In total, Holiness, Pentecostal, and Wesleyan churches claim 225,997 adherents, about 9.4 percent of all confessional adherents. Despite being difficult to categorize

---

4. Smith, *Baptist Republicanism*. Chapters 4 and 7 of Smith's book cover the vital Baptist Republican partnerships and alliances that shaped the nature of campaign finance and other forms of political participation. In chapter 4, Smith also identifies key differences between a variety of fundamentalist political groups that apparently compose a fundamentalist "bloc" (e.g., separatist fundamentalism and movement fundamentalism), and more strictly evangelical political involvement.

using traditional approaches, these churches grew substantially in Oklahoma City. Another small yet burgeoning group, the Salvation Army in Oklahoma City, grew by 646.9 percent.[5] According to the American Religious Identification Survey (ARIS) 2001, the weighted estimate of residents claiming the category of No Religion has also grown considerably since 1993, encompassing 14 percent of the total population in the state of Oklahoma.[6] Recent Pew Forum survey data have confirmed this latter finding—to be sure, the number of persons in the United States claiming the category of No Religion has grown considerably in the past twenty years.

With regard to the coordination of disaster-response efforts, the geographical layout of church buildings turned out to be an important factor. Two church buildings stood within 130 feet to the immediate east and west of the Murrah Building. Among those that received substantial media coverage were the First Methodist Church, St. Joseph's Old Cathedral, First Christian Church, and St. Paul's Cathedral (Episcopal). Nonetheless, other downtown churches in general received extensive print-media attention.

DISASTER RESPONSE

At 9:02 a.m. on April 19, 1995, a homemade fertilizer bomb located inside a Ryder rental truck exploded at a north-side loading lane of the Alfred P. Murrah Federal Building in Oklahoma City. The entire north face of the nine-story building was reduced to rubble, with the third through ninth floors pancaking, one atop another, until finally coming to rest at street level.[7] The reverberations of the blast were felt as far as thirty miles away, with topographical factors augmenting the trajectory of the blast so that numerous buildings more than one mile away from the attack site suffered more damage than some buildings only a half-mile or less away (such as Leadership Square). Two church buildings, the First Methodist Church of Oklahoma City and St. Joseph's Old Cathedral and Rectory, flanked the Murrah Building to the east and to the west respectively, and suffered heavy structural damage. Local police officers and passersby who eluded serious injury constituted the bulk of immediate first

5. Leonard, "Southern Crossroads," 47.

6. Kosmin and Mayer, *American Religious Identification Survey 2001*, 41.

7. ODCEM, *After Action Report*, 1.

responders, followed by local firefighters. Indeed the Oklahoma City Fire Department established an incident command system immediately after the incident in order to manage on-site search-and-rescue efforts. The incident commander (IC) set up an incident command post (ICP) at the intersection of N.W. Sixth Street and Harvey Avenue, which the district manager confirmed upon arriving at the scene.[8] The state emergency-operations center, located three miles east of the Murrah Federal Building in a subterranean site between two buildings at the state capitol complex, was fully operational at 9:25 a.m. and hosted representatives from various state agencies as well as the American Red Cross. Due to at least two bomb scares, the ICP was relocated to a vacant parking lot two blocks north to Northwest Eighth Street and Harvey Avenue. It was here that the mobile command vehicles of the police and fire departments were likewise relocated and thereafter joined by vehicles from the Federal Bureau of Investigation (FBI), the Bureau of Alcohol, Tobacco, and Firearms (BATF), and the Drug Enforcement Administration (DEA).[9]

As first responders searched through the remains of the Murrah Federal Building, members of a Catholic social-services agency gathered in a small truck about three miles northwest of the attack site and prayed about their impending involvement in this unprecedented and, at the time, undefined event. Upon arrival, the workers assumed individual positions at four corners of a perimeter boundary established by first responders. These mental-health workers encountered local citizens and concerned friends and family members of potential victims. As first responders continued to enter the wreckage in order to extricate the wounded and to treat victims who spilled over onto the streets surrounding the blast site, several command posts were established. In addition, three ministers were chosen to coordinate the participation of other local clergy or church personnel.

In terms of their physical dimensions (including both size and usable space) and proximity to the bombing site, at least four church buildings within a five-mile radius of the bombing site represented ideal spaces for disaster-response operations. These churches were well known on the urban landscape at the northern edge of downtown Oklahoma City. They were also quite spacious, and perhaps because they were used often, the buildings evoked comfort, familial intimacy, and patience for victims

8. Ibid., 2, 3.

9. Ibid., 4.

and their families. The Federal Emergency Management Administration (FEMA) offices, in this case, were quite miniscule and spatially removed from the Murrah Federal Building. From a strategic perspective, this distance was desirable so that a government office is protected from the direct or indirect effects of an attack. Incidentally, nonetheless, its distance from the attack site and its relative size made it a point of personnel deployment and very little more. The spatial proximity of various highly influential church buildings (i.e. First Methodist Church and First Christian Church) to the Murrah Building made them ideal venues for emergency service provision. First Methodist Church was used as a temporary mortuary and eventual family-support center; spaces at First Christian Church were used to establish another family-assistance center; and mobile feeding units were stationed at First Baptist Church. This initial use of church space, along with other varied uses during the recovery phase, eventuated in extremely significant social processes centered on narrative authority, which in turn furnished local churches with a pivotal role in postdisaster collective identity formation in relation to the interests of the state. The theological upshot of these specific social operations points to the potency of certain ecclesial "tactics" (a la Michel de Certeau)[10] that effectively weave theologically thick orientations into vital disaster-response scenarios otherwise teeming with technospecialists. These tactics also complexify state-centered "simple space" and as a result disperse political sovereignty through the wise use of gifts, including gifted speech.

The material in this chapter is divided into three sections that individually correspond to the guiding questions introduced in the previous chapter. The first section concerns, first, theological reflection surrounding pastoral response to the disaster; second, ministerial involvement in what I will call statist liturgies and similar events aimed at re-forming the body politic; and, third, ministerial interpretations of statist discourse that employed theological speech. The second section tackles citizen interpretations of church-state dedifferentiation, citizens' participation in forming collective identity and the cultural products they consumed toward this end, and the importance of memory work and the built environment. Interview data were gathered from thirteen residents who

---

10. Certeau, *Practice of Everyday Life*, 34.

either lived in Oklahoma City and environs or worked in the city during the attack.[11]

MINISTERS, EXPERTS, AND OFFICIAL RESPONSE

This section examines the relationship between the clergy or church-employed personnel and the governmental, official response to the bombing. The heuristic hypothesis that guided my data-gathering efforts claimed that church and state engage the same project of reestablishing the political imagination (i.e., more-or-less explicit affirmation of basic assumptions about human nature and destiny, about what sort of person contributes to the new social body, and about what actions ensure harmony), but that church personnel must denarrativize or decontextualize Christian views in order to gain public attention amid myriad claims from "expert" institutions molded by statist interests and visions. The data of this analysis draw not only on accounts of direct interaction between clergy and government officials but also on the manner in which clergy

11. It is critical to note again that this analysis was not based on a random sample; it is intended to identify crucial themes that emerged from within the population in question, not their relative or estimated presence across the entire population. Print media data were primarily gathered from a sample of relevant newspaper articles extending from April 20, 1995, until December 31, 1995. The articles were extracted from the NewsBank database of the Oklahoma City Library. The search terms "bomb" and "church" produced 287 articles, 188 of which were dated between April 20, 1995 (the day after the attack), and May 30, 1995. These terms were selected in order to capture those articles in which church activity was tied to the bombing. This approach runs the risk of missing articles that used only "terrorist attack" or "attack" in lieu of "bombing," but searches using these terms yielded considerably smaller numbers of hits. Interestingly, the majority of articles produced by a search using the terms "bomb," "church," and "government" (twenty-two articles) were found in the "bomb" and "church" search. Those that were not accounted for in the "bomb" and "church" search were also valued in the analysis. Also interesting is that all articles gathered through the search adopting the terms "church" and "government" (nineteen articles) appeared within the selection of articles generated in the "bomb" and "church" search. Originally my data-collection plan called for a selection of ten articles for each month, with follow-up searches until the point of saturation was reached. However, in reviewing the headlines of every article (and the body of most), I realized that the goal of ten articles was infeasible for all months from July 1995 to December 1995 (inclusive). The months of October, November, and December yielded five articles each, and August and September only produced three articles. July signaled a marked increase, to thirteen articles. Articles in remaining months were used to "compensate" for the scant data in the second half of the year. Twenty-five articles were picked from June, and the remainder fell between April 20, 1995, and May 20, 1995. Content analysis of print data using the software program MAX.QDA 2 produced 1,279 codes from a grand total of 110 articles.

interpreted the actions, evaluations, and legal decisions of public officials and other disaster-response experts, including engineers. Newspaper data (from the *Daily Oklahoman*) supplemented interview data insofar as it spoke to this relationship. Data from one-on-one interviews and print media dealing with clergy response and evaluations directed significant attention to the following themes: (1) positional authority and creative speech (including prayer) in emergency-response operations, (2) dissent or doubt with respect to memorial ceremony participation and public officials' engagement with theology in various relief efforts, (3) the absence of forgiveness as a normalized, ecclesial social discipline, and (4) the state's policy of financial aid to the churches. These themes, in the aggregate, partially challenged my expectations. That is, many instances arose in which theologically informed convictions or practices, church-centered visions of city prosperity, and renewed self-understanding shaped ongoing efforts to reestablish social organization. Otherwise various other findings that receive critical theological treatment below include the following: the speech acts of state actors were found to be characteristically *not* "gifted," ministers who harbored theological critiques of memorialization practices developed no venue to openly discuss such views, and the opposition between state-defined "aid" or compensation for congregations and the reception of divine gifts received important yet insufficient articulation. Among ministers and local congregations, many opportunities for ecclesial involvement were lost due to a lack of unified conviction and mobilizing structures (e.g., communicative resources and other relationships that tied congregational bodies to one another).

On the day of the bombing of the Murrah Federal Building, local ministers were assigned to various tasks related to disaster response, with primary attention toward grief-counseling services for families, stress-related counseling for rescuers, and, when applicable, giving final rites (prayer for salvation and absolution of sins). A trio of ministers regulated the ebb and flow of 250 ministers and chaplains from different denominations and their assignment to different emergency-related tasks at the bombing site and at other sites: Jack Poe, Oklahoma City police chaplain; Rev. Robert Allen of Wesley United Methodist Church; and Joe Williams, state FBI chaplain and director of chaplaincy for the Baptist General Convention of Oklahoma.[12] Robert Allen's designation to disaster-response

---

12. Gilliland, "Chaplains Reunite," 20.

service was convenient in the sense that Oklahoma City mayor Ron Norrick was already acquainted with him. (Allen in fact had served on the Oklahoma City University board of trustees and other panels with mayor Norrick. Also, on April 18, 1995, the day before the bombing, Norrick and Allen had both been present at a city-council meeting where Allen delivered the opening prayer.) Other ministers unknown to Norrick on a personal level possessed many years of disaster-response training and involvement (one of whom participated in this study), in large part due to tornado relief. Yet this anecdote about Robert Allen underscores the importance of acquaintance and friendship networks in the realm of church-and-state relations following disasters, an important topic in the disaster literature that cannot be treated here.

The use of ministers in a variety of roles is well attested in other data sources, especially in connection with relief efforts coordinated through Oklahoma City emergency management and through a number of national relief agencies with a local volunteer base. Within the realm of local government-spearheaded social services, Participant *A1*, a mental-health worker affiliated with a local church, made reference to the relocation of the Family Support Center from the main Red Cross facility to the First Methodist Church. This unavoidably brought a sizeable portion of organizational tasks, forms of speech, and practices to be performed within the church building and under the general oversight of Rev. Nick Harris and associate ministers of the congregation. In the case of volunteer work outside church buildings, clergy seem to have been involved to a significant degree as well. The Disaster Research Center interviewed a supervisor of a prominent relief organization who placed clergy within the general category of vital "volunteer workers." This sizable corps of volunteers satisfied a multiplicity of different tasks. These responsibilities were associated with a fairly wide range of tasks that usually reside in local, regional, and even federal governmental domains.[13] The relief worker stated:

> We had people working in the temporary morgues, helping with the paperwork, we had volunteers, like I said, assisting, making the FBI IDs. Um, we had 'em doing all the traditional [name of the participant's organization] things, uh the mass caring, the case work, we had opened what we call the [subagency], which now you now they're typically named a [another subagency name]

13. Allen, according to Participant *B3*, was responsible for coordinating all of the clergy who converged on the site.

where the advance notifications were done. [This organization] had basically the oversight of that center, and it was run by volunteers. We had a group of mental health volunteers, [and], *clergy*; I can just go on and on, I'm trying to think of other things. They just did it all, I mean just anything and everything that was needed, our staff was there.[14]

"Trading Off"

As a unit, chaplains Poe and Williams, along with Allen, spearheaded the coordination of ministerial functions at the Murrah site for a sixteen-day period (April 19, 1995, to May 5, 1995). Williams managed a statewide critical-response team of 140 police chaplains, while Poe directed twenty-four active duty reserve police chaplains. Allen, according to Participant *B3*, was responsible for coordinating all the clergy who converged on the site.[15] Although the chaplains did not require ministers to have seminary degrees in order to serve at the site, they did require ministers to receive training from the National Organization for Victims Assistance. This stipulation substantially dwindled the pool of potential on-site ministers and hence facilitated monitoring. During this period of time, the ministers also established at least two response-generated practices (as opposed to event-generated practices) that represented negotiations of authority that only make sense in the context of multiple and sometimes incompatible institutional discourses and practices aimed at maximizing command, control, coordination, and efficiency. Each response-generated practice was meant to serve the exigencies of a certain class of encounters, many of which are common to acute instances of organizational and cultural instability (such as those found in a disaster). The tendency to hierarchize local disaster-response personnel and relations was in full effect at the bombing site. Jim Ramsey, a police officer who arrived with a partner at the devastated Murrah Federal Building site about three minutes after the explosion to help pull out bodies, recounted the following:

> A fireman came in with a big, loud bullhorn and said to us, the guys who were in there from the first moment, "If you're not a fireman, get out of the building now." . . . I was extremely frustrated. What gives this man the right to come in here and tell

14. Aguirre, Respondent 5 interview (emphasis added).
15. Santos, Participant *B3* interview.

> me this? I had been in here since the beginning. I pulled people
> out—no, I don't know what I'm doing, but I had been in here long
> enough, so my chances are enough . . . This has been our feeling
> for a month: that we were there first, and we should have been
> allowed to help, to continue the help that we started, . . . If I was a
> firefighter making those decisions, I would have said, "Everybody
> out except for the firefighters." . . . But it's hard when you're on the
> other end, and you're not a firefighter.[16]

Within this wider context of hierachization and establishment of authority
relations in strategic and tactical matters, it is predictable that one class of
encounters dealt specifically with the lack of authority that clergy possess
in a context dominated by credentialed emergency-response experts. In
one particular case, police chaplain Poe was struck with the idea of having families report to one site instead of five, in order to receive information about a missing loved one. Surprisingly, Poe felt powerless to make
this suggestion to the police chiefs, the very city employees with whom
he works on a regular basis. Instead, Rev. Allen was able to carry out the
task: "Jack couldn't tell the chiefs to do this or that, but I could".[17] In this
instance, Allen seemed to possess some degree of tactical authority in
relation to police chiefs, a capacity most likely derived from the mayoral
appointment that placed him in that particular coordinative position. He
was not, as were Poe and Williams, an employee of a government agency.
Hence to at least a small degree, "secular" political aura was "transferred"
onto ministerial appointees. The ministers were in agreement that this
improvisational practice of alternation was important and commonplace.
With some frequency, then, a particular "responsibility" that proved to
be difficult for one minister was passed off to another with greater hierarchical leverage; or, as they put it, the ministers "traded off on playing
the 'bad guy.'"[18] This particular interpretation of the practice's impact on
other actors at the disaster site is interesting; it implies that the ministers
played the role of "spoilers," or those that questioned a well-established
service arrangement or other set of task performances.

　　These three ministers also served with a high degree of flexibility
because they were not operating under any sort of formal emergency-
response plan or task assignment; rather Poe stated that they focused on

16. Lackmeyer, "Terror Changes Lives," 19.

17. Gilliland, "Chaplains Reunite," 20.

18. Ibid.

"help[ing] people,"[19] a phrase that, despite being indistinct, is completely consistent with pastoral and Christian theological commitments. This flexibility allowed the ministers to use the vocational authority and pastoral perspective, which they already enjoyed from nondisaster contexts, in a more open-ended and piecemeal fashion at the bombing site. The inclusion of Rev. Allen in particular was largely unpredictable; the ministers consequently attributed it entirely to God's providential oversight: "I just think God planned that, because you [Allen] certainly maintained a liaison between here [the bombing site] and the churches."[20] Participant *B3* further elaborated thus: "Rev. Allen had given the morning prayer at a meeting with Norrick the day before. So, he [Allen] was already on Norrick's mind when the time came to get someone to fill the void."[21] Mental-health workers from Catholic Charities, by contrast, served in accordance with the protocols set forth by the local chapter of National Voluntary Organizations Active in Disaster (NVOAD). This, however, does not mean that Catholic Charities functioned with a disaster component already in place within their organizational scheme. The disaster-response component that is presently in place was designed and implemented after the bombing of the Murrah Federal Building.

The consequences of operating under a standardized model of disaster-response protocol are positive in the sense that a volunteer organization will not proceed in a fashion completely out of turn or incommensurate with respect to other organizations. An organization's assumed strategic perspective, responsibilities (domains), and tasks stem from a model enjoying widespread acceptance. Nonetheless, the ministerial action detailed above serves to undermine the "simple space," as John Milbank calls it, which the state maps onto the social world in order to render it malleable to a host of governmentalities, including the grossest forms of command and control.[22] Ministers are often difficult to place on such a rationalized map (unless they have been extensively trained in emergency-response operations) because persons may respect and require them for a variety of tasks unrelated to, for instance, search-and-rescue operations and other emergency-response functions. Indeed, they

19. Ibid.
20. Ibid.
21. Santos, Participant *B3* interview
22. See Milbank, *Word Made Strange*, 272–75.

are needed for "spiritual" matters considered essential to the ongoing work, especially counseling; beyond this, they are not considered essential directors of any other function from the perspective of state oversight. In the arrangement that obtained after the bombing in Oklahoma City, however, the capacity of ministers to complexify space by linking disparate citizens such as police officers, firefighters, food-service workers, journalists, and other community members outside the disaster-impact zone was readily discernible. Insofar as the ministers succeeded in circumventing and cutting across hierarchical barriers through the wise exercise of gifts, they were able to capitalize upon emergent opportunities. Over time, this complexification of space also undermined centralized political sovereignty. It forced ground-level practitioners to question plans and methods and to receive innovative alternatives from persons not included in the hierarchy, all the while preserving some measure of efficiency. As a common ecclesial-pastoral practice before and after disasters, this barrier crossing has the potential to undercut the only seemingly inevitable stereotypes, geoeconomic barriers, and enduring intergenerational animosities that preclude the formation of a truly universal church at the local, community level.

Public Prayer for the Traumatized Polity

Both interview data and print media confirmed the centrality of public prayer, a well-worn practice in American politics since the early days of nationhood.[23] First, prayer was publicly recurring and even concretely situated within an ad hoc memorial site. At least in the period during which Allen, Poe, and Williams headed ministerial operations, chaplains prayed with police officers before their shifts and every single morning at 9:02 (the time of the blast) at a memorial site located at N.W. Sixth and Hudson [Avenue?]. Hence, the moment of the blast was daily remembered in prayer and pondered through regularized theological reflection.

This practice was crucial in sacralizing the Murrah building site. The transformation of a site at which death and mortality were suddenly thrust upon a city is vital: it must somehow be carried into God's presence. Chaplain Poe asserted, "This whole area became kind of a holy place . . . There was more prayer for this eight-block area of Oklahoma City than there was for the whole world during that time. That's what I think

23. Waldstreicher, *In the Midst of Perpetual Fetes.*

sustained us."[24] Prayer, in fact, was at the center of a bit of media-centered controversey surrounding the degree to which "God-talk" was invoked at emergency-relief facilities. One key newspaper article features a rebuttal of a previous article that had covered the widespread doubt and anger about God's role in the disaster. The responding editorial writer, perhaps taking advantage of the opened hermeneutical space caused by the disaster, sounded off on the misinformation, quotations out of context, and otherwise supposedly erroneous argumentation of the previous article. He stated that there was actually "rock solid belief in God" at the attack site and its relief facilities. Moreover, on April 20, a registered nurse and volunteer stated that all volunteers "prayed together as one group from many different faiths," acknowledging that the relief work "'was much bigger, much harder than any of us had ever done before—we needed spiritual help!'"[25]

The importance of public prayer and its role in the cultural production of a theologically informed, postdisaster public discourse and identity would be missed if the extent to which prayer was publicized were ignored.[26] In terms of a word count in the data set, at least forty-two allusions to "prayer" (or cognates, e.g. "pray" or "praying") were contained in 110 articles, two memorial speeches, and a special memorial edition of the popular magazine, *Oklahoma Today*. Prayer was mentioned in highly varied contexts, including but not limited to closing statements in ctizen response pieces, descriptions of memorial ceremonies in cities surrounding Oklahoma City, interviews of relief-agency workers, and overviews of the content in the *Oklahoman*'s Access Line. The Access Line (by telephone) offered interested Oklahomans the opportunity to listen to songs

24. Gilliland, "Chaplains Reunite," 20.

25. McReynolds, "Post-Bomb Murmurs," 10.

26. It is difficult to proceed in this analysis without mentioning the crucial role that the most popular local newspaper, the *Oklahoman*, played in shaping public theological discourse and, therefore, in providing symbolic resources for the construction of a postdisaster identity. The data concerning ministerial improvisation was almost entirely based on newspaper coverage, which did not shy away from providing sizeable coverage of the theological interpretations or views of these ministers, along with views of others such as Reverend Nick Harris, and Most Reverend George Back, dean of St. Paul's Episcopal Cathedral. The newspaper was already quite conservative in its religious leanings, and the disaster seems to have facilitated the dilation of discursive space, thus allowing for extensive usage of theological language. The specific location of the attack, one surrounded by at least five prominent churches, played a major role in this regard as well.

and prayers of consolation from respected and popular figures in country music and politics. In other words, prayer as a publicly recognizable,
socially approved practice was not limited to the highly formalized ritual
sphere of action (e.g., memorial ceremonies); it was presented as vital
and regular at every level of social organization.

Moreover, the point at which allusions to prayer intersected with
other themes in a given article is quite informative as well. The theme
"prayer as practice" was identified 31 times and, interestingly, intersected
or overlapped with ten other coherent themes on 25 different occasions.
Of these ten other themes, four concerned a statist operation; themes
included "God-work as official response" (constructions of God during
official performances), "church and state memorial ceremonies outside
of church space," "statist allusions to the Bible," and "Governor Keating's
performance" at memorial ceremonies. The remainder of the themes
were linked predictably to church involvement and to theological interpretations by clergy or citizens; however, within this group the subtheme
"church and state familiarity" appeared as well (signifying reconciled
church-and-state cultural relations. For example, a poster titled "Heroes
of the Heartland," endorsed by the governor's wife, featured an image of
a cross superimposed over an outline of the state of Oklahoma). What
all of this indicates is a measurable dedifferentiation, chiefly through
public ritual articulations, of church-and-state cultural production. As
a spiritual discipline, prayer was appropriated in a vast number of projects of reorientation and thus became central to the postdisaster *religio*
of statist organs. It appears that the state enacted the cultural opposite of
what early Christians executed as subjects of the Roman Empire: Early
Christians co-opted focal symbols of one lifeworld and appropriated
them for purposes different from their original ones.

Most relevant to the present interests, however, were various sources
that provided extensive material about key ritual events at which ministers and politicians enacted joint cultural productions. One such event
was completely concerned with prayer as such. On May 4, 1995, just over
two weeks after the bombing, a National Day of Prayer service was held
at the steps of the Oklahoma state capitol building. In this event, a total of
at least six speakers spoke about the primacy of prayer. The program included Rev. Randall Faulkner's plea, based on New Testament Scripture,

to pray on behalf of those in government.[27] Republican senator Howard Hendrick, Lieutenant governor Mary Fallin (who also served as master of ceremonies), and governor Frank Keating expounded upon prayer and likewise read New Testament and Old Testament passages concerning God's "plans" for his people (Jer 29:10–11) and the necessity of obedient response as people "called by God's name" (2 Chr 7:14). Senator Hendrick specifically identified Oklahomans with "those called by his [God's] name."[28] Although the scriptural allusions and applications of each political actor were rooted in the Hebrew Bible, the recontextualization of the passages (from ancient postexilic Israel to twentieth-century Oklahoma) was unproblematic from the viewpoint of media coverage and the ongoing postdisaster project to reconstitute the body politic of Oklahoma. This stripping of covenantal identification with the particular Jewish people seems to be precisely what Scott Bader-Saye considers quintessential to American exceptionalism in his study of the "politics of election."[29] The political goals of the speakers and organizers are considered paramount, whereas the actual legacy of the covenantal promises is ignored because the demands of the historical moment (and years of neglect among churches) warrant indifference to the covenental legacy. In this public service, however, divine election is granted to Oklahomans proper, not to Oklahomans qua Americans. Oklahomans, as the forthcoming section will elaborate, took up a process common in postdisaster scenarios marked by generous sharing of resources and emotionally intensive encounters between vulnerable citizens: the differentiation of local from national identity as an attempt to substantively recognize the "goods" that locals are able to produce. This grassroots project, when engaged with the characteristic features of statist imaginative and physical spaces, claims devotion to prayer and election as essential qualities of the individul citizen and of the corporate body politic. Yet the grassroots project can only affirm that these graces are actually intrinsic to group life in a highly contested cultural landscape.

Along these lines, it is important to note that a survey of the print-media data revealed that prayer as a practice for the sake of a body of citizens with reference to national identity, or for the sake of binding

27. "Weary Nation," *Oklahoman*, 7.

28. Ibid.

29. Bader-Saye, *Church and Israel*, 64–68.

Oklahomans as a body politic, was always advanced, with one marginal exception, by politicians and ministers. The exception involves the "interfaith prayer" of volunteer relief workers mentioned above, which carried some implications that other ethnic and confessional groups could be included in prayer as a common, public practice during the recovery-and-response phase.[30]

Significantly, we find that public performance of prayer and religious rituals in the time following the bombing in Oklahoma City was robustly evangelical in nature and yet firmly entrenched in a distinguished place of statist activity and speech, wherein legislation and other political judgments were validated and found solemnized expression. As Richard Fenn has argued, courts of law, church buildings and services, and legislative forums are physical structures that even under "secularized social conditions" still, in themselves, give certain speech acts their signifying power, namely, their solemnity and binding nature.[31]

Most important, the relational elements of prayer, in the print-media coverage of the National Day of Prayer service, were defined in terms of links between the individual citizen, the state of Oklahoma, government, and God. In other words, the church universal and individual congregations in particular were rendered irrelevant in the construction of a transcendent reality. In fact, all intermediate levels of social organization, including synagogue and mosque, were omitted. The instrumentalization of Scripture, mentioned above, including invoking the "plans of God" for "the chosen people" could only be effective because church bodies were assumed not to have a part in the political interests at hand. This makes a sort of rhetorical ventriloquism, whereby a respected (usually deceased) historic personage is made to endorse a given cause despite little to no articulation of the authority's original context or aims: a rather facile and effective strategy. Untethered from a community of faithful discipleship, the prophet Jeremiah is disregarded, in all his anguish for a people calloused to God's pleas for Israel; and God's assurances for another chosen people are broadcast for all to endorse and assimilate. Passages like 2 Chron 7:14, which calls for repudiation of sinful practices,

30. All other allusions to prayer were offered by volunteer workers and citizens that connected the practice to their growth in emotional and spiritual maturity after the attack, or by those who used prayer as an appeal for help or strength in the midst of difficult experiences while providing service to the ailing.

31. Fenn, *Liturgies and Trials.*

become exhortations to Oklahomans in their capacity as Oklahomans. This, in effect, pits the Word of God against the Word of God. It confusingly uses the words of God for aims and audiences that may be contrary to or completely unclear about the formative aims of the Word of God in the economy of salvation. As Markus Bockmuehl contends, "the implied interpreter of Christian Scripture is a *disciple*," and that disciple is formed in the congregation of the faithful.[32] Statist uses of Scripture accomplish a trivialization of God's people, in that while it would be misguided to claim that God does not have plans for the people of Oklahoma (which he does), this does not warrant the marginalization of the people of God from those very plans. Sacred Scripture is indeed designed for formative and collective reading, and as a whole "leads to life . . . by commanding and by helping," as Aquinas claimed in one of his inaugural sermons.[33] But the rhetorical integrity and thoroughness for which Aquinas argues in explicitly distinguishing "the *height* of spiritual doctrine, the *dignity* of those who teach it," the humble condition of those who listen to it, and the order intrinsic to the communication of wisdom and reception of gifts are absent from the public employment of Scripture discussed here, insofar as such integrity only makes sense in an ecclesial setting dedicated to mutual care, intimate instruction, and growth over time.[34] As it is, many liturgies of the state (such as the National Day of Prayer ceremony detailed above) direct such public reading toward a *telos* alien to God's historical people rooted in the calling of Israel and blessed through their inclusion in the church. God's people (the intended audience of the Scriptures because they are always in need of hearing that which equips them to remember and embody their calling) are also meant to cultivate the skills of discernment, dialogue, and service necessary for the sake of an end that is only intelligble within a narrative that encompasses God's redemptive activity in the world. To hijack scriptural narrative and exhortation without acknowledging this political tenet of Scripture reading only supports the spiritualization of "*a* people," (and would perhaps prevent authentic spiritualization) with no accountability to the resources by which the process of spiritualization occurs.

---

32. Bockmuehl, *Seeing the Word,* 91–93.

33. Aquinas, *Selected Writings,* 7, 13.

34. Ibid., 13–17 (emphasis original).

After the Oklahoma City bombing, public authority, moreover, was negotiated in a theological and narrative sense with little respect for any boundaries distinguishing church and state, and regardless of vocational skill. That is to say, although government officials invoked elements of sermonic exhortation, a minister and other nonpoliticians (including the general manager of the newspaper and the chair of an unnamed civic committee), who did the very same, balanced, as it were, the cultural playing field. Each speaker, whether clergy or nonclergy, introduced a narrative spirituality to supplement the ongoing recuperative efforts following the bombing, and asked all those present in the audience to do the same. Furthermore, the National Day of Pryaer service deployed Bible passages from both covenants, promoted prayer as practice, and invoked Jesus as a figure who, according to Edmund Martin (the general manager of the *Oklahoman*), "never became tyrannized by the urgent. He carved out time for the important [i.e., prayer]."[35] Thus the *Oklahoman* as a member of the audience (more than three hundred people attended) was addressed as a *citizen*, who, for the sake of emotional recovery and future blessing, should engage in prayer as a social discipline and adopt a narrative spirituality rooted, albeit superficially, in both Christian and Judaic history. The dedifferentiation of church and state in the National Day of Prayer service was quite pronounced and, I surmise, created a precedent on the basis of which certain social imaginative practices in subsequent weeks were validated or challenged (e.g., those practices that spoke of human nature, human destiny, and social harmony). The National Day of Prayer service created the general impression that political officials could confidently engage in priestly functions without any acknowledgement of their need to abundantly "receive" from the community of faith, and without honestly noting the political implications of such action: government officials needed neither the wisdom nor the accountability that comes with reading Scripture or with invoking the Scriptures of Israel and the language of their covenant. Because the state in general only accepts universalized persons, narratives, and measures of time that validate its existence, Israel and the church can receive no substantive attention, although their resources can be co-opted to give life to a wounded social body, that of "the people." In this co-optation, local churches and the specific ministerial actors and relationships that buttress such events appear to embody the acquiescence that is necessary for this cultural co-optation

35. "Weary Nation," *Oklahoman*, 7.

to persist without dialogue. The consequences of such deficiencies will become even more evident in forthcoming sections, which show that the absence of a unified and comprehensive theological front precluded the expression of risky yet important public speech.

Details about public ministerial involvement in nationalized events received scant attention in this sample of documents; that is, beside the treatment of the National Day of Prayer and the service on that day (at which President Clinton and Billy Graham spoke), there is only one other allusion to the public prayer of ministers in the context of "the nation." In this case, Jack Poe and Joe Williams were "shocked" to have two CNN reporters ask them to pray on national television.[36] The response of "shock" is entirely dependent upon the tacitly accepted standard of secularized or nontheological speech in the public (mainstream, televised) sphere. Even so, the print data as a whole indicate that the "nationalization of prayer" was overshadowed by vernacular usage for individual rehabilitative purposes and by local political usage, with respect to which both government officials and clergy held seemingly equal public authority. Yet again, the absence of heavy nationalizing should not be taken to diminish the significance of large-scale ritual events at all, only to highlight a key quantitative difference in newspaper coverage over the course of six months after the attack. The ritual events will receive more attention in section 2.

Prayer, to this day, remains a regular aspect of the experience of most tourists or pilgrims to the impact site. This is mainly due to the differential impact of various ministers who worked at the bombing site and consequently shaped the decision to build (and publicly dedicate) a small chapel next to the site. The Heartland Chapel was the first "unofficial" or vernacular memorial to the disaster and the first permanent memorial of any kind. It is an open-air chapel that sits east of the bomb site, almost conjoined to First Methodist Church. The chapel, constructed by volunteers, with donations from Methodist, Jewish, and Muslim community members, has been frequented by virtually all visitors to the site since its appearance shortly after the blast. Volunteers constructed the chapel to be ready for visiting by the Fourth of July holiday,[37] thus assuring its subsumption into ongoing cultural constructions of national identity and

---

36. Gilliland, "Chaplains Reunite," 20.
37. "A Prayer for America," Prayer Card secured at Heartland Chapel.

national history. Within the confines of the chapel, visitors will find a small box that holds handwritten prayer requests, and a slot that holds cards featuring a prayer called "A Prayer for America," which visitors can take with them. This prayer requests the following (The format below is identical to the original):

> Father God, send a spirit of repentance and let it sweep across this nation. Let purging fire of revival begin in my heart and in Your Church. Let it spread to every community, town, and city in America.
>
> Father God, we pray for our leaders, for those who have power over us. Lift them up, Father, and give them wisdom to wisely rule this land we love, America.
>
> Let the bad roots that produce the bad fruit be burned out of their lives, and ours, and establish righteousness.
>
> We thank you, Father, for those Godly leaders who have been elected to public office. We ask that ungodly leaders improve or be removed. Thank You, God, that Satan's hold on government has been broken. We thank You that righteous rule is being established.
>
> May your kingdom come and your will be done on earth as it is in heaven.
>
> These things we persistently pray in the name of Jesus, Amen.
>
> Please take this prayer for America and pray it aloud in your church, in your Sunday school, and in your home! MAY GOD'S GRACE BE WITH YOU.[38]

This prayer card appears to represent the crystallization (in material form and as a result of the efforts of a given congregation) of the degree to which prayer is employed in service of political criticism and for rebinding the national body politic following the attack of 1995. The reference to "the bad roots that produce the bad fruit"[39] is difficult to comprehend without drawing a link to Timothy McVeigh and other homegrown fellow Americans who serve in patriotic social movements that may be bent on violent action. Besides this, the prayer contains eschatological statements about the establishment of righteous rule; these statements situate the prayer in a world in which government as a whole does not have to (and should not) persist with incompetent or "ungodly" leaders. Thus

38. Ibid.
39. Adapted from Matt 7:15–18.

it paradoxically combines a full-fledged desire for change in leadership where and when necessary with an assurance of God's patient yet relentless subjection of the powers to his reign.

While the vehement request for God's active care and attention in political leadership is necessary and laudable, the role of the local church as a community of disciples of Jesus and as God's alternative politics is overlooked or obscured. Readers are rightly called to plea for God's active care for the leadership of the nation, but the church is not understood as a people who, if true to the claims of the Son who "received authority" because of the Father's overabundant love and delight, present the possibility for an understanding of politics as a function of the Creator's love for his creatures in the world. This politics, moreover, is not achieved through coercion or militant devotion to the use of tracts and handouts, but through relentlessly compassionate and self-emptying engagement with present political actors. Individual churches, despite perennial divisions between denominations, are still the bearers of a gifted self-understanding. They are, as Berndt Wannenwetsch persuasively contends, the collapse of *polis* into *oikos* (and vice versa);[40] hence the church as the body of Christ presents politics as inextricably rooted in love, faith, hope, peace, gentleness, kindness: the church presents the manner in which all the other fruits of the Spirit (Gal 5:22–23) challenge present political discourse and practice. The political character needed for politics is the very same character molded in line with the gifts received to constitute a people who rule through service and through slavery to a wisdom that instructs on how to listen, love, and trust, not on how to predict and control. These are the people God molds to reject alternative social types or schemas that vouchsafe the way politics "must work" and the type of human being needed for such politics. These people reject, in other words, Machiavelli's distinction of private virtue and public virtue—a distinction that exists for the sake of contriving the "effectual truth of the matter" (*la verita effetuale della cosa*).[41] Members of the body of Christ, as Wannenwetsch's analysis suggests, are shaped to be loving, serving, adoring, confessing, and praying at home and "in politics," because it would be unthinkable to consider life in Christ as more appropriate in a household than in public. The church refuses to consider these to be distinct spheres

---

40. Wannenwetsch, "Political Worship of the Church," 270–80.

41. Machiavelli, *Prince*, 56.

of divine activity, not in a sense that sponsors the legislation of Christian morals or "family values," but because disciples of Christ are humbly convinced that living their lives as children in God's household (1 Tim 3:15) is tantamount to actual participation in God's eschatological assembly of saints and in temple worship. Paul's blending of different layers of political identification, including the household (*oikos*), temple cult of Israel, and assembly of citizens (*polis*), suggests not only a tearing asunder of racial differentiation between covenants but also an affirmation of the unequivocal interconnectedness of household life, worship, and public or communal participation. The vocabulary and practices of one sphere enrich, serve, and incorporate (when necessary) the other spheres so that all may be "home" to God.

The Propriety of the Public Theological Response

With respect to the cultural politics of the response and recovery phases in Oklahoma City, the invocation of prayer and the use of Scripture on the part of both ministers and political actors is merely one topic of many. Alternatively, it appears necessary to ascertain what clergy thought about the use of theological speech in the service of statist concerns with social order and with the binding of one person to another. This topic received no attention whatsoever either in the sample of articles submitted to analysis or in other print media. However, clergy and nonclergy participants spoke directly to this topic, sometimes with fervor and conviction.

Most ministers made their most poignant and relevant statements with respect to events or actions of memorialization, whether at a memorial ceremony or in the construction of places (especially the national memorial) that inscribe an ostensibly permanent, public, and tangible "text" upon any reflections on the event. When asked about the propriety of the use of theological symbols and speech (i.e., "God-talk") in the context of the National Prayer service, participant *B1*, a minister of a small congregation associated with a mainline denomination at the time of the bombing, stated,

> God [in this instance] is a civil god. [After being asked to elaborate on this response, he stated], there is nothing particularly Christian about the service, even though Scriptures were quoted. Civil religion simply will not let people die, they have to become something; it is "civil" because it will not let the real theological

themes that constitute the narrative core of Christianity to come to the surface.[42]

Evidently the minister believed that "God-talk" parodied Christian theological themes without actually assuming or presenting the substance of the "narrative core of Christianity." This is highly intriguing in light of the fact that Billy Graham, a veritable cultural icon of American evangelicalism, spoke at the service. In this participant's view, the service advanced a "civil" god that bound persons to one another only for the purpose of reconstructing their identities around the cause for which the bombing victims were said to have given their lives: a cause of the nation-state faced with an irrational, government-hating group at the margins of ordered society. Participant *B1*'s statement that "civil religion will not let people die" suggests a critical position on statist processes of memorialization, including processes that render the death of citizens "meaningful." I asked him to elaborate on this point in order to discern what sorts of constructions were most bothersome to him and like-minded ministers. He replied,

> The victims were never, before the bombing, what they were made into afterward . . . It robs families of their identities. They were, at the beginning, heroes of Muslim execution, and then they found out that McVeigh was the perpetrator. But they had been heroes for too long—it could not be undone. He [McVeigh] was an American—he had to be framed as a militant extremist, not simply a dissident. They tried to attach him to some militias (even though he was a Gulf War veteran), and even Waco, Texas (because of the similarity in date). He was a "government-hating extremist." But you know what was never mentioned . . . that he was trained to act and think along these lines. They [the government] made him that way.[43]

There are at least four highly provocative and interrelated themes in this response that invite theological reflection. First, the minister's response emphasizes the state's (official) immediate and sure construction of some "other" (e.g., a minority ethnic group) as an enemy of the nation-state. Indeed within an hour of the bombing, former congressman David McCurdy was on a CBS newscast speaking about "very clear

42. Santos, Participant *B1* interview.

43. Ibid.

evidence of fundamentalist Islamic terrorist groups."[44] In addition, on the Wednesday morning after the bombing, Congressman McCurdy indicated on Oklahoma City's KWTV Channel 9 newscast that he believed Muslim students at the University of Oklahoma were involved. Hence, he implied, this sort of event should not be viewed entirely as a surprise. After all, there was a growing population of Muslims in the Oklahoma City area. This unfamiliar, non-Protestant group stood in sharp contrast to the overwhelming majority of white Baptist or Methodist local citizens.[45] Second, the minister criticized the caricature of McVeigh that was advanced through media outlets. Not only must McVeigh lie outside the mainstream, morally appropriate social types, but he must also be extremely other, namely, not like "me" or "us," not a local Oklahoman or a generic American individual unassociated with a militia. Such militias grew out of frustration with failed government policies that had aimed to support rural businesses and farmers. In certain cases, these patriot groups operated under a quasi-apocalyptic vision of resistance to statist disarmament; that is, many patriot groups believed that the federal government was plotting a campaign to systematically extricate all weapons from private citizens.[46] This construction of the violent, illegitimate, and unpredictable "other" is of a piece with the "war" narrative in which the federal government's campaign to diminish drug and weapons offenses has been couched for the past twenty-five years. The "war on drugs" and "war on crime" are emblematic of the increased militarization of federal law enforcement that has, in turn, bred a dissident counterpart that is just as entrenched in adversarial and war-based understandings of the situation. This perverted *perichoresis* of enemies steeped in congruent fears and compulsions to violence reveals how agents of sin and death, when not confronted with the triune God's mutual submission and outpouring of love, so readily embrace conflict—conflict with no ultimate winner because such violence is beholden to annihilation: it is from beginning to end an enemy of life. Third, and in the same vein, Participant *B1* questioned the integrity of the state's response to the attacker. The minister mentioned that the military, the primary manifestation of the state's monopoly over the means of violence, had trained the perpetrator

44. Quoted in Hamm, *Apocalypse in Oklahoma*, 54.

45. Cited in Cajee, *Oklahoma Hate and Harassment Report*.

46. Wright, *Patriots*, 11.

to respond with such force and efficacy. Here again we find the blindness that attends the state's capacity to create its own enemies, because at the root of the state's imaginary is not the Spirit that enters "the great deep" to bring about and celebrate the conditions of life (Gen 1:2), but one that simply turns its face away from—or sets its face against—the chaos of the world. It often does so without substantively acknowledging its role in exacerbating rebellion among God's creatures. In other words, the second and third points of political criticism in the minister's response represent a disruption of the tri-unity of God in a creational and communal sense. Under the imaginary of the state, the potential or seemingly obvious enemy is not effectively part of the world in which "we" participate, and thus all cultural productions must emphasize that this is so. The deleterious "other" is simply invading "our" world from the outside. The slogan of such an ethos asserts: "we" have (in a strict sense) nothing to do with "them," and this is precisely how cultural processes are designed to govern social life. Conflict and claims of the most unmeasured kind proceed logically from this foundational narrative about other groups or social types.

Fourth, the minister criticized the supposed conferral of false or embellished identities: those killed were presented publicly as both "heroes" and "victims" at the expense of a focus upon the actual, more ordinary or mundane aspects of their lives. These more private elements of individual lives did appear in short obituary write-ups in the local newspaper. Yet from the perspective of state-derived civic power, these ordinary qualities do not directly serve the construction of a narrative to which the political collectivity can subscribe. Their lives must serve a more compelling question: from what broader narrative frame of reference should citizens and political actions draw in order to identify the perennial collective goods that ought to be pursued during the postdisaster period? From the perspective of participant *B1*, the dead were used to serve the ends of the national body politic over the ends of any other collective identity or grouping: "At the 'national cry service,'" he argued, "they didn't say anything about the people who died, or about ordinary people—only about the national significance of the event."[47] The National Day of Prayer service, therefore, as the name of the event implies, facilitated a cultural

---

47. Santos, Participant *B1*, interview.

politics that nationalized what many perceived as an Oklahoman or domestic problem.

The import of a cultural politics pertaining to the rememberance of the dead can be articulated further through a brief consideration of one of the concluding chapters of Søren Kierkegaard's *Works of Love*. In a chapter titled "The Work of Love in Remembering One Dead," Kierkegaard notes that love is shown most authentically in one's response to those dead. In particular, Kierkegaard argues that the work of love toward one dead must be of the "most unselfish," of the "freest" and "most faithful" kind.[48] It is the most unselfish love to the extent that it cannot exact repayment ("the 'pagan' way," as Kierkegaard claims), and even still is not diminished. The ways in which we are accustomed to receiving "requited love" when giving affection and affirming devotion, especially as a parent, are not at all possible with the dead.[49] The process of memorialization, however, often seeks something from the dead in their death (or even in their mode of death). In the present case, interested parties primarily sought an example of patriotism and political devotion insofar as the persons died inside a government building and did so as a result of a sudden, brutal attack. This was only somewhat tempered by the death of the children in the daycare center named America's Kids. Even so, can the dead—whether adult or child—actually repay in some fashion; or, worse yet, is memorialization more often than not the contrivance of a repayment? Kierkegaard makes it painfully clear that unselfish love for the dead, in stark contrast to the exacting of demands from them, tests our attachment to the prospect that the dead will continue giving to us when in fact the call is to continually give to *them* without expecting reciprocal action. And, in fact, families of the deceased do just this, as do visitors to disaster sites who place flowers and all manner of objects (toys, photos, poems) on makeshift memorials along chain-link fences and in other unseemly locations. The dead do not, we often presume, tend to these objects, including flowers that are placed at gravesites over a long period of time. We know, therefore, how to give to them without repayment; but do specially prepared national services affirm this manner of giving that demands a particular disposition, most powerfully embodied in God's love for us? God first freely loved in creation and then in every

48. Kierkegaard, *Works of Love*, 320, 322, 325.
49. Ibid., 321–22.

subsequent act of redemption. As Kierkegaard noted with respect to expectant mothers, God showed that it is possible to love something that is effectively a "non-being" in the world.[50]

Perhaps most damaging to the large-scale memorialization project that ministers criticized in Oklahoma City was its lack of the freedom that Kierkegaard claimed important: the love for the dead was not given without constraint or compulsion. In other terms, when I give love and it is not due to "reminders" or other forms of pressure exerted upon me by means of cries or demands, then the love is indeed free. In relation to memorialization after the Oklahoma City bombing, the local minister's concerns elicit a vital question: do we need to love those lost in the bombing, as citizens in a national body, strictly because they remind us of some noble deed (primarily their death at Murrah Building), in the absence of which there would be no reason to recognize and love them? If so, then the love offered at such public services is not free love. Finally, in discussing the freedom and faithfulness (or the long-term commitment) of love for the dead, it is interesting that Kierkegaard notes that no authority (e.g., no governmental agency) ensures the remembrance of each dead person.[51] This is true in general but still disregards both the task forces assembled after disasters and wars to plan memorial services and monuments, and the work of churches who remember martyrs and the faithful (and sometimes the unfaithful) dead. The remembrances of churches are often of a qualitatively different kind because of the alternative knowledges that typify the church as the body of Christ. Martyrs, for instance, are witnesses so labeled precisely because they refused to accept the importance of knowing the "meaning" that the powers and authorities of the (postlapsarian) "world," when utterly unfaithful to God's vision of human life, wish to inscribe on their bodies and souls.[52]

Participant *B1*'s perceptive bit of political critique was, according to the participant, admittedly unique or unpopular. This is, as the participant further added, because the joint constructions of statist agendas with overt theological themes made "the church and nation turn out to

---

50. Ibid., 321.

51. Ibid., 323.

52. Hovey, *To Share in the Body*, 43–62. The chapter titled "Carrying Crosses" speaks directly to the issue of how Christian martyrdom completely undermines the logic of redemptive violence and the entire political-epistemological state of affairs that supports it.

be roughly the same thing."[53] Very few citizens seemed to find this conflation disturbing. In response to a question about what reasons or justifica-
tions citizens and ministers advance in support of this dedifferentiation
of church and state, the same minister, participant B1, asserted:

> The majority of people have no problem with mixing national
> patriotism with Christian identity. I mean, [name of influential,
> publicly visible minister]—he would have no problem with the
> president assuming the role [of eulogist at the National Day of
> Prayer service]—he would say that "the president, yes, he is a kind
> of spiritual leader." But many clergy had a problem.[54]

Two other interviewed clergy did in fact maintain a similar position to
that of participant B1, who considered this "unpopular" stance to be most
common among "theologically minded" Oklahoma City ministers. In the
aggregate, this ensemble of criticisms was stern yet unorganized, without
formal channels of publication, and without a single mention in local
newspaper reports contained in the sample of this study. Participant B3,
who was born and raised in Oklahoma City, sided with a noncritical view
of the National Day of Prayer service, stating (with more than a tinge of
contradiction) that President Clinton and Governor Keating's invocation
of God was "very important to Oklahomans, although no one would have
complained if it had not happened."[55] Even so, this participant considered
this service as the postdisaster "bump in the road—we [Oklahomans
with whom the participant was acquainted] were not happy with that."[56]
When asked to elaborate as to why this was so, the participant continued,
"because of an absence of local leadership. For example, they did not use
an African American leader from Oklahoma . . . It was designed for a national audience."[57] This would be only one of many assertions surrounding the centrality of local identity.

Participant B2, a senior pastor and regional leader associated with
a more well-known congregation near Oklahoma City, likewise affirmed
the view that Oklahomans "at that point in time [after the bombing]
. . . would have considered it important" to hear public theological pro-

53. Santos, participant B1 interview.
54. Ibid.
55. Santos, Participant B3 interview.
56. Ibid.
57. Ibid.

nouncements.[58] He further supported Participant *B1*'s view in response to the query surrounding the suitability of President Clinton's theological assertions, but with some apprehension:

> That is a good question. [*Six-second pause.*] I may be the exception. I would personally not be looking to the president of the United States to do that. Someone in that position is not the one I would be looking at. My response would probably not be the same as the majority.[59]

In reply, I asked, "What, then, should the president's role in the postdisaster scenario be?" Participant *B2* answered, "to give us a sense of our shared humanity; a sense of sincere and authentic unity."[60] When I asked him briefly, "Was your national identity important in your reflections about the event?" he replied, "No, no, not at all . . . Now, I can't speak for everyone. . . . [*interceding story about local Oklahomans who aggressively harassed Muslims*] It did not come to the fore in any way." He qualified this statement with, "Now, 9-11, that is when it was different."[61] Here, then, we have another instance in which public discourse that transcends institutional boundaries of sacred and secular bears directly upon the proper frame of reference for identity building; a public official of the president's social stature should only speak to the concord of humanity in this tragedy, not to identifying God's presence and how God views the event and wishes the collectivity to respond. This ought to be carried out by someone else with greater hermeneutical (interpretive) authority in the area of Scripture, theology, or spirituality (or "the sacred"). Indeed it seems apparent that these two ministers are firmly in touch with the apparently major disparity between themselves, as those who can speak authoritatively about Scripture and God, and most other Oklahomans (including ministers) on the topic of how theological speech ought to be handled and employed in periods of crisis. Yet again, there is a sense of futility in their position, a sense in which they are the minority and have only a few sympathetic ears in the cause of defending a certain form of symbolic production that carried on without any control or regulation from within the originary cultural form. Herein the ambiguities

58. Santos, Participant *B2* interview.
59. Ibid.
60. Ibid.
61. Ibid.

and troublesome aspects of negotiating the boundary between faith and politics in a modern, advanced capitalist world are most palpable: Who should say what after a disaster, how should they say it, and when should they say it? With whom lies the authority of such speech acts, especially those of exhortation (illocutionary speech) to the body politic? Should ritual experts be concerned with protecting their sphere of symbolic authority, or "sphere sovereignty"? What sort of model for social behavior is thus provided to each interested citizen?

Participant *B2*, like participant *B1*, also held a particularly critical view of the memorialization process, this time with some reservations over the national memorial's mission statement. This statement appears on the east wall of the memorial site, next to the inscription reading "9:01 a.m." (a minute before the explosion) above the ground-level entrance, as well as on several pamphlets (e.g., the *Memorial and Museum Programs* pamphlet) and other publications. The mission statement reads, in a standardized format, thus:

> We come here to remember those who were killed,
> Those who survived and those changed forever.
> May all who leave here know the impact of violence.
> May this memorial offer comfort
> strength, peace, hope and serenity.[62]

This minister, participant *B2*, requested that I reread the statement after our interview was supposedly finished. Upon reading the statement for a second time, the minister claimed, "I'm afraid we've failed miserably. Why 'violence'? Everyone knows what happened there . . . It is misplaced."[63] Participant *B2* attributed the nature of his response, albeit only in passing, to the influence of the mimetic theory of French literary scholar Rene Girard.[64] Thus, on the grounds of a rather sophisticated framework of thought, this minister believes that the memorial embraces the very thing—violence—that it and its accompanying museum and institute are attempting to eradicate. These clergy, it appears, have prevented themselves from swallowing public formulations of what is to be believed or believable about the bombing. However, the ministers did not seem to broadcast these views with others or use their views as a basis for cen-

---

62. "History and Mission."

63. Santos, Participant *B2* interview.

64. See Girard, *I See Satan Fall Like Lightening*, 11.

suring certain alternative practices among other ministers from within the same denomination. In other words, the points of contention were (and apparently still are) well known but had not received much public articulation or reflection at the group level. So it was not surprising that at two other points throughout our interview, participant B2, who has resided in the Oklahoma City area for at least two decades, stated something along the lines of the following: "I had not thought about that issue until you mentioned it." [65]With one exception (regarding the persistence of community cohesion), these "issues" were the compatibility of church and state agendas and the use of theological speech in public office. Although capable of critically deconstructing the problematic elements of statist cultural production, the ministers were still invisible to some degree. They could not, evidently, engage in a public dialogue about these concerns. This is largely due to the lack of unified care (among the congregations of the city) over speech about God, which, according to Karl Barth, is a fundamental aspect of the theological enterprise.[66] Also, the marginalization of, on the one hand, certain theological perspectives about Christian discipleship (including citizenship) and, on the other hand, assumptions concerning Bible reading that deviated from more conventional or popular hermeneutical methods also contributed to the muffling of these voices. Finally, a rigorous training in identifying the church as God's politics and its focal practices as manifested at the congregational and intercongregational levels was not identifiable in the views of these two ministers and study participants. More consideration of such ecclesial issues would have augmented the nature of post-disaster cultural politics to a significant extent.

The silence of ministers coincided with an affirmative civic response to the bombing of the Murrah Federal Building that together attested to the power of violence as a "meaning-producing" event in the sense of establishing collective identity and solidarity—indeed, as creating a long sought after history and memory that merely invoked "God" without acknowledging the plenitude and self-giving love of the triune God. Just like those who died were publicly and primarily considered victims of extremists, so the bombing became the primary referent in the public life of Oklahomans, eclipsing those things that witness to God's ways

---

65. Santos, Participant B2 interview.
66. Barth, *Evangelical Theology*, 41.

in a comprehensive sense—namely, to the fullness of God. The national memorial, for instance, attests to strength, faith (in a "civic" god), and perseverance, but forgoes forgiveness, peace, and joy. It was built against a "foreshortened horizon," as Craig Hovey aptly names the historical imagination by virtue of which we privilege military might as the harbinger of true peace.[67]

The Absence of Forgiveness

Central to the theme of public theology following the disaster in Oklahoma City is the criticism that the public theology of that time lacked robust reflection, including a well-wrought, ecclesially articulated theology of forgiveness. From the perspective of the interviewed ministers, it appears that the government was willing to publicly present various theological interpretations and biblically rooted exhortations, but only insofar as the government was tempered by the statist interest of defining friend and foe, of exacting justice and quelling all threats to the state's monopoly over the means of violence. Three participants voiced concerns about an apparent overemphasis on violent retaliation among local churchgoing Oklahomans, a concomitant underemphasis on forgiveness, and the local and federal governments' press statements about the potential maximum punishment (execution) that would be sought against the guilty offender. All such qualities of the pubic discourse were rooted in narrative concerns that sought to align themselves with lived experience after the attack.

Participant *C1*, closely associated with ministerial work yet not an ordained minister, stated that postattack visits to various local congregations for speaking engagements yielded a "shocking" number of conversations in which congregants declared the following statement (or cognates): "I can't wait until we fry this guy [McVeigh]."[68] This compulsive embrace of justice as strictly punishment seems to align itself quite well with Participant *B2*'s Girardian critique of the national memorial's mission statement. Participant *B1* reported on his church's normal postdisaster practice of praying for the victims, their families, and the perpetrators. He further claimed that the song, "There is a Balm in Gilead" and a phrase from its opening line ("to make the wounded whole") applied

---

67. Ibid., 48.
68. Santos, Participant *C1* interview.

just as well to the perpetrators as to the victims.[69] In this light, Timothy McVeigh was construed as a broken and wounded human being in need of healing, just like any other human being. This sort of interpretive practice in effect equalizes the entire social body, positing the "solidarity of sinners." However, there is something more intriguing here: this view of McVeigh is grounded upon a political imagination at odds with that of the state. Chiefly it opposes the statist imaginary's contention that social renewal is only possible if sources of pollution are forcibly eradicated from the population. These sources of pollution cannot be forgiven because they are ultimately "explanations" of evil that are intelligible to the state and therefore the proper objects of its own mechanisms of expulsion. Forgiveness is not an option in this context, because it has been privatized, whereas justice is the work of political institutions. Thus understood, forgiveness is something that the individual citizen will have to work out in his or her own way.

To be sure, the shock that participant C_1 felt about the demands of fellow church members to "fry" Timothy McVeigh was at least partly due to this participant's understanding that forgiveness is not a psychological act performed when a hurtful, traumatic, or devastating occasion makes it necessary. From a Christian standpoint, forgiveness is life—or, better yet, the source of life. A chasm often separates the statist conception of justice from what L. Gregory Jones calls a conception of justice as "virtuous habits and patterns of relationship contextualized within a wider account of the forgiveness wrought by the triune God."[70] According to this comprehension of forgiveness, justice and forgiveness are inextricably bound to each other with the same unsettling, forceful, and paradoxically hopeful logic that undergirded God's vindication of Jesus following his crucifixion. To be sure, we do not understand why Jesus, as he hung from the tree of humiliation and injustice, uttered the words, "Father, forgive them, for they do not know what they are doing" (Luke 23:34) Yet just as Jesus took up this confrontation between the justice of an imperialist state and his Father's charity and mercy onto his body (not simply into his psyche), so must Christians enflesh forgiveness (primarily because it is not simply a conception) in order to participate in Christ's sufferings as witnesses to the Spirit's continued activity within a world that can easily be considered lost to endless cycles of violence and retaliation. Jones continues:

69. Santos, Participant B_1 interview.
70. Jones, *Embodying Forgiveness*, 89.

> For Christians, forgiveness is not a first step or a final "step"; it is
> rather an embodied way of life. Christians cannot be content with
> standards of justice found in a political constitution, much less in
> popular therapeutic currency; rather, Christians learn the fullness
> of what justice *is*, and what it entails, precisely by participating in
> such things as baptism, eucharist, and interpreting Scripture.[71]

Participation in God's justice would no doubt also include the actual or
concrete practice and experience of forgiving other Christians and being
forgiven by other Christians in the congregation. When these practices
are not integral and habitual to ecclesial life, then the justice of the state
convincingly enters the ecclesial body as a parodic substitute; that is, no
confrontation or critical engagement arising from spiritual discernment
occurs.

Such communal discernment is necessary because the narrative
of the state's aggressive and confident pursuit of "ultimate" justice finds
ready and perpetual outlets among various media within homes and
businesses across a given region. More importantly, the body politic of a
region may be heterogeneous in terms of degrees of loyalty to government
law-enforcement policy, but a majority is all that is necessary to generate
a "passive" habit in the social body—or, as Thomas Aquinas would have
put it (with the individual person in mind), a habit created by what has
been done to us. In the case of Oklahoma, the use of capital punishment
has become a habit of the state. Some have decried its commonness, but
its continued application is, whether through acquiescence or explicit
support, a practice of the body politic called Oklahoma. The ongoing
executions simply follow from the murders that gave rise to them almost
as a matter of course; the bombing of 1995 only served to deepen the
inescapability of the practice. (See the final section below.)

Financial Aid to the Churches

The specific instances in which clergy seemed to publicly question the actions and terms of the state related to the determination and dissemination of relief funds for physical structures damaged by the bombing of the Alfred Murrah Federal Building. From within the sample of 110 articles and numerous other print sources, the general theme of "federal aid for recovery efforts" in itself recorded seventeen cases, while six subthemes

71. Ibid., 89 (emphasis original).

emerged that dealt with some corollary topic associated with this general theme; in sum, the data yielded twenty-nine cases. One subcode ("funds for damaged churches"), contained within the general theme, recorded eleven cases. The only subcode under "federal aid" that contained critical views, "church and state separation," accounted for eight cases.

The federal-aid controversy following the attack was centered on a Department of Housing and Urban Development (HUD) guideline, based on the establishment clause, which forbids a church from receiving federal funds unless the church in question facilitates or provides venues for the delivery of "public services." FEMA funds are also disseminated to certain qualified nonprofit organizations, such as schools or fire departments. According to Barbara Yagerman, a public-affairs official with FEMA in Washington DC, churches can only receive aid if they provide the sorts of services that the aforementioned nonprofit agencies provide, and when this is the case, funds can only be used to repair the portion of the building used for these services. Notice here an extreme form of differentiation that reaches to the tedious demarcation of material space used for certain repertoires of action and speech, either "religious" (read: private) or "public." Distribution of resources, then, depends on the differentiation of spheres; and differentiation of this sort parcels out material bodies according to the uses to which they are applied under an overarching state-sanctioned scheme.

By June of 1995, about two months after the bombing, this particular matter had not yet been resolved and had become an object of considerable debate. U.S. representative Ernest Istook, in an attempt to resolve the matter with some expedience, made a special proposal to the U.S. Rep. Bob Livingston, then chair of the House Appropriations Committee, and argued, "These religious structures were literally innocent bystanders to a violent attack on the federal government, [and should therefore receive aid] in this unique instance, to the same extent as other entities."[72] The language of this legistlative plea is couched in precisely the terms that suit governmentality under the state: the church building is deemed a "religious structure," which implies that a building typically reserved for "public" and "official" use, such as a school, legislative building, or community center, is decidedly not religious. The desire to transform the discourse of governance became a point of contention for some prominent

72. Brus and Gilliland, "Istook Wants U.S. Aid," 1.

ministers who voiced their perspective concerning the government pro-
hibition on providing funds for damaged churches. Rev. Nick Harris, who
gave Istook a tour of the damaged First United Methodist Church a week
after the bombing, complained, "I just think it's a bigger issue than just
church/state. It's an issue of our continued ability to minister to people
in that unique area, . . . With the government's help, we can come back
and be stronger than ever, and render more services and be able to do
more things."[73] The Reverend George Back, dean of St. Paul's Episcopal
Cathedral, claimed mixed feelings when considering whether the emergency legislation based on the establishment clause ought to be amended
in some fashion:

> It's hard to know, because I think the separation of church and
> state has been a good policy in general. I don't think they [the
> government] owe it to us. I think that help would be . . . if we do
> get it, it would be helpful and it would come out of generosity, and
> not out of being owed it. In general, I think our attitude toward
> sacred places in our culture probably needs to be looked at again
> on both sides."[74]

Finally the Reverend Louis Lamb, pastor of the Roman Catholic church
St. Joseph Old Cathedral, apparently sided with separation of church and
state, but only in light of a particular view of churches as self-sufficient
institutions: "I think it's up to our Christian adherents of our congregations who contribute to the restoration of our churches. I think there's
enough money out there among Oklahomans of the different faiths that
have churches downtown that the money could be obtained through the
faithful."[75]

The speaker of each of the quotations above makes an attempt to recast the work of postdisaster financial relief into categories derived from
an alternative political imagination—categories that assume varying degrees of opposition to the prevailing statist imaginary. Harris attempts
to transcend the dichotomy via a focus on the maximization of ministry
or service to the population; Back seems to favor this legally fashioned
differentiation but then questions the basic disposition with which sacred spaces are viewed, and even argues for an alteration of the legitimate

73. Ibid.
74. Ibid.
75. Ibid.

basis of recovery-funds disbursements from a legally enforceable obligation to an act of generosity and charity. Back seeks to recontextualize
postdisaster financial assistance so as to make it an act of generosity,
or even a gift, that is commensurate with any other giving or receiving
of goods from God in the interactions of friends, family members, or
community members. In effect, then, Back was wittingly or unwittingly
eschewing any possibility of asymmetrical power relations in the act of
giving or, as the negative allusions to entitlement make evident, attempting to avoid the impression that a church expects itself to be aided by
the state. This attempt at ensuring that the provision of aid does not turn
out to make any given church feel obligated to reciprocate, chiefly in the
form of positive support or acquiescence, is consistent with his some-
what-unclear statement about reconsidering "our attitude toward sacred
places." This is a vital query for all congregations to engage, if only for the
reason of rendering a public account of what makes a place "sacred." Is
it because "deaths" occurred there, or because the spot is "historic," or,
perhaps, because a sovereign power that both institutes and lives outside
the rule of law deemed it so. Back realized, perhaps only partially, that
sacrality of place seems to be a category of determination that fundamentally challenges the notion that specific calculations, techniques, and
other secular deliberations arising from within the private/public divide
(i.e., church/state and faith/politics) can actually achieve a decision about
the sacred—a decision that understands its own implications. Lamb, it
appears, supports the doctrine of the separation of church and state only
because he wishes for "the faithful" to support their own churches with
their own wealth and to bypass all struggles and anxieties over receiving
external aid, especially from the federal government. A common unspoken thread that runs through all these responses (with the exception of
Harris's) is a certain fear that dedifferentiation will lead to a situation in
which the church will become more dependent on the government than
may be desirable.

"GET OUR HEARTS TOGETHER":
POSTDISASTER COLLECTIVE IDENTITY AND SOLIDARITY

The following section tackles the symbolic appropriations of community
members, all of whom were members of churches within or in close proximity to Oklahoma City, save one participant. The guiding question asked

whether identity in the impacted community was primarily molded by cultural processes (including memorialization) in which churches played a central role, and that nationalized local places, symbols, and persons. I asked, in other words, if localism would succumb to the imaginings and operations of the state and to organizations that adopted its vision or assumptions about what human beings were needed in order to rebuild Oklahoma City.

Data, once again, derived from one-on-one interviews and print media, along with two focus-group sessions. These were employed because it was not expected that clergy interviews would provide some key information about numerous issues tied to collective identity among city residents. Analysis of data identified five focal themes, fraught with narrative constructions, associated with collective identity: (1) the importance of public theological pronouncements and interpretations, (2) Oklahoma City's "altered status" from nationally insignificant to significant, (3) place-making and memory work, (4) overlapping spatial identities, and (5) the role of a few historically important and influential churches. Findings (3) and (4), and their prominent role in relation to the other findings, were somewhat unexpected. The theological upshot of these sociological factors and poetic or cultural actions underscores the heteronomy that characterizes the life of the church: its wisdom, discipleship, worship, relationships, and patterns of speech (its politics) are part of a superabundantly generous economy of salvation that has drawn it into life that confronts, incorporates, and overcomes death.

Overall, however, the findings partially challenged my expectations. Specifically, most respondents focused on the regional or local scope of the disaster in resistance to processes of nationalization but without altering the ground from which nationalization was emerging. Even so, the general pattern of responses disavowed any surge of overt and sustained nationalist or patriotic sentiment after the event. It seems, rather, that residents shaped the postdisaster cultural milieu in such a way as to reinforce the message (and experience) that the bombing affected Oklahomans qua Oklahomans. The most provocative aspect of the data gathered was the unanticipated positions assumed by various citizens, both clergy and nonclergy, in relation to theology and politics. Perhaps most compelling was the clear discrepancy between clergy and nonclergy respondents with respect to government officials' use of theological terms and imagery in the postdisaster period for purposes of collective identity formation.

The theme of locally orchestrated cohesion, and its corollary themes, ultimately held a very prominent place among all principal analytical codes and aggregate themes identified in primary data sources. In 110 articles, sixty-one segments were coded that dealt with the furtherance of local cohesion through either memorial gestures (e.g., "Plant a Memorial Tree Week"), statements of anguish expressed during the course of relief work ("This was our town. These were our people"), newly written songs on the citizen Access Hotline, ("Get our Hearts Together"), and observations of community and neighborhood leaders at a newspaper-sponsored forum. In this last case, a staff writer indicated that the neighborhood and community leaders "believed the tragedy, like nothing else before it, brought together Oklahomans of all races and religions, and from all areas of the city, region and state."[76]

This sense of extraordinary compassion and unprecedented solidarity has been well documented in the disaster literature, as chapter 1 indicates. However, the identification of what cultural productions and items serve as the basis of this solidarity is often neglected.

Contrary to this trend, the present section identifies various cultural products of local churches, government agencies, and architectural and urban-planning experts (acting in unison or singly) that funded the register of social resources on the basis of which citizens built a postdisaster identity. In addition, this section points to the forceful nature of local constructions of politics, place, and identity that rather explicitly found coherence through theologically embedded interpretations and the exclusion or marginalization of national identity. Focus-group interview data, one-on-one interview data, and print-media data also shed light upon unwitting "grassroots" resistance to expert system co-optation of emergency service functions.

"That Is What the Country Was Founded On"

The response of Christian churches to the disaster was underscored in the very first edition of the *Oklahoman* the day after the bombing. At least three articles addressed religious topics: ministerial statements of comfort, exhortations to love the neighbor and to renounce hate, the acceptance of anger as a natural response, and the use of Scripture to find solace. This pattern gave way to one of the clearest and most relevant

---

76. Perry, "Leaders See Effort Enduring."

themes that arose from participant and newspaper data surrounding the embrace of a peculiarly theological response on the part of government leaders at every level. Participant *A2*, after declaring that government and church effectively worked in unison after the attack, avowed thus:

> Oklahomans would have considered it [invoking spiritual matters into bombing response] important. It would not be complete without it . . . everyone welcomed it. This shows that this [separation of church and state] has been dying—but that is what the country was founded on. Prayer is needed to lead officials—to make sure that money goes to the right place and correct decisions are made. It bothers me to no end—those that want to end church-and-state separation, prayer in schools, you know, [etc.] they don't have to participate. We have "In God We Trust" on our money—but they have no problem making money.[77]

This response invoked the parochial or local as the primary frame of reference for identity formation. During the course of the interview, the only and primary allusion to the United States was in the historical claim that nationhood was achieved with a strong public and conceptual pact between church and state.[78] Despite the fact that varied theological traditions (namely, Protestant, Unitarian, and Deist) informed early formulations about the divine in relation to a start-up American liberal democracy,[79] many citizens in Oklahoma City held a much more straightforward view of church and state, which was reinvigorated and polarized after the bombing of the Murrah Federal Building. Participant *A3*, a member of a growing charismatic church, parallels this sentiment:

> Yeah, I think it's fine if politicians speak about God. Sure, I know what they have said, that Bush [Jr.] has saved a good number of people. I mean, yeah, that is right for us. As for Clinton, I think the same applies. Although, you know, through the media, I heard he got involved with some, [uncomfortable laughter] things that are not right. I don't know, that's just what I heard through the

---

77. Santos, Participant *A2* interview.

78. Ibid.

79. For well-wrought accounts of religion in the early phases of "nationhood," see Nicholls, *God and Government in an 'Age of "Reason"'*; see also Prothero, *American Jesus*; and Meacham, *American Gospel*.

media. So, as long as they are doing what's Christian [they can appeal to God].[80]

When asked if Oklahomans in general welcomed the public use of faith or statements about God's involvement after the bombing, the same participant answered, "Oh, yeah, I think so."

Several participants incorporated the bombing as an event into their narrative spirituality, whereby New Testament scriptural accounts were brought to bear upon the significance of the contemporary event, and molded thoughts about actual practice. Participants C3 and C4, both members of a local nondenominational church very much dedicated to personal Bible study and prayer, carried out an interesting interchange:

> C4: The event made me really think about evil, not really issues of insecurity. Insecurity became an issue after 9/11, because it seemed as if, you know, the entire nation was under attack. This [the Murrah Building bombing] did not raise issues of insecurity, but of evil. It seemed more of an isolated case. Most of the victims were not connected to what mattered to him [McVeigh].
>
> C3: It reminded me of the Tower of Siloam [Luke 13:1–5]. It is not a matter of finding out a religious reason for why this happened, but understanding what sort of response we should have toward God when something like this happens.
>
> C4: Yeah, bad things happen all the time.[81]

Firmly entrenched in an interpretive method that employs New Testament narratives as a framework for understanding contemporary experiences of disaster, these participants embraced a hermeneutic that many Oklahomans used in the postdisaster social context as a way both of seeking comfort and of binding persons to one another. As an ecclesial rather than individual practice, reading Scripture in this way transmutes the biblical narrative into a contemporary narrative that the citizen inhabits. This sort of participation thereby achieves a certain "compression" of time, as a result of which the present saints join the ancient saints in reengaging a struggle with the "powers" and "authorities" that demand submission to falsehoods that may otherwise be uncritically absorbed by the congregation. In the postdisaster context of Oklahoma City, public judgment about guilt and responsibility became integral for most groups,

80. Santos, Participant A3 interview.
81. Santos, Participants C3 and C4, focus-group interview.

and disciplined ecclesial practice was required to sift through the cultural options. The degree to which this practice was habitual or a bona fide discipline among the city congregations could not be determined. Nevertheless, its promise needs to be explored.

A political-cultural reading of Luke 13, for instance, highlights numerous postdisaster practices that center on the public response to harm and threat. These responses are geared toward mass propagation of a particular reading of the threat—that is, they generate a postdisaster hermeneutic that establishes itself as early as possible after the impact as a "canon," or as *the* most believable story about blameworthiness and justice. Dietrich Bonhoeffer asserts in a sermon based on this passage: "People want to be the judge themselves" in occasions marked by instability, confusion, and severe trauma; the compulsion to identify good and evil, right and wrong, responsibility and innocence, is itself an attempt at social reorientation and re-establishment of moral boundaries. Bonhoeffer continues: "We are moralists to the core. We want to be able to accuse the one and acquit the other. We want to be the judge of what happens."[82] More crucially, however, Bonhoeffer considers Jesus's reply to the supposed conjectures of fellow Galileans to be completely misguided. Why? Because our solidarity with the social decay, guilt, and sin of our generation nullifies any attempt, immediately following a disaster, at marking off the good from the evil, and the innocent from the blameworthy. Indeed, Bonhoeffer is incisive in this regard:

> Rather, what really counts here is that we realize this one thing: these events took place in my world, the world we live in, the world in which I commit sin, in which I sow hatred and unkindness day by day. These events are the fruit of what I and my family have sown. Moreover those who were involved in the disaster, the Galileans and Pilate, are my family, my brothers and sisters in sin, in hatred, in malice, in unkindness, my sisters in guilt. Whatever strikes them should strike me.[83]

The proper political response en masse, therefore, is confession and repentance. Not only should I not participate in the pursuit of assigning blame or in harmonizing the circumstances of death with the spiritual condition of the deceased, I ought to turn away from my own sinful

82. Bonhoeffer, "Way that Leads to Renewal," 231.

83. Ibid., 233.

dispositions, practices, and desires to manipulate the image or stories of the victims. Each citizen is (as was each Galilean to whom Jesus was speaking in Luke 13) is responsible for the condition of his or her people. Ostensibly dispassionate judgments centered on how "worthy" some must have been for such a hideous end, or even how evil the wrongdoer may have been, are unfounded if my own repentance is bypassed.

The role of public judgments is thus crucial for political identity formation and places a city's communities and the organs of the state that handle such a community at the center of a host of discursive activities. These discourses develop from within congregations, more or less bounded neighborhoods, government offices, emergency-volunteer agencies, and a host of even smaller groups. All such discursive constructions revolve around God's response to the disaster, around innocence, solidarity, good, evil, and grief, around the proper response of any given citizen.

Bonhoeffer, once again, invites serious reflection on this matter, especially as it pertains to human beings as creatures of God and to their determinations of good and evil. In an early writing from 1929, titled "What is a Christian Ethic?", Bonhoeffer claims,

> It is an extremely profound thing that in the old story of the Fall, the reason for the Fall is eating from the tree of the knowledge of good and evil. The original—shall we say childlike—communion between God and man stands beyond this knowledge of good and evil; it knows only of one thing, of the boundless love of God towards man.[84]

Although this assertion is embedded in a spurious argument that serves as a foil against which Bonhoeffer builds his major argument later on, the insight is not unhelpful. It illumines a foundational point: human beings are first and foremost recipients of God's love and gifts and, thus, simply stand, as Bonhoeffer would say, in the presence of God here and now. This ought to be the first realization or acknowledgement. Our knowledge or discernment, in fact, is both eclipsed and constituted by the magnitude of Christ's love. Consider the no less politically charged epistle to the Ephesians. Ephesians 3:14–19 states:

> For this reason I bow my knees before the Father, from whom every family in heaven and on earth takes its name. I pray that,

---

84. Bonhoeffer, "What Is a Christian Ethic?" 347.

according to the riches of his glory, he may grant that you may be strengthened in your inner being with power through his Spirit, and that Christ may dwell in your hearts through faith, *as you are being rooted and grounded in love. I pray that you may have the power to comprehend, with all the saints, what is the breadth and length and height and depth, and to know the love of Christ that surpasses knowledge,* so that you may be filled with all the fullness of God. (emphasis added)

As Paul writes in his first letter to the Corinthians (1 Cor 13:1–3), the ability to speak different languages, the gift of prophecy and knowledge, the gift of daring faith, the gift of a generous heart for the poor, and the willingness to abdicate our bodies to the flames (e.g., in martyrdom) simply tend toward *nothingness* and disorder if *love* does not characterize the life of the worshiping disciple of Jesus. The love that *is* God provides the legitimating basis and end of all social action before and with God. We are not meant to be the autonomous judges of good and evil; instead, only as creatures trained in love and dependent on God's provision of life and light and presence are we able to rightly assume a holy form of life that is filled up with God's fullness. That is, we cannot grasp anything without the requisite delight and love that ought to constitute discernment as a practice that builds up the good and discards the evil (as opposed to identifying good and evil from a desire to control, justify, or predict).[85] When we grasp for the burden of knowing good and evil from ourselves, as humans *sicut Deus* ("like God"), we become judges of matters too weighty for us to handle properly. The first move of a human in any context is always to look to God and his Word. As Bernd Wannenwetsch notes in his exposition of Hans Ulrich's political thought, "To be ruled by the spirit means to be listening to God's word, ready to be judged and unmasked by it."[86] The ecclesial discernment necessary following disasters is one rooted in and arising from the united love of the congregation and its delight for God's challenging, revealing, and life-giving words.[87]

---

85. In this regard, see Wirzba, *Living the Sabbath*, 59. Contending for the recovery of delight, Wirzba cites Hart, *Beauty of the Infinite*, 253.

86. Wannenwetsch, "'Ruled by the Spirit,'" 7.

87. Stephen Fowl and L. Gregory Jones's book, *Reading in Communion*, makes a wonderful case for the importance of character or virtue development as a basis for wise ecclesial readings of Scripture.

Disjunctive Discourses and Practices

At this point, it appears justified to shed light on one of the more striking findings that emerged from the interview data: the bifurcation of results along the lines of formal theological training. Clergy of a particular variety held many more views that were critical of the public usage of theological symbolism or exhortation on the part of political figures, including the use of patriotic symbolism during worship services. They still consider themselves the guardians of such hermeneutical frameworks for thought and action. Outside this network of like-minded clergy with theological inclinations, most citizens interviewed held much more favorable views of "God-talk" in public spaces during the post-attack period. Most nonclergy respondents assumed that only an "undifferentiated" state of affairs would have made the response and recovery to the attack, as one participant asserts, "complete." This divergence indicates a certain level of division in Oklahoma City between ministers and citizens who understandably do not engage the same type of literature or reflection about theological matters. These clergy, it appears, had not presented their critical stance in a public form or with the backing of a serious social movement organization; which is to say, they had not catalyzed social conflict.

From Insignificance to Significance

Rather unique to the case of the Murrah Building bombing in Oklahoma City is the manner in which it jolted citizens into a heightened awareness of being associated with a nationally "insignificant" city, at least in an economic, political, and cultural sense (if by *culture* one assumes the nonanthropological notion of literary, artistic, and intellectual acumen). Such an insignificant city became the object of a highly unfamiliar degree of public attention. Up until the point of the bombing, downtown Oklahoma City had been experiencing a downward slide in economic vitality for at least a decade, with no clear plan for resurgence. Print-media data covered the debate surrounding the potential use of federal relief funds to not only build a memorial at the bombing site and retain local businesses threatening to leave the city, but also to initiate a set of projects geared toward taking the Oklahoma City downtown area to an unprecedented level of social prestige and economic dynamism. However, before delving into this specific topic, it is crucial to investigate the manner in which Oklahomans struggled to reconcile the bombing with the apparently insignificant stature of the state of Oklahoma and Oklahoma City.

The notion of altered significance can be placed into various thematic categories, most of which depend on ascribing to Oklahomans a certain degree of simplicity, innocence, and lowliness that the bombing both magnified and challenged. For instance, Participant *B1* described Oklahoma in these terms:

> We are a young state—this event took us out of the old Southern gentility; we have not developed a state identity; many of the pivotal events that occurred to a state did not occur to us. But, think about our cultural identity. We have our economics, the Dust Bowl; all of this was space that no one wanted. Freed blacks did not want it, so the Indians got the land. No one wanted it, so we got it. I mean, look at the state license plates—there is the "Show-Me State" and others like that. But ours, it says, "Oklahoma: It's OK" [*laughter*].[88]

The notion of a state's "maturation" process, or growth into a well-defined collectivity, only after responding to formidable trials seems to be crucial for several reasons. First, the notion of maturation comes extremely close to personifying the state of Oklahoma, or imagining the citizens of the state as a single entity or "corporate personality" that passes through history as a unitary subject.[89] This corporate identity, in fact, seems to be somewhat deviant or stigmatized insofar as it does not measure up to the standards of other so-called mainstream metropolitan or capital cities that are, no doubt, buckling under the pressure to become "global" cities. Second, in the same vein, it seemingly brings the state up to par with other older states that have already attained a more concrete cultural identity, which often seems to be a desire for a certain level of social honor or glory. Deliberately self-effacing comments were often buttressed by claims expressing sheer incredulity about an American perpetrator and his selection of Oklahoma City as a target. While participant *C4* matter-of-factly expressed that "we were naïve to think no one would attack us,"[90] participant *A2* rhetorically demanded, "How could someone from this country do this? What could have possibly been his [McVeigh's]

---

88. Santos, Participant *B1* interview.

89. See Linenthal, *Unfinished Bombing*, 44–46.

90. Santos, Participant *C4* focus-group interview.

motive? *There is nothing in Oklahoma.* Why not Colorado, where there's a NORAD site" (emphasis added)?[91]

Along the same lines, both the print-media and interview data testified to the elevation of Oklahoma as a state, and particularly of Oklahomans as persons, as morally exemplary or impressive to other Americans and even to members of other nations around the globe. Intriguing is that many cases involved the appropriation of "old" or enduring traits of the body of citizens (e.g., generosity, simplicity, self-sacrifice) as the basis for a "new" national identity. When asked if a swell in patriotic sentiment was evident in her neighborhood after the attacks, participant *C4* stated,

> I would say patriotic as a community, but not as a country. We stood up as a community. We were like, "We are Oklahoma City" and we're not going to be pushed around. It wasn't necessarily like Oklahoma City versus the rest of the country, but more like, if you attack us, we will defend who we are.[92]

There is a very interesting sociolinguistic dynamic at work here—chiefly, a discursive construction reveals agency. The participant altered the usual referent of "patriotic" (a nation) to a local collectivity. The basis of this collective pride is, as stated, "defensive" insofar as resilience in the face of adversity places the group in a category of distinction among other American citizens in other states. Indeed, in this statement, the collective identity is assured and not under negotiation or in a liminal phase: we will defend "who we are." This confidence, interestingly, is couched in an imagined, rhetorical public declaration to the rest of the American populace—a statement that needs to be qualified ("it wasn't necessarily like Oklahoma City versus the rest of the country") in order for its provocative and ostentatious tone to be softened.

Even in the realm of disaster-response operations, Oklahomans managed to emblazon a new standard of emergency-service provision based on local Oklahoman pride, and that bears their state's name. The "Oklahoma standard," as it came to be known, is a prominent object of discussion in the Oklahoma Department of Civil Emergency Management's *After Action Report*. This term initially appears within a list of "operational strengths" that explains "the major reasons the operation ran smoothly."[93]

91. Santos, Participant *A2* interview.

92. Santos, Participant *C4*, focus-group interview.

93. ODCEM, 33.

In a diagram featuring the shattered north-facing visage of the Murrah Building, the report stresses that one major reason for largely unproblematic operations was "simply defined, the 'Oklahoma Standard' [, which] represents the greatest asset our state offers . . . 'Our People.'[94]

Thirteen cases of this sort of moral elevation of Oklahoman identity occurred in the newspaper sample as well. In contrast to the comments of participant C4, quoted above, which differentiated American identity from Oklahoman identity, many of the newspaper occurrences patently linked Oklahoman identity with American identity. This link, in agreement with other actions involving public officials, was interestingly manifested when mayor Ron Norrick functioned as a sort of cultural curator, overseeing the release of bombing-related artistic works that spoke to the resilience and pride of the American heartland. Specifically, recurring newspaper articles that featured a section on the *Oklahoman*'s Access Line typically contained a clear reference to Norrick's then-recent announcement that a particular song had been released for fundraising purposes. From a total of at least eleven songs that could be accessed through the automated telephone system, one was called "You Can't Break America's Heart." This song employs a common imaginative construct with a rich history beginning in the early years of nationhood (between 1776 and 1820): an anthropomorphized state with a "national character" and seemingly "with a body, a psychology, and a reputation in the world."[95] Oklahoma's position in this organic metaphor of political belonging stresses physiological centrality; Oklahomans are of the "heart": of that which pumps blood and plays a vital role for the functioning of the whole. In newspaper article dealing with urban-renewal policy both before and after the bombing, the writer asserted that "although downtown is not suited for every type of business, particularly industrial concerns that need a lot of ground floor square footage . . . it is still the heart of a city that has become known as the heart of a nation."[96]

Along similar lines, at a leadership forum planned and hosted by the *Oklahoman* nine days after the bombing, "[p]articipants were united in believing that Oklahoma's response to the disaster showed the world that

94. Ibid.

95. Waldstreicher, *In the Midst of Perpetual Fetes*, 141–42.

96. "Bricks and Mortar."

this is a special place."[97] This identity transformation assumed an initially inferior or ordinary status among the states of the Union, evidently lost through the display of tremendous unity and generosity in the face of tragedy, *and* buttressed the clear theological orientation of the collective state identity. In a newspaper article that contained more relevant codes concerning politics, God, and collective identity than any other newspaper article in the study sample (thirty-four instances), a citizen is quoted as asserting, this time in support of a sort of providential necessity, the following:

> "It's like it had to happen in Oklahoma, in the Bible Belt, where people are neighbors and we do give," said John Davis of Trinity Baptist Church. "We're the innocent of the world, of America, and I think people just were really moved by what we did, so there's a lot of people who are going to go back to California or New York and see what God's like, what Christ's like, living through people."

The prominence of Oklahoma, it seems, eventually permeated every category of social existence, including the commercial use of space, spirituality and theology, and local historical narratives of overcoming adversity. This process of collective identity formation also relied on an interesting admixture of exclusions and embraces that in turn necessarily drew upon the trauma of the Murrah Building bombing. Without the bombing, it appears, Oklahomans would not have been so evidently "special" at the national level.

The combination of incredulity over having suffered such a heinous attack along with the bold affirmations of the corporate Oklahoman character that was apparently a staple quality of the people before and during the post-attack period pose a set of interesting challenges to ecclesial life, especially in light of the fact that church members are implicated in such a process of collective identity formation.

The attempt by state citizens as a collectivity to secure an identity worthy of esteem while resisting nationalization was seen as basic and necessary in Oklahoma's stage of political development. Most interestingly, however, the citizens engaged cultural processes that promoted both a developmental understanding of statehood and the present moral robustness of the local people, which was evidently brought to light in the aftermath of the bombing.

97. Perry, "Leaders See Effort Enduring," 1.

This *poiesis* geared toward building local and regional identity writ large espoused a frame of reference incongruous with that of God's ecclesial body in certain key respects. Chiefly, many collective identities constructed after violent attack can be said to seek "temporal permanence" (reminiscent of the earthly so-called immortality and glory pondered in Plato's *Symposium*) while the church when faithful recognizes that it is, in a similarly paradoxical fashion, "contingently eternal." In the quest for gaining recognition and acknowledgement, which is often mixed with heartwrenching expressions of citywide or regionwide grief and suffering, the directors of these cultural political projects must grasp for assured "universality" (for widely recognized virtues or clear affinities to already-recognized heroes from past historical events with successful moral outcomes), which assures the people a place of social honor in American history. The church, however, must embrace the wisdom that human beings live contingently in faith and trust; indeed, Christians are called to radically acknowledge that they have received everything they have and are, including the initiation and maintenance of everyday life in the city. Stanley Hauerwas, in both *With the Grain of the Universe* and *Performing the Faith,* stresses that our contingency is something that (when fully accepted) requires the transformation of the agent whose witness is effected for the sake of other agents: an act decisively and faithfully carried out in Christ's crucifixion. This self-sacrifice, upon the Father's vindication, thereby took up the contingency of fallen "enfleshed souls" into the creational transformations of the inbreaking eternal age, which is nothing less than the promised Trinitarian incorporation of concrete, human life into fellowship with God.[98] This faithful abdication of (illusory) control over the constitution of selfhood and collective identity, which always seems to be over against the other(s), opens those of the faith community to the possibility not only of belonging to God, but also of belonging to others, in bountiful receptivity, gratitude, and service. "You are not your own," Paul urged the Corinthians, "you were bought at a price. Therefore glorify God with your body" (1 Cor 6:20). This "you" that is not "your own" has not received "the spirit of the world, but the Spirit that is from God, so that we may understand the gifts bestowed on us by God" (1 Cor 2:12). Even "God's love has been poured into our hearts through

---

98. See Rogers, *After the Spirit*, 76. This inclusion is "superfluous to the Trinity, because [it is] . . . without need and at some risk and therefore by grace."

the Holy Spirit that has been given to us" (Rom 5:5). The crucial additional difference here between the ecclesial body and "the people" is that no traumatic and drastic change in historical and social status requires the people of God to alter its history or offer its virtues to the world in order to be recognized or esteemed.

Another crucial matter surrounds the relation of local (vernacular) conceptions of life and death to those of the state. Whatever the perspective, the body of Christ knows that neither mastery over death nor life are self-secured prerogatives or rights. Death, we should recall, catalyzed this intensive process of re-creating and re-emboldening the corporate body politic. It was not a process incited or channeled through juridical mechanisms or injunction, but by means of indigenous resources and local repertoires of action and speech responding to abrupt instances of death. During the postdisaster period, Oklahomans who would have otherwise held loosely to overt or sustained political involvement were initiated into a process of learning a citizen *askesis* by means of such poetics as public ceremonies, local meetings, neighborhood clubs, print- and television-media features, and so forth. This asceticism would not seem altogether strange in one respect, because of the antecedent training in citizenship that occurs in public and private schools and even in the home. This discipline, of course, does not preclude a diversity of permutations at the local level that evidence varying degrees of patriotism, nationalism, and equally impassioned regional allegiance. Indeed, during the initial twelve-month period of tremendous hermeneutic and political instability following the bombing, it was entirely possible for citizenship to be reconceived in terms of localized, vernacular agendas and wisdom, because such large numbers of persons would have been discussing the tragedy and its implications. Even in such a period of unusually high social integration (especially within a highly differentiated capitalist social order), this *askesis* of a theologically responsive citizenship "from below" fell short of social-movement status due to a lack of organized coordination, a lack of unity of purpose across class and ethnic boundaries. Instead this form of citizenship was instantiated (i.e., domesticated) in institutionalized statist spaces imaginative and physical. While respondents and other citizens issued complaints about the nationalizing tendencies of statist agents, nothing approximating an authentic grievance with a corresponding responsible party was fully articulated or publicly protested. Therefore it could not break out into uninstitutionalized social forms (that is, into forms not filtered through the state form) and so generate alternative understandings or knowledges of collective responsibility and devotion. Thus, it remained largely beholden to the interests and machinations of the state. Vernacular practices can only gain a greater public hearing through initiatives that completely reconceive not only dependency and power across existing boundaries of race, class, and gender, but especially how dependency and power relate to the institution that holds a monopoly over the means of violence and, with it, influential conceptions of who is dead and deserves death, along with who is capable, poor, or productive.

The church, when enraptured by that imagination that enables it to see through the eyes of the (eschatological) Spirit (a Spirit that does not originate with them), witnesses to a peculiar understanding of life and death that makes sense only in light of Christ's crucifixion and resurrection. Primarily, the church contends that one may be dead and lost to God yet biologically alive; and, inversely, that one may be alive to God in spirit yet biologically dead.[99] The political implications of this position are important. If the dead in Christ continue to belong to him (Rom 14:7), then the community of faith is much larger and qualitatively different in *telos* (and practice) from the political community that simply tends to identify the relevant and capable while using historical personages as instances of an idealized history that must be continually "re-minded" and rehabilitated in order not to gradually disappear. The local community, living in this political mode of existence, does not have to shake its proverbial fists in defiance and confident self-assertion at the painful experience of death when the witness of the church is alive and present—a witness that includes those who despite being biologically dead are wondrously alive in God. In Craig Hovey's words, "The dead in Christ have been raised with him and are still part of the church. They still play a role in how the church makes decisions through their memories made present to us by the resurrection."[100] More important, the people of God, as Matthew 5:17–26 makes clear, are those enjoined to deal with anger and animosities that would invalidate their worship of God if left unaddressed. They are also those who Jesus urged must "come to terms quickly with [their respective] accuser on their way to court" (v. 25)—that is, they must personally

99. Schmemann, *Of Water and Spirit*, 62.

100. Hovey, *To Share in the Body*, 51–52.

initiate reconciliation outside formal administrative bodies. The type of people God forms and summons, therefore, do not need to demand or flaunt holiness, because they have been given every good gift from God in order to humbly learn holiness with their fellow brothers and sisters. As a corollary to this, the body of Christ must also engage in efforts to reconcile themselves with any other members of the community in order to avoid the degradation of trust that renders the worship of God impossible. The state's "war" against "fringe" militias, local Oklahoman emphasis on the virtues of the citizenry, and statist attempts to nationalize places and persons, all of which occurred after the bombing, do not model this preemptive self-offering and conciliatory practice; instead, such processes fund a devotion to protective, death-embracing politics. Rather than exhibit the qualities that Jesus declared in Matt 5:21–24 must characterize the people of God, statist agencies wait for (and partly produce) a murderer to judge, without serious devotion to the insult, alienation, and public labeling that make murderous confrontations virtually inevitable.

Despite the negative aspects of local Oklahoman attempts to construct a believable account of the moral qualities of the body politic, these are not sufficient to occlude what will eventually be discussed in the next section: Oklahomans with and without confessional ties—as resistant, not docile, bodies—effectively carried out tasks normally assumed by disaster-response technoexperts and thereby somewhat unwittingly undermined statist integrity. The mainly inadvertent nature of this involvement only further highlights the magnitude of the (missed) opportunity presented to the citizens of Oklahoma.

Overlapping Spatial Identities

The significance of overlapping spatial identities in what is ethnically and confessionally a fairly homogenous population deserves some treatment. The chief importance of overlapping spatial identities surrounds the integration of roles and statuses within the individual life narrative of any given citizen. An abundance of newspaper articles and interviews revealed influential, solitary individuals, with a host of affiliations that blended confessional affiliation, government-related responsibilities, and civic aspirations. Indeed, such overlapping is to some degree common to most Americans. In the context of disaster response and relief in Oklahoma City, however, it is essential to examine how otherwise-autonomous practices and speech forms were assimilated into one another and publicly presented as one coherent entity. So, for instance, Gwen Greaves, the choir director at Walls Chapel AME Zion Church at the time of the bombing, performed a one-woman musical concert at First Lutheran Church on November 17, 1995.[101] She was, it is important to note, a supervisor in the social-security office in the Murrah Building at the time of the bombing. The committee that designed and coordinated the National Day of Prayer memorial service, at which President Clinton and Billy Graham spoke, were also members of the Inter-Faith Alliance of Oklahoma, and occupied other positions of civic leadership. Dan and Dave Demuth, a father and son duo who owned several funeral homes in the city, served as representatives of the medical examiner's office and fulfilled various tasks that usually fall within the purview of a government-agency specialist. They selected a site for a family-assistance center (a.k.a. "the compassion center") at the First Christian Church (N.W. Thirty-Sixth Street and N. Walker Avenue), and worked at that very site as family counselors and data managers. As a newspaper article observes, no one among the specialists in the center noticed that they were not "'real' medical examiner officials." Their competence confused the tacitly expected outward presentations of government specialists. They had also, upon their own initiative, spearheaded disaster-response workshops for all interested members of the Oklahoma Association for Funeral Directors before the bombing occurred. The Oklahoma Department of Civil Emergency Management's *After-Action Report* speaks to the establishment of this family-counseling venue yet fails to mention the full-time occupations or names of those who determined that the church building was adequate. In fact, it explicitly states, in compliance with the standard format of an executive summary, that the city's medical examiner's office established the center.[102]

The Red Cross, despite being manned by highly trained professional nonprofit administrators and planners, depended heavily on a large volunteer corps (six thousand volunteers signed up after April 19) and on a long-standing cooperative relationship with local fire departments. The volunteers also set up a makeshift hardware shop on the Murrah site and manned credentialing posts for the FBI. The director of human resources for the local Red Cross chapter lauded local volunteer efforts, citing that

101. Hinton, "Bomb Survivor to Offer Voice."
102. ODCEM, 6.

the ratio of paid staffers to volunteers showed between 90 and 95 percent more volunteers than paid staffers. Beyond this, the local chapter

> could not have been better prepared for what unfolded in the hours and days following the bombing. Just the week before, we'd had a mock disaster session that started in the morning and lasted well into the evening. It covered how we would respond, what we would do, who would do what. The timing couldn't have been better because we were as prepared as anyone could have been on April 19. Everyone knew just what to do and they responded great.[103]

These are merely a few of the examples that demonstrate considerable aptitude in disaster response on the part of local, nonexpert actors—local aptitude that, consequently, resisted the material and the symbolic cooptation of an outside agency. That is, such involvement by local volunteers without official or expert system credentials molds the symbolic attributions that local citizens make about the collectivity, just as the involvement of several churches in essential emergency-service functions does as well. Local stories about commitment, extreme efforts at service delivery, dedication to God, and sacrifice resisted nationalization, and thus maintained a primarily Oklahoman context even after receiving national television-news coverage. This is another way of perceiving dedifferentiation, but in a manner that speaks to subversion of statist constructions and social organization. The church building is altered in the process of hosting expert service provision: these services are now the embodiment of ministry to those in need, the embodiment of Christ's identification with those in need. Nevertheless, while the work of the rescue worker was "blessed," the church building was still a site at which the agents of the nation-state fought to reproduce its presence and disciplines.

Place Making and Memory Work

Finally, the urban landscape of Oklahoma City came under measurable scrutiny, with serious repercussions for an identity-building project to which major institutions contributed. About one month after the attack, institutional interrelations began to bear upon the matter of place making as a part of recovery.

The beginning of personal relations and the establishment of practices was not collegial at first, as at least one article (released about three

103. Dowell, "Red Cross, Salvation Army Workers Praised."

weeks after the bombing) testifies. Indeed, what Michel Foucault called the domains of "normativity" (criteria for excluding statements as irrelevant or marginal) and "actuality" (definitions of a problem and accepted solutions) initially introduced rifts into what eventually became (at least ostensibly) a united group of urban planners, architects, and public officials of Oklahoma City.[104] Mounting resistance against the state's construal of historic landmarks was the task of Bob Blackburn, the executive director of the Oklahoma Historical Society, who, in confronting statist determinations of historical worth, asserted the worth of certain buildings "as landmarks in [their] own right [that] should be treated for what [they are]—[representatives] of a bygone era."[105] Only one building among the group of damaged structures held an official listing in the National Register of Historic Places: the Journal Record Building. Federal guidelines indicate that historical-registry designation is only permitted to properties at least fifty years old. To this stipulation, Blackburn retorted: "Just because it's not in the register doesn't mean we don't consider it significant historically."[106] This member of a localized expert system attempted to subvert federal criteria in order to fund a project for *local* determination of building retention. The state, and the manner in which it maps identity, is here revealed in its entire social-historical contingency.

The eventual response from preservationists and members of historic societies was one of pleasant surprise. State officials had usually construed "preservationists as antagonists," said Blackburn, but now viewed them as "partners."[107] This signaled a shift in the normal governmental mode of seeing the urban space or city. This is most suitably exhibited through a comparison with a previous Oklahoma project of urban renewal.

The history of Oklahoma City's urban development is fraught with peaks and valleys, adversity and demolition. Near the end of May 1995, the demolition of the remains of the Murrah Building spawned a slew of recollections surrounding the city's past attempts at urban revitalization. Interestingly, as the city struggled in the second half of 1995 to determine how many of its "historic" buildings could be saved from complete destruction following the bombing, memories resurged surrounding the

104. See Foucault, *Archaeology of Knowledge* for a more "methodological" statement of Foucault's philosophical commitments.

105. Martin, "Historical Society Worries."

106. Ibid.

107. Ibid.

widespread and governmentally spearheaded demolition of 447 buildings in the 1960's and 1970s, many of which had been of "historic and architectural significance."[108] Patience Latting, mayor between 1971 and 1983, oversaw the protracted demolitions carried out by the Oklahoma City Urban Renewal Authority. During an interview conducted just before the demolition of the Murrah Building, she stated that urban renewal under architect I. M. Pei's plan for urban development was carried out "to improve downtown and was very organized," it was the effort of "people trying to surge forward . . . to make way for progress."[109] In the case of postbombing relief efforts, the goal was rather to save as many buildings as possible. Indeed, the bombing occasioned a distinct outlook on urban renewal and collective identity. Terms such as "progress" and "renewal" were, in the context of disaster response, recovery, and relief, sublimated or altered to fit a program of saving Oklahoma's past as a gesture of resistance to the damage that the bombing caused upon the social body's ("the people's") historical and symbolic awareness. In this case, history was not known until it was damaged and had to be reconstructed.

In the postdisaster setting, therefore, certain buildings had to be imbued with symbolic and narrative significance; it cannot be overemphasized that the identity of Oklahomans depended upon the deliberations and decisions of this new task force. On top of this, the interinstitutional alignment of historic preservationists, architects, urban planners, and government officials was bolstered through emphasis on expertise, and thus on a degree of exclusion. Each occupation fulfilled an important set of tasks oriented toward the renewal of the urban landscape. One set of workers ascertained the extent of physical damage, while the other determined the particular set of political maneuvers and approaches with respect to fund acquisition. Churches were notably cordoned off from consideration for federal recovery funds, while the president of the National Trust for Historic Preservation offered lobbying services in Washington DC. The vice mayor presided over this meeting; churches, in this instance, were entirely dependent on the determinations of this constellation of contributors. Viewed more broadly, this set of developments amounts to the existence of a particular rift in the post-attack institutional interrelations.

108. Aiken, "Upcoming Demolition Raises Memories."
109. Ibid.

Nevertheless, the institutions remained heavily indebted to one another in various fundamental areas.

Specifically, members of local preservation associations as well as urban-planning firms played a significant role during the postdisaster period in Oklahoma City. The identity of the Oklahoman in this city was intimately related to place making. Herein churches became highly relevant because of their high concentration in the downtown area of Oklahoma City around the Murrah bombing site. Engineering experts attempted to interpret the importance of these buildings (and many others) from the perspective of "historic" resources or "historical value." "History," in this sense, is a sort of symbol or metaphor for memory, life, and continuity. If something is "historic," then it falls under the rubric of preservation and place making, a site at which an identity is inscribed in the past, present, and future—all at the same time. In the same vein, the structural engineer featured in one article states that the historic churches and other small buildings "gave the area character," and also "they were all vital structures that give continuity to the things that make the city interesting, and their damage is a loss to all the citizens of the city of Oklahoma City and the State of Oklahoma."[110] Notice the manner in which the structures themselves are loaded with words synonymous with "life" and identity: they give the area "character" (recognizable patterns of being), they are "vital," and they provide a sort of temporal link that is unmistakably narratival in scope. The engineer implies that the church buildings, when used, connect the person with all that went on there in previous generations, thus confirming such a mode of being as a model for the future. All this enters the public light without theological articulation. It is, as one headline states, the words of an "expert."[111] These words, and accompanying actions, carry heavy repercussions for social reorientation through the expert analysis and confirmation of the link between identity and place. The recovery process thus brings specialized knowledge to bear upon the determination of what is "historic," and thus what should be linked with the construction of local identities. This is most evident in the statement that damage to these buildings is a loss to "all the citizens of the city of Oklahoma City and the State of Oklahoma." It is possible, hence, to connect a physical place (i.e., a building) to the

110. Money, "Expert Urges Rescue of Buildings,"
111. Ibid.

integrity of the collective identity of all the inhabitants, even if most in-habitants had never visited any of these sites or cared to do so. These are the sorts of claims that signify major turning points and building blocks for cultural production in service to a particular post-attack identity. An Oklahoman, and especially an Oklahoman in Oklahoma City, *must want these churches and buildings to be preserved.* Any given inhabitant cannot be an Oklahoman without them. Once again, these designations pertain-ing to the essentiality (as opposed to the disposability) of certain physical sites are executed by those with some expert capability. Determinations of this kind were completed through "symbolic inversion,"[112] whereby buildings that occupied an ordinary and mundane (even if essential) function for specific subsets of local residents were inserted into pub-lic discourse and converted into potential sociocultural icons around which postdisaster claims could be made about what best represented Oklahomans as a collectivity (thus approximating the Durkheimian "to-tem"). This capability provides hermeneutical or interpretive leverage. The expert, therefore, is able not only to determine the extent of dam-age from a fiduciary standpoint, but also to make transhistorical claims about the significance of a physical structure. City officials were the chief endorsers of this approach, affirming that those hired (or volunteering) were among the best in their field.

Nevertheless, this approach was not without critics. The Reverend George Back stated that the churches should be viewed with more depth—as "living organisms," not just "artifacts."[113] The discursive disjunction between church leaders, on the one hand, and urban planners, preserva-tionists, engineers, and government leaders, on the other hand, was am-plified through various discursive and practical means. First, as has been mentioned, although they were permitted to attend planning meetings for the National Memorial and Museum, church leaders were not allowed to attend meetings of the group that convened to discuss other monetary provisions to certain urban-planning programs and the nature of the plans. The meetings held for the planning of the National Memorial, by contrast, were actually held inside a church building: St. Luke's Methodist Church.[114] In terms of the physical space in which formal public memory

112. Procter, "Victorian Days," 133–43.
113. Gilliland, "Churches Not Eligible for Funds."
114. Perry, "Leaders See Effort Enduring."

work was executed, many gatherings (with the bombing as the main impetus and context for interrelations) occurred within church buildings. Along with the expected worship services, church buildings also served as venues for concerts, memorial-planning meetings, reunion events, and numerous psychological-improvement workshops.

Second, the public language of government leaders was unambiguously administrative, legal, and proprietary with regard to the repair of physical structures. In a statement issued to address the status of requests for additional federal funds, Governor Keating stated that the *city* "was attacked as a federal property."[115] This is an interesting collective attribution with respect to the city. Funds should be received from the federal government because the symbol of greatest relevance, or that which forms the ultimate frame of reference for funding decisions, is Oklahoma City as "federal property." The viability of this rhetorical maneuver must rest on the legitimate political actor who made it: Governor Keating. He acted as the liaison between different levels of government actors and agencies, a position not available to local ministers. Ministers entered the fray of contested recovery funds *through* their governmental representatives. When they did speak to the issue directly, they realized that they had to take a public stand about the separation of church and state. This was an ironclad issue for which innovation did not come quickly.[116] Law, evidently, served as a symbolic base of power and sovereignty for governmental financial policy relating to major recovery efforts. Discourse tied to the monopoly over the use of force further buttressed legal discourse once the investigation produced the primary suspect, Timothy McVeigh.

The Legacy of the Churches

The long wait for any sort of government determination of relief funds and frustrations surrounding the repair work in downtown churches exposed the importance of the church as physical venue and the sort of symbolic and productive power with which it had become imbued. It appears that the setting had imbued the parishioners who consider it "home," with a particular sense of security and legitimacy not found

115. Casteel. "State Gets Reassurance."

116. While federal law still prohibits distribution of funds to churches in most cases, the Oklahoma City bombing occasioned the acceptance of certain criteria that qualify a congregation for compensation.

elsewhere. Terms of ownership or attachment (quite distinct from key terms of experts), such as "their own" or "my" place of worship, are not rare in this study's sample of articles. Also, the import of the building as a context for crucial life happenings, including what Richard Fenn calls "rituals of time," was evident in the statements of many parishioners.[117] In fact, two general codes, "church space as context for crucial life events" and "legacy of the church" clearly emerged during analysis and in unison accounted for seventeen cases. The first general code also subsumed five subcodes (dealing with various views of church space as a "home," as a "gift for the people," and as "organism") that together yielded ten additional cases. The second general code represents nostalgic accounts of the history of a given downtown church building, including those presented in a defensive tone. (For instance, one article headline read "Forgetting the Churches.") One parishioner aptly summarized the chief theme contained in all church-space–related codes: she wondered when the building would be repaired so that she could die and have her memorial service there.

The political alliances aimed at altering the physical landscape of the city and the discursive and bodily practices that encouraged, and were created by, the corresponding cultural productions demand a test of theological legitimacy. The *poiesis* pertaining to the built environment of any city is not an irrelevant sphere of activity to the church.[118] The peculiar linkage of memory, identity, and physical place actually occasions, when handled irresponsibly, an epistemic crisis. This is discernible in most of the sociopolitical processes just mentioned. I will briefly focus upon two corollary issues: the chasm between expert and nonexpert and the gift of the church.

While Oklahoman officials capitalized on the revelation of Oklahoman "goodness" to the world as a result of the bombing, this prevailing theme of reconstitution efforts did not inform their struggles regarding the reconstruction of the built environment. In the context of the modern state (in both the welfare and neoliberal forms), the relationship between expert and nonexpert can be considered an extension of logical atomism. In both cultural expression and spatial organization, this gulf between expert and nonexpert creates mutually detached areas of

117. Fenn, *Time Exposure*, 2–10.

118. See Gorringe, *Theology of the Built Environment* for a masterly theologically qualified account of physical structures.

deliberation, judgment, and social interaction. In other words, it further stratifies the social world through regimes of knowledge. While evidence may show that we are dependent on the judgments of others for our well-being or knowledge of the world (including, no doubt, so-called expert others), still, as Alasdair MacIntyre notes in *Dependent Rational Animals*, our dependence should not necessitate the absence of mutual deference or regard for the practical wisdom that comes with living in a given neighborhood or land for protracted periods. [119] Far from generating functional interdependence and equality among citizens (i.e., what structural-functionalists presumed that hyperdifferentiation and specialization would produce in the modern world), the plans and judgments of experts in recovery scenarios after disasters actually reveal a host of hegemonic practices (from which no academic of any stripe is immune). These practices construct a particular orientation to life as the inevitable, necessary, or only natural course of affairs. (Such an orientation marks the absolute statement quoted above, about the buildings Oklahomans must retain in order to uphold the integrity of Oklahoman identity.) This orientation is especially characteristic of massive urban-renewal projects, which are often couched in a concatenation of ideals including progress, innovation, civilization, and advancement. (Projects of this scope often result in uneven development.) Consequently, as the mediators of sure knowledge and management of the urban landscape single-mindedly pursue the actualization of these ideals, the efficacy of other forms of knowledge and experience (a fortiori, of being) is devalued and displaced, relegated to the status of a given ethnic, age, or occu-pational group's trait, custom, or tradition. The tenor of such political engagement with expertise is the ultimate rejection of faith as a mode of being, of faith as a source of ecclesial movement across city space.

Physical space consists in those dimensions of lived reality that manifest the fullness and glory of God to sentient and embodied creatures. Those Scriptures that employ spatial dimension as a key referent for God's tangible goodness and faithfulness cannot be appreciated without acknowledging the creational context of all physical space, including space made by humans and space that fills and constitutes the natural created order. In Genesis 1, for example, space in creation first appears as openings or clefts that are to be filled with the life God creates in subsequent

---

119. MacIntyre, *Dependent Rational Animals*, 71, 94, 95.

days. Space always redounds with tensions of pulling and pushing, separating and binding—but only as passages on the way to yet other manifold
realizations of God's abiding provision of goods, loving-kindness, power,
and faithfulness. That God's *glory*, in Hebrew, is linked to a term which
denotes "weight" or density pertaining to the significance of presence is
not accidental. The New Testament with some frequency speaks to the
fullness of God, which fills everything in every way. Once again employing
spatial dimensions, Paul speaks of the ecclesial discernment of the height,
width, length, and depth of the love of Christ (Eph 3:18). The church, in
fact, is also called to be filled with the fullness of God, to fill everything
in every way (Eph 1:23). These passages are most readily spiritualized or
psychologized in order to be rendered intelligible as referring to states
of mind. However, it is possible to see in these passages the reconstitution of space, not by means of more church buildings, but through the
presence of disciples of the Messiah as the body of Christ in the world.
Followers of the Messiah transgress boundaries, hierarchies, and layers
that enfold all life happenings and, within time, Messiah followers partly
compose the narratives in which gifted place is established out of space.
Places represent the potential for growth along with, as Brueggemann
notes, temptation, promise, and gift.[120] Just as the temple served as a locus
for communion with God through sacrifice, so too does the body of the
disciple of Jesus house the Holy Spirit and serve as a site of reconciliation
with God. Hence the place at which the members of the body of Christ
meet the physical world and those other human beings are sites at which
God's "weightiness" may be encountered anew.

The church should be aware that labeling some buildings as "historic" (and hence protected or "permanent") usually accompanies the
somewhat-arbitrary designation of other structures, depending on some
developmental fad, as dispensable. This is not to say that some buildings
do not powerfully convey a turning point in the political or social history
of a city, but simply that if God's fullness is the crucial end toward which
spatial construction and understanding are geared, then we cannot simply
rely on determinations of worth based on appearance or historical legacy.
Indeed, the turning point of most cities occurs in a variety of locations
within a single city, at both well-known locations and comparatively invisible locations—and not simply in those locations publicized as "eventful."

120. See Brueggemann, *The Land*.

Against many popular criminological theories that assume one can read the magnitude of moral cohesion and criminogenic elements of a neighborhood from the appearance of the streets and buildings (e.g., the Broken Windows Theory and Situational Crime Prevention), the church situates the primacy of faith as a transgressor of boundaries and as renunciation of such simplistic spatial judgments. Faith that is truly faith in the God of creation and redemption has always translated into temporal bodily movements across racial, economic, and gender divisions (imagined and physical, which mutually determine one another), joining one community to another in a way that eschews considerations of historical worth. Movement and the bodily co-presence it fosters actually engage the four "problems" that Bryan Turner alleges all "social systems" must solve regarding the body: the reproduction of populations, the restraining of desire, the regulation of population in space, and the representation of the "exterior" of bodies.[121] In this vein, a given congregation's activity in landed community, predicated upon the extent to which its eucharistic worship, baptismal practice, and catechetical instruction is carried out as a public text, promises to affect the actual structuring of encounters at ever-wider levels. However, the transformation of the rules or norms governing the structure of encounters (of which the body is surely a basic unit) must be a collective enterprise because such rules, which relate to everything from hand gestures and eye contact to physical comportment and the use of props, arise from shared vocabularies of body idiom that are outside the body and also out of the reach of a person subject to them. The nurturing of an ecclesial body that strives to understand itself as the place (i.e., "wherever two or three are gathered") at which bodies and encounters are molded, and not simply where beliefs, values, or doctrines are heard and intellectually assimilated, is more fully equipped to understand itself in all dimensions of truthful living in God.

Faith thus construed, as at the least a therapy of desire involving bold and prayerful bodily movement toward God and others in space and time, does not mean that the sacralization of space is enough to counter the state's historical treatment of space and place as a simple palimpsest—valued and revalued according to capitalist canons, or constructed and swept away, without loving consideration of many relevant consequences to actual human beings whose lives cannot be reduced

121. Turner, *Body and Society*, 114.

to the terms of the singular financial logics of many urban-planning or disaster-recovery models. The faith that is a gift of the church enables us to see that "the earth is the Lord's and everything in it" (Ps 24:1). Even so, as Matthew Levering duly notes in his theological exposition of Ezra and Nehemiah, the land is made holy by virtue of the worship of the covenant God who forms a people with whom to dwell in the land.[122] Whether the state, a deliberately resistant citizen group, or an assembly of Christians identifies a "holy place" and thus acknowledges its power to prompt a certain set of dispositions and behaviors, it is nonetheless "from the inside, from [a person's] heart, [that] come the evil thoughts, fornication, theft, murder, adultery, coveting, deceit," and all other "evil things" that defile the places of life (Mark 7:21–23). If the gathering of saints acknowledges that among its own necessary set of ethical tasks is recognizing that addressing the condition of "the heart" of each person bears absolutely upon the holiness of the land itself, then the life of the church can be enriched in incorporating another intracreational component of God's covenantal, salvific, work. Commitment to some ecclesial practices geared toward regularly discovering and engaging what is in the heart, within the context of forgiveness, repentance, prayer, and covenanted discipleship, ensures the earnest reception of each person into the body of Christ precisely because it enacts the acceptance of the responsibility to reflect Christ in the places (those lands, homes, and other structures that nourish and sustain life) without which we are "world-less."

Ultimately, the correspondence that God seeks in space and specifically with those who bear the *imago Dei* is grounded in the faithful movements of the Trinity. As Timothy Gorringe aptly states in his endorsement of Barth's Trinitarian theology of space: "the fact that God is present to Godself, that there is a divine proximity and remoteness . . . is the basis and presupposition of created proximity and remoteness."[123] Hence, whether political bodies engage space in the context of locales (physically co-present concentrated interaction), or in the process of regionalization or nationalization after disasters, this space is a gift: ceded or granted space that comes from the Trinity's absolute creational, incarnational, and redemptive relational presence.[124] Faithful disciples of Jesus move

---

122. Levering, *Ezra & Nehemiah*, 34.

123. Gorringe, *A Theology of the Built Environment*, 43.

124. Ibid., 44.

about this space with a desire to bind together places at which particular blessings and hauntings (i.e., traumatic memories) may both reside, and to incorporate them into the sufferings and affections of the Godhead. Disciples themselves are supposed to be "enfleshed" enactments of this binding of places or physical sites, which is evident in baptism, by which the Spirit transforms the body and soul in a concrete material rite. The "fleshiness" of baptism tempts us to conclude that it merely represents or symbolizes some deeper spiritual transaction that primarily involves (and privileges) the immaterial soul, spirit, or cognitions. The presence of a *baptized body* is actually supposed to make a difference within the everyday places that provide the physical context for encounters, relations, and larger sociopolitical forms of life; the Christian's body and soul are both transformed, and this is not merely the result of a ritual nicety of strictly memorial significance akin to a snapshot. As it is, the participative role of the bodies of Christians in the material work of the triune God must be actively articulated into lived ecclesiologies.

The (Contested) Political Imagination of the Oklahoma City Bombing

This final section tackles the following question: to what extent did church-directed theological disciplines keep up with, absorb, or clash with the discourse and practice of statist disciplines; and vice versa? My guiding research hypothesis associated with this question of competing political imaginations claimed that in reasserting its functions and organs of social control or discipline after the disaster, the state would rely on an implicit theology that ensured victory, that advanced a vision of a permanent or natural unity, and that insisted on valuing institutional expertise and competence as the primary means for assembling the social body. This hypothesis was partly accurate but still required some significant qualification.

The interview responses and existing research literature pointed to a demarcation of a few specific political practices and themes that manifested the competing political imaginaries of church and state. These practices included fulfilling emergency-service functions (domains), memorializing, forming collective identity, framing perpetrators, prioritizing identities, and place making. All such categories bore upon interlocked ways of imagining human nature and human destiny and of imagining who (or what) secures salvation for "a people." This section is entirely framed in terms of differentiation and dedifferentiation. The first subsection below details the political imaginative scope of public claims and accounts of the attack as presented in state-orchestrated ceremonies; to be sure, they aligned themselves with explicit theological views. The following subsections present the political imagination of the churches as a group, the political imagination of the state, and the dedifferentiated political imaginary of church and state, whereby certain views or practices originating in one institution were adopted by another.

Parallel Discourses and Practices of Solidarity

It is important to reemphasize the similarity of discursive and imaginative scope when grappling with the general claims of church and state after this incident, especially with respect to the making of a social body in Oklahoma, or "a people" (hence geographically and racially situated) of particular moral and theopolitical qualities. At the site of the bombing, disaster response itself, from the outset, engaged in cultural productions that joined grief, anger, sadness, prayer, challenges in human-resource management, churches, crosses, and rescuers together in a mind-boggling predicament. Soon after the bombing, the U.S. House of Representatives approved a resolution to wholly condemn the bombing. The resolution's language and the Oklahoma legislative officials' comments surrounding its public disclosure were entirely concerned with incorporating various theopolitical components: the blessings of God on Oklahoma City, the "regalvanized American spirit," the outstanding character qualities of (all) local Oklahomans, and the cruciality of retribution.[125] Rep. Ernest Istook asserted: "If you come to Oklahoma City, and I hope and pray that you'll have an occasion to do so to meet the people that fit the title of being in the heartland of America, you will find that in addition to all the ribbons, there are signs all over town that say 'God Bless Oklahoma City.' And I know he does."[126] In the same congressional session, Rep. J. C. Watts voiced the need to find the perpetrators and "make sure [they] pay for this senseless tragedy."[127] President Clinton reinforced the strong nationalist bond between Oklahoma congressmen and the federal government

125. Casteel, "State Gets Reassurance."
126. Ibid.
127. Ibid.

when he asserted: "this terrible sin took the lives of our American family."[128] This represents both a mimicked attempt at the collapse of *oikos* and *polis* offered in Ephesians 4, and a collapse of familiar relations (family) with imaginary relations (nationality). However, in many local and informal contexts, the centrality of the American story was challenged. Why? Interpretations of the disaster were fashioned from within local practices of considerable precedent, which were carried out within a web of strong social ties cultivated in very influential church buildings and congregations (especially during the response phase) and in negotiation with the local citizens' confessional theologies.

The Church: Healing, Hospitality, and Local Unification

The churches of Oklahoma City, viewed as whole, conceive of humans and collectivities, map bodies, and measure time differently from the state. They offer forgiveness, prayer, and hospitality at the local level as fundamental praxis and symbol in the recovery process. Specifically, recall how the first section of this chapter firmly established the vitality of prayer as a regular post-attack practice across all sorts of institutional discourses and spatial identities. Whether by rescuers at the bombing site, ministers in church buildings, or public officials along with local citizens at memorial services, prayer was publicly promoted as a seemingly essential characteristic of a postdisaster project of social reorientation. In other words, prayer was not simply to be done in private or on a few special occasions, but was an integral practice for binding one citizen to another.

Moreover, churches entered the political imagination as agents of relief, unification, and healing, at first challenging well-worn notions of the separation of church and state in the form of federal relief-aid stipulations, but then going no further. One minister openly expounded upon the church's role as the cement of the city, as the actual binding agent of citizens; whereas others complementarily construed the church building as a "gift" or offering to the city. In fact, some church buildings served as places at which local Oklahoman identity was reconstituted around prayer and worship over against other identities, including national identity. These buildings, as many preservationists contended, could not be lost without sacrificing the integrity of Oklahoman state identity itself.

---

128. Clinton, "Time for Healing."

With its state identity forged "in steel" after the bombing, Oklahoma was able to present itself on equal ground with other states of the Union.

With respect to "healing," content analysis of newspaper articles suggests that psychological, therapeutic, and mental-health language aligned itself quite strongly with church practice and theology following the attack. This alignment was, it should be noted, an antecedent social condition that was publicly amplified. This is evidenced by the plethora of grief workshops hosted by local churches in the eight months following the attack (at least a dozen), at least one of which featured a former Oklahoma pastor as a keynote speaker in the area of grief counseling. Most discussions of therapeutic treatment were endorsed or even adopted by local ministers, although two allusions are made to the fear of stigmatization if psychological treatment is made public. The most popular themes associated with this institutional discourse were some variation on "free" or "open" expression of feelings, and "talking through things" in order to find "healing." This discourse was also used to guide the course of several memorial ceremonies held in Oklahoma City and in surrounding towns.

The State: The Public Theology of Permanence, Competence, and Patriotism

The imaginings of the state (indeed of the nation-state) on the other hand, seemed more concerned with etching a sense of permanence in the face of attack, showing competence in economy and even in spirituality, and suffusing many objects and places with nationalist narrative elements. The nation-state achieved more permanence in physical places outside church buildings, where special (nonrecurring) memorial ritual events and the National Memorial itself secured more linkages between the bombing and national identity in the public realm and hence in the newly fashioned social body. Some injections of nationalism can occur in perpetuity if certain cultural productions (and their objects) allow for it. For example, the Oklahoma City National Memorial offers pamphlets, maps, and memorabilia that explicitly associate sacrality, America, and the memorial site. A small double-sided handout that can be acquired at the Oklahoma City National Memorial Museum details the meanings encased in all the various structures and objects at the memorial site. It claims that the memorial itself is one of the "most sacred places in

America." In describing the "Survivor Tree" that lies just north of the "Field of Empty Chairs," the visitor guide quotes what is inscribed on the plaque setting in front of the tree: "The spirit of this city and this nation will not be defeated; our deeply rooted faith sustains us." The universality and tautness of the statement is meant to incorporate all the varied "faiths" that are possible within the city and the nation. Also readers are compelled to ponder Oklahoman identity as somehow contiguous with national identity. Likewise, nationality is territorially naturalized in the statement that appears on some handbags sold to visitors: "On American Soil." Here, one again, spatial identities interpenetrate one another, sharing reputations, character qualities, and histories of resilience or permanence. What is more, to write in terms that Michel Foucault would recognize, power proves to be productive in various senses: productive of material artifacts and of conceptual linkages—some of the more important stuff out of which agents are fashioned.

The state's agents also issued direct claims about the character of God, especially in redeeming the victims, exercising compassion, and exacting justice. These claims and attendant gestures were understandably couched in relatively frequent public ritual performances (see just below). As local business owners and believers openly presented Jesus Christ as a fellow sufferer and both object and agent of faithful response, officials of the state subscribed to a more generic god of universal causes, a "God of Justice" and a "God of Righteousness."

In this vein, President Clinton injected theological evaluations at White House press conferences and at the National Day of Prayer Service. Similarly, during a May 5, 1995, memorial service, Governor Keating "spoke to God" as he stood over the crater caused by four thousand eight hundred pounds of explosives and, after the event, met personally with families. Meanwhile, other government officials quoted Scripture at public events.[129] The line separating clergy from public official was muddled significantly as a new social body was announced and constructed during this liminal phase. Keating's declarations made during the National Day of Prayer service on May 4, 1995, and as he stood over the bomb-wrought cavity the following day, furnished all the requisite discursive, theopolitical, and dramaturgical elements that compose collective identity formation. On May 4, 1995, he affirmed: "The magnitude of the loss

---

129. Plumberg, "Workers Pay Respects at Ruins."

and the sadness cannot be described with words. We cannot imagine that one human being could do this to another human being . . . But one thing we know for sure: We can always depend on people. Thank you, Oklahoma."[130] On May 5, in addition, he declared: "And as awful as these days were, we have come together *as a people*. Oklahoma's example to the world is absolutely second to none. We are *a caring people*, we are *a spiritual people*, we are *a committed people*."[131] These two events were followed by yet another memorial event, which included a memorial service and tour of the bombing site for three thousand survivors and relatives of victims, on Saturday, May 6. It was estimated to proceed from 1 p.m. to 6 p.m. At this event, family members could meet individually with Gov. Keating or continue to a memorial service at First Christian Church. Three consecutive days of ritualized performance installed a rather coherent network of significations, practices, and judgments about human destiny and human nature.

Competence was further buttressed through talk of economic performance or productivity. Many words of quasi-soteriological promise were trussed to the appropriation of bomb-relief funds, betraying a confidence and urgency with respect to making downtown Oklahoma City a lucrative and appealing center for cultural and commercial development. Keating, for example, stated that the funds would contribute to making Oklahoma City "whole" again, signifying integrity and harmony involving all institutional activities, especially in commerce (as "the cornerstone"). A Republican senator mentioned that a "new day" was coming with the passage of this aid legislation. President Clinton approved of the legislation and lauded the demonstration of interpartisan agreement and collegiality in bringing it to fruition. The principal thrust for all this hope-filled speech was an intractable focus on business development and the urgency with which it was to be implemented in order to produce a "lucrative place" that would assume an important role for the self-understanding of the postdisaster body corporate. That is, the postdisaster people were to be specifically constituted through the highly anticipated success of commercial enterprise.

Emphasis switched from economic development to preservation of buildings and architectural styles throughout the summer months after

130. Ibid.
131. "Weary Nation," 7 (emphasis added).

the attack. So talk about "revitalization" and being "drawn" to downtown in a way hitherto unknown or nonexistent invited a certain tension focused on decisions about physical continuity and discontinuity. Some particular features of the downtown area, some argued, ought to be completely new, while other things ought to remain the way they are. Some new structures were offered as objects conveying the message that "we will not allow the attack to change us": hence the suggestion on the part of many citizens to build another Murrah Federal Building on the same exact site where the previous building stood. This would have marked continuity in a manner distinct from an official memorial, which was the eventual physical occupant of the site. The chief goal of all such deliberations was the determination of what will accurately capture both the past and the imagined future of Oklahoma City, and thus create a foundational theopolitical narrative.[132]

The Dedifferentiated Church and State: Exalt "the People," Speak to God, and Kill the Offender

The aforementioned suggests that both church and state maintained certain disciplined means of imagining space and time, which remained intact before and after the bombing. However, most interesting in this respect were instances of one institution's absorbing imaginings and practices originating in another institution, with perhaps prayer and views on capital punishment as most formidable. First, prayer as a practice firmly anchored in church life and well associated with "spiritual life," conceived pluralistically, made its way into many public performances of state and church. Despite being supervised by ritual experts from different confessional perspectives, the state generated captivating moments that could not but gain some sort of ritual permanence. In this vein, especially, consider Keating's prayer as he stood over the crater caused by the explosion and Clinton's well-measured theological declarations during White House press conferences (one of which appears in the title of this chapter) and just before Billy Graham's memorial sermon at the National Day of Prayer service. In actual practice, both Keating and mayor Ron Norrick served in pastoral or clerical roles, meeting privately with family members at either memorial ceremonies or memorial planning sessions, and theologically expositing at ritual events. The force of such statements

---

132. See Till, *New Berlin*, 20–23.

to bolster a certain identity and hence certain political practices (bearing on life and death) is derived from dramaturgical properties, not mere repetition or frequency.

While prayer was assimilated into the civic power of the state, other popular discourses (specifically doctrines) and practices of local church theologies struggled to be produced in dramaturgically refined or publicly presentable forms. With few exceptions, the common doctrines and practices of forgiveness and reconciliation faced major competition as cultural objects in the postdisaster fray of cultural production. This was primarily because of competition from the state's preferred narrative framework of rebinding the broken body politic, and because the cultural objects remained "objects" or empty doctrines—they were not sufficiently "enfleshed" within each congregation, as the Word in Christ is, and as Christ seeks to be in the church as a whole. A fair number of local adherents to various denominational groups, the interview data suggest, struggled to reconcile the need to achieve "justice" (to investigate, capture, adjudicate, and punish the perpetrator) with two of the most central tasks of Christian faith: forgiveness and self-emptying love. Such absence was a major object of criticism, readers will recall, among several ministers interviewed. Herein the lack of organized unity and resource mobilization among pastors across denominations was most apparent. Behind the ostensible unity of faiths, various symbols and attendant practices were never in contention to challenge the established mode of reestablishing the social body after the attack. Participant *B2* lamented the absence of a council or assembly of Oklahoma City ministers from all confessional perspectives, similar to one that existed (and continues to exist) in nearby Tulsa. It should therefore be manifest that this meeting to find unity carries a host of implications with respect to how social groups should evaluate their practices of inclusion and exclusion (which relate to valuing humans) and hence this anecdote about missing unity among ministers strengthens the thesis that the state actually generates models for social valuation and behavior—in other words, the state does not remain neutral in the debates or cultural negotiations of civil society.

This situation was exacerbated, at least partly, as numerous church memberships absorbed statist approaches to justice and security, thereby muddling alternative theological views. "Reconciliation" or atonement, for instance, seems to have been promoted from the perspective of a survivor or victim's family member who needed to "accept" the consequences of the event in order prepare for life in subsequent years. As Valerie Dana, head of Interfaith Disaster Recovery of Oklahoma City (an organization established within days of the bombing) explained when interviewed about a special memorial ceremony held on July 1, 1995: "A reconciliation point will be a place where people have time to express their thoughts about the bombing and their concerns for the future."[133] It was not publicly advanced in terms of forgiveness and reconciliation with the perpetrator, who at least some churches prayed would be forgiven (by humans and by God) in the weeks after the bombing. These churches construed Timothy McVeigh as a broken and wounded human being who needed divine healing. This element of forgiveness was absent from statist discourse, and neither was it demanded in a public and ritual manner by a single interest group, coalition of civic associations, or the Inter-Faith Alliance of Oklahoma. It is patent that forgiveness enjoys little political articulation in the statist political imaginary bent on security via punitive measures. Forgiveness as a collective practice, unlike prayer in the abstract, necessarily directs social relations toward a very specific outcome (i.e., union) that is at odds with the theopolitical imagination of the state, and hence, at odds with the implied social dynamics the state endorses. Atonement would entail absorption and assimilation of the malfeasance into the social body—something that apparently cannot happen in the contemporary liberal-democratic penal context of either Oklahoma City or the United States. This vision of social relations and control is evident in different exhibits inside the Oklahoma City National Memorial Museum. In at least two exhibit rooms open to tourists (rooms that cover the investigative efforts of government agencies), the government is presented as bent on fulfilling its primary obligation: to detect the perpetrator, detain him or her, discover the truth about him or her, and deliver the suitable punishment (i.e., removal from the social body).

In terms of the extent of capital punishment, records from Oklahoma's justice system suggest that the commitment to execute serious offenders was starting to increase before the bombing (after a major hiatus) but accelerated remarkably after the bombing. Specifically, while Oklahoma as a state ordered the execution of five offenders between 1966 and March 20, 1995 (the year of the bombing), fifteen offenders were executed between July 1, 1995, and December 9, 1999. The total number

133. Gilliland, "Reconciliation Program."

of executions climbed to twenty-five when the year 2000 is included in the tally.[134] In addition, the state of Oklahoma is responsible for one of the most recent executions of an offender who was convicted as a juvenile. Evidently, the civic power of the state manifested in the use of extreme punitive force was not lost to more localized, church-centered postdisaster processes in community formation.

REFLECTIONS FOR ECCLESIAL PRAXIS

Despite the cultural hybridity that attends everyday contemporary life even in relatively homogeneous social, political, and confessional (evangelical) contexts such as that of Oklahoma City, congregations are still bearers of imaginative practices that constitute a people able to identify and resist the sins that beset statist actors and agendas. Below I conclude this chapter with an overview of those ecclesial practices and orientations (revealed or suggested through the research presented above), which can definitively alter the political composition of a city.

First, in a dilated discursive context in which theological speech is welcomed or expected, the congregation must draw attention to its discursive practice (including prayer and preaching) as altogether creative or poetic, gifted activity. Statist speech, on the basis of many ritual speech acts reviewed here, is *not* gifted: rather than operating in a mode of receptivity, seeking God for wisdom or exhortation, it attempts to justify through proclamation; in short, it is not based on a desire to listen or remain attentive to God but on a desire to confidently proclaim what God must be thinking. The use of Scripture to underwrite an already-achieved or *assumed* theopolitical identity ("we are a spiritual people") retains an uneasy relationship with gifted speech because such speech acts manifest an almost coercive, grasping, desperate quality that falls far short of the trusting receptivity that marks life with God. What is more, congregations cannot underestimate the theological imagination that inheres in its practice of prayer and confession. Confession, in particular, reveals the politics that is the body of Christ quite clearly—which is, unfortunately, a political practice largely lost to the modern state and to many congregations. This politics of the social body takes words and assertions (illocutionary and perlocutionary speech acts) as either participating in God, the divine Word, or not. When words are expressed *in* God, they

---

134. Oklahoma Department of Corrections. "Execution Statistics."

do not legitimate either the "war" narratives or opposition or alienation that swelled over so many years in numerous (mostly rural) locales across Oklahoma and other states. Neither do these words evade responsibility; instead, they rouse disciples of Jesus to repentance and action. "If we say we do not bear the guilt of sin, we are deceiving ourselves and the truth is not in us. But if we confess our sins, he will cleanse us from all unrighteousness. If we say we have not sinned, we make him a liar and his words are not in us" (1 John 1:5–6). In order for the truth and his word (posed synonymously in text) to be in us, confession is necessary. "So, confess your sins to one another and pray for one another so that you may be healed" (Jas 5:16). Confessing sin to a member of the body of Christ enacts fellowship with God and with another. Verbalizing sin is a form of exposure to light that ties one member to another: it incites humility, love, and united opposition to sin. It leads to a consummation of agreement in a collective act of self-dispossesion. When I confess, I release my sin and dwell in the light, continuing "in his kindness" (Rom 11:22). Witnessing to sin as a living, public member of the body of Christ and not simply in the interiority of the soul, or in the enfolded conscience, which, as Bonhoeffer rightly argued, "flees from God," is to make healing a real possibility. Confession as a practice of the body ties one to another, enthralling the body in compassion, deputyship, and truthfulness. Each party to confession, having heard the humble articulation of fault, becomes keenly aware that each is responsible for the brother or sister and thus carries him or her within the heart (see Phil 1:6–7). Confession likewise avoids the docetic temptations to spiritualize and privatize what is so tragically common in humanity. In other words, it resists and witnesses against the false humility and "official optimism" that has besieged statist and ecclesial life and is so boldly employed in many postdisaster scenarios.

Second, the state effects the transformation of the dead in the absence of any eschatological longing or hope, which results in processes of memorialization that lack genuine love. Such memorial events make demands of, rather than give to, the dead. A combination of free love that repudiates manipulation and eschatological hope is therefore quite necessary in light of the gravely skewed attributions of blame that begin in the wake of most disasters. In this case, the 168 fatalities of the Murrah Federal Building bombing were named as almost certainly the victims of Islamic terrorists, and so their lives were publicly framed as intelligible only in that light. Contrary to these assertions, love as solidarity with the accused and victimized is key, as is re-immersion into the church's understanding of life and death in light of the God of Israel, the God of the Risen One. The Risen One is the Head into whom the church knows that it must grow, with each part achieving unity as it grows in love and regard for the other. It can only live in this grace by giving itself over to death voluntarily. While the reality, finality, and fear of death shapes all polities, the church refuses to be shaped by the fear of death and hence is not compelled to respond to death as the ultimate frontier. Christians know that the love of God relativizes death, because God's "steadfast love is better than life" (Ps 63:3). This is precisely why the church is called to the fullness of life, because disciples of Jesus have confronted death and realized that only a decisive orientation to loss is what brings true life—a willingness to lose everything for the sake of love for God and love for the neighbor. The saints do not love their life on their terms, and hence leave it to God to save (Luke 9:23–27).

Additionally, the punitive nature of state-administered discipline as a strategy of social renewal after the bombing occasioned the eclipse of forgiveness in some congregations that were caught unawares and un-reflective in the realm of their own forgiveness and the way of Christ with his enemies. This cultivated lack of discernment, rooted at the intersection of lived and scriptural memory, obtains in other areas as well. The transformation of the physical city (designation of "historic sites") in aid of collective identity formation is a maneuver claiming that some places can be forgotten while others cannot. One of the key issues here is the subject who remembers and forgets—the citizen individual and collective. For the human creature, in whom many lived, imaginative constructs intersect (e.g., gender, class, ethnicity, nationality, profession, and the like), familiarity with the past is something material and spatial and thus something for which said person could be held accountable precisely because it is citable. When the state erases the built environment for the sake of some idealized project devoid of any solidarity with the character of the persons who inhabited the affected places, the state assumes that it can forget the past and evade responsibility because something "greater" will vindicate the state's decisions. The state, in such instances, wants a nonmaterialist history. As Walter Benjamin argued in his third thesis concerning history, historians cannot necessarily distinguish between "great" events and minor ones, because ultimately all events are known—and this by God.[135] If we assume, validly I believe, that the same distinction applies to the spatial dimension of history, then the politico-ontological tensions of church and state must have considerable repercussions upon the physical landscape of the city. Today, for example, three contiguous physical memorials (arranged east to west) reside in Oklahoma City: the St. Joseph's Old Cathedral's statue of Jesus weeping, the Oklahoma City National Memorial, and the Heartland Chapel. These structures, in very close proximity to one another, all distinctly mediate the unadorned pain. The statue mediates the pain of Christ (i.e., it absorbs the site into the Lazarus narrative). The National Memorial and Museum mediate a blend of the assumed epistemological privileges of state-backed resources and the nationalization of soil. Finally, the Heartland Chapel mediates the hybridization of a particular confessional theology of politics and spirituality and a distinctively Oklahoman appropriation of the trope of the American body. In light of these and the many other cultural possibilities with respect to memory work, the poetics and hermeneutics of disaster response proper to each congregation is always in need of fine-tuning. Indeed each congregation ought to know the political consequences of what it is narrating and making in the physical and imaginative spaces of the city.

135. Benjamin, "Theses on Philosophy of History," 254.

CHAPTER 3

The World Trade Center Attack:
"The Spirit of America Will Prevail"

THE CHURCHES OF NEW YORK CITY

The two-pronged attack carried out on September 11, 2001, in New York City proposes numerous factors that make it quite distinct from the Oklahoma City bombing. The demographic differences between the urban populations alone raise numerous concerns about social integration and the role of churches in highly diverse, cosmopolitan cities. Did the presence and legacy of certain congregations shape social organization in New York City as they did in Oklahoma City? In what ways did both the source and sheer scale of the event—the magnitude of physical and symbolic violence—augment or facilitate processes of nationalization? This chapter takes up these concerns as it pursuits the same task as the previous chapter: of describing some integral themes in postdisaster cultural politics and the ecclesial practices that both challenge, and succumb to, the wider project aimed at (re)creating the theopolitical imagination necessary to retain power over the socio-cultural processes that attribute sacrality, whether to identities, places, times, or "events."

The American Religious Identification Survey (ARIS) 2001, administered to a random sample of 50,281 Americans, indicates that the state of New York contains the third-largest number of Catholic adherents in the country as a percentage of the total amount of religious adherents in a given state (38 percent of all religious adherents in New York). Only Catholics in New Mexico (40 percent) and Massachusetts (44 percent) make up a larger percentage of all confessional adherents in their respective states.[1] The population of the state also experienced considerable growth in the amount of residents claiming "No Religion": this designation jumped from 7.0 percent in 1990 to 13.4 percent in 2001. This percentage is actually higher than the percentage of adherents associated with all other denominations in the state of New York, save Roman Catholicism.

Despite the large numbers of Roman Catholics (about 40 percent of all adherents in New York City), New York City is a veritable "city of faiths," as one writer has put it.[2] The city contains more Hindus, Muslims, Rastafarians, Jehovah's Witnesses, Greek Orthodox believers, Russian Orthodox believers, and religious Jews than any other city in the country.[3] The number of Seventh-Day Adventists has grown 900 percent, by and large since the 1980s.[4] Next to Roman Catholicism, Baptists (about 11 percent) and Jews (about 10.7 percent) compose the next two largest groups.[5] Regarding minority affiliation, a few figures are noteworthy: 73 percent of Hispanics and 53 percent of whites in New York City are Roman Catholic. Twenty-nine percent of blacks in New York City are Baptist, and about 19 percent are Roman Catholic. When one compares whites, Hispanics, and African Americans, the African American population is more broadly diffused among confessional groups.

Immigration plays a vital role in the life of churches in New York City insofar as the congregation has generated a cultural space in which many ethnic groups preserve language and customs from their home countries within the space and activities of the church.[6] This, however, can only be understood within different scales of social organization, including the city and the nation. The dizzying array of intersecting social movements and conservative churches, including the burgeoning conservative Korean churches and their unaccredited seminaries, along with fundamentalist Hindu groups and ethnoracial activists, provide the basis for very creative attempts at competition and cooperation.

1. Kosmin and Mayer, *American Religious Identification Survey 2001*.

2. Carnes, "Religions in the City," 3.

3. Ibid.

4. Ibid., 4.

5. Klaff, "Religious Demography of New York City," 27; Kosmin and Seymour, *One Nation Under God*.

6. Warner, "Place of the Congregation," 220.

In New York City (as in Oklahoma City) we witness the heightened impact of a confessional group that otherwise makes up a small percentage of the sum of local confessional adherents: in this instance, the Episcopal Church, and to a lesser degree the Eastern Orthodox Church. Episcopalians do not make up any more than about 3 percent of all confessional adherents in any one borough of the city, while Orthodox adherents contributed far less than this.[7] Even so, St. Paul's Chapel (Episcopal), located across Church Street to the east of the World Trade Center complex, became both an imaginative and physical site of cultural production in service of a particular view of citizenship. This is at least partly due to the strong "civic presence" that Episcopalians have enjoyed since 1697, when Trinity Church–Wall Street was chartered and became the quasi-official church of colonial New York.[8] Since that time, the Episcopal churches have continued to reach "the educated, professional classes of people who exercise a disproportionate influence in the city's social and cultural life," despite suffering through the same degree of membership loss as most mainline denominations since 1990.[9]

DISASTER RESPONSE

On September 11, 2001, at 8:48 a.m., the first of two hijacked planes struck the World Trade Center's north tower (1 World Trade Center). American Airlines flight 11 from Boston, en route to California, was forcibly overtaken by a group of Islamic extremists and diverted to New York City. The new pilot of the passenger jetliner, apparently well-trained and knowledgeable of passenger aircrafts, flew the plane, slightly tipped to the left, into the building's ninety-third and ninety-fourth floors.[10] Sixteen minutes after the first strike, at 9:02 a.m., another hijacked passenger plane slammed into the World Trade Center's south tower (2 World Trade Center). This plane made contact at a lower level than the first plane, smashing into the seventy-eighth to eighty-third floors. The persons occupying the floors where the planes hit (the "zones of impact"), about six hundred in all, died instantly. About fifteen hundred men and women

7. Klaff, "Religious Demography of New York City," 33.

8. Carle and DeCaro, *Signs of Hope in the City*, 11–12.

9. Ibid., 42.

10. National Institute of Standards and Technology, quoted in Dwyer and Flynn. 102 *Minutes*, 11

who survived the destructive arrival of the planes were subsequently blocked or trapped (due to fire and other physical impediments) as far as twenty floors from the zones of impact, and were unable to find an avenue for escape. The majority of those who occupied offices below the points of impact, however (about twelve thousand occupants) survived.[11] Between 8:46a.m. and 10:28 a.m. a highly complex, distressing, and taxing multiorganizational response to the attack was assembled.

In the immediate aftermath of both attacks, firefighters arrived in droves, many of whom were off duty and yet felt compelled to enter the fray due to the magnitude of the explosions. A logjam of fire vehicles was created on the south end of West Street just beyond Liberty Street and near the intersection of Vesey and West streets almost immediately in front of 6 World Trade Center. At the same time, a sophisticated EOC (emergency-operations command) on the twenty-third floor of 7 World Trade Center was activated.[12] This EOC, however, was eventually evacuated at 5:02 p.m. due to heavy fires caused by the collapse of the north tower. Agencies were forced to move to temporary facilities before re-establishing operations at Pier 92 on the Hudson River.[13]

An exterior fire command center was established on Albany Street facing the north tower, while interior command centers were set up in the lobbies of the north tower, the south tower, and the Marriot Hotel, which was virtually nestled between the two skyscrapers. Midlevel fire chiefs directed firefighters who arrived in the lobbies. The large number of firefighters caused major communication problems as hundreds of firefighters competed over four or five channels. This logjam impeded efficient performance and speedy delivery of accurate updates. Also, a police command center was established at the corner of Church and Vesey streets, that directed search-and-rescue teams into the buildings. These efforts were not coordinated with the fire department.[14] All the forgoing challenges paled in comparison to what subsequently occurred: the south tower collapsed at 9:59 a.m., only to be followed by the north tower at 10:28 a.m.

11. Ibid., xxiv.

12. Kendra and Wachtendorf, "Elements of Resilience," 38.

13. Ibid., 37

14. Dwyer and Flynn, *102 Minutes*, 1.

The most available clergy at the time were chaplains from the fire department, such as Father Mychal Judge (who died when debris landed on his head as he administered final rites), and others from nearby Trinity Church–Wall Street, St. Peter's Cathedral, and St. Patrick's Cathedral. A minister from Trinity Church–Wall Street, who had just finished saying his morning prayers as he stepped out of his apartment, joined responders after both collapses, in search of the injured, wounded, or dead. He stated that no one injured was found in the streets that had not already escaped or reached triage sites or hospitals. Indeed, "they were all in there," he stated with tears, "they were all in there [in the World Trade Center]."[15] Taken collectively, these churches absorbed a good deal of emergency-relief functions, but none welcomed as many as St. Paul's Chapel. Unlike the analysis from Oklahoma City, New York data analysis suggested that no other churches within a three-mile radius, besides St. Paul's Chapel, served as havens for crucial emergency-response functions beyond the first ten days after the attack.

My initial article-gathering procedures were designed to assure a systematic approach, which, concurrently, did not stultify the creativity of theoretical sampling. This approach mainly involved identifying and retaining individual articles from guided database searches in LexisNexis for publications between September 11, 2001, and May 30, 2002.[16]

15. Brubaker, *Ground Zero Spirituality at Trinity Church*.

16. Before this, however, fifty articles that had already been extracted as part of a larg-er study of interorganizational coordination (a study by the Disaster Research Center) were searched for content relating to church-and-state matters, memorial or funeral cer-emonies, and other large-scale ritual events, reflection on theological matters in light of terrorist attack, the public actions of clergy, interpretations of events carried out by state officials (e.g., congressmen, senators, and the like) employing theological language or imagery, and other relevant subtopics contained within these broad themes. The search itself was worthwhile since it provided clues to the significance that journalists afforded confessional organizations that were situated within the vast, emergent network of or-ganizations involved with disaster response. This search yielded thirteen articles with relevant information.

Another set of searches was conducted using terms consistent with the theoretical sensitizing concepts of this study and testing other topics that would follow from a given city's particular sociohistorical patterns, such as a population's predominant confessional affiliations or economic conditions. A search of the Lexis-Nexus database limiting the terms "attack" and "God" to the headline, header, or lead paragraph yielded forty-seven relevant articles. A search using the terms "World Trade Center" and "government" pro-duced five articles. Another article search linked "Catholic Church" and "World Trade Center" as key terms because of the well-known, pervasive presence of Catholic parishes

The scope and nature of the attacks on the World Trade Center invite a host of considerations that distinguish it from most other disasters in United States history. These attacks challenged like no other violent engagement before it (with the exception perhaps of Pearl Harbor) the sovereignty of the modern state and the legitimacy of many notions of just war. In particular, the deliberate targeting of the twin towers in Lower Manhattan brought into question both the legitimacy of the economic primacy of the United States at a global scale and the assurance of security from any real or perceived enemies abroad. For this reason, hermeneutical or interpretive activity was exceedingly prevalent, emerging from nearly every sphere, in the United States and beyond, for a sustained period of time. That is to say, the event jolted persons quite a distance from the United States to question basic political and social symbols and practices, as well as to devise explanations or positions surrounding appropriate response. As Graham Ward argues, one effective gauge of the enormity of an event is the hermeneutical activity that the event induces—chiefly, the extent to which an event brings into question the self-understanding of well-established groups and institutions across cultural fields.[17] This point should be borne in mind when considering the tremendous range of responses that appear from various churches, groups, and officials from other nations, and from other state-government representatives, citizens, and corporations within the United States. Finally, my reading of church-and-state cultural politics after this attack is decidedly pneumatological

among all the boroughs of New York City. Catholic parishes are not as prominent in Oklahoma City, which contains many Methodist, Baptist, and charismatic churches. This search. The search for Catholic churches in New York City article data yielded eleven articles. A search using the terms "church" and "attack" introduced another eleven articles into the tally; these pieces shed light on the activities of many churches or parachurch groups that either were quite small or had never experienced much media exposure in their locales. In order to round out the theoretical sampling for the study, two final searches were initiated. The next-to-last search, using the terms "God," "government," and "World Trade Center" produced eleven articles. The last search employed the terms "God" and "World Trade Center," and sixteen articles were selected. Due to the emergence of the importance of Rudolph Giuliani in terms of theopolitics, a search was conducted using "Giuliani" and "World Trade Center," as well as "Giuliani" alone. These yielded one article each; the other articles were either irrelevant or already selected from previous search results. Content analysis of print data using the software program MAX.QDA 2 produced 1,276 codes (just three less than the total for the Oklahoma-City analysis) from a sum total of 114 articles. A total of twelve participants provided interview data—three church workers, seven focus-group participants, a firefighter, and a New York citizen.

17. Ward, *Cultural Transformation*, 61–63.

in its shape, and no less ecclesiological. I comprehend the work of God's Spirit as most fitting because one of the more integral (and ambitious) of the nation-state's postdisaster projects attempts what Scripture testifies to be the province of the Spirit in Pentecost: to truly join and reconcile the nations in worship of God. The Paraclete, as Jean Vanier wisely reminds us, is "the one who hears the call."[18] The Spirit binds us together—the rich and poor, insider and outsider, male and female—drawing us into the mutual love, delight, and harmony that characterize the relation between the Son and the Father. The same Spirit is the source of freedom for those who depend solely upon the wisdom and governance of God. This freedom is resolutely unpredictable in view of the rigidity and fear that mark a life seeking security and reputation (see John 3:1–8), and this freedom is also God's power to generate the conviction, trust, and mutual indwelling needed to have one person speak on behalf of another. God's own life is marked by a handing over of "all that the Father has" to the Son and all that is the Son's to the Spirit for the sake of truthful declaration (John 16:12–15). It is just this declarative unity spanning periods of contentment and stability (as well as periods of loss, failure, and threat) that mark out the ecclesial body as participating in all the vicissitudes of life. The unity of the body of Christ does not depend upon treating threat (extreme or minor) as a reason to be united or integrated, because this actually impedes the persistence necessary in daily *becoming* God's people in actual endurance and obedience, and in crossing boundaries of loyalty to a specific identity in order to speak not what is "our own" but only whatever we hear from the Spirit of truth.

Churches, Clergy, and Official Response

This section examines the relationship between clergy or ministry personnel and state-orchestrated response to the attack. The heuristic hypothesis that framed the previous chapter's analysis remains the same here: that church and state engage the same project of social reorientation, namely, shaping the political imagination (i.e., more or less affirming basic assumptions about human nature and destiny, about what characteristics members of the new social body ought to adopt, and about what actions ensure social harmony). However, church personnel must denarrativize or decontextualize Christian views in order to provide a believable public

18. Vanier, *Befriending the Stranger*, 126.

account of the situation amid many so-called expert institutions that are highly dependent on statist visions of social life. The data of this analysis draw not only on accounts of interaction between clergy and government officials, but also on the ministers' interpretations of the actions, evaluations, and legal decisions of public officials and other disaster-response experts. Newspaper data from the *New York Times* and the *Daily News* supplemented interview data insofar as it spoke to this relationship. Viewed as a whole, data from one-on-one interviews, print media, and church videos about clergy response and evaluations directed significant attention to the following themes: (1) normalization and social honor of confessional practices at Ground Zero, (2) the centrality of three churches as sites of theopolitical cultural production, and (3) the localized focus and creative practices of smaller churches. Prayer, as in Oklahoma City, became a normalized social discipline, but a section is not dedicated to this phenomenon, because of redundancy in the general conclusion. In sum, these themes did not so much challenge the validity of the guiding hypothesis as they demanded a sort of qualification of it. That is, although theologically informed convictions or practices achieved much public attention, church-centered visions of the city's and nation's future were coterminous, with the former most often collapsed into the latter. Large churches, with ministers of high social status (St. Patrick's Cathedral, St. Paul's Chapel, and St. Nicholas Church) served as sites at which the American citizen was openly theologized—that is, made to automatically possess certain godly virtues and other characteristics of global importance. Smaller, local churches, however, seemed less concerned with the parodic "infused virtues" of American citizenship and concurrently were less important in the public realm.

The coordination of disaster-response services at the World Trade Center is well noted as massive in scope and logistically complex like no other disaster in U.S. history, especially in terms of interorganizational coordination and emergent domains of response tasks.[19] The contributions of confessional groups in the immediate environs of the World Trade Center complex, in the Lower Manhattan area especially, chiefly involved gathering citizens who were either confused, or injured by falling debris; establishing triage-like areas for the injured who required prayer and counseling; and using church buildings for emergency services. St.

19. Kendra and Wachtendorf, "Evacuation of Lower Manhattan," 316.

Patrick's Cathedral, St. Peter's Church (both Roman Catholic), and Trinity Church–Wall Street (Episcopal), for example, were used as temporary morgues in the hours following the initial attack. Many congregations farther away from the attack site gathered funds and donated them to relief causes or charities; others sent workers to wander the edges of the perimeter around Ground Zero when they could not attain official entry into the site. One Episcopal priest associated with Trinity Church–Wall Street started what he described as "an impromptu service of Scripture readings, hymns, and psalms" only after having contemplated that he has been in this sort of situation before and hence "knew what to do."[20] At the Church of St. Michael the Archangel on North Street in Greenwich Village (a congregation with fifteen hundred families), an "impromptu mass" commenced in the evening after locals arrived in tears and "stunned in silence."[21] The initiation of such worship services, already within the repertoire of planned responses to crisis among some congregations, is an interesting instance of social organization from a theological perspective. In these instances, acts of worship are meant to present all that is occurring, in all its urgency, confusion, shock, and bewilderment, to God. Such acts do not answer to notions of task delineation from a technorational perspective: the worship is perceived to be as real in its effects as the attack to which it is oriented. Furthermore, it introduces a transcendent element in its scheme of accountability; that is, something that thrives autonomously outside rationalized response and planning must be fitted into the ongoing, precarious situation as a major priority. While the sophisticated sacramental and liturgical theology on which this sort of ritual action depends is central to Catholic, Anglican, and various other mainline denominations, worship services are comparatively less formal among many modern evangelical and Protestant churches.

The viability of a postdisaster public theology emerged from a notion of discursive advantage or exclusive capability. In other words, many ministers (in the course of media coverage of "religious resurgence") argued or implied that one discourse or set of terms entrenched in a particular community was better able to deal with attack-induced challenges than other, more abstract discourses, such as humanism. One rabbi, six days after the attack, stated outright: "Some things cannot be expressed

---

20. Brubaker, *Ground Zero Spirituality at Trinity Church.*
21. Gordon, "Parish Pulls Together to Mourn Its Own."

without a religious community."[22] This qualification about the credibility of religious speech carried out both a legitimizing and explanatory function. Besides this, pluralism entered the discussion in order to take account of the response of many humanists, atheists, and agnostics, which, at first sight, seemed highly ironic: these responses were often introduced within a discussion about increased "religiosity." Including ministerial speeches, however, the broadest frame of reference was most frequently a national one: many citizens addressed how *Americans* had to cope with the attacks religiously or theologically. The cruciality of American identity was also bolstered through the widely publicized apology of Rev. Jerry Falwell after claiming thus:

> The abortionists have got to bear some burden for this because God will not be mocked. And when we destroy 40 million little innocent babies, we make God mad. I really believe that the pagans, and the abortionists, and the feminists, and the gays and the lesbians who are actively trying to make that an alternative lifestyle, the A.C.L.U., People for the American Way, all of them who have tried to secularize America, I point the finger in their face and say, "You helped this happen."[23]

In response to public outrage, Falwell issued a statement in which he conceded that during a time when conventional terms of political and racial division had been abandoned, he should not have singled out any particular group for criticism. Furthermore, he claimed, the only label that should have been used was "American."[24]

Normalization and the Subordination of Divine Discourse

That some churches had access into Ground Zero while others did not sheds considerable light upon the particular attention paid to, and valuations associated with, certain interpretations of church member practices and other cultural objects linked to church workers. For instance, the much-maligned Church of Scientology, based on the teachings of the former science-fiction writer L. Ron Hubbard, experienced extraordinarily positive status attainment, or increased social honor, after securing access to Ground Zero and implementing various techniques, such as

22. Niebhur, "At Houses of Worship, Feelings are Shared."
23. Goodstein, "Falwell's Finger–Pointing Inappropriate."
24. Niebhur, "Excerpts from Sermons."

"locationals" and "nerve assists." The locationals demand that a person concentrate fully on a certain object, a glass of water, or even picture in order to muddle or block out all other stimuli. It is meant to generate a respite from an overwhelming barrage of distressing or noxious stimuli (both internal and external), thereby eliminating fuzzy or muddled thinking. These and related practices are actually based on a set of assumptions and tenets about humans that are staunchly opposed to standard psychiatric practices in the United States. The Church of Scientology has a well-known history of organized opposition to psychiatric diagnostic methods and use of medications for the treatment of mental illness. Yet the social dilation that accompanied the liminal phase after this disaster afforded numerous social groups the opportunity to rehabilitate their public credibility in the process of contributing to a particular view of faith, God, and religion in its encounters with others. Viewed another way, a group was granted a degree of normality and, when certain conditions and agents converged, prestige, in the public sphere.

The emergent positive view and normalization of scientological interventions, despite their tie with a controversial organization and the so-called unorthodox nature of their basic doctrine within a confessional context suffused with symbols from Christianity, Judaism, and Islam is all the more fascinating in light of some negative assessments directed against well-known Christian evangelistic practices. Rev. John Carmichael of the Church of Scientology in New York City claimed innocence to the charge of proselytizing, asserting, "It's not proselytizing . . . It's us trying to help."[25] To the contrary, many groups, especially the more well-known local churches with evangelical leanings, handed out "gospel tracts" to passersby and rescue workers as they exited Ground Zero. Consequently, evangelism actually became an activity that generated a fissure between local churches and hence became an activity that revealed what a given church collectively deemed to be basic in their public process of self-identification after the disaster. Clergy from St. Paul's Chapel, who on the basis of a rich history of American patriotism were able to link the September 11th attacks to an ongoing national and church narrative of resilience and victory, considered the dissemination of evangelistic tracts to be reprehensible. Rev. Lyndon Harris, without identifying any specific group, argued:

25. Waldman, "Changed Lives: Religious Leader."

If there are opportunists seeking to prey on people's fears, I think
that's unfortunate. . . . I think inviting people into a community
of integrity and equality is a different thing than what they're doing. If they're proselytizing and motivating people by fear, I think
that's wrong."[26]

St. Paul's Chapel, instead, focused on overt gestures of compassion, regular interaction with rescuers and other volunteer workers, food preparation and delivery, provision of cots for rest, and other services.

This controversy invites consideration of a set of discursive matters relating to theological speech and ministerial roles after disasters
that both engage and go beyond the issues stemming from ministerial
improvisation in Oklahoma City. In New York City, in short, fear of manipulation and insincerity met the urgent need for life-giving words. To
what extent could someone, filling in the role of "grief counselor," speak
about God and various narratives or views from a particular confessional
perspective without crossing a supposed boundary—that is, without
proselytizing? The criteria used to determine this transgression is often
dichotomous, distinguishing the disclosure of information that is completely instrumental or geared toward the alleviation of psychological
distress from the use of this "information" to compel the person in need
to fully embrace a confessional perspective—that is, to convert. Evidently
the line is clearly crossed when someone becomes pushy or coercive in
some manner, thereby forcing views upon another.

The construction of this dilemma, including the form and content
of the arguments employed to sustain it, betray the sort of public sphere
that served as the prevailing discursive context of the postdisaster liberal
social body. Its shortcomings and incoherence with respect to theological
practice require treatment. First, it appears quite possible for many views
pertaining to, and seeking to establish, "mental stability" to be forced upon
persons in contexts of verbal interaction that would not be conventionally judged as religious. Yet the old assumption that religious discourse is
inherently divisive due to its inescapable incommensurability is certainly
at work here. The oft-cited solution is to adopt a more neutral language,
which steers clear of these faith-based opinions or mere beliefs, in an attempt to gently attain to mental stability and healing. One of the key implications here is that spiritual discourse ought to be instrumentalized for

26. Wakin, "At Edge of Ground Zero."

psychological purposes, thus rendering theological speech the maidservant to the greater task of serving purportedly neutral, psychopragmatic ends—namely, to help any given person feel better, cope, adjust, achieve mental stability, and the like. In other words, all such mental states can be achieved with the use of concepts referencing God, heaven, angels, spirits, suffering, mortality, and peace (of mind)—under the condition that these concepts are entirely optional and do not require an appreciation of the metaphysical assumptions or narrative from which they spring. The governing presupposition is that ministers at the disaster site addressed a particular mental phenomenon in humans that did not need any particular theological substance for fulfillment. When the goal is constitutively a mental "condition" and nothing more, then religion at the disaster site is most certainly in two of its most common and interlocked modern niches: therapy and grief management. As such, it resides in a disciplinary space dominated by the state—a friend indeed of therapy, management, and the sacred in the most abstract, neutral, and dispersed forms. This does not detract from the importance of gentleness, patience, and presence in all verbal intercourse after disasters but points out the muddled state of political, discursive, and practical affairs that marginalize these virtues as gifts of the Holy Spirit. Ministers working in this muddled state of affairs grasps for a rationalized discourse ethic that hopes to avoid the existence or political consequences of its anthropological and imaginative assumptions. The discourse and life of the Holy Spirit, by contrast, knows fully what type of human it is attempting to form and from whom that person originated. The "neutral sacred" of the state names the social space within which we struggle to help others while gripped in fear of pushing our views upon them. This social space encourages a discipline often rooted in a fear and in the rejection of our vulnerable creatureliness, and is rooted in the assumption that a person is "inhabited" by others, or by what David Ford calls "the community of the heart."[27] Accounts of liberal discourse ethics, whether in practice or in coherent theoretical form (as in the work of Jürgen Habermas), seek intersubjectivity without striving for the life-giving mutual indwelling that the Trinity brings to the church as the communion of the meek, broken, and mourning. Intersubjectivity, apparently, is not enough for God's fallen yet graced creatures. The practical upshot of the state-endorsed ethic as it disjointedly operates in a

27. Ford, *Shape of Living*, 35.

disaster-response setting is a practice that addresses an emaciated human being, one without substantive origin or *telos*,[28] who seeks the sacred in myriad forms as the means toward some positive mental state. As Erika Doss has claimed, "An American public that is often hesitant and fearful about death and dying has equated the visual and material culture of grief with the transformative milieu of the sacred."[29] Nonetheless, it is worth mentioning that this was not the way religion or theological notions were viewed in all sites of cultural production or creativity during the postdisaster period, as subsequent sections will show.

The presence of other confessional groups along with their practices and discourses were challenged in other ways as well. Whatever the criteria may have been for gaining permission to near Ground Zero, many groups were sifted out of the area by means of police-supervised credentialing measures. A table at the corner of Fulton and Church streets, or at the southwest corner of St. Paul's Chapel, staffed by pastors and advertised as a "prayer station," was removed at some point before September 30, 2001.[30] Either the ministers who ran it were not credentialed, or it was deemed unnecessary in light of the fact that St. Paul's Chapel was just a few feet away and could serve the same purpose, yet not nearly in such an open-air or informal fashion.

The "Publicly Authorized" Churches

Unlike numerous churches within a two- to three-mile radius around the Murrah Federal Building in Oklahoma City, very few churches in New York City actually served as venues for the provision of relief services beyond the first three weeks after the attack. Many recovery and relief functions distributed across three or four churches in Oklahoma City were all, in general, concentrated in one church building in New York City: St. Paul's Chapel. Nevertheless, three churches, which will be reviewed below, stood out as "publicly authorized" churches, or those that due to long-standing social honor in the area, close association with civic or economic power, impressive resources, and a fortuitous role in the disaster-response period, were able to directly engage the workings of the

28. The origin and *telos* are not incidental to the work of assisting others through tragedy but constitutive of the words and gestures, of the works of love, through which Christ approaches the grieving.

29. Doss, "Death, Art, and Memory," 69.

30. Wakin, "At Edge of Ground Zero."

nation-state at different levels of its manifestation or its social disciplines. In all these cases (albeit to varying degrees), the clergy relied on appeals to national symbols, on statist views of response to enemies, and on dramatic street processions. In some key episodes and relationships, typically "profane" realms were joined to sacred instruments and their uses.

The Centrality of St. Paul's Chapel

"This is the emergency room for our nation." This statement was delivered to a meeting of clergy at St. Paul's Chapel shortly after the attacks on the World Trade Center.[31] The speaker, Deener Matthews, claimed to be quoting a Jewish man that entered the chapel a few days after the attack, having prefaced his "national statement" with the words, "this place is holy . . . this place is sacred." St. Paul's Chapel (Broadway Avenue and Fulton Street) is a parish of the Episcopal Church's Trinity Church on Wall Street and Broadway. St. Paul's Chapel was originally constructed in 1766 as a relatively small worship site within close proximity to what at that time was a rapidly expanding urban center. Evidently St. Paul's Chapel did not cease to use its urban setting with ingenuity; presently, the context of St. Paul's Chapel is one of the premier, globally renowned hubs of cosmopolitanism.

During the immediate response period, the church welcomed the injured and frightened, and was within a week transformed into a round-the-clock human-services facility. The church building was used as a kitchen, a sleeping area, and a worship site for rescuers. The preserved pew of George Washington was transformed into a podiatric station, and massage therapists made regular visits.

Simultaneous to the wide-ranging provisions of response services within the building was the intensive construction and identification of symbolic material (bodies) and practices. The interior of the chapel was transformed into a veritable pantheon of global gestures of compassion: items were received from virtually every state of the United States, as well as from scores of nations; specifically, offerings from Japanese peace groups, a banner from Oklahoma City, and myriad other items from other ethnic and confessional groups were displayed on the walls, in the galleries, and on the pillars. The building gave tangible and creative shape to the expressions of concern from persons across many social and

---

31. Brubaker, *Ground Zero Spirituality at Trinity Church Wall Street.*

economic boundaries. The chapel's fence, which contains the building and the cemetery that surrounds it, became the site for spontaneous, vernacular expressions of condolence, anger, faith, love, and the like. Families of missing persons or victims also pinned photographs of the beloved to the fence. In this practice there is an obvious parallel to the vernacular expressions and objects pinned to the chain link fence placed around the Murrah Federal Building site in Oklahoma City. In both cases, the individual items were periodically removed, assigned a catalogue code, and finally stored in a separate warehouse or large storage facility.[32]

Participant *H2*'s answer to initial queries about the chapel's response to the federal government's public pronouncements was framed from the outset in terms of the congregation's apparent exceptionality (reminiscent of some interviewed Oklahoman clergy).[33] This participant almost immediately claimed that the chapel is part of a "liberal protestant congregation" that had a different response from others, especially when it came to "war." The Episcopal Church apparently assumed a stance very much against war, a stance that remained throughout the response and recovery periods. In formulating a position about military counterstrikes, the church intimated that some stance centered on the legitimacy of war became a primary factor upon which postdisaster identity formation depended. This makes sense considering the role that all popular media played after the attack: around-the-clock coverage and presentation of a massive array of stories tackling human life after the disaster, many of which seemed to single out "the nation's response" as especially worthy of comment. The chapel, however, never seems to have aggressively promoted this view at a public level, not even in two church-produced videos, despite the undoubtedly impressive number of ministers, locally and nationwide, who tried to temper the anger and vengeful desires of local congregants during the first week after the attack. Rather, it sought to promote this message through commodities, namely, a group of small wallet-sized greeting cards that depict interfaith messages of peace and are sold in the chapel gift shop.

Could this have been the case because, incidentally, the church building became a meeting place of many discourses and loci (standpoints) of cultural production? The legal-investigative personnel of the FBI

32. In particular, see Doss, "Death, Art, and Memory," 67–72.

33. Santos, Participant *H2* interview.

introduced and symbolically necessitated the monitored entry of persons, because the church building sat next to a "crime scene." The identifying marks of expert systems personnel were actually absorbed into the typical trappings of the church and its agents. This not only generated new directions for particular interpretive practices but also reinforced the conflation (rather than the separation, as it were) of the profane and the sacred. For instance, on display at St. Paul's Chapel is a vestment, usually worn by qualified clergy, with patches from virtually every conceivable governmental service and rescue agency (from the state of New York and abroad) that worked at the Ground Zero site and benefited from one of many services provided at the chapel. The vestment was actually worn during an interfaith service at the chapel and is now preserved for viewings at public exhibits.

Cardinal Egan and St. Patrick's Cathedral

Coverage of Edward Cardinal Egan's participation in various events during the response and recovery periods revealed the subtle alterations to discourse that became common due to certain pressures to sustain the link between the state and the public sphere as a disciplinary space. Cardinal Egan garnered perhaps as much public attention as an individual as the Roman Catholic Church did as a whole; although this does not count allusions to funerary services held in Roman Catholic church buildings. Cardinal Egan was the central, dramatic persona of one of the major memorial services held soon after the attack. In the sample of 114 articles analyzed, the term "Egan" appeared thirty-two times, a fairly high number, considering the range of topics addressed, even when other matters concerning the Roman Catholic Church were the objects of reportage or discussion. He himself became a cultural object who proffered politically important public speeches and performances that in unison served as a fertile seedbed for numerous dedifferentiating actions in service of a specifically defined collectivity. Nevertheless Egan was the topic of at least three newspaper articles that covered what at that time was considered off-limits speech: critical remarks that challenged Americans at large to consider what role our own policies may have played in inciting the attacks. Egan suggested, "It is not necessarily that the explanation is that there have been some misdeeds on the part of the United States, but that

is a possibility."[34] Interesting is that these claims were made two weeks after a well-publicized Mass (discussed below) as Egan attended a bishops'
conference at the Vatican.[35]

While Egan did not explain the basis or intentions of his remarks at
length, his other public appearances as a central theopolitical object associated with a particular picture of American citizenship occupied a vital,
pacesetting position among memorial ceremonies. He appeared in the
Yankee Stadium memorial service and was in the audience at President
Bush's address to Congress during which the "war on terrorism" was
lauded as the most appropriate political response to the attacks. More specifically, on September 16, 2001, Cardinal Egan led a Mass for the victims
(another Mass was held the following day for firefighters and emergency
workers who died) before more than two thousand worshipers, including
the secretary general of the United Nations, the city police commissioner,
United States senators, Mayor Giuliani, and others.[36] Citizens or residents
in attendance brought vernacular expressions of patriotism, including
miniature flags and denim jackets with stars and stripes sewn on the back,
to a worship service that united explicit theological pronouncements and
priestly performance with unequivocally distinguished statist identities.
Dignitaries of the state were all seated near the front of the cathedral.[37]

The beginning of the Mass, appropriately perhaps, set a dedifferentiated narrative tone: a color guard with roots in the Revolutionary War led
a very long procession of priests into the center aisle. During the homily,
Egan affirmed:

> We were stunned and confused. We were not, however, shaken.
> Rather, the best of us donned hard hats and workmen's gloves and
> face masks to deal with this horror as decent, civilized human
> beings. And the rest of us supported them, applauded them and
> prayed for and with them.[38]

He further stated thus:

> I am sure that we will seek justice in this tragedy as citizens of a
> nation under God in which hatred and desires for revenge must

34. Williams, "Reflect on Reasons."
35. Ibid.
36. Barron, "Cardinal Egan Leads Prayers for Victims."
37. Ibid.
38. Ibid.

never have a part . . . I am sure that we'll allow no group or groups
in our diverse but united community to be accused or abused because of the outrageous misdeeds of individuals. I am sure that
we will not harbor thoughts of war of any kind without careful,
careful consideration of what is right and just before the one God
and father of us all.[39]

This reaffirmation of an already-united social body of New Yorkers qua
Americans "under God" blended theological and national identities, attempted to temper vengeful sentiments by means of "assured exhortation,"
and invoked the possibility of war, in just a few contiguous statements.
The emphasis is on the actions and identity of the "we," or the "nation,"
"citizens," and "united community" that are compelled to action through
parenesis: the reminding of instruction already learned or known. This is
one central form of collective identity formation previously witnessed in
Oklahoma City; that is, the public exaltation of an ideal type to which the
collectivity has aspired (e.g., diverse yet united), without mention of the
extent to which members of the collectivity have actualized the ideal in
practice, or precisely how the ideal is to be achieved at all.

As Egan stepped down from the pulpit near the conclusion of the
ceremony, Egan embraced New York governor George Pataki and New
York City mayor Rudolph Giuliani—a gesture with glaring political consequences. As representatives of a body politic, carrying the imaginative
load of a heterogeneous group within a dynamic individual/corporate
interchange, the government leaders at that moment vouch for the inclusion of God and allow theological articulation to contribute to, at the
least, what a public account of the dead, the "decent," and the "civilized"
human beings after the disaster ought to include. As a result, a host of
other matters (e.g., assessment of terrorism, foreign policy, and the like)
also came under the influence of both the presence and absence of concrete engagement between churches and statist agents. Later, Cardinal
Egan walked along Fifth Avenue and led a crowd in singing "America
the Beautiful."[40] These actions, reminiscent of the actions of an American
public official, round out a sound example of dedifferentiation emanating
from the activities of one interpretive and ritual expert, or someone from
which others may gain some bearing as to how to speak about God and

39. Ibid.
40. Ibid.

social life during the aftermath of tragedy. Egan's actions also exemplify the concurrent and rather uninhibited spiritualization of Americans per se and the nationalization of a Mass for the dead.

Also deserving treatment as major players in the realm of memory work and public theology, the Roman Catholic Church exerted considerable influence over the symbolic constructions on the Ground Zero site itself. Besides a large number of masses held on Ground Zero, various masses were held in front of and in dedication to the famous Cross of the Two Girders. The beams, which were welded steel girders located within the internal structure of World Trade Center 1, crashed through the ceiling of World Trade Center 6 as the former collapsed. Two days after the attack, a local rescue worker discovered one cross and claimed that as he beheld it, his burdens were lifted. Rev. Brian Jordan, a local priest at St. Francis of Assisi Church in midtown Manhattan, became the virtual guardian of the icon and, after the recovery period had ceased, demanded that the cross be removed, preserved, and eventually reintroduced into the site as part of the official memorial. This battle for the public permanence of a cultural object that shaped the political imaginings of many workers at Ground Zero was merely one among many in the ensuing memorialization debate involving the victims' families coalition, civic representatives, and urban-planning authorities.

These debates often involved the employment of strategies that would link otherwise incommensurable discourses. In the present case, the crosses were solemnly blessed and were the object of a special Vatican ceremony. Roman Catholic clergy stressed that the crosses were sacramentals, or elements of the world that reveal and place humans before the presence of God; as sacramentals, these objects were linked to, yet more profound than, the actual material elements composing the beams. The obvious incompatibility between this view of material bodies and technorational or modernist views is manifest; yet the power it held for the formation of a social body (its "civic power") was welcomed. Giuliani acknowledged this to a degree, claiming that the integrity of the cross as an icon in the days after the tragedy needed to be preserved. Once again, the object needs to be reframed as a memorial icon in order to dovetail with a prevailing postdisaster narrative bereft of specific theological narrative content.

In this regard, the central difference between this case and that of Oklahoma City is that in Oklahoma City the churches surrounding the

Murrah Federal Building site established their memorials before the official memorial was even approved for construction. Such churches (St. Joseph's Old Cathedral and First United Methodist Church) did not submit to any notion of deference to official plans and then seek permission to offer their memorials for inclusion. This, however, does not necessarily make the obvious difference between their respective memorials any more understandable: one is completely free of allusions to Oklahoman or American identity (the Jesus Wept statue), while the other is overwhelmingly concerned with both Oklahoman and American identities (the Heartland Chapel). The fascinating result, as we know, is a series of adjacent memorial structures that testify to different theopolitical perspectives on the same event. In New York City, however, the Roman Catholic Church has pushed to have an ostensibly unalterable object with clear theological and narrative intentions included in an official, public memorial and has made appeals to other symbols of solidarity (e.g., to former mayor Giuliani) in order to gain entry.

St. Nicholas Orthodox Church: Humanity Renewed

St. Nicholas Orthodox Church was located on the south side of the World Trade Center complex (at 155 Cedar Street), almost completely overshadowed by the giant skyscrapers (one of which was only 250 feet away) from an aerial perspective. During the collapse of both towers, the content of the building was virtually completely destroyed, save a few liturgical items, a book, and two icons of Orthodox saints. The significance of the church swelled after it met its demise and was swept into the "riptide" of collective, spontaneous memorial gestures of local New Yorkers and affected confessional groups. It also received attention from the *New York Times* five days after the attacks. Apparently due to the fact that the church building, and by extension the Orthodox adherents who worshipped there, were deemed victims of a terrorist attack, the site was hallowed various times, and an encyclical was issued that laid out various components of the Orthodox diocese's response to the loss. Once again, a fixed, material, and theologically charged cultural object staked a place within the public-memorial dimension of an unstable political context. Therefore, the stewards of this cultural object entered contested, perilous, and highly delicate discursive terrain.

Among the many public actions of the Orthodox diocese of America (headquartered in New York City) within a year of the attack, one involved the release of a composite document titled, *In Memory, in Faith, in Hope*. It consists of three separate short writings, including an encyclical. One piece is a commemorative essay, another focuses on the Orthodox Church's response to the attack, and the third is focused solely on St. Nicholas Church on Cedar Street. The first document confesses that the "Life-giving Cross" provided the many authors with strength to write the letter, and then proceeds to condemn the "cowardly acts of terrorism" on "American soil."[41] The authors further charge all Orthodox churches in America to conduct a memorial service at the end of the "Divine Liturgy" on the September 8, 2002. They added, "Let us offer prayers for the eternal memory and blessed repose of the souls of victims of the barbaric attack and those who heroically fell."[42] Then, the document reads, "We take solace knowing we have grieved not as individuals hopelessly scattered across America, but as a family united in the Body of Christ." This statement takes on added significance in juxtaposition to those that come soon thereafter:

> Who can explain the manner in which . . . seemingly perfect strangers waling in the streets of America suddenly realized their true identity as spiritual brothers and sisters, children of God? Who can ignore the amazing and generous offerings and the unwavering determination of people to raise from the ruins where the old Church stood, a new Church with a universal mission?[43]

This piece ends with statements of gratitude with about the amazing metamorphoses that occurred in "the human race" since the attack: e.g., hatred has turned to love, and ugly hatred into beautiful compassion. This piece is striking in terms of both what it does and does not mention. First, its broad embrace of humanity and human beings without a single mention of New Yorkers (or other local or regional identity) is part of its attempt to subsume a certain vision of spiritually awakened humans into the politico-ecclesial family of God. The slight ambiguity evidenced in the statements that seemed to place the Orthodox believers as family members in Christ, and then "perfect strangers in . . . America" as brothers and

41. *In Memory, in Faith, in Hope*, 3.
42. Ibid.
43. Ibid., 4.

sisters and children of God may be intentional. Whatever the case may be in this respect, the document makes clear that human beings, in the aftermath of the disaster, were granted a revelation in which their true identity was manifested—one that transcends all local and regional identities and is centered upon the politico-ecclesial family of God. Quite remarkable is the manner in which this polished writing contrasts with the ground-level responses of Rev. John Ramos, the seventy-two-year-old pastor of St. Nicholas, and his wife, when they were asked twelve days after the attack, "Where was God?" Ramos replied, "God was in the same spot, but we never opened our hearts to let him inside. We must go to God."[44] His wife, Lorraine Ramos, endorsed her husband's statements, adding,

> We don't know why God does certain things. But everything is done for a reason. Maybe he's doing this to wake us up and get us back to our faith. God was in the same spot, but we never opened our hearts to let him inside.[45]

It is evident that the work of the pastor at the local level, especially as it pertains to theodicy, did not enjoy the benefits of the more detached observer or of those who did not have direct responsibility over a site stricken by tragedy. While the encyclical issues no negation (neither direct challenges to faith nor questions seeking God's wisdom), Ramos's challenging words approach the apophatic and demand humility.

Expansive visions, however, were not lost. The purpose of the small "old Church" that was crushed under the weight of fiery debris culminates this essay, assigning St. Nicholas Church with a "universal mission." Here is a church-centered, outwardly focused dynamism that is difficult to miss and is comparable with that of the churches in Oklahoma City. However, while the much larger churches of Oklahoma City restrained their focus to the local Oklahoman region, this small "new Church" was tied to a "universal mission." The church, as opposed to the individual believer, is the locus of agency. The efforts to construct a viable body of interaction and source of effective action are unmistakable. However, as the document makes clear, America cannot be forgotten, and the "soil" still serves as a crucial trope by which American identity is anchored in the ostensibly fertile and permanent. The document, in other words, upholds a composite of American, human, and spiritual identities but

44. Haas and Moritz, "Church Ruined, but Not Faith."
45. Ibid.

attempts to place this aggregate within an ecclesiocentric account of the disaster-response period and of a promising future.

While the Roman Catholic Church held numerous ceremonies that presented the Ground Zero cross as the basis for unity, hope, and perseverance, Orthodox clergy held various ceremonies at the site of the destroyed church building. *In Memory, in Faith, in Hope* features a photograph of Archbishop Demetrios, of America, at the site, flanked by rescue workers, a soldier in camouflage fatigues, and various priests. In fact, similar to the emphasis placed on the "spiritual soldier" at the Yankee Stadium service (see below), this picture is followed by another that features the archbishop with the same soldier, yet this time the soldier is reverently kneeling before Demetrios. The picture is meant to elucidate the Orthodox Church's local and national response as prayer centered, supplemented by numerous church-operated charities, and as offering help "to our nation and its leader."[46] Beyond this, the hierarchs of the archdiocese called "all of our churches to conduct 40 day memorial services for the victims."[47]

Also important here was the involvement of various clergy of the Orthodox Church besides Archbishop Demetrios, who appeared at Ground Zero the day after the attacks and offered prayers for "the victims, the families and the relief and rescue workers."[48] His All Holiness Ecumenical Patriarch Bartholomew also conducted a memorial service at Ground Zero six months after the attack, during which he condemned terrorism and offered consolations to the families of victims.[49] Demetrios served as a public figure of some importance, along with Cardinal Egan, even though Orthodox adherents make up a very small percentage of all confessional adherents in New York City. Demetrios also gave the benediction for the large memorial ceremony held in Yankee Stadium. In contrast to words on prayer cards or gestures of local Oklahoman churches, at this service no critical remarks were made about political leadership or any "prophetic" desire to oust those unfit for leadership. To be sure, local Orthodox ministers contributed to the transformation of the dead into heroes of a cause greater than that of which they may have been aware.

46. Ibid., 6–7.
47. Ibid.
48. Ibid., 7.
49. Ibid.

At a service in the Holy Trinity Orthodox Church in Brooklyn on the first Sunday after the attacks, the Reverend Vladimir Alexeev asserted: "Today is a day of sorrow, but today is also the day of the victory of love. These people who died by the terrorist attack aren't victims, they're heroes. They're heroes of love and true humanity. We want them to hear us: We love you, too!"[50]

The final piece of the three-part document called *In Memory, in Faith, in Hope* opens with a short paragraph and a picture of a well-attended ceremony (with a huge American flag as the backdrop in the photo) held on the feast day of St. Nicholas: December 6, 2001. Orthodox clergy were granted the opportunity to continue to worship on Ground Zero, celebrating a somber vespers and memorial service. This event was one of various concerted efforts that intimated to the public at large that the rebuilding of St. Nicholas Church was vital. Indeed the small church received donations of $2 million and pledges of reconstruction materials. In addition, the church received a total of $1 million from the combined donations of the city of Bari, Italy ($250,000) and the government of Greece ($750,000).[51] Most important, from the perspective of the Orthodox Church, Governor Pataki met with Archbishop Demetrios and provided assurance that a new St. Nicholas would be included in the redevelopment of the World Trade Center complex. These efforts reflect the convergence of various narrative strands that shaped public cultural production at Ground Zero: the essentiality of having a church "home," a theology that frequently remembers the dead as "heroes," American pride, and the need for an actual concrete structure that carries memories of destruction and renewal. The words of Archbishop Demetrios echo the most salient of these themes and frame the course of the rebuilding process as a matter of "spiritual destiny, so that millions of people who will visit the historic site of Ground Zero may find marking the place of national tragedy, a sanctuary of solace and prayer, a concrete testimony of renewed faith and hope."[52]

These words, expressed in writing and in public vocalizations, also brought to the forefront an important characteristic of solemn, disciplined ritual actions carried out at Ground Zero and nearby public areas—quite

50. Niebhur, "Excerpts from Sermons."
51. *In Memory, in Faith, in Hope*, 10.
52. Ibid., 11.

simply, that such events were open and public as opposed to carried out within a church building. As in Oklahoma City, prayer, faith, and love were constantly presented as benchmarks of behavior that had to negotiate their place with other models of behavior offered at other sites of cultural production—and all within a context of tolerance and multiculturalism desperately seeking unifying threads.

While it is important to recognize the praiseworthy aspects of these liturgical and textual acts, they nonetheless fall short of actually shattering the friend/foe dichotomy: chiefly, they neglect to definitively establish that the church is a transnational body and that not simply Americans, but all peoples and nations (including the nations of those who carried out the attacks), are likewise called to be brothers and sisters in the household of God. As followers of the Risen One, who was killed at the hands of his own people *and* of the Romans who subjugated them, there is no basis for fashioning solidarity among "my own" in a way that endorses or (even inadvertently) allows hatred toward "the others" or "our enemy." Christ asked for both to be forgiven (Luke 23:34), and in one body offered to God on the cross destroyed the wall of hostility separating his murderers, thereby becoming the source of the "new human being." Indeed, as Eph 2:11–21 suggests, Christ is "our peace" because in one body he took up the violence and hatred that marked the relationship between two groups (Jews and Gentiles) and, in doing so, established the means by which to gain access, in one Spirit, to the Father. Rather than asserting one's own newfound insight, resilience, and unity amid unbearable pain as a strategy to ensure maintaining a united front against the other, God in his wisdom actually joins adversaries within the One who preached peace to both. God's Spirit finds fitting only one christocentric path to the Father, not a multiplicity of self-consoling and self-congratulating modes of unification that carry no real devotion to the love of enemies as a daily practice, and that as a result offend the perfect Father (Matt 5:47–48). That is, if Americans are to worship God in spirit, they will only receive access to the Father in a spirit of concord with the enemies that Christ also forgave. As Eph 2:19 makes clear, the designations of *foreigner* and *noncitizen* are rendered worthless in the face of the citizenship and adoption that mark the life of a people in whom God's Spirit dwells. Put another way, Christ in the flesh, as the only pure offering, enacted the forgiveness that the Spirit grants as a gift of healing to the nations. Now, God may be worshiped by one whole body, which is the body of Christ, in the politics that resolutely and painfully joins not only strangers but enemies. Therefore, in all writing and preaching in the postdisaster period, the congregations are called to enact the law of Christ all the way down, as it were, and to affirm their love for enemies, as the Father does.

Equally evident in New York City as in Oklahoma City was the lack of unified cultural presentation on the part of local churches. Many churches offered public symbols and constructive views of the tragedy, yet in a discordant manner. There was no reference to a compact of local ministers from across denominations in New York City. It appears that a formal agreement among churches may have been deemed unnecessary because of the ecstatic nature of the generosity-based solidarity that had persisted since the day of the terrorist attack. Aided by a lack of agreement in cultural production, the proliferation of unanchored and decentralized theological and patriotic symbols in New York City was both an impediment and an aid. The variety of symbols normalized theological reflection, yet the symbols did not center in any unified vision of social interaction or power. It appears as if the state was granted this unifying role, and the state fulfilled it with its own involvement within churches, as the presence of political leaders and dignitaries confirms, including an important speech by Mayor Giuliani that will be the subject of analysis in the final section of this chapter. Many local churches, as the next section suggests, allowed the larger narratives to be handled by authorized, politically connected churches, while they narrowed their focus to local matters.

"Nonpublic Churches": Preaching, Mourning, and Serving

Participant *H1*, a pastor of a relatively small church outside Manhattan, affirmed the following as his principal faith-informed view of the attack:

> God is in control of the events, that even though these men worked evil, as I heard stories [about survival, heroism, and altruism], [I noticed that] God could work out the good. We used it to reach out to people that would otherwise not be interested in our church.[53]

The focus of this particular church's efforts was highly localized, which was understandable, considering both the sheer size of New York City and the magnitude of the event in terms of the scale of affected lives.

53. Santos, Participant *H1* interview.

These factors, or the manner in which the scale of the attack interacted with the population density of New York City and its boroughs, in some sense forced many churches to simply focus on local concerns. This meant directing their efforts to entirely local needs for grief counseling, funerals, worship services, fundraising, and collection of goods. Such was the case with *H1*'s congregation:

> We gathered money, and gave a $1,000 or $500 to victims' families or survivors [from this immediate neighborhood] . . . [A few months later] We had a memorial service for those that received money. We let the people know we are here for them and are here to help them. We had about 120 people—that day—but the church only seats 80. A missionary did most of the work during the service.[54]

This pastor's words may seem ineffectual in view of this study's central purposes, but in fact they carry major consequences for the public role of churches with the location, monetary resources, and historical legacy to secure narrative authority in public performance. The importance of ritual gatherings meant to shape collective imaginings at different scales of social organization, sometimes simultaneously (e.g., when city and nation overlap), generated a sort of authority for provision of a public account—an authority to which many could have access. The local church for which participant *H1* worked maintained a localized focus even in worship services dealing with victims and their families. The minister stated that aside from holding the memorial service mentioned in the quotation above, church members made no special changes to the song service, physical building, or altar decorations in order to incorporate or remember the attack in some way. When asked if his American identity was important, the participant replied, "Not really, I didn't really think about it. We are very diverse around here. We did quite well that way."[55] In contrast to other churches facing the "mass mediation" of their messages (e.g., the early St. Patrick's Mass for the victims was televised), this church did not concern itself with reinvigorating any sort of American loyalty.

With regard to assessments about the use of God-talk in public events, the same minister replied, "I don't have any problem with it as

---

54. Ibid.
55. Ibid.

long as they are sincere."[56] When I asked him to elaborate on this case, he answered plainly and briefly, "It's kind of a Western thought to keep God out of every aspect of life. But in a situation like this, why would you keep him out?"[57] Notice the somewhat exaggerated criticism of Western thought in terms of its propensity to evacuate God from many apparently integral aspects of life. This participant deemed that when a people is faced with a tragedy of this scale, such normal or typical prohibitions must collapse. The sort of avoidance or resistance that this minister seems to have adopted actually reserved a social space in which the church could exercise social disciplines that resisted or confronted the prevailing circulation of mass-mediated objects and symbols that emerged from dedifferentiated church and state productions.

The variety of possible responses by local churches was evident in other neighborhoods across the New York City area that held locally planned and coordinated funerary ceremonies, some of which were spontaneous. These services occasionally featured vernacular assemblages situated in the physical milieu of expert systems and yet subject to cross-racial, intraneighborhood processes of cohesion and consolation. One service, for example, hinged upon the themes of theodicy and love for firefighters. Specifically, the minister invoked the heroism of local, beloved firefighters while also attending to a defense of the presence of God, despite widespread anger and confusion about God's role in the events. The gathering of several hundred in front of Engine Company 226 on State Street in Boerum Hill, Brooklyn, was critical as a site of social body making and theological legitimacy with the potential to evade statist interventions. The Pentecostal preacher, based out of a church building just around the corner, took advantage of the tremendous "gathering force" of firefighters as symbols of compassion and gratitude. He placed himself in the doorway of the Pentecostal church building and declared,

> Many of us ask, "Where is God? Where is God now?" Just because we don't always understand life doesn't mean we don't go on with life. God is where God has always been. This is beyond the point of anger. This is beyond politics. It's beyond culture. It's beyond even religion itself. It's one common cry for the human predicament.

56. Ibid.
57. Ibid.

> Some of us are standing here today because a firefighter saved our lives, and we didn't know him, had never heard of him."[58]

These highly public attempts at reconfiguring social solidarity through a defense of God and appreciation for individual role players (firefighters in this case) showcased some of the possibilities inherent in negotiations with the larger cultural world after the disaster. The same concerns or efforts found in other speeches mentioned in this chapter arise here as well: the minister attempts to elevate some very basic category to which those in the audience can link themselves in the process of understanding God's role and the irresolvable dilemmas of the tragedy. This service was not Americanized or centered on citizenship or terrorism, but was tied to the "human predicament." Interesting is that the preacher identifies emotional pain, "politics," "culture," and "religion" as incapable of unifying his hearers and hence in need of supercession; the ultimate horizon turns out to be the human quandary that renders us exceedingly vulnerable and thereby in need of redemption. This indicates that appropriating symbols was not a matter of top-down hegemonic imposition but of active contestation by which the spiritual discipline and faith of an individual congregation and its leadership were put to the test of public proclamation. Hence, acquiescence to the more popular products of church-and-state dedifferentiation and patriotism resulted from how much thought individual churches gave to their collective self-understanding and to the geographic scope of ministry. This process, in turn, hinged upon how integral a dense theological narrative was deemed to be for their everyday existence, upon the role and significance of secularization, and upon the church's view of itself as a political entity, among other questions. In short, churches had to decide in what political imagination they would participate.

BUILDING A CITY ON HEROES: POSTDISASTER COLLECTIVE IDENTITY AND SOLIDARITY

This section treats the reception and handling of cultural objects and other theopolitical symbols on the part of community members, all of whom were members of churches within the boroughs of New York City. Two of the participants were in the city when the attack happened. The guiding supposition of this sociological question posits that local interpretive

58. Maeder, "All Over City, Healing Sought."

frameworks were confronted with a vision that extended the local to a national (often ambivalent) space, thus making them more public than ever, and altering the importance of certain elements of a community member's sense of identity and citizenship. Of greatest relevance here is the role of churches or confessional representatives in such negotiations, and how they challenge or absorb statist aims or views. A certain level of resistance was evident, however, to large-scale memorial services; so, e.g., attendance at the Yankee Stadium service was much smaller than anticipated.

Data, once again, were derived from one-on-one interviews and print media, along with one focus-group session. As in the case of Oklahoma City, so in New York City, clergy interviews provided some key information about numerous issues relevant to collective identity. Analysis of data identified seven major themes rooted in multiple narrative constructions: (1) a struggle to establish a hierarchy of overlapping identities; (2) an increased global awareness, or a decreased sense of global exceptionalism; (3) the redemptive and social organizational power of New York mayor Rudolph Giuliani, (4) an essentialized separation of the population into categories as model heroes, on the one hand (e.g., firefighters and police officers), or as those that live in their shadow, on the other; (5) citizen concern over the sincerity of politicians who invoke God-talk in public performance; (6) apocalypse; and, finally, (7) for the sake of solidarity, continual material investments through large-scale national events vernacular shrines, semi-institutionalized memorials, and commodities. (Topic 7 is more closely analyzed in chapter 5.)

By and large, the data confirmed the supposition or hypothesis. Unlike the public accounts situating Oklahoma City's fate, New York City's fate, in the public accounts, was often linked to or collapsed into the fate of the United States of America. Theological views that engaged the cosmos or, as turned out to be more likely, the "world," became very popular cultural objects in a post-attack public realm teeming with expressions and symbol that openly conveyed assumptions usually unspoken in quotidian life. At a practical level, as the previous section has shown, many churches focused on concerns at a neighborhood level. Hence, localized views about the tragedy were confronted with the cultural products emanating from large-scale ritual events over which a select number of churches presided. The solidarity of the most important social body ("the people" as a nation) was less church centered in New

York City than Oklahoma City, yet just as dependent on some extensive theologizing on the part of political actors.

Characterizing the Collectivity

The characterization of New Yorkers and other collectivities involved with the attacks of September 11, 2001, was inconsistent on many fronts, although citywide cohesion consistently melded into the nation, humanity, and even the globe in most public ritual actions. Sometimes a sense of universality was amplified through interlacing terms or concepts from many different strands of moral and political thought.

The theme of locally focused cohesion and its corollary codes retained a tense or strained relationship among other principal analytical codes and aggregate themes that focused on national and international scales of social life. In 114 articles, 54 segments were coded that pertained to affirming and rebinding the social body. These intersected with 32 other codes and subcodes, 12 of which dealt specifically with state-sponsored memorials, national anthropomorphisms, and theological imagery and identity. Fifteen subcodes were also devised to account for a multitude of descriptive and also normative statements engaging unity or solidarity at a national level ("Our nation is united as never before.") and at a global level ("Our unity is extending across the world."), and even communicating anxiety over possible neglect of New York City's needs due to excessive attention to national issues ("It is not possible for you to tell us enough times that what happened to us happened to the whole country."). Of greatest relevance are the subcodes, four in total, which together carried the greatest proportion of segments and confirmed the general picture of all data collected. These four subcodes represented important cultural processes around which theopolitical action was organized. This group of codes included "blending of national/theological identities" (thirteen cases), "kinship/family metaphors" (14 cases), "artifacts/artistic constructs (e.g., songs, poems, posters) for rebinding" (14 cases), and "nation as frame of reference" (ten cases). The variety of codes concerned with national identity far exceeded the number of codes about national identity from the content analysis of Oklahoma City sources. The code "blending of national/theological identities" actually had a corresponding code of the same name under the principal category "clergy and church involvement." That principal, church- activity-related code ("clergy and church involvement") yielded twenty-three cases. Hence the blending of confessional perspectives and practices with American sentiments figured prominently at the public level. One volunteer worker at St. Paul's Chapel in New York City asserted: "in the midst of this tragic happening, it is not black, white, no more color—everyone's just all one color. It's red, white, and blue, so to speak."[59] In the same vein, Participant *G1* considered the following to be the most important messages of public official statements: "that New Yorkers are united; Americans are united—on TV they were showing people helping each other—in tragedy."[60] The kinship metaphor, furthermore, appeared almost always in the context of firefighter memorials and, in fewer cases, in nation-building projects that offered the consolations of the so-called American Family.

The firefighters' appropriation of "fraternal bonds" turned out to carry major repercussions from the perspective of dedifferentiation. At the center of many such dedifferentiating processes stood firefighters themselves, who aggressively applied their code of fraternal unity during a period when many families lost fathers and mothers. The single theological usage of kinship came when the bishops of the Greek Orthodox archdiocese of America invoked family in a special pamphlet commemorating the September 11, 2001, attacks, declaring that on that day "seemingly perfect strangers walking in the streets across America suddenly realized their *true identity* as spiritual brothers and sisters, children of God."[61] All in all, however, public accounts pertaining to identity formation stressed a robust conception of American identity that assumed New York identity and yet went beyond it. At the same time, this does not entirely overshadow key forms of resistance or alternative interpretations.

"How Special Are We?" New Yorkers in Global Perspective

One of the most remarkable findings regarding unity and status was the sustained tension between the deflated and sober views of numerous respondents about their regional identity and the more triumphalist conceptions of New York identity advanced through nation-state memorials. One Roman Catholic congregant at a memorial service asserted, "You know you can't shut out the world . . . One thing September 11 taught us

59 Brubaker, et al. *Ground Zero Spirituality at Saint Paul Chapel.*

60. Santos, Participant *G1* interview.

61. *In Memory, in Faith, in Hope,* 4 (emphasis added).

is we're part of the world community, and it's scary, but it's something we have to deal with. We're not special" (emphasis added). Participant *J5*, commenting on his own views about America, avowed,

> Look, we have freedom of speech. I'm proud to be an American. But we get involved in things that are not our business. Otherwise, it's a wonderful place to live. Now 9/11, it opened my eyes to the world. Most of the time, I would only think about my little area. I realized there are other people out there. There is a whole world of people that are not just like us.[62]

Other members of the focus group nodded in agreement, adding "we're not alone" (participant *J4*).[63] Participant *G1* actually used the attack of 9/11 to criticize the American cultural project as a whole, claiming it is devoid of nerve, courage, and even genuine "culture":

> I believe people [in his church] did get together to pray—but it wasn't a formal event.
>
> We were drawing closer to God, but we reached out to people because they were suffering. They needed to be encouraged. But after a few months, people weren't as urgent. So only in the face of terror, people were like, "God help us." And in a nation that is all about church and state, it's odd we have "In God We Trust" [on our money]. Now they [certain endorsers of the separation of church and state] want to take it out. So in terms of culture, people would prefer to have it on money, or monetary instruments, instead of it being taught to children. So, the pledge of allegiance [contains the motto] and it is on our money. I mean, you can have a homosexual group, [on a campus] but if a group of evangelical students committed to discipleship [with Jesus] is there, it is banned.
>
> Look, there is no battleship on the Hudson. Are there fighters in Jersey? I don't know. Are things different? I don't know. With the war, they have a lot of resources out there [in the Middle East]. But if you push Iraq, then more of our people will get hurt. We'll push the guns, but not the culture. They value their culture. How many Americans do suicide bombings? It [Culture] is more valuable there than here. Here it is the dollar bill. Our history is about paying taxes. We say it is freedom, but it is not. People in America are not willing to die for their religion. Children's minds are built

62. Santos, Participants *J1*–*J5*, focus-group interview.
63. Ibid.

through culture, not the military—so that is the question: who is
going to get further with culture?[64]

The scathing and fervent rant of this participant is wide ranging. The
entire diatribe of sorts hinges on the idea of "culture." This participant
seems to identify the absence of teachings about sincere devotion to God
with an absence of culture. In this construal, culture actually initiates
persons into what is really at stake in the world, what is worth living and
dying for, and so seeks to defeat or preclude a certain fickleness of faith.
Sadly, the participant claims, Americans are thoroughly confused: we
place God squarely in the center of our mottos but then allow organized
opposition against the use of such mottos and their practical corollaries.
We have declared war on "terror," but, in this participant's view, he is
not sure that military defense is really improving any situation, on the
"homeland" or abroad. The key misallocation, as the participant finally
claims, is in the amount of energy and resources we pour into wealth and
its investment, and not into teaching "culture," or true devotion to the
cultivation of some core, dire theological sensibility.

   These responses herald a collective awakening and still hold total
negation at bay. To be sure, some of these assertions are anathema to
the statist project of social reconstitution following the disaster—they
would not be heard in any public memorial event. In particular, the responses grope for a politically transparent *metanoia*, for transformation
that takes up responsibility for the actions of the national body politic
irrespective of the status of citizenship as active or passive. Because we
are accustomed to viewing repentance as a "strictly spiritual" practice
carried out in the capacity of discipleship or spiritual formation, it is easy
to neglect that transformations of will, desire, emotion, and intellect can
be occasioned by national actions in regard to which we may seem to be
mere observers. The urgency of respondent *GI*'s complaint is sufficient
to convince us that something must change beyond global awareness.
The ecclesial practices of confession and repentance, in this case, are not
needed to repair nationalist devotion, but to provide the "brokenness"
that ensures blessing, wholeness, and truthfulness and thereby is capable
of permeating socially enduring forms of life (like citizenship) with
the presence of the body of the Christ while also not denying, among
the members of a nation like the United States, the historical or landed

---

64. Santos, Participant *GI* interview.

nature of that national identity. Repentance that follows the pattern set forth in 2 Cor 7:10–11 ("godly grief" producing "no regret" but only "eagerness to clear yourselves") occasions the awakening from collective sleep, as Walter Benjamin once contended: an awakening that eliminates the filters we have allowed to incapacitate our faculties of experience. The shock of modern life prior to the attacks of September 11, 2001 had already generated both a fascination about violence (especially virtual or electronically mediated violence, however "real") and a thoroughgoing aversion to encountering actual violence, destruction, and death. Viewed another way, cultural politics prior to the attacks did not privilege the citizen willing to confront the implications of his convictions in the light of death, sacrifice, or suffering, but privileged the patriotic consumer, who happens to have political interests, as the center of national life. The church, by contrast, knows that change is predicated on repentance.

Further consider, in this vein, the implications of the *metanoia* achieved in the life of the Apostle Peter in Acts 10 and 11, which echo the sober and yet inchoate realizations about global vulnerability of many interviewed citizens. This section of the Luke-Acts narrative sets out some important figural parallels and conveys the promise that such a repentant transformation proffers. Peter's awareness of Gentile inclusion in God's reign undermines Peter's own vision of election as essentially beginning and ending with Israel as the "master race." It becomes clear that outside of the gifted illumination that God's reign crosses ethnic and territorial barriers, there are racialized or exclusionary lenses by virtue of which the presence of others is not perceived as demanding the ethical task of being (or abiding) with them—a task that, in the christological sense, entails a willingness to embrace the person encountered in hope, peace, and mutual encouragement toward one end: life with God (see John 1:38–42). Not only this, but Peter must persuade others of God's approval. This requires a language and grammar that takes seriously the eschatological urgency of the world God is building and concurrently manifesting among those who faithfully embody and articulate such a vision. Ched Myers deftly portrays the profound struggles intrinsic to such strivings in several passages from the Gospel of Mark, passages that treat Jesus's ministry to Gentiles on "the other side" of the Sea of Galilee. During each account of a boat trip to the "Gentile side," the apostles' prejudiced loyalties are reflected in their blindness and deafness to Jesus's teachings on hypocrisy.[65]

The aforementioned discussion of prejudice points to a certain theme of interest common to a wide range of data sources in this study: the relationship between inclusion and prioritization of identity. A poignant instance of this emerged in the curious blend of family, death, and nation in media coverage of discussions about hope or "moving forward." This suggests that assimilation into the "American family" is assured in the act of dying for it, an outstanding example of totemic devotion and blood sacrifice as explicated in the work of Carolyn Marvin and David Ingle.

Whether to include in the American body politic foreigners, minority residents, or those who did not appear to fit the major physical schema of an Anglo American was also a very important topic for public consideration after the disaster. Accounting for the executive actions of the federal government and its domestic war on terrorism, many aliens decided to apply for citizenship in order to become nondeportable. To be sure, citizenship applications from Arabs and Muslims increased by a third between mid-September 2001 and January 1, 2002. In the eyes of other writers and civic leaders, it became clear that even in light of the perennial commitment to tolerance, pluralism, and inclusion of all variety of social groups, limits had to be drawn on some grounds, whether moral, spiritual, or some other rooted in the general good. In one editorial, John O'Sullivan demanded loyalty from resident aliens over tolerance, and hence, assimilation over cultural self-protection.[66] A Muslim leader from a national Muslim coalition also subscribed to this line of reasoning:

> In the World Trade Center incident, we have suffered a double grief. Many of us lost friends and relatives. And now some of us face the stereotypes that because we are Muslims, we are somehow to blame. You have to know that most of the calls we have gotten here have been from people supporting us. But we have to act as Americans. Most of you are American citizens. Fly the flag, donate money to help. If you don't want to act as American citizens, give up your passports.[67]

---

65. Myers, *Binding the Strong Man*, 185.
66. O'Sullivan, "Muslims in U.S. Should Proclaim Loyalty."
67. McFadden, "In a Stadium of Heroes."

In this case, the impetus to join the American body politic evidences an odd admixture of fear and brazen exhortatory speech.

Despite the plethora of discursive formations, catchwords, and catchphrases that circulated through social networks and media outlets, various benchmarks for social reconstitution were ultimately identifiable. The boundaries between these identities and most social institutions were highly fluid in most cases. These fundamental symbols include the elevation of (a) mayor Rudolph Giuliani to the status of a charismatic, redemptive figure, (b) firefighters and (less so) military personnel as models of social behavior and spirituality, and (c) other New Yorkers who must build upon the sacrifices of their public servants, or live in their shadows. A related subtext to the reconstitution of social relations also emerged from citizen responses: the effect that the attacks had on the impoverished. Responses from homeless persons about the monetary compensation due to families of victims raised some vitally important theological questions about social exclusion and determinations of social worth after the terrorist attack. Due to the importance of this material for the more comprehensive ecclesiological assessment of the state's cultural politics after disaster, undertaken in the last two chapters of the book, the discussion of the poor has been relegated to chapter 6.

Rudolph Giuliani: "The Essential Man"

The reception of mayor Rudolph Giuliani's public actions and speeches (as opposed to an overview of the specific actions and speech acts themselves, which will be covered below) usually occurred in the context of regularly occurring public statements at scores of funeral services in the months following the attacks. Giuliani, in many such moments, introduced the interests of patriotically centered social body formation into a conventional "sacred" space, chiefly, church buildings. Many lauded Giuliani's concern for virtually every sphere of life in New York City; one commentator claimed that "he has personally overseen almost every aspect of the attempt to reconstruct the city's infrastructure, economy and psyche as well as comforting families who are waiting to recover their loved ones."[68] Indeed, Giuliani's redemptive character was confirmed through his involvement with rather intimate family matters. For example, he executed an extremely rare feat for any public official: after

---

68. Wakin, "At Edge of Ground Zero."

Giuliani was informed that a young firefighter named Michael Gorumba had died at a Staten Island fire, Giuliani, acting in the place of her deceased brother, walked Gorumba's sister down the aisle at her wedding. Giuliani also frequently visited hospitals and comforted women who had lost their husbands.[69] Giuliani kicked off the Macy's Thanksgiving Day Parade amid a slew of citizens who were apparently willing to follow him anywhere. A resident of Staten Island claimed, "He's quite a hero to us these days." The reverence with which the mayor was viewed in the first two weeks after the attack is duly captivating. One woman, at Central Park West, proclaimed that Giuliani's presence in the days following the attack made her surmise not that he was *like* a god, but rather that "He is God."[70] Another female New Yorker, appraising the credentials of several mayoral candidates, affirmed, "They look so trivial, compared to our king."[71] Even in press-conference statements, it appeared that governor George Pataki would defer to Giuliani.[72]

Overall, then, Rudolph Giuliani fulfilled the role of an allegorical leader, through whom citizens could find resources for their own stability, on whom citizens could bestow desires to praise and defer, and through whom citizens could participate in redemptive actions throughout the city—actions somewhat removed from the immediate personal-bodily sphere of any given citizen. This focus on a soteriological and charismatic figure, whose political career and physical health had taken a turn for the worse in the year before the attacks, underscores the significance of liminality. Giuliani not only rehabilitated his public credibility, but he was happily received as a poetical figure in a state of activity, dynamically moving the course of a drama that unfolded before the eyes of New Yorkers and the world at large. During heightened uncertainty about the future of the city, Giuliani was evidently the fulfillment of permanent and enduring needs, as well as a visible individual whose agency and initiative satisfied the American vision of individual autonomy and efficacy.[73] Orrin Edgar Klapp argues that what he calls "symbolic leaders" of a practical, concrete sort (as opposed to leaders with a real impact apart from any veritable

69. Herbert, "In America; The Right Answer."
70. Ibid.
71. Ibid.
72. Ibid.
73. Klapp, *Symbolic Leaders*, 53, 54, 64.

actions) must move "some group through a status relationship that can be specified."[74] Indeed, Giuliani, as a limited individual human being, nonetheless carried massive corporate power: New Yorkers took him as a gauge and model for their own collective ascendance from lowly and distraught to tough and victorious. He was viewed as someone who satisfied "functions far beyond those of particular organizations and structures."[75] Elevated above the body politic, Giuliani served as an actual means by which the narrative of the political imagination was reconstructed. As with most phenomena generated in the context of hypermodern cultural poetics, the effects appear to have been short-lived. Participant *H3*, a minister of a large church in New York City, asserted: "New Yorkers have largely forgotten about Giuliani. Bloomberg is so strong and generous. Not that what Giuliani did was not great. But New Yorkers have moved on."

Remember the Firefighters: Building a City on Their Blood

Two striking elements were taken for granted in many texts covering the funerals of firefighters (all of which occurred in church buildings) or that spoke about the extraordinary efforts of rescuers. First, there was the manner in which the personal or emotional and the professional or job-related requirements were assumed to occupy different cognitive or existential spaces, albeit in no specified or well-articulated way. This is consistent with the modern fragmentation of ethics into a wide variety of supposedly autonomous spheres of social activity and decision making; although, theologically speaking, this fragmentation affects the whole person, and creates the impression that performance in multiple social contexts accounts for all the richness of social interaction, with no apparent overarching transcendent drama to carry ethical commitments, and without any apparent *telos* to human life beyond professional allegiance or group membership. This fragmentation is most evident in emotion-management techniques that emerge when a struggle for faithful performance of the professional script meets powerful sentiments of anguish and concern. For example, a firefighter claimed the following at a memorial ceremony dedicated to the New York City firefighters who had died during rescue attempts: "We're confused. We feel guilty. We feel deprived.

---

74. Ibid., 53.

75. Ibid., 21.

We are angry. But we are also professionals."[76] Another firefighter stated that the tragedy forced this division to rupture: "we hold our emotions back and do our jobs. But we can't hold it inside all the time."[77] Second, the job is regarded as the "greatest job in the world," and is further qualified with a bit of essentialism: "we are one because . . . it is who we are."[78] This is the second important discursive practice that turned out to be embodied or materialized in cartoons, posters, commercials, memorial ceremonies, and public speeches: firefighting is not what firefighters do, it is who they *are*. This stretches into a realm beyond functionalism, performance, and vocation; indeed a global attribution about their character and even ontology is being advanced; that is, something was asserted about being and existence per se. This practice of shoring up the existential or ontological value of certain persons and their vocations created a stabilizing effect after the collective trauma. That is to say, citizens could say to themselves, "we know we have bravery and strength and devotion around us (or in us); the firefighters show us that this is surely the case. It is who they are; this is inscrutable, beyond challenge, and inherent." As the New York City Trade Waste Commission chairman Ray Casey, who represented the mayor at a funeral service in November 2001, declared, "They had no choice in their hearts when they got the call to duty. They leapt from their truck and ran in to save lives."[79]

In at least one-half of memorial-service accounts in the sample of documents, a particularized profile of firefighters as friends and family members led into a discussion of how they died responding to the September 11, 2001, attack of the World Trade Center. Speakers at memorial ceremonies usually furnished various details about their personalities and joined these with theopolitical imagery. In one instance, at a funeral service held at St. Patrick's Cathedral, a pair of firefighters was described as patriots that served their nation, not simply their city or local community. They died for the nation and met "their God."[80] The notion of the patriot, echoing the Revolutionary War, and all wars since, ennobles the work and efforts of the firefighters within a nationalized

76. Spielman, "'Our Family Is Suffering.'"
77. Wakin, "Attacks Spur a Surge of Interest in Religion."
78. Ibid.
79. Shelby and Kates, "'God Called for Heroes.'"
80. Farrel, et al., "They Lived and Died Together."

context. At a funeral service held in November 2001, one firefighter was characterized as a "true American patriot who served his nation."[81]

Through the Americanization of funeral services, the frame of reference against which the firefighters' and police officers' lives could be symbolically constructed was equipped with added social and political power. In some cases the dead were presented as humble, everyday heroes who were not recognized until September 11, 2001. One police sergeant stated the following about his fellow officer: "[He] didn't become a hero on Sept. 11. He was a hero all his life."[82] The brother of another firefighter claimed: "[this firefighter] let us in on a secret Sept. 11. He has been a hero for quite some time, but kept it to himself."[83]

Many times, moreover, firefighters and police officers were set forth as models for behavior or virtuous character traits: "'Even if they knew the fate that awaited them they would've eagerly and willingly done the same thing to save one life,'" said one firefighter at a brother's funeral. "'They gave us all a loving lesson in how to be best friends and how to treat people and care for people.'"[84] "'What mattered to Dennis most were human beings and all living things,'" claimed the Reverend Bruce Powers at a memorial Mass in Melville, New York: "[The firefighter] was naturally a rescuer—it was a God-given gift he had."[85] The wife of one firefighter stated that "he always knew in his heart what was right.[86] In a service held in the West Side, a Catholic priest stated, "'Now [this firefighter] has another great experience. God is breathing life back into him, giving him another chance that will last forever. We can keep his spirit alive by the way we conduct ourselves for the good of other people.'"[87] Another pastor at a nearby funeral asserted, "What these people had in common was their willingness to put the needs of others ahead of their own—their ability to act honorably, in spite of their natural fears. Most of us will never be called upon to display the bravery shown by the New York firefighters or passengers of Flight 93, but they will be our inspiration in the weeks and

81. Ibid.

82. Engels, et al., "Hundreds Bid Farewell."

83. Gest and Moritz, "'Heaven Has a Heck of a Fire Department Now.'"

84. Farrel, et al., "They Lived and Died Together."

85. El-Gobashy, "Tears, Cheers for Fireman."

86. Ibid.

87. Gearty, et al., "Tearful Pay Last Respects."

months ahead."[88] Finally, at Father Mychal Judge's funeral, Cardinal Egan asserted the following, to which many gave nods of approval: "New York is going to be rebuilt stronger than ever before in the blood and sweat of our heroes."[89]

Rudolph Giuliani's hermeneutical and symbolic significance (that is, his status as a cultural object through which others could interpret the tragedy) served to strengthen the role of firefighters in the attack's aftermath as well. Usually Giuliani served as the spokesperson for the regional and national collectivity. At one memorial service, Mayor Giuliani reminded a father that his son was a hero for all New Yorkers: "'You should feel a tremendous pride in this man,'" he said. "'[O]ur firefighters conducted a rescue operation that reencouraged America during its hardest hour.'"[90] Even when the mayor was unable to attend a funeral, he sent surrogates who read written statements. At the Maranatha Church of the Nazarene in Paramus, New Jersey, where one thousand people gathered to honor a firefighter from the Bronx, deputy mayor Anthony P. Coles, read: "'Bruce did not die any death that day. He died a hero, and he died for a purpose.'"[91] At another service, Mayor Giuliani paid tribute to a firefighter and other terror victims, tying the death of rescuers to an American political virtue: "'Every time I feel grief, I feel this quiet sense of pride, a sense of strength. They died for freedom.'"[92]

The aforementioned are only a sample of the hundreds of ritual events at which solemn statements were made about the ultimate value or meaning of almost four hundred firefighters. However, it is clear that these rescuers served as symbolic resources for both the reconstitution of ethical standards and the maintenance of the American political system. More important, the citizen's moral vision is reestablished through a construal of the exemplar's total life, which undoubtedly culminates with sacrifice for the nation.

In the sample of documents and speeches analyzed here, this whole process (recognizing the admirable traits of the firefighter and the general ethos that these are meant to generate for the postdisaster social body) is

88. Spielman, "'Our Family Is Suffering.'"
89. Niebhur, "At Houses of Worship, Feelings Are Shared."
90. El-Gobashy, "Tears, Cheers for Fireman."
91. Murphy, "Nation Challenged."
92. Engels, et al., "Hundreds Bid Farewell."

not framed as a gift of God, save with the reference noted above, in which the firefighter's vocation is deemed "God-given." While the praising of virtues is needed for the edification of any social body, disregard for the origin of such virtues is not simply a matter of divine offense, but as the previous chapter noted, a display of love that is not free, and a reflection of politics as self-referential and self-sustaining in the extreme. Chris Huebner is quite right, in his essay on the ecumenical movement, to contend that the achievement of unity or solidarity is not often viewed as a grace although this is precisely what it is.[93] Unification around a common ethical outlook cannot simply be achieved without some incalculable and nonrational set of realizations rooted in a radical heteronomy (i.e., in personal submission) that cannot be claimed as real in abstraction from the flesh-and-blood encounters of vulnerable yet faithful human beings. In other words, divine agency must be viewed not only as ultimately "other" but also as more determinative than human agency in faithful, material action; making divine agency more determinative than human agency nonetheless does not in the least offset the roles of human potential and creative action. Inasmuch as such agency is exercised within a church building, during a memorial ceremony in which death and finality must be translated into new memories and beginnings, simply reinforces the capillary acumen of the state's political imagination and its capacity to create (in the Foucauldian sense) both individuals and collectivities. To claim that a city is to be rebuilt on the blood of heroes is to virtually foreclose the role of divine initiative in eschatological hope—specifically, that which compels us to admit that only in the *coming* of God, not in marching toward him, will a communion of joy and charity come about. One could note the cries of the martyrs in John's Apocalypse to draw an interesting contrast. Yet when clergy and state actors jointly participate in the constitution of a model of social re-creation that casts heroism, democratic principles, and even the biological elements of the touted heroes ("blood and sweat") as the basic aesthetic and mimetic building blocks of the city after disaster, the role of substantial theological narratives or doctrines (e.g., the incarnation, sin, the Trinity, salvation, forgiveness, resurrection) becomes more ambiguous. The heroic statist aesthetic likewise undermines or disregards our understanding of the gifts of the Spirit as radically decentering the agent from being the originator and

---

93. Huebner, *Precarious Peace*, 76.

singular bearer of such virtues. Hence what is a given congregation to do? Are the doctrines to be ignored, eschewed, or harmonized with the prevailing discourse and practice? What must be done if a congregation acting collectively is to wisely set some narrative or doctrine against a specific aspect of the state's project considered in need of confrontation, without challenging or disregarding the unbearable grief of some who have lost loved ones? The beginning of an answer to this query must begin with the implications of John 8:30–32, which is elaborated in the Kierkegaardian (incarnational) conviction that the Christian is called to "live in" the doctrines and patterns set forth in accordance with the rule of faith, as "something that is bound up with the deepest roots of [one's] existence." Otherwise, the doctrines simply remain ideas or postulates external to Christians, as mere objects of agreement or assent.[94] Without this as an antecedent condition to disaster, the congregation is exposed as the mere custodians of pious utterances and beliefs to which it subscribes, not as disciples who "teach [the nations] to obey everything [Jesus has] commanded them" (Matt 28:18–20). Consequently, in the realm of cultural poetics and politics, the church has no authority (which is precisely what the Risen One declares having received prior to the baptismal and pedagogical commission at the end of Matthew's gospel), because the doctrines do not translate into the dynamic presence of the body of Christ. Without this presence, therefore, nothing of the basic interactional elements by which disciples relate to one another enters decisively into the reestablishment of the political order. The question here does not concern whether firefighters should be praised for courageous deeds that many persons cannot imagine performing, but concerns the absence of the church as an augmenting presence in the process by which the objectified "firefighter as heroic patriot" is entrenched in a narrative of restoration that appropriates character virtues as the basis upon which the *mythos* of a "nation of agents" is restored to a body politic. Before this is addressed more fully below, one needs to consider how many firefighters perceived the political and spiritual elements of their lives after the attacks.

Spirituality Forged in Disaster

Primary among the findings relating to the practices of specific social groups or institutions outside church buildings and congregations is the

94. See Kierkegaard, "Early Journal Entries," 7–9.

emergence of what can be named "disaster-centered spirituality" among firefighters. Participant *F1* (a veteran New York City firefighter nearing retirement) painted a picture of postdisaster firefighters as having learned, most for the first time, to incorporate spiritual matters into everyday conversations at the firehouse. Specifically, the firefighter mentioned that many firefighters began to speak about God openly for the first time in their lives. Some began to attend Bible studies in the firehouse while others only spoke of God in the context of the death of fellow firefighters.[95] This latter comment catalyzed a series of probes and responses whereby participant *F1* highlighted an important series of community activities, political stances, and other cultural links. First, neighborhood residents provided spiritual guidance for dealing with frustrations surrounding recovery work at Ground Zero:

> The [labor] union didn't help at Ground Zero. The guys [firefighters] felt as if they were being walked over by the city. Guys worked at the site and were gradually pulled away. But at the neighborhood, folks visited the guys and they held vigils for us and prayed with the guys. I prayed with them. This helped the guys a lot during this period, especially when the union was not so strong.[96]

Second, in relation to the fire department's view of the federal government's response to terrorism, participant *F1* explained:

> Folks who were not particularly with [supportive of] the fire department didn't say anything at first, but later they did. You know in the fire department, there is, you know, there is a mindset of conservatism as opposed to liberalism; they are conservative because they want to better their opportunities in a way that liberalism doesn't offer. But months later, guys started to complain about some of the government's actions.[97]

In terms of the invocation of theological language on the part of political figures at memorial events, the firefighter asserted:

> I supported what he [Giuliani] was saying, at least God was included, unlike others who don't include him at all. [Interviewer: "Were there any objections to this in the firehouse?"] No, not really. But I was like "wow," he is bringing God into the picture. We

95. Santos, Participant *F1* interview.
96. Ibid.
97. Ibid.

are trying to take it out of schools and here they are talking about
God. . . . I think those memorials [i.e., memorial services] had a
common effect on the men. Considering what they went through,
it had an effect on all of them.[98]

When I asked about the degree to which firefighters became focused on
their American identity or citizenship, the participant, surprisingly, asserted that it was not much of a factor among the firefighters he knew.[99]
Regarding the burgeoning interest in God or spirituality, he said:

God was at the firehouse for a while, although it did drop off eventually. You know, guys switch stations and a new group comes in.
Anyway, God can only be there to the extent that people have him
in their hearts. And when hard times came after 9-11, there were
plenty of times that anger or frustration would set in. But when
anger sets in and answers are not coming in as we want them,
people would rather get even than, you know, think about God
or pray.[100]

Several key matters are thus illumined. First, what institutional arrangement serves and was served through the firefighters' newfound spiritual
curiosity? Quite definitely, it seems, the state crafted itself through these
very workers who engaged in unprecedented reflections about God. This
is at the core of what Michel Foucault considered the more insidious,
capillary nature of power and technologies of self. Engaged in a decidedly
new project of rudimentary theological reflection, many of the firefighters to which participant *F1* alluded obtained a spiritual orientation heavily shaped by a militaristic and hierarchical institution itself historically,
politically, and organizationally linked to statist concerns for security,
management, and even spirituality. This is clear from the firefighter's
statement that persons who were not supportive of the fire department
would not make any critical comments about the federal government's
agenda against terror until much later. This participant also spoke to
the "going concerns" of firefighters in politics, which was essentially
tied to the secure establishment of regulations or policies that promote
"the lifestyle they have as firefighters." Political concern, for firefighters,
resolutely engages the maintenance of "lifestyle"—of work schedules,

98. Ibid.
99. Ibid.
100. Ibid.

vacation time, salary, benefits, insurance, and time with family. Their political concern was not, as a result, focused on any critical matter of what
sorts of motivations, images, or normative assumptions are produced (or
reproduced) from within the linkage of firefighter, church, and government. Indeed firefighters' concerns were not even focused on how the
church and state relate to each other in any substantive sense. Most surprising was the lack of concern about American identity at a time when
so much about it was being produced for memorial services, newscasts,
and other public events.

For firefighters, the cultural resources from which the nexus of
spirituality, politics, and identity was (and is?) constructed was decidedly
liturgical—chiefly, through the speech acts, bodily actions, and symbols
produced in the seemingly endless slew of official memorial processions
and services held for firefighters. Yet this series of rituals was divorced
from an ongoing communal life geared toward the development of faith,
wisdom, and love. Participant *F1*, the interviewed firefighter, acknowledged the impact of these ritual events upon the cadre of firefighters.
Most important, most of these ceremonies were executed within church
buildings, not necessarily sites of civil religion. Thus, unless any given
firefighter began to read Scripture or engage in consistent study of biblical, spiritual, or theological topics outside of funerary experiences tied to
the World Trade Center attacks, the social imagination conveyed in such
processions and speech acts provided the bulk of the content for spiritual
consideration in the life of the individual firefighter. Consequently, in
turn, this internalization of symbols and public accounts of truth promoted a particular theology and politics of identity, even if participants
carried an acquiescent or indifferent attitude toward specific features of
such accounts as they were publicly presented. As participant *F1* made
clear, the challenge to modify prevailing thought patterns in the context
of extreme grief, frustration, or emotional exhaustion after the attacks
did not easily lead to sustained commitment to theological or spiritual
discipline. For many firefighters, therefore, the focus remained insular.
They were mainly concerned with "lifestyle" opportunities; exercised only
nominal engagement with issues linking God, spirituality and politics;
and submitted to the aggrandizing constructions of other institutions
concerning the importance of firefighters to the American legacy of
bravery—that is, of human agency detached from an ecclesially mediated ontology of participation and divine eschatological initiative. The

noticeable absence of an assertively faithful congregational engagement with these public processes served to bring the hegemonic character of the nation-building project into bold relief. Recall that many citizen responses, and responses of firefighters to some degree, questioned or denied some key aspects of the politics of glory represented in the speeches and actions of the messiah figure of Rudolph Giuliani. This inaptness of statist politics sheds light on the criticality of ecclesial acquiescence for the effective portrayal of an ostensibly well-integrated public cultural project. This compliance entails both the abdication of cultural agency *and* acceptance of a discursive field that favors indecisive and disembodied theological doctrines rather than a faithful community that enacts Scripture.

"Sincerity" and Public Invocations of God

The use of theological symbols or biblical references in public, political performances received consistent treatment from focus-group participants, many of whom were high school– or college-aged youth. When asked for their views about so-called official God-talk pertaining to "God's role" or "divine will" in the attacks, almost all participants agreed that "sincerity" was the key criterion (just as participant *H1*, the minister of a small church outside Manhattan, had stated). Participant *J3* pinned his response on God's close involvement with the governmental functions of Israelite monarchies: "If you look at Kings [1 and 2 Kings], you notice how closely David sought after God's will and desire for the nation. That's important to me."[101] Participant *J4* quickly added, "You should be able to talk about God if it reflects your life. But not simply to comfort Americans, [simulating a sad tone] 'Oh, God is with us, God will help us' [*some laughter*]."[102] Participant *G1* addressed this issue at some length:

> I think they should talk about God more often but they need to back it up with action; either with funding or with a decision to do something. They could be in office, but they stay out of controversy. So they stay out of it [controversy] but no one knows where they stand. I need to see that—for them to live as if they lived for God. But they have tough decisions—so I respect them. How do you protect a country with all these waterways? If they really do believe in God, then they'll make something happen.

101. Santos, Participants *J1–J5*, focus-group interview.
102. Ibid.

In the Middle East, it is different. Do you see any politicians here dying for something they believe in? If you really wanted to see something through no matter what. It is all about culture. The one that requires faith will last longer. This country teaches works, not faith.[103]

As the minister in the first section (participant *H1*) also posited, the demands of the situation and the actual integrity or sincerity of the speaker ought to determine whether any public figure speaks about God or invokes "God's views" about the tragedy at hand. Consistent with numerous comments made in Oklahoma City interviews, citizens in New York appeared leery of God-talk when internal motivations and other aspects of a political figure's life were not deducible or transparent to some degree. These views as a whole suggest the existence of a scripturally driven, subversive yet private transcript of typical state-sanctioned public dramas and performances. These private yet subversive views remain enclosed within church group discussion without taking on the so-called establishment of compliant theological discourse. A public transcript centered on measured, nonecclesial appropriations of a generic god with superficial biblical ornamentation remains the prevailing mode of presentation. This established discourse refuses to consider the unsettling counterdiscourse of the private but subversive sector. These approved presentations usually project as much of the political figure as possible for public modeling and consumption. Even if the public figure projects private or intimate matters, this is acceptable so long as the projection is consistent with the project at hand rather than an answer to public accountability about motives and honesty.

Fear of the Apocalypse

The attacks on September 11, 2001, coincided with a development in popular theology and evangelical writing that burgeoned in response to the advent of the new millennium: resurgence in end-times and apocalyptic theology. The public culture of the postdisaster period in New York City, especially during the first month, was teeming with public preachers and fundamentalist church groups that staked out pavement space in Lower Manhattan and began to make strident claims about the imminent

---

103. Santos, Participant *G1* interview.

"end of the world."[104] A female preacher, Dorothy Ivey, warned crowds of the coming apocalypse while a man nearby held up a sign that read, "Repent Ye and Believe in the Gospel."[105] A survey of five hundred bookstores, administered about two months after the attack, by the Evangelical Christian Publishers Association discovered that the number of nonfiction books about prophecy sold in the eight weeks after September 11 had increased by 71 percent compared with the previous eight weeks.[106]

This appeared to have captured the imaginations and molded the social relations of numerous focus-group participants as well. Participant *J1*, a Hispanic single mother of two, asserted that in her neighborhood, "people were talking about 'the end of the world.' I thought 'I got to go to church . . . Is the world going to end?'" Elaborating on the heightened religious sensibilities of neighbors, she added: "people spoke about God, but not after two months."[107]

Following this, the fear and insecurity of a large-scale war between the United States and a somewhat nebulous enemy became a major topic of discussion for many focus-group participants. Still speaking in terms of popular conceptions of "Armageddon," a climactic, divinely initiated war during which good defeats evil and its earthly emissaries once and for all, participant *J1* asserted, "When I went to pick up my daughter at school, she came screaming with the other kids, 'Are we in a war, are we going to die now?' So I felt real panicky, yesterday, today, tomorrow . . . when?"[108]

Participant *J2*, a college-aged participant in the study who grew up in New York City, followed up on *J1*'s comment, offering, "Perhaps this is the beginning of the end." After about a ten-second pause, I asked him to elaborate on why he thought this was the case. He replied,

> I got that from people, adults, the media. . . . magazines in the supermarket . . . you know, [*deepens his voice and gestures upwards with his hands to signify grandeur*] "The End of the World!" Then I thought, wait, this has happened before. In hurricanes, World War II, the stock market crash—"this is it!" To tell you the truth, though, when I think about all of these things as a series of events,

104. Wakin, "At Edge of Ground Zero."
105. Jacobs, "Delivering the Gospel."
106. Sack, "Apocalyptic Theology Revitalized by Attacks."
107. Santos, Participants *J1–J5*, focus-group interview
108. Ibid.

> [e.g.] the Tsunamis and 9/11, and going to church, reading the
> Bible, . . . I am starting to believe it, something is going on.[109]

It is evident that the traumatic scale of the event as one among several before and since September 11, 2001, has enthralled this participant within
a popular yet roundly chastised form of apocalyptic understanding. For
many New Yorkers, this was potentially a matter of great urgency and
frequent discussion. Although it subsided as a topic of community talk,
for a time it promoted solidarity through commonly reinforced anxiety,
confusion, and uncertainty.

Rituals of Solidarity, Rampant Hybridization

Significant degrees of apocalyptic anxiety and confusion hold an important place in the broader social context within which nationally oriented
rituals of solidarity were performed. An impressive ensemble of gestures
and practices of solidarity appeared in Lower Manhattan in the twelve
months after the attack. The cultural appropriations of attenders at the
Yankee Stadium memorial ceremony as most notable. Also of considerable
importance was the incorporation of the attacks into regularly occurring
ritual celebrations or festivities, such as the Saint Patrick's Day parade.
The Yankee Stadium prayer service, perhaps like no other, forcefully promoted, under the banner of "religious diversity" (1) Americanization of
nonnatives, and (2) elevation of uniformed military officers. Additionally,
although affirmations of the social body were strong based on participant
comments, the underwhelming attendance for this service suggested that
local, vernacular ceremonies were just as popular.

Twelve days after the attack, a memorial services coordinated by the
city government was held in Yankee Stadium. The ceremony was called
"A Prayer for America." Attended by twenty thousand persons, the event
was replete with prayers, singing, acclamation, defiant protests, and hor-
tatory flourishes. The prestige, aura, and credibility of various celebrities
(e.g., Oprah Winfrey, James Earl Jones, Plácido Domingo, and numerous Broadway stars) mixed with a formidable band of local confessional
leaders, which included Rev. Calvin Butts, Edward Cardinal Egan, Imam
Izak-el Mu-eed Pasha, and Jewish, Buddhist, and Hindu leaders.[110] For
many New Yorkers, the five-hour televised event turned out to be an

109. Ibid.
110. Heisler, "20,000 Join Hands, Hearts."

extravagant national rally subsuming celebrity-led entertainment under a universalized religious unity centered on the glorification of American heritage. One attender noted: "When 'The Star Spangled Banner' was sung, it was like a prayer for me. I don't know why so few people came out. Maybe they feel safer praying at home. But I needed community with me."[111] A woman in attendance considered the event one that had mass psychological benefit and that dignified New York City, adding, "This coming together is cathartic, rather than retreating into our own hollows and into ignorance and fear. Only in New York can you bring this out into the open. This is truly important." In a similar vein, the brother of a missing firefighter expressed the following: "Emotionally, it helped a lot. Mentally . . . I'm still working on it."[112] Mothers held aloft posters of their missing firefighter sons, families stood behind large American flags, and many others linked arm in arm as a long chain across the stands. Representations of the flag were myriad: on T-shirts, hats, and posters; in hair buns and sticking out of pipes.[113]

The subordination of distinct confessional affiliation to American identity and the looming military interventions in the Middle East was acute. One observer noted that men wearing pins that read "I am Sikh. God Bless America," actively reached out to men wearing uniforms.[114] The crowd roared and rose to its feet when Imam Pasha admonished all those present to embrace tolerance, saying "We are Muslims, but we are Americans. We Muslims, Americans, stand today with a heavy weight on our shoulder that those who would dare do such dastardly acts claim our faith. They are no believers in God at all."[115] Other New Yorkers in attendance held up signs that intimated war; one person held a placard reading, "Pray Today, Fight Tomorrow."[116] In two different articles covering the event in the *Daily News*, military figures were depicted praying alongside thousands of others, and a caption read, "in reverence." Graphically, the soldiers were spiritualized and presented in this mode at large.

111. McFadden, "In a Stadium of Heroes."
112. Heisler, "20,000 Join Hands, Hearts."
113. Ibid.
114. Ibid.
115. Ibid.
116. Ibid.

The Yankee Stadium so-called prayer service, therefore, not only further naturalized spiritual expression but also enmeshed it in a matrix of collective patriotic vocalizations and material presentations of grief, anger, and exuberance. Moreover, the service furthered the universalistic disposition of American patriotism as something that all should welcome (including those born outside the United States), because, as it were, loyalty is its own reward. The need for apophatic humility is dismissed in the absence of any overriding *telos* that governs and is evident within citizen practices (such as in those practices that disciples of Jesus are called to embody in concrete community). By working toward a *telos*, such practices carry theological (and thus cultural) legitimacy. The absence of a governing *telos* did not prevent a model for a kind of spirituality from being proffered: as religious leaders, military officials, and celebrities exhorted and prayed, spirituality was geared toward establishing consensus around the guarantee that our celebrities, religious leaders, and military officials were in agreement about who we must oppose and who we undoubtedly are. (Whether consensus is actually achieved is irrelevant.) This erasure of distinction between the famous, the religious leaders, and the military officials, all of whom may be commoditized for surplus profit, is essential for the projection of integrity onto the social body in events of this type. Although the majority of residents present are mourning, this does not lead the collectivity to acknowledge either a lack of knowledge of God or severe limitations that come with being a creature. This is, at its zenith, a spirituality of surety amid anguish. Because it makes no room for, as Frances Young puts it, "the gulf between God's 'Otherness' and our creatureliness bridged by the saving *kenosis* (emptying) in the incarnation,"[117] this type of event relies on the comfort of immanence: stardom, celebrity, and pseudocosmopolitanism provide both solace and a political imagination by which to anticipate the future. Moreover, the sheer visibility of the celebrities operates as a mode of ordering the world: "to be in the media frame is to be at the [center] of things, an idea so heavily naturalized that it often, paradoxically, seems difficult to *see* (through)."[118] Celebrities are mobilized as "priests" or intermediaries who legitimize all manner of ventures, because the contemporary body politic realizes active agency as a collectivity of fans and not necessarily as a group of citizens or as

117. Young, *Brokenness and Blessing,* 63 (emphasis original).

118. Redmond and Holmes, *Stardom and Celebrity,* 5 (emphasis original).

followers of Jesus. The celebrity/fan dynamic of identification is today's parody of the Christ/disciple dynamic of identification and participation, yet the former has successfully flowed into everyday life in a way that the latter has not.

As the above suggests, collective identity was hardly a given after the World Trade Center attack. It underwent a rigorous process of activation, bolstering, binding, and separating, especially in public, dramatic performance. Even if public officials did not provide the content for American devotion in public life, local residents served as highly driven and often ingenious cultural creators. Meanwhile, solemn pronouncements at formalized ritual events introduced many powerful social models into circulation (firefighters, Giuliani, and others) amid localized, ephemeral utterances and practices.

These vernacular expressions, to be sure, are still worthy of analysis. The massive upheaval of cultural production across many spheres, including the increased use of theological and apocalyptic language, complemented with inscriptions of anger and grief on city walls, facilitated the overtly public comparison of numerous visions of ideal social life with concrete reality. Due to the volume of material associated with such phenomena, chapter 6 will offer closer coverage of the material culture of solidarity. That chapter takes up local efforts at institutionalizing emergent memorials and commodification of memorial items as its dual foci.

THE REENCHANTMENT OF THE AMERICAN WORLD: THE (CONTESTED) POLITICAL IMAGINARY OF THE WORLD TRADE CENTER ATTACKS

To what extent did church-rooted practices and disciplines parallel, absorb, or clash with the discourse and practice of statist disciplines, and vice versa? The hypothesis associated with this query of competing political imaginations claimed that in reasserting its functions and organs of social control after the disaster, the state would rely on an implicit theology that assured victory, that proffered a vision of a natural and romantic unity, and that insisted on valuing expertise, competence, and visibility as the primary means for assembling the social body. This expectation was largely confirmed.

The analysis that follows is framed in terms of differentiation and dedifferentiation. The first subsection below details the predominance of imaginative dedifferentiation in many different spheres of social life after the disaster, as exemplified in urban search-and-rescue operations. Dedifferentiation made the infusion of statist disciplines that much easier at both the broadest and narrative spheres of public life. Topics of the subsections that follow include the political imagination of the churches as a whole, the political imagination of the state, and the different manifestations of the dedifferentiated political imagination of church and state whereby certain views, practices, and relationships from in one institution (where an institution is an embodiment of theopolitical imagination) were adopted by another institution. This final section tracks dedifferentiation of church and state by political figures, in the commercial and economic spheres, and in concrete institutionalization of church- and state-personnel bonds.

Private and Public, Imaginary and Familiar

Throughout the course of the analysis, the political and social weight of dedifferentiation emerged in many different realms of social life apart from the focus of the study. Most intriguing were the nontechnical, informal, and symbolic actions required for activity coordination and resource sharing between local and regional governmental organizations, on the one hand, and federal entities, on the other hand. Interviews conducted with members of the FEMA Urban Search and Rescue program suggest that a certain set of institutional boundaries had to be addressed in narrative or symbolic fashion if well-coordinated activities were to materialize. One group of search-and-rescue specialists recounted how appeals to compassion and to participation in the common "brotherhood" of firefighters dismantled barriers between local firefighters and visiting FEMA rescuers. One of the federal rescue specialists involved in the response to the September 11, 2001, attacks explained that a reference to a training experience he had shared with the local leader some years prior to the disaster, and not a specific delineation of technical credentials or federal authority, actually accomplished the trust and closeness needed to include the visiting federal group in the ongoing locally managed response operations.[119] In this case, the local, aggrieved fire chief from New York City needed much more than a simple recitation of technical capabilities to accept a certain group of workers into his tactical and strategic scheme.

119. Santos and Buck, Respondent 6 interview.

He needed to discern an analogical bond (i.e., "I'm a firefighter too . . . Those are my brothers as well"[120]) that consequently generated formal cooperation, emotional solidarity, and an effective dedifferentiation of institutional resources (in this case between local New York firefighters and federal rescuers).

This brief example aims to show merely that utterance helped collapse the familiar into the imaginative so that institutional barriers could be crossed regularly during periods of disaster response. That is, the claim that one is a brother of another, in the absence of genetic connection, is an imaginative claim of the highest order because it draws a forceful picture of reality not immediately apparent in the relationship between the workers as institutional representatives. Fraternity is especially not apparent when the persons in question are not friends in the conventional sense and have no substantial history of interaction. The imaginative claim of brotherhood evoked a pattern of disciplined and intimate interaction not attainable by the usual method of flashing federal qualifications. Among rescue groups, the extreme variability of morale, leadership style, present and former political affiliations, and idiosyncrasies is analogous to the variability among persons composing a faithful community or city, who require gestures of coherence and solidarity during periods of radical instability. Social integration, therefore, at every level of social organization depends upon initiatives that demand intimacy, trust, and (perhaps better) *faith*, as an act that welcomes the presence of the Risen One.

The Church: Alternative Citizenship and Economy

Just as in Oklahoma City, local churches not in the public limelight, especially church-based groups or organizations external to New York City and surrounding suburbs, conceived of humans and collectivities, mapped bodies and their purposes, and measured time differently than the state did. Especially among local churches like the one reviewed in the first section above, offers of forgiveness, prayer, hospitality, and financial assistance to victims in the vicinity of the church served as fundamental praxes and symbols in the recovery process. As in Oklahoma, so in New York, private prayer and prayer vigils were promoted as a seemingly essential characteristic of a postdisaster project of social reorientation. Beyond this, however, churches also rose to the occasion of offering alternative

---

120. Santos and Buck, Respondent 6 interview.

views of American devotion and even of economic interaction. In terms of the latter, the predominant contractualist, administratively heavy, and credit-dependent relations were subverted through gratuitous giving. The difference between the Roman Catholic Church's political vision and that of statist agencies was stark in this respect; for instance, while the state emphasized the importance of patriotism, resilience, and unity at the expense of aiding many poor locals (see below), the Catholic Church openly struggled with placing terrorism on the global agenda ahead of the problem of inequality.[121] In fact, a document issued by Catholic bishops shortly after September 11, 2001, argued that the attacks were partly due to common and far-reaching social inequities; the bishops decided to retain a focus on durable inequalities.[122]

"Above and Beyond this Country"

Data from interviews and print media furnished ample intimations and direct examples of how theological perspectives altered the normal course of economic and political affairs in numerous and scattered instances of social interaction. This distinctive orientation to social existence is reflexive and self-conscious, as one study participant noted in response to the question, "Were there struggles in the congregation with respect to how one should view the perpetrators—should they be forgiven?"

> You won't see [such struggles] with disciples, because we are citizens of something above and beyond this country. If our citizenship is only about a group of people, then we are in trouble. It needs to go beyond that—it needs to be universal.[123]

The alternative frame of reference here for universal citizenship is grounded in something "beyond" the group of human beings itself. Alternative perspectives also arose in other realms of human life. A preacher from Kentucky, one of several who formed a loosely knit alliance of evangelical ministers, delivered financial aid in unusually large quantities after a simple face-to-face encounter, without the commonly expected, cumbersome bureaucratic procedure. Consequently this practice generated tremendous leverage toward the destabilization of predominant norms

---

121. Henneberger, "Cardinal, at Rome Synod."
122. Henneberger, "Social Justice and Terror."
123. Santos, Participant *G1* interview.

for determining trustworthiness. One recipient of two thousand dollars responded, "You don't get that around here much. Being here in New York, you get real cynical." To be sure, the goal, according to the ministers, was to send out a message of "God's love": they signed "Jesus Loves You" on the bottom left-hand corner of each check. The amount given and the informality of the interaction subverted all the expectations of the recipients and introduced alternative views about the potential for human generosity. Recipients were required only to sign their names and to note the amount received on a sheet of paper. In order to be considered for aid, the owner of a business simply had to state a need, or an employee had to avow a need for work. This form of giving produced a sort of moral imperative toward qualitatively different conduct. As one recipient responded after receiving one thousand dollars, "Thank you, I'll *do good things.*"[124] Conversely, a refusal to offer support was equivalent to a rejection of certain behaviors. For example, the ministers gently turned down a tavern owner who sold liquor.

This giving spree, however, also occurred in a liminal phase and did not require a reciprocal engagement or countergift; it did not demand the genesis of new, permanent social relations or binding obligations. Neither did it lead to any institutionalization or organizational form within New York City. It did receive some criticism from Catholic Charities, the workers of which deemed such practices as unprofessional, as opposed to their own, which are based on a "professional social work" model.[125]

Forgiveness, Compassion, and Preaching the Gospel

Appeals for forgiveness toward the perpetrators were ubiquitous in the first two weeks after the attacks. These were overmatched by appeals to focus upon God and communication or relationship with him. Word-count analysis revealed that the term "God" appeared 220 times in 114 total articles: hence God-talk was not sparse. More than half the allusions emanated from clergy, which still left a substantial amount among citizens and political figures. Data revealed that a substantial cross-section of denominations shared similar views on judgment and forgiveness during Sunday worship services. Most remarkably, preachers attempted to reorganize and assert solidarity around God's love and also exhorted the congrega-

124. Wakin, "At Edge of Ground Zero (emphasis added).
125. Ibid.

tion to refrain from making ultimate judgments about the perpetrators, a task which is reserved for God.[126] On the Upper West Side, Rev. Charles Kullman of the Church of St. Paul the Apostle impressed upon the audience the need to grasp that "God's love and our hatred cannot coexist in our hearts. Jesus came to save all sinners, even terrorists."[127]

These appeals were sincere and urgent but occurred simultaneously with mass-mediated productions that intimated war and the necessity of retaliation. Other appeals were muddled in humanistic and civilizational language. Even so, the open preaching of gospel messages circulated symbols of renewed concern for theological topics. Local journalists documented the distribution of over ten thousand Bibles and the newfound freedom with which New Yorkers began to discuss spiritual matters in public.[128] Even so, much of the renewed fervor waned, which some ministers predicted, as they upheld another elementary teaching of most Christian theology; namely, the change of the heart or soul as fundamental to any change of social and political structures.

Considering all the data concerning the practices and discourses that emanated from New York City congregations, one notes that the political imagination of local churches and of others who contributed to public accounts of the situation often embraced gift giving and compassionate presence as subversive to contractarian relations; churches admonished citizens to forgive and give; and churches spearheaded radical forms of hospitality and assistance across cultural barriers without eradicating difference. Hence the seeds of a counterpolitical order were planted but were also subject to challenges of the waning moral effervescence that characterizes a postdisaster period once dominant political and economic institutions seek to reestablish a cultural presence consistent with the status quo ante.

The Nation-State:
The Global Agenda, the Towers, and the Inevitable War

Taken as a whole, the data pertaining to the practices and discourse of statist agencies and public memorial ceremonies endorsed an intrigu-

---

126. Maeder, "All Over City, Healing Sought."

127. Ibid.

128. Rosenberg, "Faith, Tested and Abiding"; Goodstein, "Falwell's Finger-Pointing Inappropriate."

ing global conception of America as the romantic and civic nation par excellence. America was "romantic" in the sense that many viewed it as a "communal totality" that "at once natural and historical gives rise to and morally justifies the sovereign state."[129] In many public performances, this "totality" was construed as the target of the World Trade Center attack. "Civic nationalism" also appears to have played a role insofar as public constructions of unity amid diversity and an emphasis on the virtue of democratic processes elevated notions such as "free polity," "popular will," and "rights" to the stature of symbolic weapons.[130] By virtue of democracy and unity we differentiated ourselves from the so-called terrorists or enemies. All such differentiating characteristics were rendered on a global canvas as the now obvious, ideal social order. That this level of social organization should receive so much attention was almost completely due to the symbolic nature of the attack; even from a disaster-relief standpoint, the imagined community was essential: Giuliani's and Pataki's official tours of the Ground Zero site with congressmen was meant to impress upon the visiting legislators that the target of the attack was "the nation as a whole" and therefore "ought to help pay for" relief.[131]

Kofi Annan, the secretary general of the United Nations seems to have suitably captured this notion in a short piece published in the *New York Times* ten days after the attack. Annan carried this message to all his public appearances, including to the Mass for the victims, at St. Patrick's Cathedral on September 16, 2001, and at numerous other services in mosques and synagogues. The essay bespeaks the attempt at an international compact or community that transcends all social divisions based on race and religion. Interesting is that Annan is quite adamant about convincing his readers that terrorism is not based on religion or national descent, but he does not offer an alternative perspective. He seems to press this specific matter in order to further exhort readers to avoid discriminatory practices. Two points are made quite clearly: an international effort is needed to protect what the terrorists so aptly exploited (our "open, free global system"[132]). The overarching picture is of a universal community focused upon eradicating "enemies" that challenge the social order, which

---

129. Lockwood-O'Donovan, "Timely Conversation," 379.
130. Ibid.
131. Steinhauer, "Giuliani Reports Sharp Increase."
132. Annan, "Fighting Terrorism on a Global Front."

again actually remains undescribed by any articulation and without substance. The actual goal of unity remains unstated and assumed. The only time Annan even mentions a goal in passing, he alludes to Mayor Giuliani's assertion that divisions between and within societies based on region, religion, or "peoplehood" are "exactly what we are fighting here."[133] The unity of September 11, then, is a unity wrought in tragedy and in response to an attack, not one forged in (armed) peacetime or in view of some other mass emergency such as a famine. This is unity unabashedly defined in response to an enemy. The only thing that is unequivocal is the need to fight "terrorism." Giuliani's quoted assertion promotes the notion that America is stoutly against divisions of any kind based on religion, race, or region. The American nation, then, is itself an eradication of all such divisions. The vision apropos of social relations after the attacks, hence, is global and appears to demand the eradication of difference per se; that is, its emphasis on homogeneity sponsors a sort of universal homelessness. This homelessness, in turn, funds a construal of the particular as merely instrumental to the universal mission of the United States government to wrest political order from militarized lawlessness.

Given this amorphous global perspective, two themes and attendant practices appeared to most adequately represent the disciplines of the nation-state as a supposed autonomous realm: (1) glorification of the twin towers, and (2) inevitability of war. Dedifferentiation occurred at a very broad level of social organization, yet in some key respects was dissimilar from such dedifferentiation in Oklahoma City.

The Transcendence of the Towers

The World Trade Center towers have taken on more explicit authority as totemic symbols (as symbols around which a massive amount of social and emotional energy has been dedicated for the sake of social integration) than they likely possessed before their destruction. Even today, various panels stand aloft against the viewing wall surrounding Ground Zero: panels that together articulate the political imagination of the local governing authorities. The panels contain a chronological rendering of the attacks and consequent tragedies that took place on September 11, 2001, in New York City, Washington DC, and Shanksville, Pennsylvania. The panels contain much textual commentary and many photographs

133. Ibid.

featuring buildings, memorial images, and disaster sites. As a product of the Port Authority of New York and New Jersey, and other local-government planning agencies, the panels make a series of interesting political, anthropological, and implicitly theological claims, although this time without ever mentioning God. One of the introductory panels focusing upon the World Trade Center attack offers the heading: "No History is without its Heartache."[134] The panel reads:

> World Trade Center—Now gone, the World Trade Center towers represent something more. Still the dynamic, thriving *soul* of a city—but even more, the enduring strength that will define New York City for centuries to come. (emphasis added)

By designating the towers the "soul" of the city, the authors publicly grant them an irrevocable, defining role in collective identity formation ex post facto. The towers animate the city as a bodily organism; moreover, as the "soul," they are connected to but distinct from the body. One cannot get rid of the soul, in this sense, no matter what has been done to the physical aspects. This overdetermination of the towers' meaning for the narrative identity of a people (this narrative constitutive of identity covers past, present, and future) is open to many different forms of cultural manipulation dependent on metaphors of physical (and soulful) bodies. Similarly, on the panel dedicated to the attack in Washington DC, the Pentagon is characterized as "the core of our nation's democracy and defense." Just as the previous panel, so this panel highlights, using powerfully evocative and familiar terms, that which is most vulnerable and most important. Another panel, titled "Message from the Port Authority of New York and New Jersey," carries some of the same metaphors but introduces a touch of intimacy:

> The World Trade Center was *our vision* and *our home*. We know that although we built the towers, they were not ours alone. They belonged to everyone—those who worked inside their walls, who walked in their shade, who used them as landmarks, and who recognized their significance in the great landscape of New York City and the world as a whole.
>
> Through the investments we make, the jobs we generate, and the infrastructure we develop, we help the region grow. We are

---

134. I copied this quotation and the following extracts from the fence panels at Ground Zero in February 2006.

here so people can succeed, so ideas can be realized, and so communities can thrive. (emphasis added)

The World Trade Center is here the locus of comfort, hope, security, and universal charity. The towers were given to everyone, and everyone could share in their global significance. This enduring significance then lends legitimacy to the agency that constructed it: the Port Authority presents itself as an organizing principle that realizes, as it were, the good for the many. Its contributions are singularly vital to everyone. What all this seems to indicate is that the scale of social organization to which a person qua citizen symbolically attaches herself, and which she even helps to produce, is the same scale of social organization that seeks recompense after violence is done to that citizen: in this case, the nation seeks to address grievances linked to the destruction of the World Trade Center towers.

"You Picked the Wrong City. You Picked the Wrong Country."

Amid the attempts of confessional leaders to temper a hasty move to military retaliation or war, state agencies were forthright in their promotion of military strikes as a response to the attacks on the World Trade Center. Public talk of retaliation occurred concurrently with the highly lauded advent of egalitarian relations and of ostensibly unadulterated unity at the disaster site as well as in televised masses and memorial services. It was all initiated through two declarations by President Bush. First, claiming "the continuing and immediate threat of further attacks on the United States," the president declared a national state of emergency after touring Ground Zero. Second, the president declared war on terror in a session before Congress. Indeed, the inevitability of retaliation became an internalized operating principle of the Bush administration as a whole. A senior administration official claimed that after a White House meeting at which various initiatives connected to education and prescription-drug coverage were discussed, the president claimed that all these issues would "pale" in comparison to the war on terror, which was "the purpose of this administration."[135] Senator Charles E. Schumer, a Democrat from New York, said, "[President Bush] has told me several times that he is staking his entire presidency on this—that the mark of whether he's successful is whether he can succeed in his goal of wiping out terrorism."[136]

135. Bruni, "For President, a Mission."
136. Ibid.

President Bush, however, was certainly not alone in his sentiments. Former president Clinton also declared that the United States should act swiftly to root out terrorism.[137] Even emergency relief legislation was rooted in images of war. Rep. Bill Thomas, a Republican from California and the chairman of the House Ways and Means Committee, asserted in relation to the victims' relief bill (which would offer, among other tax breaks, forgiveness of income taxes for victims of the terrorist attacks): "The package is self-evidently necessary, it is a response to an attack that was tantamount to war."[138]

This emphasis on military response impelled the emergence of a cultural milieu given to the honoring of military personnel. During the analysis of texts, the code "deference to military personnel and other experts" yielded 12 cases. The analysis also revealed adamant statements about inevitable reprisals. At the Yankee Stadium memorial service at which clergy and other confessional leaders spoke and prayed, Adm. Robert Natter, commander in chief of the Atlantic Fleet, delivered this warning: "To our terrorist enemies we say: You picked the wrong city. You picked the wrong country."[139]

Data dealing with the response of New Yorkers suggest that the flood of talk about war and about its necessity captured the popular imagination, but to only some extent. For instance, consider the flag, signed by local American residents and citizens, which was sent to Afghanistan as an "inspirational and emotional memento" to those in combat. Some signed, "For all the victims at the Towers, give them hell."[140] In other cases, inevitability was the bedrock, as it were, upon which doubts were formed: "I've got this sick feeling right here," a paralegal from New York shared "*I knew we had to do this.* We all knew it was coming. But that doesn't make it any easier to think about what we're doing over there, and what the cost is going to be back home."[141] "I'm terrified by what I'm seeing and hearing," a psychological counselor stated. "I cannot foresee a good outcome. It feels like a runaway train. It feels like a new kind of war that doesn't fit any linguistic definition. *But I also see the necessity of taking*

137. Steinhauer, "Giuliani Reports Sharp Increase."
138. Ibid.
139. Heisler, "20,000 Join Hands, Hearts."
140. Ibid.
141. Firestone, "Sunday of Muted Cheers" (emphasis added).

action, although I just can't see an even partially good outcome."[142] Along the same lines, a mother of three, married to a soldier, fearfully said, "*I want the country to be doing this*; part of me wants him to go. The country needs to stand up against terrorism, and the people who go and do that are the military."[143] Another man interviewed by a *New York Times* reporter claimed the following, as he sat in front of a huge American flag:

> Obviously we need to do something, but going and bombing scares me because of what other Muslim countries might do. I think we're right, but they don't like us much over there, and it scares me that they are going to retaliate in this country. Terrorists could strike anywhere, even here in the middle of nowhere; they could strike and people will feel if it happens here, it can happen anywhere. It's psychological warfare.[144]

The mixed feelings toward military operations in Afghanistan revealed deep tensions between the already-embraced ideal of peace between nations and an equally deep-seated requirement for aggressive retaliation that would rehabilitate the sovereign state and the global reputation of the United States as the country that would "rid the world of evil."[145]

The Dedifferentiated Church and State: The Redeemers, the Nation, and the Blessed American Economy

As expected (in contrast to the Oklahoma City bombing), the dedifferentiated cultural interrelations of church and state chiefly sacralized American agents involved with what came to be considered quintessentially godly *and* American practices. Many discourses and practices that constituted this dedifferentiated cultural production were presented above. So this final section will focus on the theopolitical gestures of New York mayor Rudolph Giuliani and U.S. president George W. Bush ("the Redeemers"), and on the sacralization of capitalist and commercial activity. The chapter concludes with a summary of joint church-and-state cultural productions.

142. Ibid (emphasis added).
143. Ibid.
144. Ibid.
145. Perez-Rivas, "Bush Vows."

The Political Theology of Rudolph Giuliani

A word count covering all articles and speeches (114) employed in the study indicated that the name "Giuliani" appeared 90 times, while "government" and its cognates appeared 55 times. That the mayor occupied a powerful symbolic and functional role is thus beyond argument. This section reviews some of his claims and actions that shaped the reconstitution of the political imagination of the social body in New York, with special attention directed toward his farewell speech.

Giuliani's farewell speech represents a quintessential example of statist incursions into church spaces for theopolitical purposes and for shaping narrative assumptions about the nature and destiny of human lives. This speech culminated several months of almost mythic social prestige for Giuliani. In this speech, delivered in St. Paul's Chapel, Giuliani carried out the most explicit theologizing of a statist kind, while fulfilling his Leviathan-like charismatic, spiritual, and redemptive leadership role.

Although initially Giuliani spoke about his general outlook on the city, the majority of his speech focused upon what occurred just after the attacks. With regard to general political goals, Giuliani asserted, "It seemed to me that what I had to do was to totally change the direction and course of New York City. Maybe I was right about that, maybe I was wrong about it. But that's the way I felt I had to operate."[146] With this daunting task in mind, he spoke at length about memorialization and city development, through a spiritual and aesthetic prism not common with many public figures in metropolitan hubs. He also spoke, at various points in the address, of St. Paul's Chapel as a sacrament representing New York City and America. (God was not mentioned.) Before Giuliani addressed the principal matters, he claimed, as a politician-pastor, that his main goal as mayor was to effect a

> change in the spirit of the city. That city that used to be the rotting apple, that 60, 70, 80 percent of the people wanted to leave and nobody wanted to come to, that city now is very strong and it is a confident city. It's a city that has withstood the worst attack of any city in America or in the history of America and people are standing up as tall, as strong and as straight as this church.[147]

146. Giuliani, "Giuliani Talks of City's Spirit."
147. Ibid.

Giuliani argued that the physical structures of the city had to be rebuilt like the "human structures of the city."[148] Despite the fact that Giuliani did not immediately state what this approach entailed, it appears justifiable to infer that his discussion about memorialization and city development amounted to an explication of this perspective. He admonished the audience to view the memorializing and redevelopment process as one that should not focus on economic development but on building a certain memorial structure:

> And it's not going to happen if we just think about it in a very narrow way. How do you replace the offices? And how do you get the jobs? There is plenty of—we can do all that. We've got to think about it from the point of view of a soaring, beautiful memorial. And then if we do that right, if we do that part right, then the economic development will just happen. And millions of people will come here. And you'll have all the economic development you want. And you can do the office space in a lot of different places. And I feel very, very strongly about this. And it is something I'm not going to forget and something I'm going to continue to speak up on because I feel I owe that in a very, very personal way. Thousands of people died there. And hundreds of them died as rescue workers . . . So I really believe we shouldn't think about this site out there right beyond us right here as a site for economic development. I think we should think about it this way: we should think about how we can find the most creative minds possible who love and honor America and can express that in artistic ways that I can't, but they can. And we should think about a soaring, monumental, beautiful memorial that just draws millions of people here that just want to see it and then also want to come here for reading and education and background and research.[149]

Giuliani's approach, as the lengthy quotation indicates, favors a connection between education, nationalism, and inspirational physical forms; in particular, the mayor urged for the development of a memorial of overwhelming aesthetic or mythical proportions. As Giuliani continued, his description of the ideal memorial took on a greater historical and theological shape, yet devoid of specifically Christian or Jewish narrative themes.

148. Ibid.
149. Ibid.

> Long after we are all gone, it's the sacrifice of our patriots and their
> heroism that is going to be what this place is remembered for. This
> is going to be a place that is remembered 100 and 1,000 years
> from now, like the great battlefields of Europe and of the United
> States. And we really have to be able to do with it what they did
> with Normandy or Valley Forge or Bunker Hill or Gettysburg.
> We have to be able to create something here that enshrines this
> forever and that allows people to build on it and grow from it . . .
> [T]his place has to be sanctified. This place has to become a place
> in which when anybody comes here, immediately they're going to
> feel the great power and strength and emotion of what it means
> to be an American.[150]

The memorial site is likened, in this vision, to a site at which loyal patriots
died in battle. This superimposition of sacrifice in battle as a source of
continued life is totemic (in the Durkheimian sense) and also intriguing
to the extent that it ignores the actual level of patriotic loyalty of those
who died. As earlier quotations suggested, from an interview with a firefighter, nationalistic zeal was not high among many firefighters even after
the attacks. Yet Giuliani's speech verbalizes the statist desire to build a
narrative that must live in tension with or even in contradiction to lived
reality and in tension with or in contradiction to the transient character
of even the most loyal citizen, regardless of confession.

Giuliani concludes by invoking St. Paul's Chapel itself as an instrument for the distribution of sacrality:

> The place George Washington prayed when he first became
> President of the United States stood strong, powerful, undaunted,
> at the attacks by these people, who hate what we stand for because
> what we stand for is so much stronger than they are. Well this
> chapel stands for our values and I hope you return here often to
> reflect on what it means to be an American and a New Yorker.

Giuliani, in this closing maneuver, employs this "house of God" as a
touchstone from which sacrality extends to New Yorkers, to objectified
American history, and to Americans proper as divinely approved citizens.
He constructs, in Weberian terms, a this-worldly, nationalistic "asceticism," which was also apparent (in a slightly different form) from the postdisaster ceremonial discourse in Oklahoma City. It is also important to
note the resolute effort to affirm a particular identity for commemorative

150. Ibid.

and rehabilitative purposes, without any reference to being a Christian or to some other theological virtue such as love, peace, gentleness, or patience. Despite being delivered in a church building, Giuliani's farewell address betrays the poetic capacity of the state to turn any sacred object into a space or site at which it re-members the body politic, especially in its concrete geographical and physical embodiment. Indeed the figural anchor for this closing portion of the speech is the personage George Washington, and the first president's own theodevotional activity in the chapel (which some historians claim was quite sparse at best).

As one of many public theopolitical events involving Giuliani, the farewell address demonstrates the viability of studying an institutional alignment under a common, imaginative project that places a premium on a particular character and that allocates bodies across space and time. But more broadly, the actions of allegorical leaders exemplify the porous and dynamic boundaries between the individual and collective, the universal and particular. As Giuliani also remarked, "My strength and energy comes entirely from the people of the City of New York." This assertion adequately rounds out Giuliani's last few months: Almost like Thomas Hobbes in *Leviathan*, Giuliani envisioned himself as corporeally dependent on "the people" as he went about fulfilling his obligations to the dead and the living, carried by a hope to animate all of them with a spirit that he had taken upon himself. More intimately still, he also said on Thanksgiving Day 2001, the only way he could effectively carry out his duties as mayor is if he had a "love affair with the people of New York."[151] This assertion and scores of others like it were heavily publicized and hence provided an emergent register of charismatic discourse, in a pastoral-redemptive key, from which citizens could draw as they sought to enter the national body or, better, the national *life* after the disaster.

Finally, Rudolph Giuliani's speech served an important post–terrorist-attack social process also apparent in Oklahoma City: to establish a predictable arrangement of interaction subsumed under a broad collective interpretation of an ideology, that is, a shared set of beliefs that another group has imposed upon the whole. Even the initial frame placed on the response to violent attack carried significant repercussions for subsequent ritual action and interaction between clergy and officials. For example, what difference would it have made if the immediate interpretation concerning

151. Giuliani, "Giuliani Talks of City's Spirit"; Colangelo, "Rudy Finds Plenty to Be Thankful For."

the September 11, 2001, attacks had been not so roundly concerned with an evil attack on democratic values and freedom but instead had focused on issues of foreign policy, international financial interests, and cultural misunderstanding? This predominant frame for interpreting the violent attacks received nuanced attention in many ritual settings in which ministers and public officials appeared together and, as a result, became a script by which interaction and general relations were established, standardized, and judged. Agreement over this very script presupposes ritual events like that of Mayor Giuliani's farewell ceremony.

The Gospel of President Bush

The presidential administration of George W. Bush contributed heavily to the reconstitution of the political imagination after the terrorist attack. It is difficult, to be sure, to separate Bush's symbolic frame for his war on terrorism from his theopolitics, to whatever extent one reinforces or supplements the other in public performance. It is sufficient, however, to focus upon his speech on the National Day of Prayer and Rememberance: September 14, 2001. It sets the symbolic and imaginative precedence for other speeches.

President Bush's primary contributions to political imagination surrounded the anthropomorphizing of the nation (i.e., treating the nation as a protagonist); this included articulating a national character and its control over historical events. Also, the theological character of Bush's speech posits views about God and prayer yet is conditioned by statist concerns for universal inclusion. Bush spoke at this event, along with Billy Graham, in the National Cathedral in Washington DC.

As Bush delivered his speech, he invoked a corporate entity, apparently subsuming all Americans, with specific intentions and emotions. He declared, "This nation is peaceful, but fierce when stirred to anger," and "Our purpose as a nation is firm."[152] More thoroughly, he also avowed:

> It is said that adversity introduces us to ourselves. This is true of a nation as well. In this trial, we have been reminded, and the world has seen, that our fellow Americans are generous and kind, resourceful and brave. We see our national character in rescuers working past exhaustion; in long lines of blood donors; in thousands of citizens who have asked to work and serve in any way possible. And we have seen our national character in eloquent

152. Bush, "President's Remarks at National Day of Prayer and Remembrance."

acts of sacrifice. Inside the World Trade Center, one man who could have saved himself stayed until the end at the side of his quadriplegic friend.[153]

As became quite common in the ensuing months, a corporate personality was built on the deeds of the deceased heroes, patriots, and victims. As Clinton had in Oklahoma City, Bush summons an interesting rhetorical device: a reminder of the character of an American that may have been somehow forgotten but was in the person all along. One of Bush's more memorable statements was followed by one of his national anthropomorphisms: "This conflict was begun on the timing and terms of others. It will end in a way, and at an hour, of our choosing."[154] These types of statements came to typify a forceful approach to historical control, an outgrowth of a desire to reassert national sovereignty and self-sufficiency.

From the perspective of rebinding the social body, Bush opted for national identity as superordinate in relation to other backgrounds. He actually stated that "national unity" was the unity of "every faith and every background." This sort of unity, then, was more basic, at the narrative level, than faith itself. In the same message, nonetheless, Bush appealed to God

to watch over our nation, and grant us patience and resolve in all that is to come. We pray that He will comfort and console those who now walk in sorrow. We thank Him for each life we now must mourn, and the promise of a life to come.

As we have been assured, neither death nor life, nor angels nor principalities nor powers, nor things present nor things to come, nor height nor depth, can separate us from God's love. May He bless the souls of the departed. May He comfort our own. And may He always guide our country.

God bless America.

Such speech acts, which once again extract scriptural witness from its originary interpretive link to the church, actually constitute a national level of social organization. Various church-based groups, including Christian-based corporations, rallied to extend the symbolic apparatus and narrative that Bush (along with Giuliani) had enacted, which included the inevitable war and positive support of God. This paralleled the more self-initiated actions of Methodist and Baptist pastors in Oklahoma

153. Ibid.
154. Ibid

City. For instance, one largely evangelical national retail chain released the following e-letter to some of its clientele:

> Dear_____,
>
> I saw today on the news that President Bush has openly asked for prayer. How amazing and wonderful that he would do that. It moved me such that I wanted to share that request with everyone we could and in that light, I hope you don't mind "yet another email."
>
> Mindful of the current situation with Iraq, our President has requested the prayers of those he has been called to lead. On behalf of Family Christian Stores and FamilyChristian.com, I would like to encourage you to take time this evening, or in the days ahead, to gather with your household in prayer for the leadership of our nation.
>
> President Bush specifically requests prayer for:
>
> - Wisdom for he and his advisors as he considers leading the effort to disarm Saddam in light of the safety of our people and the peace of the world.
> - The soldiers who are being deployed to be acutely aware of the value of their training, their honor and the appreciation of the American people. May God's strength, help and protection literally dwell with our troops.
> - The leaders of the FBI, the CIA, Homeland Security and the Department of Defense as they follow the President's orders to develop a Terrorist Threat Integration Center that will gather and analyze information about all kinds of threats to America in one place. Pray that God will guide them in the process of making our nation safe from terrorist threats.
> - For our nation, pray that America will realize that it is mightiest when on its knees. May this be the year that America turns back to God.
>
> Thank you for your time and concern. We are grateful that God has placed a man of faith in the White House and we celebrate the freedom we enjoy in America to pray openly. May God continue to bless America.
>
> An American and Brother in Christ,
>
> Dave Browne
> President & CEO
> Family Christian Stores[155]

155. As I recall, this form e-mail was sent to consumers enrolled in Family Christian Stores' Pastor's Perks and Family Perks Program in January 2003.

It is patent that, in this postdisaster period, theological engagement of some sort confronted most persons, challenging the privatization of faith. Yet at the same time, this e-mail message came as one practical and discursive package among many, including to some who sharply disagreed with fundamental elements of the presidential response. Most decisive in a milieu rich with hermeneutic schemes is the nation-state's aim to create a unified whole abstracted from citizens' actions with one another in light of specific collective goods. While this abstraction is the proper reference point for all universal utterances, it is not the proper reference point for agendas of victory or glory. Nationalism often engages in great deception and self-deception through its "emaciated piety that is insufficiently specific and embodied."[156] This lack of specificity goes unrecognized because, as many of the postdisaster speeches argued, the American citizen is assured of right standing in the world and before God, and sufficient justification of the fact appears in the form of "our heroes," in official rhetoric of resolve and optimism, and in divine approbation, regardless of abundant doubts and questions among the citizenry. The lack of specificity, moreover, serves the project of population surveillance and territorial legibility, which reduces citizens to units of production and compliance. As Ernest Gellner put it:

> the basic deception and self-deception practiced by nationalism is this: nationalism is, essentially, the general imposition of a high culture on society, where previously low cultures had taken up the lives of the majority, and in some cases the totality, of the population. It means that generalized diffusion of a school-mediated, academy-supervised idiom, codified for the requirements of reasonably precise bureaucratic and technological communication. It is the establishment of anonymous, impersonal society, with mutually substitutable atomized individuals, held together above all by a shared culture of this kind, in place of a previous complex structure of local groups.[157]

The *ascesis*, therefore, that the state requires of the citizenry appears to be uncritical and superficial and quite detached from the veritable skills and practices that many citizens have themselves devised at the local level in response to concretely felt or perceived needs.[158] From a cultural-ecclesial

156. Pinches, "Stout, Hauerwas, and the Body of America," 9.

157. Gellner, *Nations and Nationalism*, 56.

158. The volume *Christianity, Democracy, and the Radical Ordinary*, by Stanley

perspective, the question remains the same: does the congregation facilitate the robust claims making and *poiesis* of the state, or does it redirect cultural politics through its own *praxis* or discipleship practices that mold character toward some good in the context of a graced church body?[159]

Capital and Commerce as Sacralization Tools

One of the more confusing and intriguing aspects of the spatial and practical demarcation of holiness as they related to the molding of theopolitics at the World Trade Center site involved commercial and profit-driven activity. Stated plainly, while signs on the viewing fence surrounding the site prohibit the sale of items and the donation of funds, only about two hundred feet away, heavy commercialization and commoditization is being practiced within St. Paul's Chapel. Here a small gift shop (basically comprising a glass counter with interior displays and racks) lies about fifteen feet to the left of the altar. This arrangement appears to convey at least a minor measure of social confusion and conflict. Incorporating the view of institutional dedifferentiation, however, opens two avenues for exploration. First, the admixture of commercialized experience with remembrance of sacrifice is facile given tourist-industry expectations; given the cluttered and compacted spatial arrangement of retail stores, homes, and offices in Manhattan; and the powerful narrative background of Christ's sacrifice contained in virtually all things Christian. Within these cultural and physical contexts, market activity became a benchmark for regulating sacrality at particular points of uncertainty after the attack. In the first three weeks, for example, dedication to work and commerce signified loyalty to the American nation-state's "way of life" and defiance to the terrorists "out there" who were responsible for the attack. By the end of 2001, however, viewing the attack site as an impetus for economic redevelopment was deemphasized at Giuliani's farewell speech, and signs placed on the fence just outside Ground Zero discouraged the sale of any items and the solicitation of funds.

Second, St. Paul's Chapel, it seems, was exempt from such official attempts at curbing economic activity. Macrolevel or broad collective

---

Hauerwas and Romand Coles, which opens the series Theopolitical Visions (a series that includes this book), convincingly portrays the products of ingenuity and attentiveness arising from many citizen-led, grassroots organizations.

159. I am indebted to Peter M. Candler's discussion of *poiesis* and *praxis* in "Tolkien or Nietzsche: Philology and Nihilism," 7.

imaginings of free market capitalism were, essentially, granted a quasi-ontological primacy while commercial activity in the city was used as a tool for gauging public sacredness. St. Paul's Chapel, already called a house of God, could offer disaster commodities without public censure. Why? Theological legitimacy extended to the production of retail goods that promoted a particular politics and theology in line with the prevailing statist project of renewal.

Indeed the institutional models of life presented for commercial consumption after disasters imaginatively framed social relations in some manner—that is, they supported the cultivation of a particular kind of person. After the disaster at the World Trade Center, for instance, a person's unyielding dedication to carrying out occupational duties or tasks (especially if they were for a multinational corporation) promoted the American ideals of freedom and prosperity for the national body. Those who worked on or near Wall Street were resolute about their duty the Monday after the attack: "I'm ready to go to work. I really see this as a patriotic duty," affirmed a New York Stock Exchange (NYSE) employee of fourteen years. "It's important for Americans to know we will continue to function as a free market economy. The NYSE is a global symbol."[160] Also, said Cynthia Driskill, chief executive of CDG & Associates, a Dallas-based consulting firm: "The terrorists targeted *the fabric of our society* through our businesses. If we stop business, then we're giving them what they tried to achieve. We're not going to do that."[161]

Second, and more essential at this point, a crucial Weberian theme emerged that ought to receive more attention in future disaster studies: what Marcel Henaff designates as "the opposition between generous relations—acts of gift exchange—and profitable relations, i.e. market activity."[162] This issue, remarkably, raises numerous related questions tied to theology and the welfare state. The generosity of volunteer work and selfless heroism at the attack site was construed as evidence of God's tremendous grace, which in turn was meant to epitomize American character. It seems, then, that any hostility between relations of generosity or gift giving, on the one hand, and market relations, on the other, was sublimated under the harmonic nation-state facing a disaster. So, what

160. Associated Press, "New Yorkers Return to Work."
161. Associated Press, "Business Leaders Driven by Patriotism"; emphasis added.
162. Henaff, "Religious Ethics, Gift Exchange and Capitalism," 306.

Max Weber described as distinct forms of social relations (the predominantly Catholic ethic of fraternity, on the one hand, and the perennially Protestant and individualist "worldly asceticism"[163] on the other hand) were interwoven in practice, and newly hailed within a different scale and nature of social organization, satisfied with its own justified means and ends. In fact, the new nature and scale of social organization was purportedly the only scale of social organization that could deal with a disaster of this sort: the nation-state and its disciplines and technologies of identity. The nation-state managed to effectively create a storyline to which most cultural production conformed, in that an unmistakably simple ethos circulated through social groups and persons: an ethos that conveyed a reconciled sphere of gift giving and market transaction and admitted no contradiction.

Bonds of Church and State

As this chapter has demonstrated, the dedifferentiation of church and state was formidable after the World Trade Center disaster, and depended upon the formation of certain mass-mediated cultural gestures. Among these were the cultivation of the spiritual soldier (the soldier at prayer), the speech acts of Mayor Giuliani in St. Paul's Chapel, and the commodities sold to those visiting New York. Data further revealed that the symbolic and affective bond between church and state was itself nearly institutionalized. Dedifferentiation actually crystallized into a very interesting alliance of governmental and theological interests and practices. Despite some vagaries, this alliance emerged in specific and noteworthy forms in New York City after the attack. Bronx borough president Fernando Ferrar appointed Rev. Raymond Rivera chair of the chaplain's office, an officially recognized post of borough governance.[164] The office is to identify noncompensated chaplains from a variety of faiths, who will assist the community in the event of a crisis like that of September 11, 2001, or of a smaller scale. The September 11 attacks served as the impetus for creating a chaplain's office; in particular, it was the cumulative efforts of clergy that inspired Rivera to put together a proposal, to which the mayor agreed.[165] Interestingly, the proposal makes no mention of explicit

---

163. Weber, *Protestant Ethic and the Spirit of Capitalism*, 149.

164. Weil, "Ferrer Has Faith in Clergy Office."

165. Ibid.

practices; the post of chair is viewed through the lenses of public service. All the same, the idiom "keep the faith," used in the first line of the article that covers this appointment, suggests a theologically oriented act on the part of the borough president.[166] That is, the president's institution of the chaplaincy is an act of faith (presumably in God, although God is left unnamed in the article).

One of the most important ritual enactments and modelings of state-and-church dedifferentiation was also discernible in the response of priests to important speeches. After Giuliani's farewell ceremony, a priest from the Anglican tradition made a string of remarkable comments about Giuliani's speech on a video produced by St. Paul's Chapel:

> He used the word *soar* over and over again—*soar* is a spiritual word. Let your spirits soar [Image of statue of liberty with flag appears on screen.] The word *soar* is a spiritual word. "May you soar into the heavenly kingdom" [gestures upwards with his hands]. "Soar on wings like eagles." All that fits.[167]

Although Giuliani's use of the term *soar* was not central to the speech reviewed above, this interpretive evaluation highlights the favorable and formidable public alliance formed between a number of churches and the mayor. Whether this alliance was public insofar as it primarily consisted in planning and discussion concerning postdisaster ritual events, in reputation and image management, or in other matters of policy agreement is not as relevant as what the alliance produced (in terms of citizenship, ecclesial life, and governmental responsibility) within the persons and groups who witnessed such a relationship. To borrow Graham Ward's approach to cultural hermeneutics, the burgeoning commentary on Mayor Giuliani's words and actions can be said to have effected the transition from Giuliani's self-production to the invention of a culture and historical position by other people.[168]

---

166. Ibid.

167. Brubaker, et al., *Ground Zero Spirituality at Saint Paul's Chapel.*

168. Ward, *Cultural Transformation*, 31. Ward actually makes an almost-identical observation about the veritable plethora of experts and secondary writings simply bearing upon the work of Karl Barth.

REFLECTIONS FOR ECCLESIAL PRAXIS

The foregoing analysis of cultural politics about the September 11, 2001, attack in New York City demonstrates the parity of imaginative scope between ecclesial and statist projects centered upon the reassertion of basic assumptions about human nature and destiny. From within a matrix of power relations that implicate the life of all congregations into a wider and putatively uncontrollable set of cultural processes, ecclesial bodies are tested in their ability to "pay close attention [themselves] and [their] teaching." (1 Tim 4:16), lest they enter unprepared the bewildering fray of discursive and bodily disciplines joining patriotism, stardom, sacrifice, grief, and redemption—detached from any clear, overriding good, which ultimately is the God of Israel, the God of the Risen One. In this challenging context, the *leitorgia* of some clergy involved participation in constructing public accounts of the situation that relied on patriotic, celebratory processions and the execution of memorials in the honored presence of public officials. In this way and others, the churches played an important role in the nationalization of local places, symbols, and persons. In reestablishing social disciplines after disaster, the state employed an apparatus of security dependent upon a theology that assures victory, advances a vision of an uncontestable or primordial unity, and insists on valuing institutional competence or expertise (economic competence, e.g.). Through the pastoral politics of Rudy Giuliani and the blood of "patriotic firefighters," the body politic was provided a basis for civic gratitude, and hence were provided the vulnerability or openness-in-wonder that is a condition for assimilating a reconstructive discourse. These figures, which also included police officers and volunteers, gathered in a string of seemingly endless funeral services in scores of church buildings and in doing so set forth ethical standards, built public memory, linked individuals to the nation, and developed a particular view of God and humans. In not simply depending on "civil religion"—its own sites, norms, and terms of God's role in the city's and nation's (now coextensive) fate—the state was able to more forcefully develop an *image* of full social integration across all classes, ethnic groups, and even "civilized" or free nations. This image was built around themes that in actuality only attain to some coherence in the life of the Church, incorporating the weak and strong, poor and rich, and those of all nations who have been added to the Body of Christ, not through an assumed universal optimism (despite serious doubt) and ability to successfully retaliate to threat, but in the blood of the only true victim that reveals our abased, scarred nature in a world that God is making new. The action and presence of the Crucified and Risen Christ in a new creation is a narrative that applies equally to large influential churches that are able to generate and distribute considerable cultural objects (ideas, physical artifacts, programs, etc.) for surrounding communities and to others more focused on local needs without engaging the implications of the actions of larger, "publicly authorized" churches. The smaller churches as a whole did not, in their avoidance of nationalistic matters, contribute any countervailing, coherent counter-narrative able to call the larger churches to give an account of their making or mis-making. These large churches in New York were much more resolute in their blending of local, national, and theological themes and hence required a decisive counterwisdom.

This counter-wisdom is all the more vital in light of the unsettling conflict between the seemingly endless recitation of victory stories relayed by statist agents and the extensive doubt and confusion among New Yorkers about the United States' global status; all such citizens were compelled to deal with the confusing array of discursive constructions aimed at social binding (some emphasizing humanity, others spirituality, and still others national pride or capitalist prowess) through reliance on some concrete, familiar relations and institutional leaders that ensconced god-talk into recovery discourses.

In contrast, the disciplines of the assembly of saints are those that engage a sort of *ontological* depth; they define what is *being* in the presence of God and not simply "talking" to or about God, understood in the Kierkegaardian sense as a word, gesture, or activity that crowds out, muzzles, or disregards God's presence—regardless of how often "God" and correlate themes are mentioned in a festive or somber key. God's reign through the Risen One incites the destruction of such "god-talk" because the kingdom is not demonstrated in "idle talk" or any particular patterns of consumption, but in power and in the "righteousness, peace, and joy in the Holy Spirit."[169] The New Yorkers whose disquieting comments betray a lack of inner cultivation of power and peace in the body politic were abruptly, violently, and tragically awakened to the sad state

---

169. This claim melds the content of two passages of Scripture: 1 Cor 4:20 and Rom 14:17.

of our "cosmopolitanism." We think we know about the world and its nations—the human members of the earth—and the privileged position we share as those that steer or guide the course of its life, but we in fact don't *know* these 'others' because we have not delighted in them, as the Father has in sending his Son in glorious weakness. A congregation not schooled to deal with divisions or bitter roots of its own as part of its on-going collective life will be absorbed into the state's narrative enactments in national or international conflicts. Statist pretensions and grandeur fill the void of local practices of forgiveness because nothing else seems plausible or feasible. Thus, the best alternative in the case of disaster response turns out to be some version of territorial exclusion akin to many criminal justice policies of the neoliberal city. These policies favor an account of community health as dependent on the refined ability to identify a stranger who must be promptly questioned and, if necessary, excluded. Evangelism (as in catechetical instruction in the context of friendship) and outreach is an authoritative antithesis to such a strategy: it can embolden an otherwise insular citizen-consumer to initiate rela-tionships with 'the other' that disrupts the routine activities and social bonds that prevent activity in solidarity with those from another class, ethnic background, neighborhood, or nation. Consumption is likewise redirected to the degree that goods may circulate through the citizen *for the sake of others* with whom the disciple of Jesus seeks a divine bond of friendship. This practice, along with baptism and Eucharist, challenge the greater creational division that divine eschatological action seeks to remedy: heaven and earth must serve in mutuality in God's reign. While the church is concerned with touching, hearing, and understanding *in vivo*—a movement of bodies in love—in embrace, singing, or service, the action of the nation-state's universal project needs celebrities, threats, posters, and parasitic relations with the particular. Jackson states it best in his rhetorical and textual analysis of the public language of counter-terrorism following the attacks of September 11, 2001: "[o]ne of the most noticeable and ubiquitous features of the language of counter-terrorism is its invariable appeal to identity . . . the clear implication of this language is that identity rather than deliberation is the basis of human action."[170] Interpreted in Christian terms, the response to attack that must be resisted is one of unequivocal assurance in personal integrity and sacred approval

---

170. Jackson, *Writing the War on Terror*, 59.

that consequently precludes the logic of love—the possibility of friendship or of the expansion of God's reign in each potential interaction.

Indeed, the concomitant conferral of a sacralized identity and de-emphasis on communicative encounters centered on humility and wise speech, which in theological terms must emphasize a bodily presence, brings us to a final consideration of how *personal* the state really is in terms of both its negative and constructive role in the creation of a postdisaster political order and, more specifically, a particular human being. The state's surety in building up the sacred American citizen to whom universal assent is deemed self-evident runs counter to what, in a Kierkegaardian paradox, could be understood as the meek and "unsettled decisiveness" of the disciple of Jesus. More elaborately, the disciple of Jesus is always *becoming* faithful; she is always on the way, as a pilgrim seeking to be received. To the degree that the gospels are read in the presence of Jesus as a contemporary (another key theme in several of Kierkegaard's writings) is a disciple always on the way to Jerusalem. The disciple faces the cross at each Eucharist and in baptism, confronted again with the decision of whether to join the evaders, judges, and cowards—of whether to send Jesus to his death. National identity, pride or anger cannot bring this journey to a halt until God's eschatological initiative settles the accounts of the nations. This is the quality of the gospels that haunts and frees, judges and cleanses: our *life or being in it*. This journey is necessary because of the changefulness or fickleness of human beings. This journey or carrying on "in the way" is also necessary, as Kierkegaard contends near the end of *Practice in Christianity*, because the church can only speak the truth if it understands that "to *be* the truth is the only true explanation of what truth is."[171] The Church Militant, in order to avoid proclaiming itself as already triumphant and in possession of truth as something preeminently *known*, can only *be* in truth by going along the way of Christ—by the actuality of suffering. Put simply, the persons that compose the church cannot revel in triumph because they have come to know the truth as vital lessons or "information" assimilated and retained, or have rightly judged the *results* of Christ's life and the subsequent centuries of theological reflection as indisputably good. Ultimate celebration only comes to a people that, as if starting from the very beginning with Christ, are "willing to be developed in like manner, to be tried,

171. Kierkegaard, *Practice in Christianity*, 205, 212.

to battle, to suffer as did the one who acquired truth" for them.[172] The love for nation, therefore, which translates into resentment or distrust toward a given enemy, no doubt a substantial test for each citizen in a period of disaster, requires the counter-action of the Spirit who Christ pours out and who enables us to love others and marvel in God (Acts 2). This speech of wonder and praise subverts the discourse of bombast and is capable of ringing out among those of every nation because rather than establishing "our" love on the foundation of hatred, suspicion, or ignorance toward "them," love for the other is set against enmity toward the sin in *the Christian* that occasioned the suffering of Christ, the Risen Other (see Acts 2:33–38).

Another paradox applies to the universal magnitude or "grandeur" of the state's claims inasmuch as they occlude Christ's words about the significance of the insignificant. There is nothing that so disarms us (or summons mechanisms of evasion) as the little and the "insignificant," including the poor, the disabled, the child, and even "the lily and the birds." It is precisely to these that Jesus points as a sure cause of the disclosure of the "thoughts of the heart" and a chief reason why Jesus must be, contrary to statist appropriations (or expropriations) of "religion," an object of faith or a sign of offense.[173] Can the grandeur or scope of the nation-state as it currently operates ever be commensurate with these words of Jesus: "let the little children come to me, and do not stop them; for it is to such as these that the kingdom of God belongs" (Luke 18:16)? What epistemological-political framework guiding a postmodern and postindustrial nation bent on defeating terrorism is able to incorporate or engender the practices that make political orders face their own weakness in the disabled, and thus receive gifts from them, and direct sufficient attention to children so as to point them to a place of blessedness. Kierkegaard, in an address entitled, *The Lily in the Field and the Bird of the Air,* painstakingly highlights how the "infinite qualitative difference" between humans and God must occasion and vouchsafe the importance of *silence*. In disdain, Kierkegaard notes how the infinite and the temporal remain apart in the lives of many human beings precisely because we cannot keep quiet when we suffer.[174] Our mimetic efforts must thereby be directed at the "trees . . .

---

172. Ibid., 203.

173. Ibid., 126.

174. Kierkegaard, "Lily in the Field," 336.

in the thickest growth," the lily, or the bird "that is silent and suffers."[175] Due to its incapacity in relation to speech, the bird "exempts itself" from those speech-acts that make "the suffering worse than suffering, into the sin of impatience and sadness."[176] As a sign against the all-too-human tendency to "[accuse] God and humanity in suffering," the bird cannot supplant listening to (or depending upon) God with a gripe, threat, demand, or agenda.[177] Because incessant speaking makes the suffering indefinite and quells the hope of acquiring wisdom from God's Word and living creatures, it is no surprise that the political consequences of such ignorance is the formation of peoples that instrumentalize and intensify their sufferings by making them the basis of a claim against another without regard for the presence and work of the Triune God. Assuredly, the Father knows the sufferings of all and embodies them in the Son in order that suffering will effect self-giving service and bold love, not accusation and brazen claims-making.

175. Ibid.
176. Ibid., 337.
177. Ibid.

CHAPTER 4

Hurricane Katrina:
"I Am Not a Refugee . . . I Am a Survivor"

The Churches of New Orleans

According to the National Religious Identification Survey of 2001 (NRSI), Baptists (35 percent) and Roman Catholics (28 percent) laid claim to the two largest numbers of confessional adherents in Louisiana. In the city of New Orleans, Roman Catholics constitute the largest denomination in terms of membership, with Baptists closely following. Due to some appreciable population shifts (e.g., the Mexican population's increase is mainly attributable to the influx of migrant construction workers[1]) and a large number of church closings and moves, most figures collected before 2005 (and since then, including the Pew Forum's Landscape Survey released in February 2008) must be accepted as provisional until newer figures are generated some years from now. Of considerable interest, along these lines, is the extent to which the African American population, which made up about 64 percent of the total population of New Orleans[2] before the hurricane, was geographically displaced and politically destabilized. Significantly, the NRSI study confirmed the findings of the Pew study pertaining to the increase in survey participants who chose the category "No Religion" as an option. Furthermore, in Louisiana, this category represented the largest number of "confessional adherents" after Roman Catholics and Baptists. That is, more residents chose this option than those who identified themselves with any other mainline, evangelical, Jewish, Muslim, or "other" confessional group. As in many

1. Fletcher, et al., "Latino Workers and Human Rights," 108–10.
2. U.S. Census Bureau, 2000.

other states for which this pattern also obtains—that is, two or three denominations compose the majority of confessional adherents while those of "No Religion" assume the next-largest group—a major drop-off of affiliation or active involvement beyond the prevailing two denominations is apparent. But the implications are not altogether straightforward. The United Methodist Church, although certainly not a major presence in terms of sheer numbers, operates a well-established disaster-response agency using resources and financial backing attained from congregations that span all regions of the United States. This appears to be the case with most mainline Protestant denominations with congregations in New Orleans. With respect to upstart congregations, independent Bible churches, or even sizable, locally prominent groups with an insubstantial interstate social network, a disaster of this magnitude is capable of completely eradicating a confessional group. Therefore, the "No Religion" category of participants represent a group worthy of consideration insofar as a noncommittal or ostensibly neutral attitude with respect to religious devotion, in light of the cultural and theological assumptions advanced here, places a citizen squarely in the illusory civil space that is dominated by the state and capitalist consumptive practices. Most New Age spiritualities, following a similar tack, disregard the political implications of so-called self-realization or self-discovery or positive thinking; most often, such programs have only minor or derivative influence on the way an adherent thinks of politics or public cultural processes because of the often extremely abstract self-referentiality of their technologies of the self. The basic upshot of these demographic figures for ecclesial self-understanding and faithful (united) action is that if such a large number of neighbors are truly of "No Religion" (which is distinct from "undecided" or "refused to answer"), then the communion that is meant to characterize the fellowship of Jesus's disciples is faced with another popular tendency that questions precisely what the church is politically: a common union that traverses private/public boundaries and insists upon living in and with the Resurrected One, not simply *the teachings* of the Resurrected One.[3]

3. See Kierkegaard, *Practice in Christianity*, 123, 127–29. In the process of making a case for the necessity of indirect communication with respect to Christ—because as the God-man he embodies a contradiction that suspends human understanding and demands a decision of faith or rejection—Kierkegaard emphatically claims that in Christianity the teacher is more important than the teachings. Indeed, the communicator must live *in* what is communicated. It is not possible without doing violence to Christianity to simply speculate about the unity of God and humanity in Christ or to simultaneously

This further elicits questions about the consistency of a given congregational member's involvement with worship in the body of Christ and how this involvement contributes to a desire for the actual presence of the Word in the day-to-day life of Christians and of those whom they serve. This actuality, if you will, of the body and the Word that is Christ, is the church's proper mode of participation within a world subject to great trauma. Actualization of the Word made flesh in the life of the church demonstrates how judgment and compassion, mercy and wrath, and even humility and courage, cannot be understood as mutually exclusive moral categories but as fundamental components of the dynamic life of God's pilgrim people as they live between curse and promise.

DISASTER RESPONSE

The Labor Day weekend of 2005 will perhaps forever signify a gamut of emotionally charged recollections involving pain, misery, relief, joy, and anger for a large number of Louisianans. Hurricane Katrina was not the "perfect storm" in terms of magnitude or force, but the towns and cities which it struck had less-than-desirable topographical qualities and (as became obvious in the case of New Orleans) suffered from years of government inefficacy (via jurisdictional disagreements) or inactivity with respect to key infrastructural projects, including levee construction, maintenance, and assessment. Storm surges from Hurricane Katrina destroyed towns on the coast of Louisiana and Mississippi and flooded New Orleans East. Levee breaches along the southern edge of Lake Pontchatrain ensured the flooding of most parts of the rest of the city. Numerous levees were built with poor-quality materials or were not correctly installed; some levee structures were actually lifted off of their mounts by water that traveled underneath them, causing massive amounts of water to rush into homes just beyond the levee walls.

This was a weekend during and after which the hopes, prejudices, strengths and weaknesses of American confessional communities and political systems were exposed in most unsettling circumstances. While New Orleans received most of the televised attention from the major

take Christ's teachings and reject Christ. Hence, I would claim that confronting Christ's words always entails confronting Christ himself, who, as the sign of offense or the object of faith, necessitates the exposure of the heart before the God-man. This makes clear that the political existence of the church goes beyond conceptual or theoretical understanding and places it squarely in the realm of encounter, dialogue, discernment, and love.

networks due to the botched large-scale evacuation, inadequate provision of goods to evacuees at the Superdome, and other visually appalling cases of suffering, abandonment, and confusion, many smaller towns along the Gulf Coast, in most of which lived residents of considerable poverty as well, were disregarded at the national level. News coverage of the disaster, then, proved yet again that the "newsworthy" is the sensational or extreme, especially when the object of attention is a break-of-bulk city of major economic and cultural importance to the United States.[4] In the hierarchical arrangement or social stratification arising from capitalist differentiation of city and hinterlands, and the (wrongly) assumed lopsided cultural innovation that follows from this split, cities (and hence citizens) become the objects of varying degrees of televised attention because news-related scrutiny is itself implicated in the process of profit maximization and in the construction of spectacle.

Still, it became evident in the weeks that followed the disaster that most local, state, and federal governmental agencies remained apprehensive about the very matters that furnished the conditions for destruction: government valuations of economic vitality in terms of property value; taxes; and actual human worth, often based on numerical indicators and other statistical or probability-based evaluations, along with suspicions rooted in New Orleans's poor political reputation. In the meantime, nonprofit and confessional relief groups, some of which possessed no credentials or accreditations for social recognition in a broader field of expertise or vocation, entered the city and conducted the majority of debris cleanup and initial rebuilding.

Although not as expansive as previous chapters, this analysis of the postdisaster period after Hurricane Katrina explores a number of cultural political processes that roughly parallel those that emerged after the Oklahoma City bombing and the September 11, 2001, attack in New York City. However, while overlap is crucial for the sake of generating insights that encompass all three occasions, the case of New Orleans introduces a few matters at the intersection of sociology, politics, and theology that are quite peculiar to it. Therefore, this chapter serves as a bridge to the final, more theoretical and theologically driven chapters, in that it begins

---

4. A break-of-bulk location is where a particular good is turned over from one mode of transportation to another; say, from ship to truck. A good, or "the bulk," at this location may also be stored or processed in some way to make the next phase of transportation more affordable.

to draw together and devotes more space to some of the key political and theological problems to which we granted less concentration in the previous two chapters.

To be specific, this chapter examines, with ministerial responses and interpretations in mind, the promise of an ecclesial hermeneutic of judgment. This initial section treats the speech acts and conduct of clergy in relation to the task of rebuilding entire communities, and clergy's critique of official statements concerning God's judgment. The second section lays out some aspects of the challenge of displacement and abandonment for Katrina survivors, and this time situates the theme of God's judgment within an emergent theology of the neighbor, which guided ecclesial response after Hurricane Katrina. This emergent theology became possible when congregations decided to circumvent bureaucratic and administrative structures designed to coordinate relief activities. Finally, the material in this chapter that focuses upon the political imaginary of the state identifies the rationale and ultimate shortcomings of governmental discourse and practice. I address three phenomena in particular: the militarized, command-and-control response that placed a premium on hierarchical relations and the urban-renewal plans that explicitly or implicitly opposed the resettlement of poor New Orleanians. The second topic directs critical attention to another concern: the state's subordination to capitalist-class interests—the preponderance of which, indeed, had already debilitated community relations between classes to the point that New Orleans residents who lived a mere five blocks from one another never interacted or took up mutual concerns, and hence failed to assemble a much-needed social movement to affirmatively promote citizen dialogue with the state. These urban-renewal plans further underscore the epistemological shortcomings, grounded in ontological fears (i.e., honest admissions of what statist plans assume about human beings), of governmental modes of viewing and handling mass emergencies. As the friend/foe motif finds less currency in the context of so-called natural disasters, a more creational orientation is the required hermeneutic task for members of any given congregation. Additionally, the absence of a foreign people (whether internal or external to the United States) to label and castigate actually reveals the overwrought and fragmented control embodied in the state's operations in the realm of individual and community welfare, and in intragovernmental relations.

Clergy, Churches, and the Question of Governmental Response

One cannot overestimate the crucial role of the Roman Catholic Church in the hybridized cultural forms of New Orleans, most vividly witnessed in the jazz-infused and creolized funeral processions and worship services in the city. In a fascinating juxtaposition, the St. Louis Cathedral, which held its first Mass after the hurricane on October 2, 2005, is located near the heart of the famed French Quarter. Within only a few blocks of the grand building, rows of exotic nightclubs and bars host the throng of partygoers during any given week and especially on festival (e.g., Mardi Gras) occasions. Indeed, as one local writer notes, "after the famed and raucous Mardi Gras celebration, many penitents head to the cathedral to receive ashes on Ash Wednesday."[5] Hardly a reflection of sincere faithfulness, this practice did not mitigate the assertions of archbishop Alfred Hughes, propounding the existentially indispensable nature of the cathedral: "This is indeed an historic moment in the life—not only in the church of New Orleans but in the whole city . . . The structure which harbors the soul of our city has come back to life. . .Thanks be to God."[6] Along with framing the cathedral as the generative or animating element of the physical city, the Reverend William Maestri added: "The St. Louis Cathedral is a symbol that really unites all of our city, and this is what we're going to need to move forward."[7] A visitor, in like terms, deemed the cathedral the "heart and soul" of the city and as the point of origin for rebuilding.

These statements at the first Mass after the hurricane pointed toward the pivotal role of local and external church bodies after the hurricane as potential fonts of life from which the city could receive renewal with each new interaction, encounter, and relationship. Statements likening a church to a blood-pumping organ, or deeming it a haven of souls, and an origination point, however, are mere artifice if not carried into a collective demonstration of discipleship and active engagement with the anguish, despair, and doubt that pervades citizen life after a disaster. As previous chapters have shown, this engagement necessarily involves a pastoral-political hermeneutic, often revealed (and even constructed)

5. Forliti, "St. Louis Cathedral Holds Mass."
6. Ibid.
7. Ibid.

in its various dimensions in the link among sermonic statements; public actions of resistance, compassion, or courage; and pastoral care.

Of the many ministerial evaluations or interpretations offered, this section handles only those themes that bear upon God's role as judge in the hurricane and how this bears upon ecclesial life. This debate over to what degree (and how) the hurricane was an act of divine judgment invites concerns about the destructive potential of the created order, the disaster as a potential spring of redemptive social change, and theological evaluations of governmental response in view of effective ecclesial practices of relief and recovery.

GOD'S JUDGMENT AND THE LIFE OF THE CHURCH

After offering (as a gesture of solidarity in a shared destiny) that the statue of Jesus Christ (which had lost a thumb and forefinger during the hurricane) would not be repaired until the recovery of New Orleans is completed, Archbishop Hughes tackled the question of divine judgment. Hughes insisted that the hurricane was not sent as divine retribution against sinners. Hughes, particularly, claimed that: "God tolerates evil in order that we may ultimately realize a greater good."[8] Hughes attests that evil persists as God's mercy and patience advances the good of the reign of his Son, before the promised resurrection and the final reconciliation of the nations. Maybe, he added, New Orleans would rebuild as a community with a more cohesive moral outlook, a community spared of racial enmity and pervasive hedonism. Another minister active in disaster response, relief, and recovery efforts, and associated with a mainline Protestant denomination (participant *M1*), likewise sought to distance God from the morbid and extensive damage wrought by the hurricane. He identified the centerpiece of his reflection about the disaster as the

> idea of God's providence or God's care and presence; God did not do this to us. Some thought that God was punishing us—There is a popular religious conception that everything that happens, God sends it. But when [a hurricane] occurs, it does not fit—[this view] is Sunday-school oriented, because we haven't been given the language to understand. It is part of living in a human world and a world with nature—a world that is filled with natural tragedy and disasters. So, we learned to see that God's presence is what helps

8. Ibid.

us cope with life and it's not about God doing these things to us. It gave us an occasion to think about how God acts and how suffering comes—that is, what is God's response to suffering rather than why has God caused this suffering. There were many conversations about this—it invited us to do this in terms of sermons and in terms of pastoral care. We invited congregation and community to ask where have you seen God at work—the compassion of church members, of outsiders, and not, "Oh, God is coming after us."[9]

Later, he further asserted,

Out of creation there is going to evolve disasters and tragedy; we are going to impact this world and cause some disaster. But this is an alternative to the view that God is out to get us. In the midst of this, God is out to show us his presence, we see it in submission, in caring, and all other things that get us through the tragedy.[10]

In this minister's view, it was important to perceive the situation as one in which "God was with us in the suffering" and inviting survivors to relationship in suffering, so that once established in that mode of living, they would perpetually reach out to one another. Assuredly, as this participant claimed in more ecclesiological terms, "This is a God that can start again, that can re-create. This is what it is to be the body of Christ; to empty yourself for the sake of others. As you empty yourself you find yourself filled."[11] This minister's incarnational theology named the inventive and ultimately efficacious practices of church members once they deemed the congregation the locus or base of neighborhood renewal. Yet in a manner true to the ways of God (especially in baptism and Eucharist), these local efforts participate in universally significant actions, not necessarily because they can be translated into abstract principles for action elsewhere, but because they point to the union of God and humanity. Moreover, as the next section on ecclesial and citizen response discusses more fully, this minister served as the exegete or reader of the congregation's collective actions. His reflections on having "a language to understand" speak to an earnest acceptance of a role that John Howard Yoder links to the

9. Santos, Participant *M1* interview.

10. Ibid.

11. Ibid.

"hermeneutics of peoplehood": linguistic self-consciousness.[12] On the basis of the fruit of the actions he witnessed, this minister verbally expressed theological insights that, in turn, served as a platform for yet more contemplations bearing upon praxis and a deeper understanding of God's work. Most challenging in this endeavor is the way in which the polemical or contentious nature of the topic does not govern the course of reflection so that, ultimately, the case is simply developed in opposition to those of the other group, for whom the hurricane was strictly a punishment.

Yet another minister (associated with a smaller mainline congregation) tendered an alternative interpretation of divine judgment with more direct ecclesial consequences. Like the ministers quoted above, participant *M2* did not view Hurricane Katrina as God's punitive response to a sinful people. More positively, "God is always in control of everything," he claimed. "He allows bad things to happen in order to work out the good."[13] In more closely evaluating the merits of the divine-retribution view that many ministers, along with mayor Ray Nagin and Louisiana senator Hank Erwin (a Republican from Montevallo), proffered in the initial weeks after the storm, this minister averred, "I'd say this storm was God's way of showing the church its failures in social justice. It was a wake-up call to the church to live true to its confession. The relief effort is an opportunity for the church to rebuild, [to] restore both structures and relationships."[14] Participant *M2*'s view owes much to another pattern of divine activity found in the scriptural testimony: principally, that for every instance of judgment on "the nations" that reject God, there also seems to be a case of judgment directed against God's people. This pastor eschewed the view that the church would never receive a harrowing or profound demand from God, thereby ensuring the pertinence of Jeremiah, Isaiah, and Ezekiel. Echoing this stance on God's judgment in the context of ecclesial discipline against hypocritical brothers and sisters, the Apostle Paul shared: "For what do I have to do with judging those outside? Is it not those who are inside that you are to judge? God will judge those outside. 'Drive out the wicked person from among you'" (1 Cor 5:12–13). Paul's bifurcation of responsibility in this case carries numerous implications for the modern state, most of which are

---

12. Yoder, *Priestly Kingdom*, 32.

13. Santos, Participant *M2* interview.

14. Ibid.

addressed in the final section of this chapter. It will suffice for now to comment that this view grants priority to a congregation's discernment and practices concerning renunciation of sins, repentance, and the taxing yet crucial undertaking of cultivating a deep appreciation of holiness within each member of the body. Indeed Rev. William Wooten, a moderator at an open-air worship service on the steps of City Hall at which about two hundred mainly evangelical ministers and church members gathered, stated that God spared the French Quarter and Bourbon Street because he was not pleased with "division and lack of concern for the poor" among churches. "Judgment begins in the House of God. There were more sinful acts in our churches than there were in our streets."[15] The call to repentance, however, must always be met with congregational formation, facilitated through the rhetorical end of *movere* (which moves the soul to action and thereby validates that the words of God in worship have convinced the disciples to believe). To be convinced is not to give assent or agreement, but for the will to be taken captive and moved to action. If one has not been moved to action, then persuasion has not obtained.[16] This task of congregational formation is often avoided due to ambivalence, fears, and distorted understandings about what Christian friendship, especially in its political dimensions, entails—namely, to paraphrase Paul in interrogative form: are we "competent to instruct one another," and do we "teach and admonish one another in all wisdom" in order to present one another complete in Christ (Col 3:16)? Worship services, whether of a special memorial kind or of the regularly occurring variety, are carried beyond the confines of church buildings through the active bonds of disciples of Jesus, for whom the Lord's Supper, baptism, song, and peaceful embrace guide daily action. Beyond these matters, this minister was also somewhat concerned with what he deemed the traps (noted in Kierkegaard's comments at the end of the previous chapter) inherent in an overly contemplative point of reference to the disaster. With this in mind, he issued the following:

> People in New Orleans had no sense of purpose after Katrina. Families, homes, and businesses were devastated; people were without money and resources—hopeless. God sends His people on a

15. Nolan, "Pastors Pray for Spiritual Rebirth."

16. See Candler, *Rhetoric, Theology, and Manuduction.*

mission to give people a sense of purpose by serving others. People should be outwardly focused rather than inwardly reflective.[17]

This participant's pastoral and evangelical approach was tested in that it had to adequately respond to the demands of an extremely high membership-turnover rate; somewhat matter-of-factly he shared that church members regularly move in and out of the area within one to two years. As a result, this minister found it most helpful to simply have the congregation adapt the staple New Orleanian orientation toward festivity and celebration, together with the openness of front porches as sites of interaction rituals, into planned weekly or biweekly gatherings. He found that regular "parties" or gatherings rapidly assimilated newcomers to neighborhood life and hence, at the least, provided the conditions necessary for the cultivation of awareness and presence to the needs of the many neighbors encountered.[18] This embrace and adaptation of the settled celebratory disposition of New Orleanians dovetails quite well into the celebratory nature of the kingdom of God and the manner in which liturgical and practical theological understandings of the "eschatological banquet" can deepen what Randall Collins calls, "interaction ritual chains."[19] These chains of regularized interaction at homes, front porches, and businesses produce fruit if instantiated by means of a disciple's concern for encounters with neighbors that eschew vain displays of impression-driven hospitality or the mere recitation of platitudes. These interactions assume, but go beyond, mere performance of prevailing social norms and actually generate love, friendship, trust, and the possibility of new bonds beyond the established group, which, in turn, may occasion new cultural interpretations of the political situation in the city. This could be somewhat aptly named, again following Randall Collins, the "social process of thinking."[20] These times of sharing in and reasoning through life together are not simply "fun" but take seriously the work of God's Spirit to join persons together beyond "civilized" niceties. In this case, the

17. Santos, Participant *M2* interview.

18. Ibid.

19. Collins, *Interaction Ritual Chains*, 184–96. Collins privileges the role of emotional complementarities in interaction ritual chains in an attempt to steer clear of many problems posed by rational-choice perspectives that seem to neglect emotions altogether. Importantly, this emphasis draws us back to consider how the manner in which a person engages the other is reflective of the way the person engages God.

20. Ibid., 183–96.

minister cited above rightly grasps the subversive nature of the flexibility with which locals in numerous neighborhoods in and around St. Charles Avenue view their business schedules. The participant shared zealously about the somewhat-unpredictable business hours of local shops that have evaded the incursions of McDonaldization (those social arrangements that embody hyperrationalized modes of efficiency, standardization, and inflexibility; in other words, those which often disregard the creativity and agency of the local community). It is clear to this particular minister that such a collective interest in resisting global-capitalist cooptation plays directly into the work of the church as a people that are willing to first build mutuality, and with it trust and joy through regular expressions of celebration with others. These celebrations and informal gatherings collectively and cumulatively pose an alternative to reasoning and practices that honor competitive edge and "the bottomline." *If* such practices can be carried out over a protracted period, then the very legibility of the community to the state's organs will decrease, because space and bodies will grow less and less answerable to the policies that depend upon simple space, easy classification of identities, and predictable concentration of goods and wealth. The primary challenge here, the minister perceives, is to remain "strong in the grace" over time; to habituate the disciples-in-the-making to interaction ritual chains, which are better expressed as "liturgical interaction chains" in the sense that they are a work of the people occasioned in and growing out of worship in God. In worship and fellowship with the brothers and sisters of Christ do we not receive God's gracious provision of wisdom for the purpose of forming love-bonds, whether in joy, sadness, or reconciliation? All political reasoning *in* God springs from this wisdom because it is built upon the commitment to live together in a loving vulnerability that invites the cultivation of bold, truthful speech for the sake of the other. As a collective commitment or oath to a specific interaction order, and not simply to abstract ideals, goals, or mission statements, the regularized meeting of citizens formed out of this dissident subculture can become a communal habit. This habit of interaction involving disciples of Jesus takes up vernacular resources of political resistance and ingenuity (such as that which drives the Krewe Du Vieux parade) and works them into a decisively Christian mode of reasoning through friendship, confession, faith, and self-giving charity. This nature of interaction provides safeguards against turning prophetic critique or immanent criticism into cynicism and insult. Habit in this case invites suspicion perhaps because of the all-too-common experience of regular meetings of church members that only loosely maintain congregational unity. This is the sort of habit, to place it in Kierkegaardian terms, which can actually oppose genuine love.[21] This occurs when an ecclesial habit (such as worship services, meetings at homes, community outreach) actually promotes ecclesial vice inasmuch as it no longer serves as a ground or condition for greater depth or devotion. "No," Kierkegaard claims, "only the eternal's 'You shall' and the hearing ear which will hear this 'shall' can save you from habit."[22] Habit thus understood remains a disposition or power that is subject to too many changes, while love in an eternal mode is unchangeable: it has undergone a transformation into "duty" and henceforth participates in divine freedom. That is, it does not depend upon the whims of the subject or the flux of responses, both negative and positive, of subjects and objects in the external environment. Kierkegaard therefore fears the loss, through habit, of the intentionality, deliberation, and courage needed to completely bind oneself to another in love. Precisely in this case the interaction order that persists before, during, and after the gatherings of citizens serves as the essential bulwark upon which this intentionality and boundedness is reproduced. This requires an appreciation of both the goal of the gatherings in general and the nature of the interactions therein. This does not require top-down accountability procedures; rather, it further requires ecclesial dialogue and prayer, or a collective habit, in the Thomistic sense of the word *habit*, in which the quality of one's interactions is not considered privately but tested in the context of communal discussion and discernment, of the worshipping people's desire to become more attuned to loving action.[23]

Positively, with respect to the statist imaginary, yet another interviewed minister (participant *M4*), this time from a mostly middle-class evangelical Protestant congregation with a legacy of involvement in social

21. Kierkegaard, *Works of Love*, 52.

22. Ibid.

23. One may also reflect on the nature and outcome of ecclesial habits by following John Dewey's distinction between a "routine, unintelligent habit and an intelligent habit or art." The former remains rigid and insensitive to changing circumstances, while the latter can amount to "intentional responsive adjustments" that answer to shifting circumstances but remain fixed on achieving certain ends. See Dewey, *Human Nature and Conduct*, 77.

justice, commented upon the distinctive advantages of ecclesial resources (in contrast to governmental actors) during the disaster-response phase:

> The church knows the people who live here. The church knows what it takes to do business here and what it takes to get things done. The government doesn't know that very often. I went to speak at a church in North Carolina and left there with two thousand dollars in my pocket; people were just approaching me afterwards and placing checks in my hand, saying, "Here you go," because they trusted me. That trust capital was there. You see, the government has to earn trust, but the church, most of the time, already has it.[24]

The governmental welfare agencies are here construed as detached and unaware of the informal (perhaps dissident or oppositional) subcultures that persist according to a sufficiently different set of interactional norms, vernacular, and practical wisdom that frequently eludes the organs of the state.

This minister also contributed an important "negative" dimension to the festive attitude of New Orleans residents, citing the popular response to many storms as one of playful disregard, often leading to large "block parties" during which massive amounts of food was barbequed because residents assumed it would go bad once the power was lost. Due to this general tendency favoring cavalier disdain (combined with considerable distrust of authorities), the minister claimed that he was unsure what else could have been done to evacuate more residents in the face of Katrina, with the exception of an earlier citywide call for evacuation. This consideration, although not intended as demeaning, was the foil against which the participant presented what he deemed to be the vital civic commitments that a post-Katrina New Orleans must instill in its citizens. These commitments were conveyed in the context of criticisms for state actors, pastoral insights aimed at curtailing resentment in the congregation, and the thriving presence of numerous grassroots groups. Particularly, while Participant M4 developed clear-cut views about the failures of government, he did not use the pulpit as a site for criticism. He shared:

> All the prognostications were wrong . . . the predictions of public officials, city hall, and the mayor. That's all we talked about for months . . . Our future as a city. So, I decided to not preach about

24. Santos, Participant M4, first interview.

that [government intentions for rebuilding]. I wanted to think about "us," not "them." And we had a number of FEMA workers and other volunteers from major agencies [worshiping] here; in fact, I told them that, "you're safe here; we want everyone that's here to know they can worship with us."[25]

With specific reference to Mayor Nagin, the participant added:

I was in a meeting with him, sitting [very] close to him, with other ministers there; I was wondering, "Are you really listening?"... All we told him was, "Look, we don't want you to do anything for us, we don't want jobs from you, we don't want kickbacks from you, we just want you to lead." We didn't say it exactly like that, but you understand—we simply wanted him to know what was needed badly at the time. And he made some [gestures of acknowledgement], but there was no follow-up—none.[26]

This experience with the mayor only deepened the participant's general contempt toward "big government." The discursive, purposive, and relational gap between the ministers from this particular meeting and the mayor is disheartening. The minister apparently attempted to eschew all the ethical expectations (including corrupt ones) that he construed as a staple of local political discourse and involvement (favor-granting, kickbacks, economic promises) in order to clearly relay a specific message. The ministers had to exercise gifted self-understanding and remain focused upon godly intentions in order to extricate themselves from this prevailing political orientation and to set themselves beyond it in order to speak with *parrhesia*, or bold (free and truthful) speech. Participant *M4*, moreover, drew on pastoral experience in preaching and providing aid through numerous grass-roots efforts as the bases for reflection on citizenship: "I believed in the incredible resiliency of the human spirit; I believed in it and I witnessed it. There was a vacuum during this time— and it was a time when someone, if they had the audacity, had to step up."[27] Indeed, the participant made a case for a "diligent citizenship":

Our focus should be upon self-reliance, citizenship, and people saying, "I am responsible. I don't know how to do this, but show me how to do this . . . and if someone can't do much for themselves, I'll do what it takes to get them there." Some of the best

25. Ibid.
26. Ibid.
27. Ibid.

stories coming out of Katrina have been stories about citizens who have rallied, and as an interracial [group], to seek changes in important areas.[28]

Some terms in the minister's admonition could certainly be interpreted as a marginal endorsement of the civil-defense model (which grew immensely in popularity during the 1950s) of self-reliant, private, and family- or home-centered preparedness, if not for the inclusion of two corresponding ethical tasks: the humble disposition to accept help and a willingness to give of the self to other residents in need. The actualization of this dual task has made (and will make) all the difference for ecclesial involvement in disaster-preparedness policy reform. For instance, the minister pointed to the work of Common Good, a civic organization originally composed of fourteen ministers, of mixed ethnic backgrounds, who agreed they were "tired of the race card" and the manner in which it had prevented effective grassroots action across class and ethnic boundaries.[29] Evidently, the organization has grown well beyond the original fourteen members. They have hosted debates, and a representative group of women from a local Presbyterian church have coordinated public discussions geared toward effective levee reform. As virtually all other research participants mentioned, Katrina introduced an opportunity for change in the shape and nature of city politics—an opportunity that had to be seized. Participant M4 asserted, "Katrina accomplished what ten years of denominational-relations committee work did not."[30] This participant claimed that besides bringing one congregation into close contact with other congregations within its denomination (and even beyond), the disaster also incited an" incredible redeepening" of what it meant to live in New Orleans and "love this place."[31] In consequence, there was no "God Bless America" motif running through the labors of restoring the body politic. It was a more "regional fervor." Understood differently, the disaster judged the church by means of a reawakening to the primacy of unity and freedom in truthful speech that the politics of God demands as a primary end before and after a disaster. This truthful speech is first and foremost the political outgrowth of friendships within

28. Ibid.
29. Ibid.
30. Ibid.
31. Ibid.

the church dedicated to encouraging others toward love, good deeds, and the rejection of self-deception (Heb 3:12–13, 10:24–25).

A number of other occasions arose during the recovery-and-relief period for sustained dialogue or bold critique of the speech acts and strategies of statist actors. In one specific instance, William Willimon both addressed divine retribution and verbally confronted an influential proponent of the view: senator Hank Erwin. In a weekly column, the senator wrote:

> New Orleans and the Mississippi Gulf Coast have always been known for gambling, sin and wickedness. It is the kind of behavior that ultimately brings the judgment of God . . . Warnings year after year by godly evangelists and preachers went unheeded. So why were we surprised when finally the hand of judgment fell? Sadly, innocents suffered along with the guilty. Sin always brings suffering to good people as well as the bad.[32]

What is more, Erwin added, "As harsh as it may sound, those hurricanes do say that God is real, and we have to realize sin has consequences."[33] As a rebuttal, Bishop Willimon stated thus:

> I'm certainly against gambling and its hold on state government in Mississippi, but I expect there is as much sin, of possibly a different order, in Montevallo as on the Gulf Coast. If God punished all of us for our sin, who could stand? That seems to me a much more appropriate Christian response than that of the senator.[34]

Willimon places the onus on Erwin to account for the sins of his own locale and thus to reconsider the theo-logic of his view. Why would God punish this particular city, its poor and rich, while sparing another city (which no doubt hosts a government leader) that is most likely just as spiritually destitute? Another key consideration here may not merely surround the *why* of judgment, but even the timing of the questions and presuppositions that govern the line of reasoning about divine judgment. Questions centered on judgment may be more appropriate once the works of service and mercy (which need to be present regardless of doctrinal views on divine judgment) have been carried out for some time. Willimon also suggests, rightly in my view, that even amid uncertainty

32. Erwin, "Alabama Legislator: Katrina was God's Wrath."
33. Ibid.
34. Ibid.

about judgment, God's mercy remains unquestionably present and in-carnate. That is, whether this is an act of punishment or not, we should perhaps be even more resolute in acquiring an awareness of divine clem-ency and kindness. The immediate suppositions of God's vindictiveness or wrath may be the projection of our own proclivity to violence and retaliation.

Willimon's rejoinder is simply one of numerous cases of ministe-rial criticism. Most accounts of criticism directly pertained to the local, state, and federal governments' response to the disaster, which was, by most accounts and with few exceptions, quite inept. Participant *M2* con-fidently declared, "The federal government is 100 percent responsible. If the federal government messed it up, they should fix it."[35] With spe-cific reference to the management of the Army Corp of Engineers, he stressed, "The subcontractors may have been using bad materials, but it was the federal government who was overseeing the whole operation."[36] This attempt to lay blame entirely on the government, after having as-serted that the hurricane was more properly understood as a judgment against the church, seems contradictory but can be comprehended in part through a conception of civic responsibility and integrity to which this minister believes the church should call all government agencies. It implies a conception of judgment whereby the state is judged *through* the church. Or, put differently, the state is only fittingly judged if the church is assured that it needs judgment, but only if the fear of death or rejection has not conquered or severely hampered its own ability to loose and to bind. Hence the church cannot judge the actions of statist agencies or actors and simultaneously escape God's judgment or discipline (see Matt 7:1–5). In one respect, the controversy surrounding divine judgment is only further compounded with the realization that the French Quarter, the haven of decadence that Senator Erwin confidently designated as ripe for destruction, was by-and-large spared of major damage. A second look, however, offers the promise of yet more insight into a hermeneutic of judgment in the case of Hurricane Katrina: primarily that those of the privileged economic classes often owned businesses in this district that rested on higher ground. Putatively, then, they were somehow able to avoid the so-called lessons contained in God's judgment, while thousands

35. Santos, Participant *M2* interview.
36. Ibid.

of others suffered either the loss of life, home, or other basic goods due to their low-lying residential location. Considering this disturbing observation in tandem with, say, Matthew 25:31–46, is sufficient to cast considerable doubt upon Senator Erwin's assertions, and leads us to consider, in a more prophetic and eschatological-ecclesial perspective, the roles of both political economy and race in this disaster. These are considered more fully in the following section, which shifts our attention to the cultural political experiences of New Orleanian survivors and ecclesial responses within a milieu that devalued statist presence and yet could not escape the statist political imaginary, because capitalist undertakings parasitically seized this imaginary for the sake of profit.

COMMUNITY RE-FORMATION, THE POWER OF CAPITAL, AND THE POLITICS OF RACE

The case of post-Katrina community formation unfortunately showcases the consequences of the rapacious disregard that distinguishes most forms of capitalist opportunism, both as an antecedent social condition and as a social form generative of asymmetrical relations in the aftermath of the hurricane. As an antecedent condition, for example, the gradual embrace of neoliberalism initiated in the late 1970s, which promoted strong private-property rights, free trade, and free markets, led to the eventual abandonment of land-use regulation, an essential component of the National Flood Plain Insurance Program.[37] This deregulatory ethos also encouraged a haphazard attitude toward the revision of flood zone maps, which resulted in inaccurate appraisals of risk. Coastal development in extremely vulnerable zones ensued, thereby ensuring the extensive weakening of natural barriers that would have been capable of offering significant resistance to hurricanes and tropical storms.[38] A number of attempts to improve flood-insurance regulations in the 90s, and most recently in spring of 2006, also failed due to strong bipartisan support for property rights, and due to an inability to resist developer and trade group ploys aimed at rendering reform virtually meaningless. The predatory nature of investment was most evident in the Manufactured Housing Institute's attempt, after Katrina, to have wind-safety standards (which only apply to homes built after 1994) suspended in order to expedite the installation

37. Steinberg, "Disasters and Deregulation," 62.
38. Ibid.

of mobile homes in affected areas—zones still susceptible to oblitera-tion. Within this context of submission to the neoliberal agenda, then, investors or real-estate developers from California and other states were able to quickly pounce upon many possibilities for profit partly because only those with financial wherewithal were able to continue living in the area with relatively minimal disturbance. It is precisely these persons who, generally, are unable or unwilling to speak for the impoverished thousands who evacuated and were compelled to reside hundreds of miles from home. The result in terms of life as a body politic is entirely adverse to rebuilding the city toward a fulfillment of the goodness of God in creation; there is, in David Dante Troutt's words, the undeniable absence of a "village sensibility, a reliable means of reaching exiled resi-dents in the cause of meaningful participation, and a protective purpose to preempt greed."[39]

Consider further, for instance, Troutt's account of the relation be-tween two New Orleanians whom he encountered during a walk through the city after the flooding began to recede. Troutt came upon a senior African American woman for whom the section of the city adjacent to the cemetery had been home for at least fifty years; dejected and disori-ented (she referred to Mayor Nagin as "the president") despite having been spared the total loss of her "brick-front shotgun shack" on Seventh Street, she complained of having no neighbors present for companion-ship, save one that was filling his vehicle with belongings in preparation for departure.[40] Troutt noticed the deep-seated pain and confusion she was experiencing when shortly thereafter Troutt encountered a young New Orleans-born real-estate agent who was anything but confused. As a witness to a bewildering inversion of affect and outlook, Troutt recounted that the young white male tried to hide "a shrewd grin inside an embar-rassed smile" as he described the many highly profitable investment op-portunities that had emerged just after the hurricane. The young investor was able to pinpoint on a map the exact locations adequate for gentrifica-tion projects in the coming years.[41] Important is that this young man had never entered the elder woman's neighborhood, despite living only eight or nine blocks away. This disjunction and fragmentation in community

39. Troutt, "Many Thousands Gone, Again," 14.
40. Ibid., 13.
41. Ibid., 14.

life is widespread, the consequence, in large part, of unbridled capitalist investment that effects uneven development, which, in turn, creates
sharp geographic divisions between the lower and upper classes so that
those who ought to know of one another are in fact worlds apart, with
little sense of a collective good for the landed community. Indeed, large
stucco walls separate the young realtor's well-kept neighborhood from the
cemetery and surrounding neighborhoods. Citizen life, in these contexts,
merely adapts to capitalism's advance and abdicates a hopeful imagination of a counterreality in order to reap some (however minimal) reward
from such "development." Another major rift, according to Participant
M2, persists between the "city" (Orleans Parish) and the Metairie and
Kenner suburbs lying northwest of the city. "The prevailing attitude," he
claimed, "pits these areas as opposites: Metairie has the hard workers, the
city has the lazy folks; we're black, they're white; we're poor, they're rich."

In the eyes of many residents, the state-endorsed *religio* of capitalism, which binds persons only if profit is anticipated, even infiltrated the
work of relief agencies. What is more, the advantages of the business class
in the French Quarter fulfilled a disintegrative function in the postdisaster period. For instance, a female graduate student from New Orleans
(participant *N1*), who returned to collect whatever belongings could be
salvaged from her apartment, commented thus:

> Many NGOs and relief agencies that were nationally recognized
> moved in to make money without any appreciation for [the char-
> acter of] the people and their culture. Imagine, who among them
> realized that Mardi Gras is actually a family-oriented event?
> Families actually get together, have a barbecue, and give gifts to
> children. But, the first businesses to open, even before supermar-
> kets, were strip clubs. Relief workers, who had nowhere to go for
> food would go to these clubs and there received the impression
> that this is what the city is all about. They had no food, so this was
> the only place many could go.[42]

The capitalist impulse finds ready expression in these forceful words.
Buttressed by stereotypes and tourist-friendly generalities, capitalist commitments detached from substantive community or collective goods and
telos justify almost any action for the sake of "survival," a term that often names a desire for continued profit. From the vehement perspective

---

42. Santos, Participant *N1* interview.

of this young woman, the logic is simple: the strip club opens, business remains viable, and the end product is a distorted representation of New Orleanian cultural life. It is distorted insofar as it casts a shroud of ignorance upon the not-so-profitable elements of local life and concurrently endorses the state's complicity in the commodification of carnal pleasures and women. More to the theological point, it completely negates the possibility of such a thing as communion, solidarity, or mutual indwelling—save a thin liberal conception of the social whole composed of self-interested individual nodes with only voluntary (mostly contractual) obligations. Inasmuch as congregations have tolerated (or even endorsed) this mode of living points to the urgency of collective acts of repentance that rehearse united action in the city.

While national identity lacked stable anchorage in the New Orleanian cultural milieu (French and Creole allegiance still claims many, evidenced in many home-front flags), and the federal government became the object of vitriolic criticism, the state still did not lack presence; nevertheless, even this presence invited censure from many communities in the process of reestablishing some sense of social coherence.

The statist political imaginary was discernible first and foremost in the construction of binaries via the absorption of white creoles into the city's privileged class, and in other historically relevant policies with lasting influence (e.g., highway construction and housing policy). More specific to this disaster, the deployment of military personnel to the Superdome revealed the statist imaginary in pronounced terms, even without the totemic patriotism and sustained attempts at theologizing or spiritualizing "the American." Also, the "creative word" of public officials made an unfortunate appearance not for good but for the perpetuation of racial stereotypes that impeded rebuilding plans; it was, in Augustinian terms, anything but borrowed speech.[43]

A local citizen wrote to criticize the unsound absence of skepticism on the part of both media outlets and governmental agencies with respect to rumors of "carnage" and frequent rape in the Superdome. He poignantly drew attention to the stark and exceedingly disturbing inconsistency between, on the one hand, the government's lack of urgency

43. In describing the conversion of the well-aged Victorinus, Augustine asserts: "How much less should he be afraid in proclaiming your word, when he used to feel no fear in using *his own words* before crowds of frenzied pagans" (*Confessions* 7.2.5 [Chadwick, 136–37]; emphasis added).

even as numerous residents (at least twenty) died outside the convention center waiting for basic goods; and, on the other hand, the heavy military operation mounted once mayor Ray Nagin and police chief Eddie Compass hastily relayed rumors of widespread rape and violence in the convention center.[44] The militarization of disaster response is most amenable to the prevailing imaginary of disaster-response policy (and even to civil defense and police protection, the forerunners to emergency management), because militarization is couched in a well-worn myth about how humans respond to emergency: as brutish, inconsiderate, irrational, self-absorbed actors who view all other persons as potential obstacles to survival. This is one central reason many disaster-preparedness plans are privatized, despite the considerable social-scientific research affirming the commonality of altruism, calm, and concern for maintaining pre-existing social bonds even during emergency evacuations.[45] Yet because most government agencies at all levels have yet to fully assimilate these findings, and because the motion-picture and video-game industries see no profit in depicting altruism not balanced against large doses of hatred and macabre recklessness, the only seemingly plausible protocol for statist agencies and citizens alike involves hierarchies of command and control, not public participation.

The unilateral display of force and confidence did not impress all citizens. The young graduate student mentioned above shared this account:

44. Protevi, "Thomas Confuses Two Aspects of Katrina,"

45. The strength of the social bond, in fact, accounts for many of the tragic and horrific aspects of emergency evacuations gone awry. A number of researchers have challenged commonly held misconceptions about human action in emergency, including E. L. Quarantelli. "Behavior of Panic Participants," 187–94; Johnson, "Panic and the Breakdown of Social Order," 171–83; and Johnson, et al., "Microstructure and Panic," 168–89. These researchers have found, among other things, that in many instances of emergency egress (exiting), when an evacuee realizes upon exiting a burning building that his or her mate, friend, or family member remains inside, he or she feels compelled to reenter the building and rescue the loved one. These attempts, cumulatively, may cause a collision of bodies at numerous entrance/exit points of a building. A back-and-forth, wavelike dynamic is generated whereby individuals attempting to enter or exit lose their balance, fall down, and become susceptible to trampling. We do not, therefore, have to conjure up the barbaric evacuee or pliable member of the maddening "crowd" to convince ourselves of the legitimacy of disaster-response policy that must impose or fabricate order. Compassion and devotion, in the context of severe physical limitations, which we may face in many other contexts of lived experience, are sufficient to produce deadly consequences.

> I felt more at risk once I returned home; when you go back home and members of the military approach you with guns and tanks, you will feel like the enemy. A member of the military approached me with a gun drawn and stated that there had been a black suspect stealing purses, but that I ought not to worry , because they would protect me. I felt more threatened by him. I though to myself, 'I'd rather be mugged.'[46]

This account was of course not unique. In another case, a visitor to the city shared that numerous SWAT teams escorted her and her colleagues out of a downtown hotel, evoking comparisons with warlike rescue operations.[47]

The military intervention and armed escort service for visitors was directly tied to race politics and the rhetorical power of the public figure, which, in concert impeded rescue efforts and subsequent rebuilding plans. Race politics were problematic in two respects: (1) immigrant workers willing to receive the minimum wage flooded construction projects, while displaced residents remained scattered about in Louisiana and beyond for a month or more after the hurricane; and (2) the public statements of mayor Melvin "Kip" Holden of Baton Rouge served to be the proverbial salt in the wound of an internally discordant political culture that attempted to mask completely racialized political conditions with an allegedly nonracial mayor.[48] According to participant *N1*, racial relations had improved tremendously over the previous decade in New Orleans but then worsened dramatically shortly after the hurricane, not least because of many relief workers who were "incredibly racist." One of the ministers interviewed shared an account of a racist white volunteer from a church in a southern state. The volunteer refused to enter a home in need of major repairs, because African Americans were present. Fortunately, the worker slowly changed his views and ultimately initiated frequent conversation, spending time with the African American worker during break periods.

---

46. Santos, Participant *N1*, interview.

47. Cashin, "Katrina," 30.

48. White, "Persistence of Race Politics," 58. White contends that because Holden's primary support came from a mixture of blacks, progressives, and business-oriented voters, he was pressed to both counter the presumption that he favored black citizens and reassure the racist elements in his constituency that he would protect the city from criminal evacuees.

Commodification processes capitalized on the magnitude of this problem: for example, small shops began to sell T-shirts with the words "F.E.M.A., Find Every Mexican Available" emblazoned on the front. One recent publication comments that a considerable number of Honduran Latinos began residing in New Orleans fifty years ago,[49] although the alleged mushrooming of the Mexican population has sufficiently challenged stereotyped perceptions of New Orleanians, especially of African American residents. These stereotypes led to a sea change: the once optimistic and inspired giving of funds for rebuilding projects has turned into relatively underwhelming donations. The fearful words of Mayor Holden, no doubt, were a key catalyst in this process of "contraction"; on the eve of the arrival of Katrina, as evacuation efforts were underway, the mayor stated: "'I want to make sure that some of these thugs and looters that are out shooting officers in New Orleans don't come here and do the same. I am not going to allow a New Orleans situation, shooting at people and looting, to happen here in Baton Rouge.'"[50] These statements, offshoots of a hermeneutic of judgment detached from grace, catalyzed a series of rumors of rape and bedlam that were publicized and embellished through radio and television outlets, eventually inciting a SWAT-team operation at Baton Rouge's River Center convention center, where five thousand evacuees were being housed. These events, in turn, impeded rescue and evacuation efforts in New Orleans. John Valery White, a Louisiana native and professor of law at Louisiana State University, construes the wider effects of these epideictic statements both as a reflection of the enduring political limitations of key black actors and, most formidably, as a foreshadowing of the contradictions that would dominate rebuilding plans.[51] The very residents who were the target of these statements from the black mayor of the state's capital city were primarily the working poor; that is, those residents who work the minimum-wage jobs that are the backbone of the city's multibillion-dollar hotel and restaurant tourism industry. These are the same residents who have often sustained the music, food, and street-side entertainment culture that all interested parties wish to keep. Yet the rebuilding plans, without being publicly honest, have intimated the desire to attract as many low-wage workers as possible (on

49. Sothern, *Down in New Orleans*, 264.
50. Quoted in White, "Persistence of Race Politics," 41.
51. White, "Persistence of Race Politics," 42.

which it must depend for rebuilding efforts and the tourism industry) without the poverty or corollary "urban problems" that follow from consequent welfare dependence. That is, rebuilding planners do not want the black working poor to return. These are residents framed as the unwilling workers occupying space, teeming with violent tendencies, and unable to control urges or passions in adverse circumstances. It is no wonder, in this light, that the temporary villages needed for these residents to gradually rebuild the city (the best alternative to leaving the state altogether) were denied them. The reason for this denial is, unfortunately, racial in its key dimensions. The North Shore parishes that lie at the northern edge of Lake Pontchatrain (the most agreeable to longtime residents who wish to rebuild the city but are unable to actually move back in) are actually the areas that received "white flight" in the years preceding the storm. These parishes did not accept the construction of any temporary trailer villages. The state's lack of remedial action in this affair, sadly, confirmed the negative reputation and perpetual suspicions (actually supported in some cases) of corruption that have marred city politics ever since black politicians gained positions of influence in the 1960s and 70s. Hence the state has remained beholden to class- and prestige-related interests, which simply reproduce the fears and prejudices that led to the exclusionary practices in the first place.

Thus reconstruction plans were troubling when they were released after four months of silence: the city would be divided into districts, the most flooded of which would be subject to a rebuilding moratorium until at least May 2006. The moratorium could be lifted on the condition that residents sufficiently demonstrated an intention to rebuild their communities. For the middle-class homeowner, this goal appeared more-or-less feasible, but for the working-class poor of New Orleans, two-thirds of whom were renters, reaching this state of rebuilding at the prescribed pace was highly unlikely, for reasons just cited. The absence of any sort of mechanism by which a resident may track down a neighbor precludes even the mere initiation of the process. This plan, it appears, merely fosters the social and economic conditions that will reproduce inequalities, albeit in a more intense and spatially uneven manner. As more affluent members repair and restore homes and environments at a relatively rapid pace in their sections of the city, the poorer citizens, who may be delayed in returning, or who may have access to fewer resources, must rebuild at a slower pace and thus remain extremely vulnerable to another disaster.

Many of these non-elite residents have not been welcomed back, and few voices have demanded redress. Simply recall the story detailed above of the young real-estate agent and local elder of the city; it begs the question, who will embrace the working class and the poor, and speak for them in their absence?

It is in this unsettling and embattled context that the ecclesial practices detailed below form the foundation for the more radical interventions required in the rebuilding plans of New Orleans. These practices draw on the work of the divine Word to invite Christlike kenotic love (especially in speech acts shared at cafes, dinner tables, and public events) that seek to repudiate stereotype, reconstruct root metaphors, and encourage service to the neighbor. These and other works of love place the *ekklesia* at the center of the city's rebuilding plan, because such an assembly speaks to the city's goodness in God's purposes, which in turn requires truthful and up-building speech for all citizens. In other terms, speech and practice must repudiate ultimate security in economic prosperity, the approval of public figures and of the affluent, and (as the Lukan witness suggests in the account of the rich man and Lazarus), by extension, death (Luke 16:19–31). Faith communities are called to appropriate God's eschatological vision that reverses the destinies of the rich and poor.

The Theopolitics of Life as Neighbor

Ecclesial responses were multifaceted: some of the most important response-related social processes considered in this section include (1) congregational intervention on behalf of the displaced in the context of racial prejudice and the arduous initiation of new relationships, (2) the construction of a working hermeneutic of judgment and grace in opposition to that of statist agents, and (3) the imaginative contrivance and implementation of recovery activities that eschewed governmentally administered relief projects. The upshot of these extremely demanding interactions is that they served as the crucible from which political reasoning could be learned in terms of Alasdair MacIntyre's "virtues of acknowledged dependence"[52] An eye toward learning the requisite skills that

52. See MacIntyre, *Dependent Rational Animals*, 118–28. Macintyre dedicates all of chapter 10 to an exposition of how training in the exercise of an interlocked set of virtues (including mercy and charity) is necessary to sustain relationships of gracious giving and receiving that challenge the assumed and exclusive normality of rational persons without disabilities or dependencies.

undergird such virtues enables Christian citizens to encounter the other, to identify agreements and disagreements, and eventually to enter into efforts for the collective good as an ecclesial unit. That is, in Augustinian terms, in learning the virtues, one hopes to make the boundaries of the earthly city much more porous to the movements of the heavenly city.

Churches operated in an environment in which the state-as-*soter* (savior) served a socially integrative function; it was a living icon, an entity worthy of citizens' submission, respect, *and*, increasingly, contempt. This was evident in the rhetoric of journalistic reportage and in expressions of dependence upon state aid and recognition, not only for evacuees but also for citizens in other Louisiana cities and in other states, for whom the uncertainty of whether their expenses would be reimbursed influenced their delivery of service. The national government or some other higher level of administration was objectified and esteemed in the process of creating a direct link with an individual citizen, and in this capacity it is expected to provide recognition of services. This recognition is conflated with the actual person-to-person service rendered to the displaced in need. For example, a director of a mission in Oklahoma simply wanted the evacuees and government to tell him "thank you," and this would have made weeks of demanding work with evacuees worthwhile.[53] One journalist employed the phrase "search for salvation" to capture New Orleans residents' desperate anticipation of positive news about the prospect of rebuilding the city.[54] This was an apt statement in key respects, most of which were not intended by the author. Disasters deepen our understanding of salvation as more than personal attainment of forgiveness. (Jesus seems to indicate the encompassing nature of salvation often in the gospels after healing the sick, with words such as, "your faith has saved you.") Indeed, salvation as a corporate or social matter alters the course of lives through the attainment of wholeness or *shalom* that accordingly alters economic and governmental activity. The Christian scriptural witness about the early church has clear indications of such as well, as a cursory reading of Acts 19 and 20 demonstrates. In the present case, instead, the citizens of New Orleans were looking for salvation from the government, from its plans for infrastructural renewal. Such a longing for salvation persisted unsatisfied for months. Finally Mayor Nagin

53. Wilkerson, "Scattered in a Storm's Wake," 1.
54. Associated Press, "Nagin Updates Hurricane-Displaced Residents."

released the disappointing rebuilding plans, which had been formulated without consulting citizens or external advisors. After this, for the first few months of 2006, Nagin directed his energies to accomplishing reelection. Once this was attained, Nagin took up, as Rudolph Giuliani had, the task of official speech in the context of worship. Hence the salvational longings did not go unprompted. Mayor Nagin, just after attending a Mass at St. Peter Claver Church in the city's Treme neighborhood, claimed, "We now have the economic stimulus that will happen at unprecedented levels in the city, for us to expand the economic power and for everyone to get a piece of that pie."[55] Nagin conveyed his intentions "to reach out to every segment" of New Orleans, envisioning a city "where whites and blacks and Asians and Hispanics are all working together to expand this pie."[56] These assertions, like others that take the same form, offer promise of ethnic reconciliation *vis-à-vis* the pursuit of that highly coveted pecuniary "pie." No mention is made of the actual relations between these groups that must obtain if such reconciliation and shared economic prosperity would continue for the long term without collapsing under the weight of historically powerful animosities or lingering distrust.

Many congregations were compelled to deal with the promise of governmental assistance, just as the churches in Oklahoma City had. Yet again, the views were mixed: "I have never seen a government program that does not have strings attached," said the Reverend J. Brent Walker, executive director of the Baptist Joint Committee for Religious Liberty. "It's an ironclad rule: What government funds, government regulates. There's just no way around that."[57] Conversely, many state governments (along with major cities such as Houston, Texas, and Chattanooga, Tennessee) have developed nonprofit, faith-based initiatives or even local government offices, in the case of Chattanooga. One Mississippi nonprofit agency hosts workshops that instruct church administrators and pastors how to secure from their state governments grant funds earmarked for faith-based initiatives. Aggressive attempts to procure funds in Louisiana will probably only grow in coming years, unless some new policy or legislation prevents it. This much was implied in the statements of one participant, a young woman from Africa who works for Louisiana State

55. Nossiter, "New Start for Familiar Face."
56. Ibid.
57. Kunzelman, "On Gulf Coast, faith-based groups."

University, and who is a member of a traditionally apolitical, medium-sized nondenominational congregation (without a church building):

> We have actually thought a lot about getting a grant form the state
> . . . yes, to help restore the involvement of the church and resettle
> a few families. Initially, and I think this was pretty common; we
> were in survival mode, but now I think we're more clear headed
> about what can be done.[58]

If this sort of adaptive delay applies to other congregations, the partnership between churches and government will almost certainly grow stronger. Many congregations have established separate nonprofit organizations as a method by which to sidestep the ethical quandaries of governmental funding for what on all accounts would still be considered Christian service; many, indeed, find this approach evasive, not convincing. The repercussions of this church-and-state collaboration, however, have raised yet another slew of questions bearing upon justice, citizenship, and the proper conception of "religious" assistance.

Commentators both within and without the state of Louisiana, starting only a month after Hurricane Katrina, debated how to properly conceptualize "religious assistance": if the right hand does not know what the left hand is doing, then how can faith-based groups accept government reimbursement or support for initiatives? One writer from Boston, James Carroll, presented a view fairly representative of one particular position against funding churches. Carroll noted, "On the scene of the catastrophe itself, religious organizations have provided heroic relief, often in stark contrast to hesitant government agencies. The value and values of religion have been on full display during this crisis."[59] Despite this, Carroll argues that churches are able to benefit from providing public functions with "antipublic values."[60] He cites support for Pat Robertson's relief agency, an organization linked to a man who "supports assassination as a tool for foreign policy," as one example among many.[61] "The crux of Carroll's argument deals with how this problem is amplified when religiously based deeds of service supply fundamental needs in place of

---

58. Santos, Participant *L2* interview.
59. Carroll, "Church, State, and Katrina," A15.
60. Ibid.
61. Ibid.

government responses. He argues that in this case, "something essential to democracy is at stake." Carroll contends:

> The rights of citizens to basic relief, especially in times of crisis, are rooted not in charity, but in justice. Charity can be an affront to the dignity of citizenship. Citizens in a democracy, after all, are the owners of government; therefore government help is a form of self-help.[62]

Carroll thereby posits antimony between charity and justice insofar as the latter provides the necessary and sufficient justification for a citizen's right to basic relief. The right cannot, therefore, be premised on love. Now, a theistic vision of justice cannot possibly seal off love from the act of relief, at least not in light of the parable of Good Samaritan. The primary disjunction here is between a theoretically or philosophically articulated principle of justice and a conceptualization of justice that arises from the socially embedded authority of Christians' narrative spirituality or faithful performances. Such spirituality begs the question, why can't love or charity ground the act of assistance? Perhaps the specter of pure formalism or proceduralism lurks about, seeking to foreclose the debate. If one has a right to basic relief, then Carroll assumes that it is all "said and done" as a work of justice; but if love compels the same act, then citizenship is supposedly undermined. Under this conception, charity is somehow either too weak to ensure that relief will arise, or it is too strong, overdetermining (and hence imposing) the act that brings relief upon the recipient. The parable of Good Samaritan, in fact, when appropriated from within a communal hermeneutic, confronts such a thin and anxious notion of assistance, because the Christian understands the occasion to help as one that precludes assessments of the worthiness of the victim or recipient, and that instead leads the servant to *ask* herself if she will be a neighbor to the one before her. The calculation of fairness or proportion is precisely the target of criticism in this parable: "I must help even if the person is a detestable individual who belongs to that larger group of folk who held my religious heritage [or lifestyle or political views or whatever] in contempt." While Carroll hopes to ensure relief through formal justice, christological wisdom sets forth the lesson by confronting and challenging the very desire to self-justify and set limits to assistance—a trend so common to the neoliberal, consumptive

62. Ibid.

body politic. Carroll's argument is fine for the insular and settled body of citizens infatuated with self-help, yet does nothing to touch citizen orientation toward those who lie outside the validations of citizenship and formal propriety. The christological argument pierces the habits of the heart that blindly reproduce inequalities and ensure loyal and commendable behavior toward insiders. Christ's teaching additionally challenges the notion that citizenship does not demand that a person face either individual weaknesses or prejudicial tendencies (that is, sinfulness) or the ways in which loyal citizens victimize others out of loyalty to their own. Christians of God's commonwealth realize that formalist or procedural justice does little to engage the narrative entanglements of wounded human beings in quotidian life. Once an encounter emerges that calls for assistance, will justice, as Carroll construes it, complete the task, or does charity necessarily come into play? Carroll is afraid of letting the "religiously motivated" become an imposition, thus betraying the conception of the human being (and citizen) as fundamentally atomistic, "objective," and consequently alienated.[63] Spiritual formation, or "religion" in its simplest, reductive sense, is here simply an add-on to citizen life and even bare existence as a rational agent. A concern over freedom conceived as a possession or property of the individual person's constitution also underpins these concerns. However, as the parable just cited intimates, freedom is itself what arises from this encounter of costly *caritas*. Dietrich Bonhoeffer informs or interprets this position well. In his commentary on Gen 1:26–27, he claims that

> Freedom is not something man has for himself but something he has for other. No man is free "as such"…Freedom is not a quality of man, nor is it an ability, a capacity, a kind of being that somehow flares up in him…it is not a possession, a presence, an object, nor is it a form for existence—but a relationship and nothing else. In truth, freedom is a relationship between two persons.[64]

If humans are created out God's own freedom, then we can never claim that freedom is *within* a person in a mode somehow isolatable from relation or being-for-the-other. The parable of the Good Samaritan exemplifies the freedom that arises from the decisions and acts of service performed for the sake of the neighbor, while the absence of freedom is

63. Ibid.

64. Bonhoeffer, *Creation and Fall/Temptation*, 40.

evident in the moral calculus of those who question Jesus, by which questions they seek justified limitations of engagement with those in need. Most interesting then, is that both state agents and confessional leaders worry about what strings are attached, so to speak, to disaster relief or assistance: church leaders worry that the state will impose its expectations on a given congregation, and citizens worry that churches will do the same to recipients of assistance.

Another form of argument that questioned the practice of reimbursing church groups for relief work isolated an ethic intrinsic to Christian service: Help others, and expect nothing in return. Critics used this injunction to endorse the notion that "big government" needs sound (or neutral) financing options to carry out its own disaster-recovery work and, besides this, President Bush could have rolled back tax breaks on the wealthy as a source of funds but instead chose to pour money into faith-based groups. Regardless of the economics of this situation, which indeed require attention, the situation itself again exposes the lack of consensus among confessions. If it is volunteer work, why would someone expect pay for it? Government funding seems to assume that the government will support the maintenance of a faith-based relief operation, which may or may not be viewed as distinct from the government's paying someone to do volunteer work. In the present case, writers such as Carroll criticized the federal practice of large-scale payments for faith-based relief work, afraid that the policy would set a precedent after years of consistent policy against the practice. Indeed, numerous leaders pointed to city and state governments overwhelmed (e.g. Denver, Colorado), and called for churches to reach out without receiving aid.

The Theopolitics of "the Encounter" after Hurricane Katrina

Bearing the aforementioned in mind, it is important to note that many churches went beyond the debate concerning the separation of church and state in noticing that cultural authority is equally inherent in the creative, faithful, and resilient actions that, as divinely grounded *poiesis* and *praxis*, redefine the elemental components of community. That is, the cultural politics instantiated in the church, contrary to capitalist and statist policies chronicled above take care and time to create both internal states that are pleasing to God and cultural products that speak across class differences to a person's relation to God. Many congregations found authoritative witness in faithful action to be sufficient as a font of insight into what was most essential in the recovery period. For example, the "adoption" of churches or other confessional groups was a crucial means by which some semblance of continuity could be afforded parishioners of churches forced to close doors, even if major problems of internal ecclesial culture made such moves painfully necessary. Specifically, one set of relocations or closings was not simply a consequence of lost membership but also of factors connected to the political-economic consequences of litigation. Participant *L1* regretfully commented: "A priest that I've known for many years told me, 'They [the Catholic Church] had to decide whether to pay for flood insurance or for child-molestation cases, and they chose to channel funds to the child-molestation cases.'"[65] In other cases, congregations made space for displaced groups for worship. One rabbi receiving assistance commented gratefully, "We will bring over the ritual objects we need to make it temporarily a Jewish space, and we are grateful to have such beautiful surroundings for our services."[66] This statement describes actions that typify the importance of liturgical or ritual enactments of faith in a disrupted social environment. Even if the space becomes only "temporarily" Jewish, the identity of the people is buttressed or imbued through the manipulation of material bodies. Most important, in this case, the narrativization of the space involves a transformation of a place that has been used for alternate sacred services. One group crosses the boundary of another in a state of liminality, which opens space for transformative social interaction—that is, for encounters that more fully open the other to the presence of God in moments of compassion. A Jewish group that transforms a Christian space into a site for the celebration of the Day of Atonement has some parallels in Jewish narrative history. They are already quite familiar with wandering or estrangement from a homeland; that is, they are familiar with exile. Such elements coincide with disaster-response experiences: detachment from home and land, as well as disorientation. Entering the narrative of God's providence calls the exiles to confront this situation with grateful reception of assistance, God's promises for deliverance, and expressions of praise. It is not enough for the group to enact such a story individually— it must be done as a group. Many churches realized just this as they en-

---

65. Santos, Participant *L1* interview.

66. Taylor, "Storms to Heavily Influence Jewish High Holy Days," 1-F.

tered into works of service for evacuees or displaced residents of New Orleans. Congregations were confronted with the necessity of learning, and hence partially inheriting, the historical and cultural struggles of the displaced.

Given that many evacuees had never traveled outside New Orleans, their experience of being transported away from their homes and familiar surroundings raised suspicions of a return to direct subjugation. As a hotel maid and her daughter were being transported to a remote mission in Oklahoma (mentioned above), she uttered, "'They trying to slave us. They going to make us pick cotton. We gon' die.'"[67] Others realized just how extreme was the taken-for-granted quality of life in their hometown, which was now considered a merely hoped-for destination. For most, it was, and remains to be, the work of creating social relationships that was most difficult to accept: the dreaded interaction with "the other" that unnerves the conventional technologies of the self that rely on stock metaphors of self-reliance and, for most minority evacuees, that painfully exposes a considerable distance from many aspects of mainstream social life. The mainstream represents the coveted yet out-of-reach goods of the social world that are the source at once of attraction or seduction and of frustration.

In the sample of sources analyzed for this study, a host of trials emerged, involving everything from culinary matters to involuntary dependence. Evacuees were often compelled to face their own interior demons in light of the extreme changes in diet that they experienced as residents of evacuee camps. Likewise, food-service workers from states outside Louisiana struggled with the decision to provide familiar foods, because they considered the required ingredients to be too expensive or difficult to attain. Evacuees often tackled, at some point after arrival, the strange challenge of becoming the object of pity; this was followed by a major drop-off in services and in sympathetic listeners. "It's was like we were a fad," said one evacuee.[68] For some evacuees who ended up in camps, the loss of a sense of time and of any proper sense of direction came about as a result of extensive travel combined with preestablished schedules for sleeping, eating, and excursions into host cities to look for homes or jobs. These experiences of loss were exacerbated by weeks of

67. Wilkerson, "Scattered in a Storm's Wake."
68. Ibid.

living in close quarters in the company of persons they had not chosen as friends or companions, all the while being required to abide by curfew rules (common in homeless shelters) and to fulfill chores. These rules, in the case of some camps, were the parameters established by volunteers with experience as camp directors or counselors, not by social workers or psychiatrists.[69] Perhaps most difficult were situations in which a service provider seemed to take responsibility for something they believed the evacuee should take upon themselves to carry out. Over time, competition grew between residents, and frustrations often boiled over as a result of diminishing job opportunities and confusion over government relief rules. Those serving evacuees, moreover, became embroiled in estimating how much more might be given if the government opted to only reimburse a certain percentage of expenditures. These evacuees were faced with the types of questions that the church has been welcomed to treat as familiar territory: the acceptance of external standards of holiness for the sake of others, the assimilation of friends one did not choose but with whom life must go on, and the struggle over estimations concerning the limits of giving and forgiving; all these are constitutive of communion. Reaching out to the stranger is thus the risky but Christlike movement that tests collective resolve in God.

Welcoming the stranger (it is often forgotten even in the church) is a taxing and trying task. The solidarity communicated in the initial gestures of compassion, and the costs they produce, were (and are) only the beginning. The continued support of evacuees, when this entails a level of familiarity, intimacy, and especially tenacious dialogue amid confusion, misunderstandings, and even offense, calls for greater corporate worship and refined discernment: those things that share in Christ's interventions as "the pioneer and perfecter of our faith" (Heb 12:2). Yet in following Jesus through disaster, it is easy to miss the political ramifications of accepting the lesson that those who serve have their brokenness and vulnerability exposed in their acts of service to the needy. The paradox of the power of weakness, which conceives of the strong as in need of the weak just as much as the weak need the strong—for God chose the foolish in the world to shame the wise, and the weak to shame the strong (1 Cor 1:27)—is the deep resource for emancipative political reasoning.

69. Ibid.

This reasoning starts with the actual practices of the church that place it, as Kierkegaard assumed, in contemporaneity with Christ.[70]

This is partly evident in the twenty cases among the media sources analyzed that set off successful local initiatives against governmental programs that could not accomplish similar ends due to formal, policy-driven, or bureaucratically based limitations. The common thread that ran through many of these treatments of grassroots responses versus (mostly ineffective) government aid appears to be that most forms of government aid did not demand anything from citizens outside monetary contribution. While some local or grassroots groups offered their own homes to displaced families, FEMA sought to provide a hermetically sealed solution; that is, one abstracted from the many other possibilities of assistance that exist in the dense network of goods and practical wisdom. Paradoxically, the government's financial disbursements are always presented as the aid that settles matters once and for all; meanwhile, all other forms of aid, including temporary shelter and time spent with unknown others, maintains only temporary utility, although it is precisely these forms of aid that blur social boundaries and test unexamined political principles and affections, that expose racism and elitism, and that thus generate the possibility of social change, albeit only through the often emotionally and intellectually grueling demands of concrete encounters. It is these encounters that develop political reasoning in its more refined forms. The subsection that follows more specifically identifies the praxis of specific congregations, and in particular their political engagements with the statist political imaginary. This engagement ultimately constitutes a journey into, as Bonhoeffer demonstrated, the judgment and guilt of our generation.

Compassion, Judgment, and Confession Outside of State Intervention

Many observers praised the work of confessional groups. Jim Towey, indicating both the power and the excruciating demands of compassion, asserted: "compassion isn't easy, and there's a lot of fatigue out there."[71] Towey lauded the work of smaller churches that needed the weekly contribution of members in order to operate, and that of larger churches that abandoned the "rulebook" to welcome the dispossessed and desperate

70. Kierkegaard, *Practice in Christianity*, 62–65.
71. Taylor, "Shout-Out for Churches."

evacuees. While a rather tremendous degree of dependence on bureau-cratically administered government services was recognized in the sourc-es analyzed for this study, ecclesial groups undermined such dependence in a variety of ways. Participant *M1* shared that

> It took us until December in order to figure out how to run that of-fice, but the local churches were doing the work and going around the bureaucracy. A pastor would call with people that can help and in theory, they were supposed to call [the central office] and they would parcel the jobs out. But we said, come on down, because it was more important to keep it going and not stop. The theory was that everything would go through BR [Baton Rouge] and they would schedule it, but folks would call and never get a call back. So folks would call the pastors and tell them what we have.[72]

For a number of confessional groups, this observation amounted to a striking realization and subsequent change in community practice:

> During Katrina, the government did not care if you talked the-ology or not. They were so interested in getting any help in any form. The church frames its response on the assumption that we are people of compassion, because we care. The government frames the question of aid as a matter of "helping because no one else will." They didn't think that the local communities would be able to help and not only help, but do it more effectively than the government.[73]
>
> The local churches realized that the power to respond to this was not in government, but in being a neighbor. They started being neighbors, and they realized that their neighbor was in Maryland, or Kansas, and this occurred when folks realized that the larger bureaucratic responses were not coming.[74]

Only upon confirming the failure of governmental relief services did the displaced citizens and church members turn to the practice of neigh-borliness, which, upon repeated usage, turned out to be a formidable practice that initiated vulnerable and trusting social relations. It likewise generated theological insight into the difference between the compas-sionate and hopeful basis of giving as Christ enables us, and the negative assumption that (at least to this minister) informs state-led assistance.

72. Santos, Participant *M1*.

73. Ibid.

74. Ibid.

The church knows that it must risk communion. This level of vulnerability and interdependence is an extension of the trust that inheres in local ecclesial friendship bonds, insofar as regional and local boundaries of age, race, and gender are rendered irrelevant. Participant *M1* stated that the local churches started "being neighbors" and altered their cognizance of neighbors to include those beyond the local, concrete realm.[75] They opened themselves to actively receive and become the object of giving. For a people to take on this orientation during a period of tremendous disorientation is an act of patience and submission—certainly, a living psalm. However, another crucial question is whether this period trains a people to, in the long run, live trustfully and in submission to God in periods of suffering. Does their comfort overflow in comfort to others? This is markedly relevant in the case of well-to-do congregations, like St. Dominic Catholic Church and St. Paul's Anglican Church, that were able to quickly repair their buildings and reactivate ministry. The continual initiative on the part of congregations such as these to be unsettled and to invite the possibility of offense represents a necessary condition for the prospect of cross-congregational ties that effectively undermine established racial, economic, and political boundaries between parishes and neighborhoods. As Participant *M1*'s comment below indicates, seeking encounters and bonds that foster *gracious reception* of help formed the heart of effective recovery work:

> FEMA would get so caught up with admin tasks that it paralyzed the folks getting help. The people started using personal relationship to get help. The administration and bureaucracy only started coming after the local institutions and groups starting doing the work. The local groups initiated personal relationships, business relationships, and institutional relationships to get people into the city, and then the government realized that they should just let them do what they can do. All the larger institutions learned this—church, state, regional—they were amazed at how well it happened. These things [relief efforts] happened better without their presence.[76]

Not only did the establishment of these relationships engender the possibility of aligning organizations, companies, and nonprofit firms that

75. Ibid.
76. Ibid.

often operate according to wildly different logics and discourses, it actually formed the foundation for organizational structure: the ties between the usually highly differentiated firms served as the initial basis for administrative design geared toward sustaining those linkages. When asked why the large governmental agencies would have been so concerned with the success of local efforts, Participant *M1* replied,

> It [the concern] occurs on the basis of their power in the culture. They [the state] think, "Well, they have to have us"—they have to validate their own power and existence. But when the bureaucracy did not respond—the people decided, "We are going to do this and we'll ask for forgiveness [later] and not for permission."[77]

The power of large statist agencies stimulates, according to this participant, an anxiety over its precarious "existence." This existence is construed chiefly in terms of autonomy and citizen compliance. Most interestingly, the participant chose to describe the state as constantly striving to rehabilitate not only its legitimacy (a hallmark of postmodern politics in advanced capitalist social formations) but also a metaphysical vision of itself as *necessary*. This assured necessity, in Kierkegaard's terms, is owed to a willful forgetfulness or disregard of origins that facilitates "a deification of the established order."[78] Herein we find a most telling feature of the statist imaginary as deified: the state, as the purported "institution of institutions," naturalizes a compulsory super-vision of individual human beings. If the modern state is necessary, then the atomization of the citizenry is a logical outcome: all other allegiances are relativized before this subject-object totality of knowledge, administration, and safety. Kierkegaard further argues,

> The established order began with that collision between the single individual's relationship with God, but now that is to be forgotten, the bridge cut down, and the established order deified.[79]

A few lines later, Kierkegaard maintains,

> Every human being is to live in fear and trembling, and likewise no established order is to be exempted from fear and trembling. Fear and trembling signify that we are in the process of becom-

77. Ibid.
78. Kierkegaard, *Practice in Christianity*, 88.
79. Ibid.

ing; and every single individual, and likewise the generation, is
and should be aware of being in the process of becoming. And
fear and trembling signify that there is a God—something every
human being and every established order ought not to forget for
one moment.[80]

As the previous chapter noted in relation to that pilgrimage of becoming
that is discipleship, the churches of faithful disciples of Jesus must place
their relationships and their own will, emotions, and thoughts—their
heart—at the mercy of those practices of the church that uphold humility and love as the chief virtues: confession, the preached word, and the
transforming practice of Eucharist as the feast of the world's redemption
and of baptism as sharing in the death and resurrection of Christ. And
indeed, it behooves the congregation to see this as a thoroughgoing matter of individual worship and surrender before God that in its collective
outcome assures an ecclesial body that is, as Paul exhorts, "united in the
same mind and same purpose" (1 Cor 1:10). As the body of Christ, such
an ecclesial body submits to its head and realizes it shares in the greatest
of blessings of wisdom, love, and hope *as a body*. When a congregation
operates more as a loose conglomeration of believers, virtually each member is, at their core, unsure about whether it matters if he or she enters
God's grace in worship, prayer, and faithful instruction for the sake of the
neighbor. The result most often is inconsistent attendance at worship and
very little contact outside regularly scheduled services—put simply, the
body does not live *as a body*. Consider Participant *L2* as she describes the
midweek worship services of her congregation after the hurricane:

> For . . . I'd say, the first few weeks after the storm, our midweek
> services were basically about confession and open sharing.
> Christians shared frustrations about, well, delays in getting help
> from government or even anger at the whole situation. I think
> a lot of people began to realize that their lives would never be
> the same again. I mean, they found themselves living in another
> home with another family. But the church in that period grew so
> much—as the brothers and sisters confessed and prayed openly in
> the room, they were also learning from God about what it meant
> to be faithful.[81]

80. Ibid.
81. Santos, Participant *L2* interview.

The service to neighbors that were not members of churches is not possible, in the short-term and certainly not in the long-term, without such practices. The trust and love that undergird these practices require regular interaction. Indeed, this participant stated that at least 80 percent or more of the church members attended all worship services before the hurricane. While in some nondisaster contexts it must be granted that the therapeutic nature of some forms of group worship may sacrifice *la vita activa* on the altar of some form of overly detached contemplation and self-referential piety, it is the work of the body as it grows into its head, carried out in regular person-to-person encounters, that forms the groundwork for substantial and faithful service to the neighbor. With confession comes a renewed focus on God and a willingness to share in the guilt of all neighbors. This willingness makes it a grave mistake to assume that such an ethic of being a neighbor is akin to the popular, sentimentalized, and nonjudgmental brand of pleasant neighborhood acquaintance. The postdisaster situation, indubitably, demands more than that. This need is partly due to the many residents (inside and outside Louisiana) for whom widespread flooding, unexpected deaths, and home loss were the result of God's wrath on the city. Some residents, including a couple that was interviewed for this study, attempted to explain this away by referencing doctrinal differences between denominations ("I am Catholic, so I don't go that route, but my Baptist friend is all about fire and brimstone."[82]) or through a minimization of sin ("I don't think God would do that; we are not that bad, at least not in comparison to any other city."). The distinct impression this left on the course of social relationships was even inscribed, literally, into the material bodies of the environment—signifying the hermeneutic reverberations and trials that the storm introduced to a resident's sense of membership in the body corporate. On a toilet-paper dispenser in a bookstore in Metairie, Louisiana, a brief yet intense dialogue was written between residents—a dialogue that exemplified the intersection of divine judgment, race, despair, and hope. In clear, uppercase letters (covering about ten inches of horizontal space) along the edge of the dispenser, words read, "Why do I live in Jefferson Parish?" Juxtaposed against this expression, one person wrote, "The storm came so that you would pay for your sins." Below this, a query appeared: "Will we rebuild?" Yet another (or not) answered, "You

82. Santos, Participant *L3* interview.

won't because you are black and you are poor." Someone who came across these phrases, perhaps one of the original "writers," attempted to scrawl over the words "black" and "poor." Off to the right side, positioned diagonally in relation to the vertical arrangement of exchanges, words read, "Judge Not." Taking this into consideration, we can recast our discussion of judgment more squarely in a theological and ecclesiological frame of reference, with some guidance from scriptural wisdom that provides the needed starting point: God's ways with us.

One of the most common points of reference in talk about New Orleans's supposedly well-deserved punishment is the Genesis account of Sodom and Gomorrah. My account of the church as God's politics cannot be complete without some treatment of Abraham's plea for the city (Gen 13). On the one hand, the complete eradication of a city bent on practices that on the basis of Genesis, treat the visiting stranger as a potential object of abuse is consistent with the biblical witness against forms of life centered on death, chaos, and self-interest. On the other hand, Abraham's intercessory plea is a crucial component of the entire narrative. Indeed, God's own apparent deliberation about whether to inform Abraham is quite significant. Most significant, perhaps, is not the actual number of righteous required to save the city, but Abraham's bold requests, which are prefaced by Abraham's complete endorsement of God as the "judge of the whole earth" (v. 25). While God is concerned with the outcry over blatant sin in the cities named and with Abraham's knowledge of this concern, Abraham is focused upon God's integrity with respect to the righteous of the city. This dialogue is sufficient to show that the God who places the destiny of nations upon the posterity of a single couple wishes to hear the pleas and expectations of those who live in full trust. Abraham presents successive pleas in accordance with his understanding of God's justice, and God listens to each and every one. The dialogue does not end until God has heard all Abraham's potential salvation scenarios. Hence, our understanding of judgment must take into account the intercession of the church, or the lack thereof.

Furthermore, perhaps it would be fruitful to surmise that judgment did not occur in the coming of Hurricane Katrina but in the aftermath, when men and women engaged, tested, called, rejected, shunned, or received one another. Such contexts are those in which we are more likely to find Christ—among the naked, hungry, and thirsty (Matt 25:31–46). Judgment occurred inasmuch as clothing, food, and water were or were not provided to Christ, when his face was not seen in the people. The claim that Christ is found among a group of others, centuries removed from the Jesus of Nazareth who asserted the things recorded in Matthew 25, is both a controversial and compelling one. Kierkegaard, for instance, found that whether the absolute nature of Christ is either an offense or an object of faith is fundamentally a matter of contemporaneity. Christ could not *be* of history conventionally understood, because this would relativize him (that is, would place him on par with any other human being who once lived) and would subject him to judgment according to the "outcome" of his life.[83] Christ as the God-Man appeared in lowliness and in opposition to all standard historical conceptions, thus determinedly making himself an object of faith or a sign of offense. He cannot be esteemed or judged as someone strictly "in" history. If this the case, then can my solidarity with a certain group be so profound that I find myself in them and they find themselves in me, so that the notion of a stable, singular individual identity that simply contains impressions or recollections of others is undermined? Indeed, if Christ, as Matthew 25 suggests, so intimately identifies with the poor and needy, then he is always in fellowship with them in their struggles. If we are in fellowship with Jesus, then we can also join the poor and become convinced that service to one is service to the other, so much so that divine judgment seals the pact. Herein, perhaps, we find the nexus of disaster, memory, and community. Participant *F1*'s account of displaced citizens is instructive:

> I live forty-five minutes out of the city. It is made up of folks from St. Bernard [Parish]. They still have the perspective of being a neighbor. They live in the idea of being connected with those around them—they have a story and want to hear the story of their neighbor and their life and, even [in carrying out this practice with new neighbors], they will return home [to St. Bernard]. "My neighbor is still in St. Bernard"—they'll still connect to the experience and to the people who stayed behind. They have compassion for their history and for their future; a special hope.[84]

83 See Kierkegaard, *Practice in* Christianity, 42–51. Kierkegaard presents a series of hypothetical, though certainly not entirely fictitious, speeches in which citizens and statesmen assess Christ as if he were in their midst, as a contemporary. In all cases, because of his failure of logic, questionable mental health, strange personality, poor political strategy, or shortage of reputational benefits for partners, Christ is derided and rejected as too offensive.

84. Santos, Participant *M1* interview.

The eschatological significance of this cannot be missed or dismissed. Just as Christ can claim to be found with the poor and destitute precisely as the eschatological Christ (that is, as the One coming to us from an utterly whole and fulfilled life), so can the displaced citizen claim solidarity with the destroyed and somewhat-desolate community he or she once inhabited. What is more, the citizen can carry out the robust and compassionate life of the neighbor—a neighbor immersed in the life story of others. The manner in which this gestures Christlikeness is crucial because for many citizens it is their initiation into an encounter with the divine. It should not be strange, furthermore, that the human person lives as someone inhabited, as it were, by many others.[85] Disaster does not create this condition; it sufficiently destabilizes our usual cultural orientation to the point that it becomes obvious and even desired to be inhabited by others. But just as individuals shun long-term interdependence and deep intimacy, so the enhanced community-level sharing and giving requires a particular ecclesial vision in order to continue. The principle of subsidiarity highlights the need for local and intermediate community groups, already dependent on a number of preexisting relationships, to carry out such work. Here the work of God's care is a work of a people that God may awaken to the task of rebuilding in solidarity. In fact, in this task a certain form of political congregational discernment is quite crucial, because the recognition that the restoration of "the land," that is, of the physical structures, and the corollary sacramental significance of those material edifices, and the complex web of judgments and practices that the structures facilitate and represent, is not identical to the restoration of the persons in community. They are, to be sure, intimately connected. However, achievement in one facet does not simply assure deliverance in the other. Michael Levering suggests this much in his treatment of Ezra and Nehemiah, setting forth the restoration of the worship of God's holy people as the ground for the return of holiness, or for "the promise of divine indwelling," to that very same land.[86]

---

85. See Ford, *Shape of Living*, 35.

86. In discussing the Israelites' rejection of assistance from the "peoples of the land," Matthew Levering posits: "Were the peoples of the land to assist in the rebuilding of the temple, then no return to the land could actually take place, because the land becomes itself . . . only when the returning exiles seek it for the purposes of true worship" (Levering, *Ezra & Nehemiah*, 34).

The Gift of Membership: Guilt, Responsibility, and Renewal

Within Christian ecclesial practice, consequently, the most hopeful model for church disaster preparedness is tantamount to what the church may call the gift of membership (or living toward a destiny in collectivity), which includes the gift of responsibility; and this only comes with the gift of guilt and confession as guided by the Holy Spirit. Perhaps the single most important gesture of governance is an admission of guilt and embodied humility. A concession to wrongdoing is a primary practice of the church. This does not mean the church can only hope to embody a holy way of life *in theory*, or can engage in longwinded apologies for its complicity in every malfeasance; rather, in the admissions of faithful followers to contributing to the guilt of the world, it is opening itself up to the possibility of forgiveness and repentance, which are radical acts of release and social change. This confession is not "institutional" but something to which each member is committed—members who welcome others to listen, pray, and move forward within God's gracious strength. The state, in this respect, requires forgiveness but finds it difficult to ask for. It often does not see itself as a group of human beings that require such practices as centrally constitutive of governmental work. The churches are meant to practice this as a way of displaying what life can be like when responsibility and guilt are not eschewed or turned into tools for reputation management, but accepted and redeemed within an eschatological vision of human family. This notion of human family is covenantal, echoing at once God's proclamations in Genesis 9 ("I will require the life of every animal and every man for your life and your blood. I will require the life of each man's brother for a man's life"), and the ecclesial-covenantal injunctions of Matthew 5 (e.g., "First go and be reconciled to your brother and then come and present your gift") and 18 (e.g., "If your brother sins, go and show him his fault, when the two of you are alone"). Human beings, in other words, discover they are brothers and sisters in a covenantal family *within* the life of community, while the families of the nation-state struggle to engender cohesion from within the swirling and often unmerciful demands of subcultures found within the global market, within profession, and within entertainment, government, or neighborhood. It is not so much that these subcultures demand and expect compliance to group norms without compassion; rather, they often lack the internal imagination, radical commitment, and poetic resources necessary for the immanent criticism to see life otherwise.

Take note, for example, of one southwestern African congregation's desire to take responsibility for the hurricane. Participant *M4* recalled a message he received from a church in Africa that apologized for what had transpired in the Gulf Coast, claiming responsibility for the hurricane.[87] Remarkably, this group was aware that tropical depressions and other early stages of powerful storm systems originated from that part of the world and thus felt somehow responsible. Whether one finds this reasoning theologically convincing or not, it is undeniably humble and uncanny insofar as it joins covenant, creation, and judgment in a noteworthy manner. So, before I head into the final section, about the statist political imaginary, I must articulate a creational component of ecclesial life that is able to supplement our discussion of judgment and, by extension, of ecclesial engagement with the neighbor after disaster. A creational hermeneutic of judgment in this case begins with God's creative work and his love and faithfulness toward his creation. Ecclesial *mimesis* finds its primal object against which to measure its actions and thoughts to be God's passion for creation.

In more ways than one, undoubtedly, Genesis 6–9 and Genesis 18 bear upon the imagination of the faithful and of the world beyond. The flood account bears the marks of a God who grieves as the responsible Creator, compelled to respond. Early in chapter 6, the text carries three allusions to the intimate, undeniable, and almost-visceral creator-creature link, two of which are in the first person: "he made mankind," "'whom I have created,'" and the plainspoken, "'I have made them.'" Creation is the product of God's hands and God's breath. Hence, he must do something. God will not simply let things be, with a sense of aloof, resigned detachment in the face of frustrating circumstances. Instead, he finds goodness in creation in the interest of renewal; specifically, he finds "favor." If God's action is predicated on a perfectly free love and concern for a ravaged earth, a love named the Cross, then the human beings that as a body act as a "priestly nation" must also accept communion with the created world.

In his lectures on Genesis, Dietrich Bonhoeffer claimed the following about the incontrovertible link between the human and the earth:

---

87. Santos, Participant *M4*. Interviewed January 7, 2008.

> Man's origin is in a piece of earth. His bond with the earth be-
> longs to his essential being. The "earth is his mother"; he comes
> out of her womb . . . His body belongs to his essential being.
> Man's body is not his prison, his shell, his exterior, but man
> himself. Man does not "have" a body; he does not "have" a soul;
> rather, he "is" body and soul. Man in the beginning is really his
> body. He is one. He is his body, as Christ is completely his body,
> as the Church is the body of Christ.[88]

Shortly thereafter, Bonhoeffer adds,

> The essential point of human existence is its bond with mother
> earth, its being as body . . . He comes out of the earth in which
> he slept and was dead; he is called out by the Word of God the
> Almighty, in himself a piece of the earth, but earth called into
> human being by God.[89]

After commenting that "the human body only lives by God's Spirit; this is
indeed its essential nature," Bonhoeffer concludes that "in his bodiliness
he is related to the earth and to other bodies, he is there for others, he is
dependent on others."[90]

The earth is like a brother; the earth is in some vital sense our kin. It
shares in our life as we share in its own life. What we label "weather systems" is the work of a created amalgam of substances, which, in a marred
and broken state, still reflect the divine glory. The Apostle Paul asserted
that the earth strives to overcome decay (Rom 8:19) like humans and
must actually "anticipate" our adoption as God's children:

> I consider that the sufferings of this present time are not worth
> comparing with the glory about to be revealed to us. For the cre-
> ation waits with eager longing for the revealing of the children
> of God; for the creation was subjected to futility, not of its own
> will but by the will of the one who subjected it, in hope that the
> creation itself will be set free from its bondage to decay and will
> obtain the freedom of the glory of the children of God. We know
> that the whole creation has been groaning in labor pains until
> now; and not only the creation, but we ourselves, who have the
> first fruits of the Spirit, groan inwardly while we wait for adop-
> tion, the redemption of our bodies. For in hope we were saved.

88. Bonhoeffer, *Creation and Fall/Temptation*, 50.

89. Ibid., 51.

90. Ibid., 52.

> Now hope that is seen is not hope. For who hopes for what is
> seen? But if we hope for what we do not see, we wait for it with
> patience. (Rom 8:18–25, NRSV)

Bonhoeffer is right in that we can assume a joint passage into a particular
destiny with the created order. Most interesting, Paul asserts that he an-
ticipates creation's eventual freedom from decay as a participation in ("set
free . . . into") the "glorious freedom of God's children" (v. 21). The pains
and laments of creation, itself an interesting anthropomorphism applied
to the earth, are discussed in the context of "our present sufferings" (v.18).
This joint destiny, moreover, comes with precedent—namely, God's covenant with Noah and all living creatures in Genesis 10. The prophets
sustain the centrality of this creationwide covenant as well. For example,
the prophet Hosea details God's intention to make a new covenant with
Israel that includes the animals of the sky, earth, and sea (Hos 2:18). This
covenant with all living creatures promises the destruction of weapons
of war and an eternal commitment from God to be with his people in
justice, righteousness, love, and compassion (vv. 19–20).

The foregoing quotations are meant to underscore two important
themes of preparedness and political identity (i.e., membership). First, the
weather is not, in its nature, merely an unfeeling enemy in the sense that its
unpredictability is a formidable test of our dominion and technorational
wherewithal. Rather, it was created to have a covenant life *with us* (Gen
9:12–16), receiving our care and attention. The perils, nonetheless, are
significant and tragic. We are like brothers or sisters who have not been
reconciled. The creation suffers with us in our "present sufferings" (Rom
8:18). It is not simply chemical compounds that can be manipulated by
God to do this or that. Indeed, God subjected "the creation" to futility in
the hope that it would be set free along with God's children when the latter undergo the redemption of their bodies (Rom 8:20–21). The fact that
"bodies" is mentioned here, and not "souls," is sensible if only for the fact
that Paul is persuading us of the anguish of the "whole creation"—namely,
the material world as we know it. Our bodies are not utterly distinct from
the material world but live, suffer, and sin in it: our bodies are of material
creation. Our bodies testify to an affinity with the earth that a soul cannot
do without. All are created by God, and all are in need of redemption. All
must live in hope. A people untrained in the endurance that hope brings
will fall under *krisis* (judgment) as well as under the crushing weight of

confusion, despair, and powerlessness that comes with living through a large storm and the test of character it exacts.

This begs a further question: in what ways do the state's organs live with the created order and suffer with it? The governmentality of which Michel Foucault spoke with respect to the "science" of government eschews such discourse of affinity or of suffering cohesion with the creation. It is forced to construe "populations" and "rates," not because it seeks evil or even mediocrity in delivery of compassionate service, but because it fails to embody any robust conception or understanding of evil and good on the basis of which to train its workers: it seeks, in other words, a confession of *ignorance* and *efficiency* (e.g., "I'm just doing my job"). It must confess ignorance because, despite the prominent discourse of expertise and control, the statist organ can only "work with the information [its] given" in any lived operational context, especially that of mass emergencies and disasters.[91] All such conceptions, furthermore, gain additional currency from the acquiescence of the people in community who live in and compose the personnel of statist organs. And this, of course, leads us again to the vitality of confession and a grammar of "godly sorrow" rather than "worldly sorrow," by which sadness leads us to substantively change our ways; that is, to salvation rather than death (2 Cor 7:10–11).

THE THEOPOLITICAL IMAGINARY OF THE STATE: KNOWLEDGE, VISION, AND JUDGMENT FALSELY CALLED SO

This final section considers more closely, through cultural-political lenses, some of the elements of the statist political imaginary as mediated in a select number of disaster-response and postdisaster reconstruction projects. The veritable truism that government at every level fell short in fulfilling many crucial emergency-service functions is not the main concern of the this section; rather, it explores, in anthropomorphic terms, the intelligence, vision, and judgment embodied in the statist imaginary linked to this disaster. These capacities of the statist subject-object are then related to Christ's reflections, longing, and embrace in his body. This comparative examination reveals that the state, operating out of a sense

91. The quotation in this sentence is derived from an interview with an executive of the state of Louisiana. Participant O1 oversaw a significant number of important emergency-service functions following the arrival of Hurricane Katrina. Interviewed January 13, 2008.

of despair and limitation to which it is unaccustomed, requires the judgment of the church.

The degree of governmental discord was unfortunately elevated during both the evacuation and the response phases of the post-Katrina debacle. Accusations and ad hominem attacks were exchanged with great frequency. Local and state government claimed that FEMA failed to communicate directly with members of the mayor's office and with the Louisiana state government. The basis of many criticisms leveled against FEMA director Michael Brown (who, for his part, claimed that a major rift between New Orleans mayor Ray Nagin and Louisiana governor Kathleen Blanco encumbered the response process), was one of surprise or disbelief: "people thought there was some federal expertise out there. There wasn't. Not from you,"[92] stated Rep. Gene Taylor, a Democrat from Mississippi, during a special congressional panel planned by the House Republican leaders. Brown staunchly defended his expertise, retorting, "I've overseen over 150 presidentially declared disasters. I know what I'm doing, and I think I do a pretty darn good job of it."[93] Despite his expertise, Brown claimed that he had no authority to order a complete evacuation well ahead of the storm's arrival, and that the ultimate reason for the misery of many evacuees was exactly due to the late and disorderly evacuation. Brown insisted that a warning to that effect went unheeded by Governor Blanco. Mayor Nagin, in turn, criticized the federal government for not providing the necessary resources to care for the evacuees and to transport them out of the city. Other officials criticized FEMA for not restoring order to the city and ameliorating the poor communication between law-enforcement agencies, to which Brown replied that the communication technology necessary for the task was denied him.[94] Nagin, in fact, urged local officials at a meeting of the National League of Cities to be extremely concerned about improving the federal government's response to disasters; indeed he claimed that the federal government was typically in a "constipated" state and that pressure from mayors would serve as "Ex-lax."[95]

92. Jordan, "Former FEMA director Blames Others."
93. Ibid.
94. Ibid.
95. Whitmire, "Nagin Says Mayors Must Urge Feds."

Provincial squabbles likewise exposed the doubts and suspicions that encumbered legislative decision making. Nagin had to deal with a popular rumor that the government was planning on large-scale demolition of homes—a fear no doubt arising from the paranoia and misgivings that had prevented many residents from evacuating even when a government vehicle traveled through the city urging families to leave before the arrival of the hurricane. The rumor of a government-initiated home demolition did not inhibit the mayor. Nagin criticized the inadequate congressional response to Hurricane Katrina, citing the rather rapid dissipation of interest in rebuilding New Orleans and surrounding cities due to overriding concerns about the war in Iraq. Acutely aware of the financial problems that an economically inactive New Orleans would produce for Louisiana (he claimed that New Orleans accounts for 35 percent of the state budget), the mayor also labeled state legislators as "indifferent" to the post-Katrina plight.[96] Besides this, Nagin himself was the target of considerable criticism, most of which was directed toward the reconstruction plan released after a long period of silence, and for his proposal to construct a casino district in New Orleans that he supposed would provide a "hype and glitter" factor that investors and visitors would find hard to deny and that would, as one journalist commenting on the proposal stated, "breathe life into the ailing city economy."[97] The strongest of Nagin's efforts, it appears, were directed toward financial renewal and stability, a task which led him to censure other cities that were vying for some of the $110 billion of federal aid he expected: "Maybe let a little bit go," he said, "to areas that were less affected . . . I'm thankful that they took our people in. A little aid is appropriate."[98] Other Louisiana officials as well, not just Nagin, had to convince federal lawmakers that they were not as corrupt or incompetent as their reputation suggested in order to receive the funds they considered necessary for an effective rebuilding effort.

This review of just a few of the more crucial points of contention indicates both the fallenness of politics (something Augustine observed astutely) and, more particularly, the fretfulness or anxiety that attends to the confusing array of claims, requests, and expectations. Everything from the surprising failure of so-called experts and fruitless gestures of

96. Gyan, "Nagin: 'I'm Rowing Alone.'"
97. Ibid.
98. LaPlante and Shields, "Nagin: N.O. Should Get Most Aid."

intergovernmental dependence to fears of corruption and the inadequacy of "information" affirm the almost complete dependence of government on epistemic rather than ontological criteria or commitments in executive and economic affairs. On this scale of decision making about the provision of funds and goods to a specific region, it is not surprising that New Orleanian officials believed they were being ignored. Can government function with its eyes on two crises centered on death: a disaster at home and an armed conflict abroad? The way through this morass partly depends upon understanding the consequences of our fixation on a functionalized epistemology detached from what a people *are*: stated in other terms, how do a physical city and its government participate in the vices and virtues of its citizens? Better yet, can the question of the goodness or beauty of a people's existence be intelligibly asked in light of the economic and political aspirations of the citizens, without falling back on responses couched in functionalism and voluntarism? The questions of goodness and beauty (and truth) are quintessentially ecclesial ones and stand in opposition to all the postdisaster debate about what exactly a government agency knows prior to a disaster. All this discussion is bent on fixing responsibility on the actions of government workers: responsibility arising from their reception and assessment of information (which by nature is fragmented, incoherent, and pliable). This exposes a key weakness in the statist imaginary's conception of interaction between human persons.

As a constellation of organizations that supposedly possess many advantages over uncoordinated individual action (including the benefits of a plurality of perspectives, less memory loss, and centralized coordination and mobilization of resources), government still fails to *be with* the citizenry if it has not settled with them and listened well. A discipline of attention assures that others are not used as instruments toward some greater governmental end. Giving attention means disapproving of patronizing, pitying, or serving others (especially the underprivileged) as subordinates. The "pillar and bulwark of the truth (1 Tim 3:15) that is the church is not supposed to be made up of the pretentious or puffed up, but of those who, in Simone Weil's words, love their neighbor because they are attentive. In this attentiveness, "the soul empties itself of all its own contents in order to receive into itself the being it is looking at, just as he is, in all his truth. Only he who is capable of attention can do this."[99] This attention demands an encounter with a person in anguish before, during, and after disaster. Many statist projects boast of a universal legitimacy grounded in abstraction that simply appears to be a fear of face-to-face encounter—of a meeting that in faith exacts a test of love, faith, and hope between two human beings. These encounters make gift giving possible, not simply so-called emergency aid or entitlements. Such meetings redefine government intelligence or information analysis; the encounter between a parent and a son or daughter with extreme physical disabilities, as Frances Young movingly conveys, generates "intelligence" of a more incarnate sort: a virtue in touching and seeing in tenderness and selflessness that the state disregards in its own words of praise and expectation.[100] Indeed, the general postdisaster idealization of transcending racial and religious divisions optimistically undermines the importance of encounter, unless the encounter is violent, indirect, or speedy, with little or no cost to the body and soul of the self. Kenotic attention, to the contrary, stands in opposition to a corollary of statist "knowledge" contained in its vision of population and territory in the postdisaster reconstruction plans. Kenotic attention opposes, in other words, the implicit statist approval of docetism. This docetism is the ultimate rejection of the presence of Christ in and with humanity.

The rebuilding plans that surreptitiously rejected the return of the working poor, and the general disregard for the working poor before the hurricane, are directly linked to the government's mechanisms of population management. In one of Michel Foucault's lectures on territory and security, he details how the population as such becomes a "political subject, a new collective subject" because it is expected to behave in certain ways, and as an object "toward which mechanisms are directed" in order to generate a predetermined effect.[101] In terms of the New Orleans reconstruction plans formulated without citizen consultation, the citizens were viewed as members of a population insofar as each person is "an element of the thing [that the state] want[s] to manage in the best way possible, namely the population."[102] Viewed from the level of population,

---

99. Weil, *Waiting for God*, 114.

100. Young, *Brokenness and Blessing*, 30.

101. Foucault, *Security, Territory, Population*, 42.

102. Ibid., 43.

citizens are expected to conform to a plan, the implementation and goals of which were established beforehand without any constitutive trust, presence, or attention on the part of those officials purportedly seeking to improve the welfare of the members. The population as a collective subject is already defined in terms of productive capacity in numerous categories that are likewise subject to and the product of calculation and prediction. The working (and nonworking) poor are those who Foucault refers to as "the people" in opposition to "the population." "The people" are those who put themselves outside the population and the apparatuses by which it is regulated and defined.[103] The most appalling of rebuilding plans envisions a particular city and a specific population for it, and go about making sure that all subtleties of speech and action make it appear that no exclusion is afoot. Methods of specialization and predictability that allow for a specific population to be envisioned are almost from the outset handmaidens of manipulative practices—practices that foster detachment from actual human beings. Such practices produce high-end commodities and services, yet with a so-called ugly or delinquent subset of persons for whom complete submission is either not possible or desirable, or both impossible and undesirable. The final objective is the population," Foucault contends. "[T]he population is pertinent as the objective, and individuals, the series of individuals, are no longer pertinent as the objective, but only as the instrument, relay, or condition for obtaining something at the level of population."[104]

The church serves as a countersocial form with respect to specialization and its affinity to maximum control, which in turn leads to the exclusion of "all other possibilities."[105] Note Wendell Berry's claim with respect to the confident specifications and models of the "specialist" mode of thought concerning so-called farms of the future:

> Nowhere is the essential totalitarianism and essential weakness of the specialist mind more clearly displayed than in this ambition. Confronted with the living substance of farming—the complexly, even mysteriously interrelated lives on which it depends, from the microorganisms in the soil to the human consumer—the agriculture specialist can think only of subjecting it to total control.[106]

103. Ibid., 44.
104. Ibid. , 42.
105. Berry, *Unsettling of America*, 71.
106. Ibid., 70.

Moreover, this narrow vision and implementation of technique for the sake of controlled and expected abundance persists side-by-side with chaos and disorder. This disorder lies just beyond the boundaries within which all is in control. In the realm of the chaotic lies everything and everyone that does not "work." The specialist mode of thinking, planning, and creating, then, promotes disorder to the extent that it relegates certain things to the status of dispensable because they do not work within the specified model. Simply take notice of the prevalence of downtown business districts in medium-to-large urban settings, complete with four-star hotels and state-of-the-art convention centers, which reside within a few blocks (or less) of poorly maintained, segregated neighborhoods. Although these neighborhoods may thrive with respect to solidarity and citizen involvement, the political imagination that weds advanced capitalism and statist autonomy sees disorder at the edge of order, and with it the urge clean up the streets for the sake of appearance. This pressure to keep up appearances has played a crucial role in the criminalization of poverty. In an attempt to save the face of the city, as it were (when the city is viewed as a construct of the state), publicly visible poor persons are considered blemishes, embarrassments, and financial burdens, due to both their lack of productivity and their impact on tourism.

By analogy, we are able to contrast the logic that governs the prevailing vision of certain persons and groups in the city with the manner in which the church confronts such a vision. Whereas the state will eliminate the irreconcilable villain from "the people," the particular modus operandi of the state organs already excludes large numbers of the non-functional or unproductive before and after disasters. The state, as it is a human mechanism fraught with *our own* despair and anxiety, specializes in categorization and exclusion. Indeed, this does not happen in a directly coercive mode. The idea of the state is adopted among citizens as a solution to the tremendous challenge of dependence: when I view my life as dependent, yet only impersonally so, the claims that other lives make on me are contingent in the negative sense. That is, I do not have any substantial or demanding relation to any one human individual within the closed horizon of family, work, consumption, or government (including administrative agencies that hold information about me and provide assistance). In other words, everything outside my immediate closed sphere of existence can be chaotic but remain pristinely imperceptible. Until, of course, something ruptures that social and political vision, and disorder spills over into realm of order.

This rupture reveals in no uncertain terms the excluded bodies that live on in the social and political margins. These are the humans (the bodies, feelings, vernacular, tastes, and practices) whom we would rather do without. These are, more often than not, the black, Hispanic, and other mixed bodies we do not understand through the prism of the statist imaginary, which often privileges binaries (while tertiary or more expansive arrangements cause problems). After all, we cannot directly perceive the spirit of a any human at first sight, only a body, even if the body is, as Wittgenstein said, the "shape of the soul."[107] These are persons only known in any genuine ontological sense through contact, dialogue, embrace, and attentive face-to-face service: hence the shock of seeing the sheer mass of New Orleans residents (approximately twenty thousand of them) that appeared at the Superdome, only to be photographed and questioned as they desperately waited for food and other goods. These bodies and their neighborhoods (many of which only a mile or two away from the French Quarter and the centers of prestige and financial pros-perity) were transported—via television and Internet communication—to a new place, to be seen by other Louisianans, other Americans, and the rest of the world.

Even as the chilling and listless scenario played out in the lives of these residents, they still faced the same evaluations of worth that char-acterized their life before the disaster. Without being asked to do so, several participants took pains to highlight the apparent uncouth and at times dangerous behavior of displaced residents inside the Superdome. Participant *L1* avowed,

> And no matter what some say, it was not peaceful in the dome.
> I know a woman who cares for an elderly, sickly friend, and she
> told me that she had to drape herself over the body of the woman
> because of gunshots she heard while they were in the dome.[108]

Other participants downplayed the problem as mere exaggeration and sensationalist media. Regardless of what exactly occurred at the Superdome, the strife and disagreement over getting the story right about the conduct of "the people in the dome" reflect the struggle for a coherent

107. Wittgenstein, *Philosophical Investigations*, 178
108. Santos, Participant *L1* interview.

and believable political narrative, especially in light of what a particular narrative may require with respect to *membership*. It is trying indeed to unsettle or give up one's view of other ethnic groups, justice, business practice, and community life, because the prospect of alterations either reveals severe contradictions in our line of reasoning or punctures our ostensibly coherent political imagination. In other words, we know we must ask ourselves: will this new account require substantial change in the practices emanating from my previously exercised imagination? If my political imagination changes, this necessarily entails a demand to change my patterns of social, intellectual, and bodily practice; it may entail the beginning of new conversations with persons of a different background: that is, with persons whose access to resources, percep-tions of opportunity, or assumptions about the other engender a different context from within which community practices arise. In simple terms, this change may cause different communities to speak to one another. If the official postdisaster narrative calls for, at most, only a private rage and sentimental identification with the sad situation of the underclass or the invisible, then my views of a certain group will never appear to need alteration, especially if I surround myself with friends and family who would never expect or encourage me to actually come in contact with such groups in the first place.

The church as formed by God is a people called out from the na-tions. In practice, this calls congregations to already be completely other, because the members never cease to start new friendships and relations outside of their privileged and comfortable family circle. God the Spirit brings, as Acts 2 and 3 vividly portray, many nations and their tongues to one focus of wonderment and exaltation toward God. Moreover, as Paul the apostle writes in the context of worship, those who are considered dispensable, unproductive, or unattractive are treated as indispensable and in need of special treatment (1 Cor 12:22–24). This makes the body both relevant and irrelevant. Such an antithetical construction and mode of understanding is pervasive in Paul's writings; indeed, it reflects God's subversion of our preferred method of reason and logic. The church makes the physical body relevant in that it is disciplined for the sake of discipleship to Jesus, yet it is irrelevant to the judgments and standards of the broader cultural world that lives in itself, which means out of its own resources and horizon of expectation. The state, and its partnership with unrestrained capitalism, is god within this horizon. It does not promote transformation but mere cooperation, submission to specialization and retail services, and therefore expects trust as satiation or full consumption. By contrast, the church touches and transforms bodies so that they are with other bodies and souls, combining destinies and narratives once alienated one from another but now offered jointly to God.

Take note, for instance, of the incongruity between the words of a high school student and the statist imaginary's penchant for population management without the population's direct involvement. During the first several months after Hurricane Katrina, educators prompted students to place their reflections about the storm on paper in the form of poetry or prose. A young female student named Keva Carr wrote,

> Well, when a friend is in trouble, you do not turn your back on her. But in my case it's a city. A city that has given me laughter and tears . . . my city needs me. It needs my prayers, my hope, my words, and my strength . . .
>
> To: My City
> I Love you, and you
> Shall
> Rise
> Again.[109]

By analogically redirecting filial devotion to the city, this student amplifies the unfathomability of forgetfulness and trains herself to resist all the internal pressures and external mechanisms (whether capitalist or not) that encourage such a nihilistic practice of sublimation. Affection and concern for the city as friend is a means by which the city may be viewed as an ontological reality that may participate in the ongoing creative agency of the Trinity, or the kingdom of the resurrected Son (as the poem says, "Rise / Again") that gathers together brothers and sisters as a holy assembly. Extensions of friendship bespeak a yearning or longing for what is both good and best for the friend. This orientation to the city encapsulates the theopolitics of the neighbor to which Hurricane Katrina opened the eyes of many. Judgment and instruction to God may occur in this context because it is a context of friendship, not of oversight, technical competence, or desperation over financial prosperity.

Frankly, therefore, it is important to assert what is clear in light of the theological and biblical material in the beginning of this chapter and

---

109. Carr, "To: My City."

that which has ensued: the state does *not love* the poor. It cannot imagine such an activity; it can only speak of "assistance" and "emergency aid." Its agencies seek to help the poor in a variety of ways, to alleviate their struggle, and to speak for them at legislative assemblies, but it does not in itself embody love. The modus operandi of the state in its relations to the substantive qualities of other entities, as one government executive we interviewed asserted, is not surprising: "if a program will provide assistance to our [governmental] organizational goals, then we'll support it, regardless of what the organization necessarily believes or values."[110] This executive, however, acknowledged that changes to government start with the clarification of expectations at the community level. She stated vehemently,

> Every community has to answer question of what the government and church or NGO [nongovernmental organization] should do. Katrina should open conversation of what the government should provide and what the community should provide for itself. Louisiana has made strides towards solutions to poverty—what are our problems and what can we (the community rather than the government) provide? We need to try to bring more people to the table who don't necessarily have a vested interest in what the government is providing and get their input. Government is supposed to fill expectations of its constituents. The governmental "gaps" folks were talking about after Katrina: these gaps were created by the people's expectations of government that were not necessarily vocalized.[111]

This executive lucidly points to the need for increased dialogue, for dialogue with sufficient clarity to assure participants that the government should not be an entity detached from people (and to assure people that the government does not believe it is detached from people). Moreover, this executive lays the responsibility for allowing the government to "get bloated," or filled with resources inefficiently utilized, upon the lack of dialogue about citizen expectations.[112]

The church, however, has received its charter from Christ and so enters the dialogue with a divine expectation to embody certain virtues of mercy and service. It must love the poor because it must love Christ.

110. Santos, Participant *P1* interview.
111. Ibid.
112. Ibid.

"Must" does not imply coercion or force. It denotes more importantly a profound desire for wholeness: "To whom shall we go? You have the words of eternal life" (John 6:68). Furthermore, there is no wholeness without the wisdom of which the ancient sages speak. It is not coincidental that reading through the book of Proverbs forces one to encounter the poor, and this often. Likewise, Job cannot proceed through his both disheartening and enlivened dialogue with his so-called comforters without engaging the "hard service" of the "days of the hired worker . . . the servant longing for the evening shadow, and . . . the hired man looking for his wages" (Job 7:1–2). There is no wisdom in this world that abides between curse and promise without a deep appreciation and love for the poor.

This obfuscation of or disregard for God's wisdom in the weak and poor is most evident in the state's exercise of judgment, which bears an intimate relation to its vision of population and to its intelligence or knowledge. Discussed above, the struggle over apprehending judgment has affirmed God's goodness; God's justice in relation to sin; the failure of congregations to live justly; and, integrally, our kinship with the earth in judgment and redemption. This latter element we expect would fall beyond the bounds of statist concern. But there is more to this problem: we (in our participation in the statist imaginary) are troubled with the notion that, as Bonhoeffer argued: grace comes in judgment. This is as much an issue of truth as any other, but not in the usual, propositional sense of truth: "Truth is not something in itself, which rests for itself, but something that happens between two. Truth only happens in community."[113] These words concerning truth, which bear a striking resemblance to Bonhoeffer's contention that only in relationship with the other is freedom a reality, constitute the foundation of an ecclesial-political hermeneutic of judgment. The judgment enacted in the church between disciples of Jesus is the first premise or step toward judgment in relation to the state. Consider, for instance, Bonhoeffer's argument concerning how to properly view the state if Christ, as the center of history, consequently places the church at the center of history.

> The Church does not show itself to be the centre by visibly standing at the centre of the state or by letting itself be put at the centre, as when it is made a state Church. It is not its visible position in the realm of the state that shows its relation to the state. The

113. Bonhoeffer, *Christ the Center*, 50.

> meaning and the promise of the state is hidden in it, it judges
> and justifies the state in its nature. Its nature, i.e. the nature of the
> state, is to bring a people nearer to its fulfillment by law and the
> order it creates. With the thought of an order-creating state, that
> messianic claim dwells hidden within.[114]

Due to presence of the "messianic claim" within the state, it is the church's
prerogative to justify and judge the state. However, this judgment cannot
occur, if we take seriously Paul's injunction in 1 Cor 5:12–13, unless the
church judges itself. Although I am unsure about the hiddenness of the
messianic claim, the notion that within the church lies the meaning and
promise of the state places an onus upon the church that only those who
dwell with the incarnate Son can fulfill. This judgment, patterned after
the relations and interactions of disciples as indicated at various points
throughout this chapter, speaks a true word to the state if it arises from
ecclesial or liturgical embodiment, from the church's concrete life in the
world. Finally, then (and perhaps this is the most difficult notion for the
statist imaginary to digest), *grace arrives in judgment.* Kierkegaard frames
judgment as through and through a matter of love. In a writing titled *Two
Discourses at the Communion on Fridays,* Kierkegaard, quite enthralled
at the notion that judgment only warrants hope if it is rooted in God's
unchanged love, goes on thus:

> But therefore I take comfort in the words, and I block every es-
> cape route for me and I push aside all excuses and all extenuations
> and bare my breast where I will be wounded by the words that,
> judging, penetrate, judging "You loved only little." Oh, only pen-
> etrate more deeply, even more deeply, you healing pain . . . even
> when such is the judgment, I am in one sense aware of no pain,
> I am aware of an indescribable blessedness, because precisely my
> sentence, my death sentence upon me and my wretched love, con-
> tains something else in addition: God is unchanged love.[115]

Such impassioned and gracious acceptance of judgment is only possible
if, as Kierkegaard insists in his comments about the parable of the two
debtors, "everything remains within love."[116] This form of judgment,
contrary to that produced in apprehensive, and still violent, statist assessments of information and population management, is to be enacted in

114. Ibid., 63.

115. Kierkegaard, "Two Discourses at the Communion," 391.

116. Ibid.

the church if it is to contribute to a profound change in the politics of the world in view of the work of Christ in our midst.

REFLECTIONS FOR ECCLESIAL PRAXIS

The aforementioned leads us to consider the prospect of the politics of the love encountered in the incarnation. The love of the incarnation risks greatly and moves forward, draws all the other to itself, not for direct access or control, but to direct the other to the God of abundant life, to edify, and to show the other that her words and presence are sought out. This love may only be found in the church through the Holy Spirit, who intercedes for us and hence assures that we do not love as single, isolated persons but in pained yet faithful fellowship (Rom 8:26). This is God's own Spirit given as a gift that binds us to him; it is, consequently, the Spirit that animates and transforms the insular and alienated wisdom of our *secut Deus* spirit. The state only lives in a linear continuum that has no definite *omega*. Matters can simply get better or get worse, and this is to be determined by the force or strength of our own measures and convictions. It is only falsely suspended from the divine, because it is assured victory from God but does nothing to develop in the citizenry a love for or humility before God and the other. The avoidance of Trinity among many churches is unfortunate because the Father, Son, and Holy Spirit model the way of self-giving love, recognition, sacrifice, and wisdom that cultivate life for the other and in relation to the other. Despair, anguish, hopelessness, and all other pain are the Godhead's pain, but shared and transformed through mutual self-sacrifice or, put another way, through ecstatic compassion. It was the Father's joy to give life in the Son; and Jesus, "who for the sake of the joy that was set before him endured the cross, disregarding its shame" (Heb 12:2). Joy in God's time (and timing) transforms social and political relations insofar as this joy is subsumed within the *telos* of politics: an ordering of one to the other, and of all God's creatures, toward union with God. One cannot build political life on the assumption that I must pit one portion of the population against another, or that there must be some way to benefit the self as much as the others. Love that participates in Christ's way is also, as Kierkegaard states in the beginning of *Works of Love*, that which links the temporal to the eternal. Love, as Paul wrote to the Corinthians, is that which is the greatest in comparison to faith and hope; indeed, love abides and thus contains within itself, as Kierkegaard wrote, "the truth of the eternal."[117] Incidentally, knowledge or reason is not the chosen medium or faculty that constitutes the gate through which the eternal is apprehended. Rather, it is love. Love is the self-giving of God to humanity—it is a return to the beginning of creation and an anticipation of the consummation of creation. It is not a faculty, but a wellspring and preservation of life that originates outside the lover and beloved. This is something to which a human being can be only receptive; it cannot be earned, seized, controlled, or deduced from previously established premises or conditions. It comes from unknown depths and origins.[118]

This chapter has considered, although through a more theologically engaged perspective, the cultural politics of disaster response after Hurricane Katrina. The common thread running through these discussions was not as prominent an issue in previous chapters: God's judgment. However, the work of a called people, God's church, plays a vital role in mediating God's judgment. This judgment does not consist in a unilateral recitation of passages about God's justice with respect to sin, or in aggressive watchdog activities. The church itself is a locus of judgment, as expressed in the loving interchange of exhortation, instructions, prayers, and encounters with one another and the poor. These ecclesial practices carry within them a capacity to make new community and to compel action from the freedom and truth possible only in the crucible that is the ongoing life of the congregation. When the congregation's life takes seriously that judgment arises from love and grace, then it need not justify itself to the state. Its life as such will confront the state. In New Orleans, the statist political imaginary sealed itself off from the love of the poor and hence has precluded access to the fullness of being, wisdom, love, and friendship that *only* comes from this meeting or encounter of faces, eyes, and hands.

The ensuing chapters turn to a more social-theoretical and theological discussion of the elements of community formation after disaster, in light of material production, and particularly in light of commodification; and to the pastoral or ministerial role as a political interpreter of culture. The final chapter turns to a distillation of the key ecclesiological arguments presented thus far and uses them as a basis for a fuller discussion of the church as a source of emancipative community after disasters.

117. Kierkegaard, *Works of Love*, 25
118. Ibid., 26.

CHAPTER 5

Postdisaster-Culture Industry and
the Minister as Cultural Exegete

This study, from an analytical standpoint, has focused on the reestablishment of disciplined imaginings of space and time through institutional
differentiation and dedifferentiation following disasters. The study has
been concerned with how enduring and materially mediated conceptions of the sacred/secular divide, as expressed in the separation of
church and state, collapsed in acute ways following two terrorist-related
disasters and a weather disaster. Therefore, the reinstitution of viable
political imaginaries comes through a variety of cultural negotiations,
including through the assimilation of public accounts of truth. The case
of Hurricane Katrina introduced a case in which the cultural-political leverage that the state often enjoys in exercising emergency power was, by
and large, lost. Rather than taking part in processes of dedifferentiation,
a number of congregations took it upon themselves to disregard certain
administrative avenues for disaster relief and to establish local relations
on the basis of which administration was designed. These congregations
reversed the process of organizational socialization whereby administrative or bureaucratic stricture governs social relations; these congregations
constrained the typical process of relief and aid provision, subordinating
it to the role of gifted face-to-face encounters. These encounters and subsequent bonds restore political imagination through cultural production
whereby all the following are influenced: legitimacy in disaster response,
public performance, institutional autonomy, collective identity formation (solidarity), and the social-relational and ontological implications of
certain imaginings of space and time.

This penultimate chapter has a dual focus. From the perspective of disaster studies, it marks a contribution to an otherwise scantily addressed problem in the literature on disaster recovery, namely, "how do different cultural values affect the process [of recovery]? What role do political considerations play in the process"?[1] This study has also attempted to etch out an alternative space for further studies of "restoration," "rehabilitation" and "reconstruction."[2] What I have aimed to convincingly show is that in the case of these disasters, churches and statist agencies operate in a milieu rife with cultural conflict, absorption, and adaptation, in the realms of both embodied practice and theological reflection. This dynamic environment warrants cultivating skills of cultural exegesis, especially in the realm of consumption. To this end, this discussion features the material process by which city residents attempt to inscribe themselves more deeply into the collective articulation of pain and hope and, by extension, into the role of minister and church in interpreting and participating in the process of disaster recovery.

Material Bodies and Rituals of Solidarity

Unlike Oklahoma City, at which all major vernacular or unofficial shrines and memorial gestures were carried out in the vicinity immediately surrounding the Murrah Federal Building site (particularly on the Memory Fence), the entire Lower Manhattan area turned out be littered with a multiplicity of vernacular shrines and memorials after the attacks on the World Trade Center complex. The most fascinating processes linked to such "public expressions of private grief"[3] involved the inception of unplanned, creative, or improvised memorial artifacts that traveled along various stages of public institutionalization, commodification, and crystallization. As mentioned, the Ground Zero Cross of Girders was entirely unanticipated in its genesis but obtained iconic status. Indeed, the Cross became a site around which worship, and hence a completely theological orientation to the disaster, was pronounced and regularized at Ground Zero: the Franciscan Rev. Brian Jordan held weekly masses at the site

1. Quarantelli, "Disaster Recovery Process," 1.

2. Ibid. See Quarantelli's discussion of how different terms, such as *reconstruction*, *rehabilitation*, and *restoration*, carry differing legal and policy implications, depending upon whether the goal is to reattain preimpact social and economic patterns or simply to address social disintegration. Quarantelli, "Disaster Recovery Process," 3–7.

3. Jorgensen-Earp, "Public Memory and Private Grief."

of the cross until June 2002.[4] As the object of numerous ritual actions of blessing, including one from the Vatican, it carved an indelible mark on the landscape of Ground Zero so that the site could not be imagined without it.

Vernacular Inscriptions

At about the same time that the cross at Ground Zero was beginning its symbolic ascendance, virtually innumerable messages were being inscribed into the gray soot that covered the streets, walls, and windows of the buildings and storefronts in Lower Manhattan. Passersby, using their fingers or another blunt object, etched (among other utterances) expressions of rage, sadness, despair, the consolation of God's love for blocks extending outward from the World Trade Center site. In 71 Murray Street, locals actually inscribed messages on walls, including what follows, which corresponds to its actual format:

"The Towers Will Rise Again"
"God Bless America"
"Avenge Them"[5]

These spontaneous scrawlings take advantage of an open social space that takes physical space just as seriously as the site of cultural production and social rebinding. In a city where graffiti and tagging already provide a social antecedent that facilitate these expressions, the scale of such expressions is staggering. This is especially true in terms of centralized or administratively coordinate memorialization that may seem to preclude or discourage this sort of expression.

Makeshift memorials were also set up at Pennsylvania Station, on a fence along Canal Street (where thoughts and feelings were written out on pieces of paper stapled to yellow ribbons), in a Times Square storefront window that was spattered with cards carrying like sentiments, and in Union Square where a nineteen-year-old student taped down over one hundred pieces of butcher paper to the ground. Passersby covered this paper with "tributes, prayers, opinions, and counter-opinions."[6] This site became an uncentralized discussion and debate forum completely on

4. Barry, "At Ground Zero, Seeking Shelter."
5. Barry, "From a World Lost, Ephemeral Notes."
6. Waldman, "Grief is Lessened by Sharing."

resident initiative. Akin to these shrines was the St. Paul's Chapel wall of messages that ran along Broadway. In an attempt to copy the success of these shrines of public commemoration, the Urban Center galleries offered an exhibit named *Missing*, which comprised photographs of the spontaneous shrines, and grants visitors the opportunity to record their thoughts.

Another memorial practice that emerged on March 11, 2002 and lasted for a month included the "Twin Shafts of Light" (or "Tribute in Light"). These two large beams, formed by 616,000 watts of power pumped through over a dozen search lights, seemed to evoke a ghostly image of the Twin Towers up from Ground Zero, thereby simultaneously offering their presence and hurtful absence. The debate among residents surrounding the ending of this tribute was not simply rooted in the amount of power being consumed but in the message that it sent about the course of life in the future, a major element of the political imagination. While some residents claimed that such large commemorations are needed to prevent life from going on as usual, others declared that they needed to be removed because, "[t]here comes a point when you have to recover and move on."[7]

Theopolitical Commodities

Before I move on to a fuller discussion of commodities, a few theoretical considerations are in order. First, the commodities offered for purchase after the World Trade Center attacks were vital to postdisaster identity construction. These items, unlike images at public events or on television, can be owned and carried about. These commodities enabled, in a very crucial sense, entrance into the "national body" through a simple market transaction—primarily, for anyone who could afford to pay the price. Second, how and when an item was commodified demands attention. As this discussion avows, many items were vernacular creations that were looped into the mechanisms of market reproduction. Why could they be absorbed into the retail market with such rapidity? One reason, at least, involves what Maurice Halbwachs contended in the context of his discussion of "historical memories."[8] Collective memories arise from the subsumption of an objective event, or an event that is apparently relevant to everybody, into an individual biography and personal memory. Third, virtual nearness to the physical site, the deceased, or some other

7. Jacobs, "In Morning Sky, Seamless Exit."
8. Halbwachs, *On Collective Memory*, 59.

sacralized aspect of the event heavily influenced the exchange value of items. Items offered the possibility of "visceral seeing,"[9] a way of seeing that blurs the boundary between the viewer and the viewed on a disaster site. The closer one could get to some object on the site, the more real became the viewer's felt allegiance: that is, most of the human senses are brought into the memory-making and allegiance-creating experience. Fourth, aspects of the physical venue at which such commodities were offered (e.g., near the St. Paul's Chapel altar) and the very properties of the postdisaster commodities may together constitute a social mechanism for identity hybridization. When a person, for instance, buys a "flag of honor" at St. Paul's Chapel, do one does so as a New Yorker, as an American, as a Christian. Or perhaps a buyer takes hold of only some of these identities, or, perhaps, all.

Numerous ritual gestures of solidarity of an explicitly theological kind emerged during the eight-month ministry of St. Paul's Chapel. As expressions of gratitude to relief workers at the chapel, many rescue and debris-removal workers at Ground Zero formed miniature crosses out of scraps found at Ground Zero.[10] Perhaps modeled after the Cross of Girders at Ground Zero, and charged with the symbolic force of crucifixion and renewal, this item-idea did not remain impervious to market reproduction. Eventually, St. Paul's began to offer small pendant-sized crosses in their gift shop (see figure 1 below), reproductions of those that volunteers created from steel scraps.

Figure 1—Cross of Girders Statuette

9. See Cox Miller, "Visceral Seeing," 391–411.

10. "Out of the Dust," St. Paul's Timeline, foldout purchased at chapel.

Alongside other products incorporating the attacks one item sold at St. Paul's Chapel represents an interesting blend of high fashion, spiritual discipline, and sacrifice. Finger rosaries (figure 2) employing popular Venetian floral inlay beads offered the consumer, through mass, popular appeal, the sufferings of Christ.

Figure 2—Finger Rosaries

At St. Paul's Chapel, visitors also found a relatively inexpensive packet of wallet-sized cards containing a patchwork of images, some from other confessional perspectives (e.g. Native American), which depicted patriotic calls to virtue ("courage" and "hope"), memorial images from the disaster site, the vestment covered with rescue-agency patches (below right), and an American flag. The cards are meant to be passed on to friends, loved ones, or family members with a message that links the World Trade Center attack to some cultural object (tangible or intangible) that arose *from* the attack. The majority of images seem to be of objects that St. Paul's Chapel received from compassionate donors in the weeks succeeding the event. The images on the cards are recycled in such a fashion that they memorialize (by pulling individuals into the sights of Ground Zero) and thus simulate an experience leading to solidarity. The fact that the cards are all linked to "peace" is meant to integrate the stance of the church to the federal government's decision to engage in military reprisals.

Figure 3—Peace Cards

Merchandisers tied to the Roman Catholic Church offered an interesting theopolitical item highlighting a major patriotic motif. "An American Prayer Book" links the contemplation and devotion that typifies the discipline of prayer with a pseudo-catechistic approach to American history. Featuring a picture of the Ground Zero Cross with an American flag positioned just above the horizontal beam, this book was dedicated to all who lost their lives on September 11, 2001 and especially to Fr. Mychal Judge. It also offers a brief history of "our nation from its founding, and features prayers from various faiths, quotes from Presidents, and interesting bits of Americana." This product, then, is a package of de-differentiated reflection on politics and a universalized subsumption of "faiths."

One unique item made it through to utilization in market exchange *and* military engagement: a twelve-by-eighteen-foot American flag. This flag, originally draped over one of the surviving buildings at Ground Zero, was over time covered with personal messages from family members to the deceased (on the red stripes), sentiments such as "God Bless America" and defiant outbursts toward unnamed enemies (on the white stripes), and the actual names of the deceased (on the starry blue).[11] This item was used as a motivational icon carrying instructions and advice for soldiers in combat missions in Afghanistan. The flag was also commodified and offered for sale at the gift shop of St. Paul's Chapel. Two versions

11. Chen, "Flag to Carry Sentiments."

exist of this flag, often called the "Flag of Honor." These versions were rendered poster-sized and extremely precise in design and in the etching of names. One version includes all of those "killed in the terrorist attacks of 9.11" (see figure 4 below); the other version contains the names of the rescuers who died. The caption below the image of the flag uses the flag itself to authorize immortalization: "Now and forever more it [the flag] will represent their immortality. We shall never forget them."

The power of massified circulation and market-driven manipulation is aptly exhibited in this item. This commercial flux makes dedifferentiation that much easier to activate but much more difficult to control for any unified institutional purpose. Also, as in virtually all memorial ceremonies, theology figures powerfully in public assurances of the afterlife.

Flag of Honor.™

This flag contains the names of those killed in the terrorist attacks of 9.11. *
Now and forever it will represent their immortality
We shall never forget them

Figure 4—"Flag of Honor"

Many other commodities like the "flag of honor" reflected a reinvigorated national narrative identity that encompassed a certain theopolitical imagining of space and time. It was inherently fascinating to explore how certain commodities from, for example, the store at St.Paul's Chapel in New York City (in which Rudolph Giuliani gave his farewell speech) and other such denominational outlets conveyed a particular theopolitical identity. Different material products offered different answers to questions such as, what sort of view should a citizen have of the perpetrators? What themes are most important for a citizen at this juncture? Who does God support and why? For what should a citizen hope?

Other independent consumer outlets combined images of the American flag with the World Trade Center Towers. One T-shirt featured a large American flag furling next to an image of the towers with boldfaced blue letters asserting, "Evil Will Be Punished." An evangelically oriented Christian book and paraphernalia store I visited two weeks after the attack featured two T-shirts for sale, juxtaposed on a wall behind the cash registers. One of the shirts contained the message, "Pray for Peace," displaying the popular image of large hands clasped (as in prayer) looming over an image of the planet earth. The T-shirt next to it contained large, boldfaced lettering, superimposed on an American flag, that read, "Pray for our Troops." Yet another T-shirt (figure 5 below) deliberately links assertions typical of military sacrifice with the victims of the attacks, and these two with God's approval of the American cause and identity.

Figure 5—"Ultimate Price" T-shirt

This T-shirt, therefore, reframes the deceased as military heroes. It includes the deceased in the same company as patriots of the Revolutionary War, as soldiers of World Wars I and II and of other military campaigns since, including Operation Desert Storm and (at the time the shirt was released) of the impending "war on terrorism." This T-shirt offers the wearer the ability to publicly carry about the message that the national body is "re-membered" or reconstituted, through sacrificial deaths.

The final product of note is also for sale at St.Paul's Chapel and deliberately upholds democratic ideals. The *Here Is New York* book brings together about a thousand photographs submitted by New Yorkers (including amateur and professional photographers as well as children) to an exhibit that now travels throughout the United States and Europe and bears the same name.[12] The compendium, which the publisher deems will be "valued as the most important visual record of 9/11" is meant to capture "the most coherent sense of the whole" with regard to what occurred on September 11, 2001.[13] The sheer variety of photographs aims at exemplifying the variety of identities and backgrounds allowed expression under democratic government; the book features a "corporate author": "the people of New York." The book buttresses a democratic conception of "popular will" that is translated into a huge collection of images aimed at "speak[ing] . . . with one purpose, saying that to make sense of this terrifying phase in our history we must break down the barriers that divide us."[14] The united collectivity evidently must apprehend the significance of "the times": it is precisely the images of the people that enable the destruction of divisions. Also, the title of the collection intimates a boldness, plainness, and matter-of-fact perspective on the postdisaster period. The attacks and the New Yorkers involved should be unadorned and presented *in vivo*. An image of democracy is taken up into this stark mode of presenting regional or local identity: the main advertising image for the product features an open page with a sufficiently noticeable image of the American flag. As in other public performances during the post-disaster period, the fate of the city of New York, its residents, and the United States are seamlessly enmeshed.

12. www.hereisnewyork.org.
13. Ibid.
14. Ibid.

In conclusion, the material culture of solidarity emerging out the World Trade Center attacks is worthy of a completely separate research agenda. The above sample of items, however, offers interesting glimpses not only into some of the symbols elevated for consumption, but also into the possibilities for participation in the disaster-recovery process for those who do not reside in or around New York City. A potential consumer of such products can find them in St. Paul's Chapel and, as a result, can find an ornate tapestry of cultural objects representing sacrificial death, popular fashion and jewelry, the American flag, and worship of and prayer to God all within feet or inches of one another. This host of objects proposes seemingly infinite modes of participation in and appreciation for the disaster, while simultaneously offering a particular understanding of church life, of God, of American history, and of citizenship through a single (shopping) experience.

CHURCHES, CLERGY, AND THE PUBLIC DISCOURSE OF DISASTER

Cultural Agency and the Pastor's Political Imagination

This section begins by noting two important sociological and political factors to which the analysis of both terrorist-related disasters spoke abundantly: agency in cultural space and the "publicness" (to borrow from Habermas) of the political imagination that pastors enacted.[15] The agency of churches as corporate and cultural actors was greater in Oklahoma City and New Orleans than in New York City. This is partly due to the fact that the impact of churches in a city of such diminutive stature in comparison with New York City could be more keenly followed at a public level. The almost-bewildering variety of confessional groups scattered about Lower Manhattan and across the boroughs generates a situation in which the emergence of a few churches with specified roles is welcomed. Whereas in Oklahoma City the practical (in terms of emergency-service functions) and symbolic productivity of churches applied to a good number of churches after the event, in New York City, a few prominent churches rose to the level of public narrative authority, in particular with respect to public, dramatic performance. Only St. Paul's Chapel carried an enduring role in fulfilling governmental functions and symbolic production. What these deliberations conveyed is the importance of the political imagination of the minister, and how this engaged the social and cultural history

15. Habermas, *Structural Transformation*, 7.

of institutions within the minister's immediate environment. In all three cities I studied, local ministers interacted with highly exigent social environments; they faced a prevailing dialectic of insignificance and significance (specifically in relation to Oklahoma's founding and New Orleans's economic decline) and the challenges of global reputation (especially in the case of New York City). Not only that, but ministers had to negotiate how to exercise their political imagination in both the response and recovery phases. Prayer seems to have assumed its already somewhat privileged place in the history of civic pride in the United States, while outdoor worship services and practices of charity created space for greater degrees of relevance and normalization. At the same time, the pressure of public performance in service to institutional alignment after the disaster (with the local, regional, and federal governments, major media outlets, and the like) made dissimulation a definite option.

Location, Space, Demographics, and Scale

Somewhat independent of the political imaginative orientation of a given pastor or priest and the cultural history of that minister's social environment, this study shows that a number of other matters related to space, population properties, and scale are also essential to a study of culture and disasters that wishes to take account of churches and government agencies. First, the course and nature of cultural production at a disaster site depended on *the concentration and location of churches around the disaster site*. Both Oklahoma City and New York City contained at least six or seven well-maintained churches within a three-mile radius of the attack site. The location and concentration of church buildings directly invites public discussion of important issues tied to the shape and extent of the volunteer base; brings media attention; and (especially) spotlights processes linked to emerging norms.

The relative presence, location, and concentration of churches means that clergy at or near the scene may or may not attain a strong foothold, as it were, on an interpretive framework on the situation—and, in considering the nature of mass communication now, at stake here is the potential circulation of privileged ideas and images emanating from direct involvement with the disaster. Viewed theoretically, such circulation immediately brings the views of clergy into a discursive space in which ministers decide (through positive action or acquiescence) whether they will deal with a multiplicity of discourses. This multiplicity, ministers find, requires a setting that clearly and distinctly conveys authoritative speech. This speech, especially that of a minister, may or may not be absorbed into the pool of thoughts about responsibility and order that swell into public spaces after disasters. It is precisely in this social and political situation that the criminal trials of the state (in the case of terrorist attacks) and liturgy of the church possess an enduring import in contemporary contexts: namely, in the collapse of the sacred and secular through solemn and collectively binding speech acts.

The extent to which the actions and speech acts of the minister gain an audience, attract media attention, and constructively contribute to a viable political imagination depends upon—and here we enter the thick of differentiation and dedifferentiation—the minister's relationship to and perception about local government and its personnel, as well as upon the relative ethnic and demographic makeup of the impacted area. The relative ethnic, confessional, and demographic homogeneity of Oklahoma City made legitimate entry into spaces and practices of dedifferentiation much more facile than in New York City. When a minister is situated in a city that not only is homogenous in industry (Oklahoma City was overly dependent on energy and agricultural industries at the time), but also serves vocationally within a fairly narrow and manageable range of other confessional groups, then institutional alignment is already easier. However, at this point we reach the import of macrolevel cultural forces, including institutionalized modes of church governance. If a church was more congregationalist in its view of decision making and autonomy, then it was more likely to remain an independent cultural producer. One found this sort of church cooperating with others in terms of sharing space and resources, but not seeking unification in deeper narrative and doctrinal matters, especially as these related to political issues of ordering social relations, justice, freedom, and so forth. This was the case in both Oklahoma City and New York City, wherein churches seemed not to be in explicit agreement in many areas, including disposition to attackers, memorialization, and debate over the secular/sacred divide.

If we reinstate the issue of ministerial engagement with the public sphere of responsibility for the event, and restoration of social discipline after a disaster, which includes the formidable presence of expert, credentialed, technically savvy government agencies, then the issue of *available space* within the church becomes significant. In Oklahoma City, the majority of church buildings around the Murrah Federal Building site were spacious, and clergy invited use of the space: they were, as the data analysis showed, the locus of a good many crucial life happenings on a daily basis. Oklahomans were accustomed to using churches for all sorts of events. More important, local Oklahomans with aptitude in disaster response and intimate knowledge of church life assisted with the inculcation of important emergency-response functions into church operations. The availability of space, then, interacts with the competencies of individuals with overlapping spatial devotions to create the possibility of church spaces that can absorb and redefine otherwise expert functions. I argued in chapter 4 that actions like these actually generate resistance to statist co-optation of local spaces and elevate the symbolic force of the church. In other words, if clergy happen to offer their churches for a large variety of emergency-service functions, then what they say about God, the church, faith, and politics will more potently enter the contested political imagination. At the same time, however, churches have to deal with their own absorption of discourses, including ontological assumptions, which are not indigenous to its own discursive tradition.

The final factors that affect the cultural actions of a minister and a church involve the *scale of the attack* in physical and symbolic sense, and the nature of the response by statist personnel. In terrorist attacks, the state response most relevant to churches comes when statist personnel interpret the level of damage inflicted upon the monopoly over the means of violence and upon control over the prioritization of identities. Soon after attacks, public officials and symbolic leaders fill the airwaves with comments, complaints, adamant pleas, and semi-insolent declarations about such matters. Public officials do not so much mourn as announce that "the authorities will be relentless in their pursuit of justice" and "investigations and security measures have been doubled." Meanwhile, exhortation and global attributions emanating from mayoral and gubernatorial podiums raise questions about identity, implicitly and explicitly asking, who is a citizen and who is not? Who does God help, and why? Why is God involved at all? This and more, I hope this study has demonstrated, is the province of ministerial work that grasps practical, political, and theological matters at once.

CHAPTER 6

Conclusion

THEOLOGICAL LEGITIMACY AND CULTURAL RESOURCES FOR IDENTITY CONSTRUCTION

In this concluding chapter, I will set forth at a few, more narrowly framed, corollary matters that emanated from the analyses concerning solidarity, the re-formation of a body politic, and the cultural politics of the church, with an eye toward how the ecclesial body may understand and tackle these issues. The question of the theological legitimacy of the response to each disaster introduced a common concern over postdisaster collective identity formation and, in turn, a struggle over what social formations and discursive repertoires would steer the production of symbolic and material resources. The establishment of a legitimate post-attack project in service of social order necessarily invited issues of corporate identity. The most vital public question became: what sorts of persons are needed to respond to this attack? This question arose is primarily due to social-historical factors. First, the multiplication of intermediate social associations (e.g., trade guilds, unions, civic associations, business alliances) in an urban area in the postindustrial era assumes that a multiplicity of discourses, statuses, and roles are intersecting on a daily basis. The need to establish one overarching identity as a legitimating umbrella for other identities served the state's interest of a legible polity.[1] Second, as the populace takes into account the powerful narratives of American exceptionalism, resilience in adversity, and expansion, certain cultural traits (typical patterns of interpretation and belief) originating from national imaginings became simply of a piece with the state's interests. In these

---

1. Scott, *Seeing Like a State*, 2, 3, 32.

cases of disaster, these imaginings were also used to subvert statist disciplines. As it is, it behooves us to recall the importance of *local narratives of statehood*. Undoubtedly, narratives of all sorts collided in postdisaster narrative constructions, to which all institutions attempted to make a lasting contribution. The data as a whole showed that after disasters, citizens attempt to prioritize identities, and this effort is mediated through rituals, speeches, civic practices, and observation of church-and-state relations during the recovery process.

With respect to collective identity, the cases of Oklahoma City and New Orleans conveyed some major theoretical points quite vividly. I believe the theopolitics of recovery in these instances showcased the power of church-centered localism in the ongoing struggle between the interests and concerns of the nation-state (captured in a constellation of discourses and practices) and the concerns articulated in the local, theologically embedded narrative and practice. This finding sternly challenged my first heuristic hypothesis. Despite the hierarchizing tendencies of expert systems, pastors of local Methodist churches (Harris and Allen), Baptist congregations (Williams), and Catholic gatherings (Lamb) were still able to forge a distinctive position from which to make a differential impact on the social organization and symbolic-production processes at the disaster site and beyond. Even Mayor Norrick and Governor Keating contributed to this localization. This simply marked the beginning of what in the next six to eight months became a crystallization of institutional (and hence cultural and interpretive) formations whereby local citizens were caught as actors within a web of cultural (creative) tensions. These tensions called for ingenuity from citizens witnessing the crossing point between (one the one hand) a public theology stressing localized faith, the importance of church ministry, psychological reparations, and pride in Oklahoman character, and (on the other hand) the assemblage of expert determinations in the somewhat-buffered legal, legislative, and technorational realm closely linked to statist ritual events of nationalization and permanence. Statist operations claimed that buildings, ceremonies, memorials, and so forth had to speak to the permanence of these people, and to how they wish to live. The fanatical others and paranoid militias are not what Oklahoma or America is about: indeed, the state denies in its framings of the perpetrator that it created Timothy McVeigh. The state, in this case, remained true to Carl Schmitt's vision: identify the friends and foes that cannot be reconciled, and especially not here in the United

States of America. The crystallization of institutional formations in the public sphere, and the state's actions mentioned above, applied equally to the response and recovery periods in New York City and New Orleans as well. Theoretically, the cultural objects are passed on to citizens who incorporate inside/outside designations as part of their recovery-phase project of reconstituting identity. The *ekklesia* of the saints moves beyond binary designations of friend and foe in an attempt to live into the vision of God's reconciliation with the nations, or into the Pentecost reversal of Babel by virtue of which a member of a nation is a potential gift and worshiper of God in the church. The saint's first response to a citizen of another nation is thus one of expectancy, welcome, and dialogue (as Jesus interacted with the Gentile demoniac): indeed, a risky and faith-demanding venture.

Citizen Grammars of Accountability

Across at least two categories of social relationships (local citizens and ministers), I found among participants (notwithstanding subtle differences) a desire to assemble a grammar of accountability. Responses from these citizens' and ministers' groups carried implications of this sort. Simply ponder the resolute criticisms of local clergy about public theological statements: participant *A2*'s claim (from the Oklahoma City focus groups) that prayer assures correct governmental decisions; the prophetic petitions of the prayer card at the Heartland Chapel; participant *C4*'s confident affirmation that "my faith makes me a better Oklahoman." In New York City, participants imposed criteria of integrity and sincerity onto God-talk that aims at upholding theological discourse itself and the transparency of leaders. In other words, a certain institution should hold itself accountable to (or be held accountable by) a certain other institution and the narrative identity it proffers. Of course, this did not occur in a straightforward and neat fashion. The messiness revealed often-veiled relations of power and hierarchy in cultural production, of which citizens may or may not be aware. Oklahomans, New Yorkers, and New Orleanians did notice, even if not explicitly, the tension between theologically-charged understandings of American history and the importance of "local places." More particularly, these citizens also displayed sensitivities bearing on the primacy of Christian identity and the essential connection between certain narratives and a specific level of social organization (e.g., a group, organization, or city), that is, a concrete *place* of devotion and offering. Even if that place is a nation or state rather than a city, the level of fidelity can still be quite high. Churches both put these narratives to use and are themselves inscribed into them (sometimes regardless of the views of individual members) to advance an integrated picture of how social life ought to proceed after the disaster. This, theoretically, represents the theopolitics of recovery proper, from the perspective of the local resident or citizen.

The grammar of accountability, from an ecclesial standpoint, is principally the upshot of a compassionate memory, an *anamnesis*, in an eschatological register. The most significant articulation of this memory appears in the worshipful vision of the cries of the martyrs waiting on God's consummation of all things in the book of Revelation (6:9–10), and is also well informed by Walter Benjamin's *Theses on the Philosophy of History*. Particularly, theses 4 and 5 bear upon, among other things, the "force" of the past. In the former, Benjamin asserts that the spiritual things are not a by-product of the class struggle for "material things," but are manifested in the "humor," "courage," and "fortitude" of those involved.[2] These characteristics of the "strugglers" will be adopted as a standard against which the deeds and words and victories of all rulers in the present will be judged. Thus, the class struggle is ever present, but an eye must be kept on the "spiritual" qualities generated within persons. The latter thesis lends itself to a fascinating interpretation: when the past is revealed, in an instant, for what it truly is ("the true picture of the past flits by"), certain dispositions facilitate the grasping of the lesson. Historicism may designate certain foci of study, all the while positing the permanence of history. However, Benjamin argues, this perspective neglects the fact that lessons from history come in instants, in snapshots. Historical materialism wishes to remain open to the lessons as they appear, primarily because it is concerned with the movement of people and material things: that is, with concrete life. This is missed within the flamboyant musings of the historian unaware of the sober truth that we can selectively appropriate lessons from the past by cutting ourselves off from particular concerns. The church's calling to live with and for its neighbors places it in a situation to remember those whom the victors have forgotten.

2. Benjamin, "Theses on the Philosophy of History," 255–56.

Compensation for Families and the Maintenance of the Underclass

An important theme that emerged throughout the course of content analysis dealt with class divisions, especially in New York City and New Orleans. In New York City, the response to the attack seems to have trivialized class differences. This was not as much of a problem in Oklahoma City, due to a relative lack of conspicuous wealth and of displays of wealth-related prestige in the downtown area, and due to the comparatively narrower range of income. Although only two of the data sources directly linked the response of the poor to churches in New York City, the New Orleans disaster made it clear that conflict over what narrative about social life and social worth will dictate collective life inescapably carries implications for the underclass.

The response of the poor to the New York City attack primarily concerns the context of discussion about the monetary compensation directed at the families of attack victims, and what these figures say or do not say about the welfare of those already poor. One group of poor residents grounded their views on issues of deserts and restoration. A homeless woman offered, "I know, if you go to school for a number of years, you go for a reason. They were used to making hundreds of thousands of dollars a year. It's a lifestyle choice. If that's what they worked for, I think they should get it. If charity gave it for them, they should have it."[3] Numerous persons interviewed at a food pantry and soup kitchen in the Bronx, called Part of the Solution, offered no complaints. One Hispanic woman dependent on welfare programs asserted, "Those are different categories, I think they should take care of those families before me."[4] A man waiting for food-stamp allotments based his view on the fact that he did not lose his wealth in a sudden, unforeseeable tragedy. Other poor individuals opposed lower compensation amounts because they could not imagine how someone from the upper middle class or above could settle into a lower- middle-class or working-class lifestyle.[5]

However, some poor New Yorkers who claimed to have seen on evening newscasts widows who lived in mansions believed that such women and their families did not deserve to be supported "at a level far above the

3. Dewan, "Among the Poor, Sympathy for the Families."
4. Ibid.
5. Ibid.

average American income." One man stated, "When my father died, we went through a lot of changes, too, it's called life."[6] Others believed that the families of victims need extensive support but balked at the compensatory figures (many well over $1 million). In this case, the problem was exacerbated by the demise of many soup kitchens that closed down in the months following the attack due to major declines in donations. At Part of the Solution, operations have slowed down because they were dependent on a church in Rye, New York, that lost seven members. In addition, for many who lived in or around violent encounters on a daily basis, the overflow of charity and sharing so evident around the Ground Zero site and in association with human-service employees has not reached them. A food-pantry director angrily claimed, "Our folks live in violence, [our people have been saying] what do you mean, the world has changed? Our world hasn't changed."[7] A sizable amount of frustration has also arisen from the absence of federal funds that seem to be abundantly available to those involved with the attacks but that do not seem to be arriving for the underprivileged.

The alleged lopsidedness of generosity and recognition was also felt among blue-collar workers and others in the local health-care industry. A Mormon woman protested, "I feel like, even in my church they've [i.e., the underprivileged] been neglected. They have the nerve to say, 'For Christmas, Ms. Murphy, we're going to sing to the firefighters and the policemen.' More people got killed than the firemen and the policemen. Sing to the blue-collar workers."[8] Dawn Bryan, the executive director of various Momentum AIDS lunch programs forced to close two Monday meal programs because of city budget cuts and a decline in donations, said that AIDS and World AIDS Day (December 1) had become "invisible."[9]

The primary importance of the above comments relates to how and why certain cultural processes reach or develop within particular social strata and not others. Disasters may bring established social inequalities into question, but collective assessment of the depth or extent of the problems depends on whether (as Doug McAdam has argued with respect to social movements) certain agents can permit a grievance to enter peren-

6. Ibid.

7. Ibid.

8. Ibid.

9. Ibid

nial public discourse.[10] Among the responses, the power of meritocratic and wealth-based forms of status attainment was obvious. Furthermore, many did not see themselves as victims or as the objects of exploitation. Others, on the other hand, claimed that the response and recovery periods exposed the one-sided consumption of symbolic and narrative constructions that seemed to be universal in relevance but actually detached from the lives of the working and lower classes. The grievance mentioned above concerning a lack of recognition paid to "blue-collar workers," along with the complaint about the New Orleans rebuilding plans that indirectly opposed the return of the working poor, reveal to some degree the manner in which the postdisaster project to rebind citizens and establish certain norms of even charitable interaction and universal compassion can, in practice, become narrow, and can exclude some groups who cannot easily digest the social models presented. This is undoubtedly important in view of the political imagination and its assumptions about the proper worth of humans and about the norms of social interaction. The political imagination itself seems to value some humans over others and may not even assume that some people can, should, or will be able to know what is at stake in the world. This is why for some poorer members of New York, September 11, 2001, may have been a trying and terrible day, but it did not introduce anything into life that might have lifted the veil from their eyes upon the world. What must be borne in mind, hence, is that lack of access to numerous cultural resources and practices otherwise available to many in the middle and upper classes (through churches, government agencies, and even television) left many New Yorkers with no material from which to tap the process of collective identity formation. A lack of extensive social network linkages, which are very common among well-to-do professionals, also prevents poorer residents from achieving the social contact or assimilation needed for such projects.

    The actual language and social vision by which the permanent underclass, as an enduring "trait" of democratic capitalism, interpret the plight of disaster victims is linked to the very language used to evaluate them as cases or files. Hence, the poor cited above did not often speak out of pain or relational intimacy; when they did, the words were forceful and, at times, somewhat bitter. Their lives as social-welfare cases, and the evolving calculus used to determine how worthy they are for help,

---

10. See McAdam, "Conceptual Origins, Current Problems," 23–27.

adequately correspond to what Walter Brueggemann calls a "contractual theology," a notion introduced in chapter 1.[11] Namely, the predominant theology of human community in the state (including in the "civil or public sphere") is a "contractual theology" whereby a foundational construct sets out a sense of "orderliness and coherence in life, the interconnectedness of acts and their results . . . There are orders, limits, and boundaries within which humanness is possible and beyond which there can be only trouble."[12] Contractual theology lends itself to ideological constructions and to the legitimation of an exploitative order. For this very reason it must be sternly resisted. "The reason that the contractual theology must be sharply criticized," Brueggemann argues, "is that it lacks a human face when it is articulated consistently. It is a system of reality that allows for no slippage, no graciousness, no room for failure."[13] Any pain or suffering arising from a contractual theology, which, according to this conception, may be linked with technocratic rationality, is deemed as disruptive and must be silenced.

Here again emerges the notion of human failure, a potentially disturbing course of critical reflection, considering the pervasiveness of optimism linked with the persistence of enlightenment notions of progress, perfection, and technical mastery. Instrumental reason does not wish to deal with failure, only with trial and error, or the laboratory experiment. It cannot engage the potential social change and regime change that human failure implies. Nor can it handle the concrete difficulties, casualties, and unforeseen consequences to public trust, unity, and day-to-day friendship patterns—that is, the lifeworld. The problem is not with the pretensions of coherence, precision, and uniformity that find expression in modern practices of time keeping (seconds, minutes, and hours) and technological reproduction or capital investment, but with the notion that the coherence allows for no failure, for no ability to deal with failure in a constructive manner that brings about enduring social changes and upholds a valid anthropology.

Brueggemann posits the desire to control and manage the products of labor in certain ways, including the products of land, as a dangerous inclination because it resists the inherent and valuable dialectical tension

---

11. Brueggemann, *Theology of the Old Testament*, 15.

12. Ibid.

13. Ibid., 17.

within human existence. This struggle maintains a sense of wonder, gratitude, and graciousness essential to all human communities. Contractual
theology therefore employs the notions of cosmic order to stabilize the
established political and social formation while the spiritual qualities,
or things constitutive of an enduring and remembering community (to
which Benjamin alludes in thesis 4), are ignored. These elements are disregarded because the language of technical evaluation permeates, in a
reified mode, all language of community building and voiced pain that
may bring the expert systems of the state into question. The community
rather is judged on the basis of its ability to self-sufficiently contribute to
the overarching system of capitalist production and its false theological
contract. In elaboration, Brueggemann claims thus:

> The contractual theology of coherence and rationality offers a
> world in which pain need not occur . . . it is a world of perfect
> symmetry in which God's will is known and can be obeyed. Such
> a theological system . . . is also as modern as religions of "possibil-
> ity thinking," as *consumerism*, in which the right product makes
> whole, and as *competence* linked to technical reason, in which in-
> competence is unnecessary and unacceptable.[14]

Brueggemann considers this enterprise of technical competence, of which
late or advanced capitalism is the exemplar identified by the Frankfurt
School, as a denial of the narrative in which all humankind is grounded
and of which Israel is the representative and pedagogical manifestation.
In this sense, the enduring significance of Israel is not due to the fact that
it posits "timeless truths" encased in its Scriptures for all other nations
and cultures, but simply because it has embodied the historical experience of many peoples and has overcome.

The task for the congregation (and for scholars in aid of the church)
with respect to assessing their view of the poor in relation to disaster is to
first clarify the elements involved in postdisaster solidarity projects from
the level of cultural action. What do persons and other citizens outside
the church purchase or produce by way of material bodies that expose
their interpretation of property, consumption, and prestige? What do
citizens actually say about God-talk in the public sphere? The responses
to these questions speak volumes about a person's orientation toward,
and agreement with, specific valuations of select human activities, and

14. Ibid., 18 (emphasis original).

about what it will take for them to contribute to a particular vision of the future; that is, it reflects their estimation of who is worthy of imitation, who should die, who should live, and what sort of attention should be paid to wealth and prestige-dependent class boundaries.

Transition from Gift Relations to Market Relations

One topic introduced in chapter 3 that requires theological elaboration and further investigation is the issue of gift relations and market relations during the response and recovery phases. Key questions involve not only how the nation-state reconciles the two, but also how the residents of affected communities emerge during the reconstruction phase with a somewhat unstable set of expectations (expectations resulting from generous and gratuitous support from volunteers, neighbors, and charity agencies) while next facing realities of administrative red tape that once again functionalize social relations and enforce the pressure of reentering market relations in order to survive. In other words, one cannot live off of generosity; differentiation assumes its course of redividing labor and identities, and reengaging the bases of capitalist relations. This has already become apparent in the post-Katrina challenges associated with FEMA's provision of small, trailerlike homes that eventually sank into the ground on which they were huddled: What were once gifts given to those left without homes after the hurricane are now securable only through an application process.

Precisely at this point the Durkheimian theme of mechanical solidarity giving way to organic solidarity finds tremendous relevance—not in terms of organic solidarity replacing mechanical solidarity, but in terms of organic solidarity becoming the predominant mode of social interdependence. This interdependence, stemming from pervasive social differentiation and specialization, can be understood most accurately as impersonal dependence, or a dependence that links the individual directly to the state. But this link is mediated by mechanisms devoid of human presence. Paper applications, automated telephone responses, electronic transmission of personal information, and mail-only correspondence when a potentially life-altering occasion is at hand, while seemingly necessary, also represent an abdication of local avenues of generosity or gift giving. Many ecclesial communities, as chapter 4 demonstrated, provide the most compelling examples of effectively evading complete

dependence on impersonal mechanisms that overwhelm federal bureaucratic administrations, which are liable to adapt slowly to changes
in citizen status, due to insurance claims or to faults or delays in other
government agencies. As an exploitative measure, such detachment may
also serve to make obtuse, obscure, or inconsistent the logic for denying assistance to an applicant. As the case of deregulation in the wake of
Hurricane Katrina shows, a decision to aid or deny an applicant can result
from government surrender to corporate interests, which are themselves
forms of state power. This dispersed statist power propels the return to
market relations and hinders gift-giving encounters. The denunciation
of the gift is the necessity of bourgeois and bureaucratic rationality that
sees abstract cases of need (as a statistical demand, not as a member of
a community). While more localized or intimate determinations of aid
also possess certain shortcomings, the transformative potential of the
gift to compel yet more gift giving to others (and even forgiveness and
gentleness because someone knows of a local to whom they are indebted)
are remarkable. Likewise, perceiving the consequences of rejection or a
situation of dire straits calls again for local considerations of primary aid
to citizens who have faced loss in disaster. This neighborly consideration
therefore demands a resistance to profiteering at the least, and to many
other mechanisms of capitalist wealth circulation and consumption.

Perhaps the greatest resistance needed against contemporary capitalist forces before and after disaster is in what Mark Neocleous deems
the most distorted aspect of the personification of capital: the mechanism by which subjects become objects and objects becomes subjects.[15]
Indeed, the corporation as a (juridically wrought) person enjoys a certain
unity that only state power can match at the corporate level. Meanwhile,
the body politic remains subordinate to these so-called persons unless
the body of Christ, as the site of the meal of transfiguration, or abundant
and resplendent generosity, comes to practice. Here the sharing of food,
homes, clothing, and, indeed, the riches of wisdom, must defy capitalist
appropriations that attempt to turn it into yet another commodity. The
giving and sharing at this site starts with Christ, who did not seek profit
for himself but gave of his very body in the hope and faithfulness that
the God of life would restore what had been lost and add to him brothers
and sisters in communion. This is what the body of Christ offers against

15. Neocleous, *Imagining the State*, 83.

impersonal dependence and capitalist investment during the postdisaster period. From this body many nations are fed. When disciples of the living Christ, for example, regularly forsake additional expenses and meals, and redirect these funds into savings or resource pools explicitly dedicated to neighbors, then they are living up into this body that is itself a gift that God has given to the world. The members of Christ are called to live first and foremost as a politics of attentive seeing, listening, and embracing. As Jacques Derrida helpfully mused, the eyes and hands are best observed by the other, not oneself.[16] The other sees the eyes and hands directed at them, for their good and sustenance, as extensions of another life into their own. When a congregation lives with hands and eyes present to one another not simply at worship services but in the life of each member, then the schooling necessary to see all other community members through the members of the church body is well underway.

Theoretical notions that this topic invites for exploration in research are fertile and fascinating, especially when it comes to the components involved with adjusting from gift-dependent relations to capitalist and market relations. What happens in terms of group affiliation, new social-network involvement, and political views? Are there groups that form who resist such a transition? If not, why not? To what degree do those families or individuals who accept generous donations or assistance alter their civic participation? Another central point for this type of theory building and inquiry is to tap into the sociology of this transition with respect to how churches, as primary agents of charity, participate or do not participate in it.

Incorporating a Disaster into Regularly Occurring Ritual Events

In the process of dedifferentiation, this study emphasized the role of large-scale and small-scale ritual ceremonies, including prayer services and funerals, as paramount. Further theory building and research in this area of study should be directed toward how a disaster is incorporated into already regularly occurring celebrations. For instance, New Yorkers are certainly not strangers to manifold festivals, parades, and other celebrations. A St. Patrick's Day parade held about six months after the attack raised an important question about the nature of *regularly occurring* pub-

16. Derrida, et al., *Derrida*, DVD (documentary film).

lic celebrations or festivals *after* the World Trade Center disaster. These physical and imaginative events were remarkable instances of hybridization. How does these type of event (say, a parade) assimilate elements of a recent disaster into its established processions, materials, and other cultural products? After the September 11, 2001, attacks, there were a multiplicity of holidays that regularly turn up from one year to the next, which had to address the event in some way, e.g., Christmas, Hanukkah, St. Patrick's Day, Presidents' Day, and the like. Most interesting in this regard is who is chosen as the grand marshal in such events, who composes the planning committee, and the manner in which event planners incorporate popular symbols and expressions from the immediate disaster-response period into their events. For example, what if a Presidents' Day event included the presentation of a chunk of rock or steel from either of the World Trade Center towers? What language would be used, and how would it be incorporated into the event? The chosen language could include snippets or compelling quotes from important speeches and poems, or even pictures taken at the disaster site. Within this line of inquiry, theological messages could also be discerned if they were carried into the local event-planning process. Are the implicit or explicit theological views eschewed or filtered out, or are the views imported in their entirety into a novel context? Answering these questions requires further analysis.

Incorporating Local Residents into Statist Redevelopment Plans

Many articles and numerous interviews also addressed another important topic linked to the workings and imaginings of the state in relation to the role of churches and citizens in the recovery process. Put another way, how exactly should statist agencies involve and defend locals, especially those not informed about politics or theology? This refers, if considered another way, to the logjam of political and economic experts who have forged a set of strategies and decision-making mechanisms for recovery, yet without giving ordinary people even somewhat-direct access to or influence on the process. Although the matter was not addressed in chapter 3 on New York City, nevertheless the redevelopment committees in that city and in Oklahoma City were designed and agreed upon only after serving on a committee had been announced as a viable option for citizens, to revitalize "our great city." This speaks to proclivities of the state to mobilize readily available resources and activate strong social networks in the expert realm for the purpose of redevelopment. This very efficient mobilization and implementation also bears the shortcoming of neglecting citizen involvement—and hence, the categories of experience relevant to a nonexpert. This also invites a greater collaboration of place-making studies, public memory, and disaster recovery. The manner in which preservationists, urban planners, local politicians, and church leaders are or are not linked to one another reflects conflict over the hermeneutical superiority (in establishing so-called historical worth) of certain discourses and in consequence molds, and at times atomizes, the citizenry. That is, because they cannot come together to name and claim the actual places in which they will execute their personal narratives, how can they rely on the short-lived spiritual resurgence that seemed to occur after both events?

Church, State, and Reconstituting the Social

A consequential topic that analysis of postdisaster political imaginaries revealed was the apparent inadequacy of civil religious sites of worship, discourse, and material objects. This qualifies (or clarifies) Robert Bellah's claim, made in the now-famous article, "Civil Religion in America," that there "actually exists alongside of and rather clearly differentiated from the churches an elaborate and well-institutionalized civil religion in America."[17] The state's rapacious appropriations of Christian theological terminology or liturgy, then, ask: How does the state dedifferentiate itself from the sacred, as it were, without instigating a massive, longstanding, and public crisis that challenges its own identity? This query, I submit, also has a flip side that questions how churches respond to statist incursions into church space and respond to more abstract projects of narrative building using biblical drama. The degree of resistance and absorption depends on the extent to which the church conceives of itself as *relevant* to the present orderings of life, especially in terms of political power and mechanisms of social renewal. Bellah, concerned with the practical, rather than definitional or theoretical, problems that "civil religion" entails, did not often problematize this statist co-optation of the church beyond the assurance of God's judgment of the nations.[18] That is, God's divine

17. Bellah, "Civil Religion in America."
18. Bellah, "Finding the Church: Post-Traditional Discipleship."

oversight of the nations necessitates some sort of judgment for misuses, abuses, or rejections of his wisdom, justice, and attributes. Bellah, in fact, became so distressed by the tendency to equate civil religion with the idolatrous worship of state that, in the writing of *Habits of the Heart*, he abandoned the term altogether for "biblical and republican traditions."[19] This term more transparently reveals Bellah's longstanding concern with the relationship between discipleship and citizenship even as his writings became ever more ecclesiocentric throughout the 80s and 90s. Interesting is that this increased emphasis on the church as the determinative community of Christians is concomitant with an equally strong emphasis on the development of a citizen concern about the "common good" over against self-interest, as *Habits of the Heart* demonstrates. This text and its successor, *The Good Society*, actually employ examples of church activity and citizenship to exemplify practices that uphold commitment to the common good. Bellah, in fact, posits that insofar as these works emphasize the common good, readers will find "just below the surface, the body of Christ." These works, moreover, are meant to be expressions of what Paul Tillich called "the catholic principle."[20] In an attempt to appeal to a wider audience and a wider set of conversation partners, but somehow to maintain the relevance of the church, Bellah "places" the church just below the text—namely, as an expression of commitment to the common good. However, this is the sort of reductionist maneuvering that our democratic discourse ethics assumes is necessary. The church cannot enter the dialogue unless it is a particular, historical community rather than an example of commitment to a governing principle or an end of community life. This move, in turn, leads us back to the same subordinate situation in which citizenship and nation beckon the church to service; the state acts not as a willing and grateful recipient but as a parasite that assumes that church and state can live off each other. Robert Bellah is correct in assuming the relative independence of this "biblical and republican tradition" yet has not fully explored how this development, achieved only because churches made allowances for it in theology and worship, altered the mode of reasoning by which any given congregation changes its views of discipleship as a politics in its own right. We are still, it appears, afraid of the pain and promise of the cross, the actual flesh

19. Ibid.
20. Ibid.

and life of the one who died there, and of the implications of that death given to Life for all pretensions to knowledge and the "common good." Living for the common good is refracted in the cross as an encounter, as more than simply a series of service acts that demonstrate civic engagement, or agreement with democratic principles. Living for the common good through the cross is a sequence of engagements with human beings, made in the image of God: engagements capable of testing the depth of the law of Christ in each member, and hence of reaching depths of joy, gladness, and celebration that can be manifested even in the most desperate situations. The state's ceremonial sites and civil-religious dogma, or those core principles that Bellah once considered vital to biblical and republican traditions, cannot duplicate or explicate the power of such lived encounters. They are a shell, as it were, of the originary point: God incarnate, and hence not simply a text, idea, or axiom to unite an imagined community. The citizens who are the citizens of the commonwealth of God's people are built up into communion because they know well that in encountering one another, they are encountering "God with us."

In the theoretical language of disaster studies, this means that churches are compelled to enter a "domain" and adopt "high priority values."[21] *Domain* refers to that "generalized image of the organized social action held by both participants and relevant others in any instance of organized disaster response, providing an overall orienting definition of the legitimate purposes of the behavior."[22] Some organizations that would otherwise have no predisaster domain for crisis-related activity must come to adopt certain "values" or commitments (e.g., the preservation of the life of neighbors) in order to engage a particular domain of activity, such as an emergent group of rescuers who are not members of the fire department or a government-sanctioned search-and-rescue squad. It is patent that local and regional governments possess a preestablished domain for large-scale coordinative responsibilities. This is most certainly the case, if not more so, in the event of a disaster. Local churches likewise carry a mandate to assist the community in periods of crisis, whether disaster related or not; but this charter pales in comparison to the technical, logistical, and integrative scope of the governmental task. For theoretical purposes, it is crucial to recognize the massively lopsided scope of technical tasks but the even scope of social imaginative claims.

21. Kreps, "Organization of Disaster Response," 69.

22. Ibid., 68.

Nonetheless, this research has confirmed that it is these two institutions that appear at the forefront of the task of identifying those very values and traditions that inculcate actions and persons in a broader frame of reference. The respective actors associated with these institutions carry a massive burden of drawing a picture of reality that must accommodate the overwhelming presence of suffering and death, while also inciting a willingness to persevere in the face of shameful defeat. This is, I presume, what lies at the core of the logic that brought mayor Rudolph Giuliani to give his farewell speech in St. Paul's Chapel in New York City rather than in a secular, civic space such as a government building. During the course of disaster response and recovery, actions like that of former mayor Giuliani indicate that churches who considered themselves relevant in a politically imaginative sense adopted not only values that justified work in the domain involving ministerial activities in a church setting, but also values that bore upon other ultimate matters, primarily those linked to statist functions, such as responding to terrorist attacks, setting a course for the future, recognizing the ideal character traits upon which the future will be built, naming the enemy around which we must unite, and so forth. Research on the adoption of "high priority values" has usually disregarded these points.

Future research must delve deeply into this matter, considered even more abstractly as follows: what is said publicly about death at the hands of other human beings contributes largely to the generalized image in which social life is carried forward after the incident. Undoubtedly, public speech affects the "deep culture," as Wuthnow argues, upon which social organization is premised.[23] Churches showed glimpses of an alternative vision of reality, of a *Weltanschauung* advanced not only for the sake of practical and integrative purposes but also to define the social as such. In this sense, the church is a threat to the nation-state, and (when churches desired or were allowed) revealed an alternative politics, economy, and social body emanating from its own narrative practices. Interestingly, as in Oklahoma City and New York, churches were presented mostly as institutional friends of the state, with criticism of quintessential statist views withheld, or only partially expressed and without any organizational coordination. Indeed, the only way of covering over this threat was through ritual events within "sacred space" (e.g., churches) that blended

23. Wuthnow, *American Mythos*, 12–15.

and created symbols that simultaneously renationalized and retheologized a space, city, and identity.

WHAT ABOUT HURRICANE KATRINA AND OTHER NATURAL DISASTERS?

The final way in which the complex cultural workings of church-and-state interrelations can be elucidated is in thinking about their respective roles in the context of what are called natural disasters. This, perhaps more than any other comparative context, reveals the importance of statist constructions of enemies and friends—in other words, of its affirmative, institutional role in generating allegiance, in ordering social relations, and in constructing group boundaries. After natural disasters, there usually has not been any Other, besides perhaps God, Mother Nature, or the laws of meteorological and geological phenomena, which must be brought into a consideration of responsibility, blame, or justice. The aftermath of Hurricane Katrina, however, poses an exception to this. Following that hurricane, heavy criticism and scorn was directed toward many different levels of the United States government. In this case, the state was content to back off and allow churches to perform many important recovery operations. Why? When it is possible to reinforce the solidarity of a people through definitive judgment and even violent expulsion from the social body, then the state is in its rightful place, with churches as local assistants and the models from which the state has constructed itself, its powers for ordering life, and its prerogative for sending representatives of the harmed national body to redress its grievances. Natural disasters do not usually situate congregations and the state within this set of symbolic productions linked to identity, although they readily provide material for narrative constructions of grief, suffering, and renewal.

The main theoretical conclusions surrounding the dimensions of dedifferentiation follow: First, facilitation of theopolitical dedifferentiation depends upon a destructive challenge or affront to the state's monopoly over the means of violence, including its role to competently identify threats and protect citizens with the very use of such exclusive violence. This affront, of course, is jointly material and symbolic (e.g., note the political imaginative role of the World Trade Center towers) to the extent that both materiality and symbolism must be summoned to trigger the sort of dedifferentiation at issue here. When this challenge to the state's sovereignty in relation to violence does not obtain, then churches are either free or enabled to complete many relief and recovery functions without the formidable presence of statist projects for collective identity formation. It must be kept in mind, however, that this freedom of the church to act does not assure the public that the theological imagination of churches will receive pubic attention. Usually these efforts will be viewed as humanitarian aid on par with that of any other relief agency. Yet when attacks on the sovereignty of a state *vis-à-vis* the welfare of the national body occur, the state must move into myriad social, discursive, and physical spaces to reassert, through liturgical events and processes of dedifferentiation with churches, the authority it needs over the body of citizens to thrive yet again. The state needs a certain type of citizen or person in order to remain alive and objectified; or from a less passive standpoint, human beings find it necessary to cultivate identities that create new levels of social organization, that join together a larger body of persons separated by considerable distance, in order to maintain a particular circulation of narrative discourses and practices that buttress an entire perspective on human life, what motives and goods drive it forward, and who or what protects it. Ironically, human agency is used to personify and historically objectify a state that in turn diverts and augments the agency of human beings. It does this by binding persons to one another in such a way that persons are only so bound through their own antecedent dependence on the state's organs and its narratives, practices, and ways of speaking and seeing. These depend, as this study has shown, on expulsion of violent enemies with the use of violence, on construction of a citizen body through the marvels of technical competence, on unquestioned support from God, and on the narrative creation of sacrificial heroes to whom are attributed motivations and actions that each successive generation should emulate. The state, as we have seen, needs churches to accomplish this feat, because they provide the ideal types, as it were, for such efforts.

The second vital theoretical point is that dedifferentiation of church and state across all dimensions (say, narratival, material, social-relational, and ethical) depends upon shifting cultural pluralism into a cultural monism. In this respect, certain degrees and forms of dedifferentiation are possible in the United States that may not be possible elsewhere. The state needs to neutralize and define *difference* in such a way that *sameness* under the nation and its systems of economy, executive decision making, and other major institutions can be achieved only if (1) the narrative content of other institutions can be rendered flat and malleable and (2) the existence of reconciled or harmonious social relations between virtually all cultural groups is heavily publicized. In other words, competing narratives are suppressed, and longstanding or stark differences between groups become trivial.

A third theoretical point that this study raises is that the process of relativizing or eliminating the narrative particularities of group and assuming their mutual coherence within the cause of the state, in turn, depends upon the degree to which citizens are convinced that a dire or emergency situation is at hand, and that the state is the only institution capable of defining the problem and dealing with it. In contrast to hurricanes or other severe weather patterns, human attacks can be, theoretically, rectified through the obliteration of those who committed the act, or can be prevented through the elimination of those who plan on carrying out attacks in the future. This *simplification* generates other simplifications: that the knowledge of the state exudes surety (when in most instances it militates against encounter), and that the violence of the state is redemptive—that is, it is ultimate justice. This form of justice addresses a problem but has no collateral or residual effects; or if it does, they do not outweigh the benefits violence brings. This positive view of violence facilitates the easy entry of talk about war and justice in postdisaster projects for reconstituting the national body. The state hopes that identities will be built around a redemptive view of violence. This conception of violence, paradoxically, thrived alongside and even within the equally redemptive elements of rescue efforts and generous outpouring of volunteer assistance that persisted at the very site of the World Trade Center attack. The church and state, then, can form a cultural partnership after disaster that reconciles all things for every level of social organization.

The body of Christ, as a body that suffers with the world, repudiates a commitment to redemptive violence, to materially detached valuations of a population as a privileged mode of representation, to planning and ascertaining worth detached from God's goodness, truth, and beauty, and to portrayals of the world as hopelessly ridden with emergencies. This body forms communities dedicated to numerous focal practices that emanate from worship, Eucharist, and baptism. Baptism, undeniably, enacts the most important death that a person will ever face; it defies death as the end of natural life, including any death in tragic or unexpected circumstances. It does not deny or diminish the extreme struggle and finality that accompanies the death of any single person, but simply, yet powerfully, challenges the nature of the "end" brought about in any such deaths. Most important, a church that makes baptism public introduces into the surrounding community an audacious affront to the presence of death in that community, regardless of the means by which death is occasioned.

This community holds that the open expression of pain cannot be muffled. True amazement, in the case of massive trauma, can come only by way of true negativity. Thus, the analysis of history must embrace lessons emanating from the sadness stemming from manipulative practices, even if such an embrace means the end of a regime and its disciplines of memory.[24] This is only possible if memories are preserved that constitute the cultural histories of various peoples who form landed communities. These stories are likewise the benchmarks of many subcultures of opposition. These cultures embrace an alternative consciousness that eschews the views presupposed by an economy of affluence and a religion of immanence[25] that in concert reject the incursions of God. This project must enjoin the formation of (1) a radical institution of accountability predicated on compassionate listening to the neighbor, not on moral self-justification or simply standardized criteria; and of (2) evaluative political work that will appeal to courage and fortitude of communities of the past and apply these qualities to the work of present and past rulers. "Material compassion" is the relational/moral component that prevents the polarization of technocratic accountability. These refined attributes within the persons cannot be forgotten in the name of progressive or advanced technological policies. The historical materialism of the church, as it were, therefore grasps the pain and hope of a community of people who are keenly aware of the dangers of conformity and of uncritical absorption into a larger story of the triumphalist nation-state. Yet this compassion is founded upon a great love. The politics that is the body of Christ is grounded, first and foremost, upon God's self-giving love, and so those who are members of his body cannot demand or expect love, so as to attempt to control it and channel it toward the self. It is love that

24. The resurrected Jesus, according to Brueggemann, spelled the end "of the nonhistory taught in the royal school [while] a new history begins for those who stood outside history" (Brueggemann, *Prophetic Imagination*, 113).

25. Ibid.

can only be *given*; any other type of love, such as the "spontaneous love" that Kierkegaard deems subject to many changes over time and especially in response to the apparent rejection or approval of the other, actually crushes a person's vision of life, because it is a love that wants everything for itself.[26] On the contrary, those who follow the Risen One share in the love that abides between the Son and the Father, which is given to us by the Spirit. The church when faithful is a most vulnerable people—a people who truly pray the psalms as songs of surrender in order to receive the life that cannot be generated immanently or autonomously. Because the church is not self-generating, the disciples that compose it are, para-doxically, only free to bind themselves, while any divergence from this *being* denies that the church is primarily a called, wooed, enchanted, and embraced people. The church is a rejection of humanity *secut Deus*—of humanity "like God." The church does not want to attain triumph or to boast in the face of disaster; it simply hopes to participate in filling every-thing, in every way, with God.

26. Kierkegaard, *Works of Love*, 46–52.

Bibliography

Aguirre, Benigno. Interview of Respondent 5. March 5, 2000, electronic transcript, Okla-homa City, OK.

Aiken, Charlotte. "Upcoming Demolition Raises Memories of Others in Past." *Oklahoman,* May 14, 1995. NewsBank Database, Oklahoma City Library.

Alexander, Jeffrey C., et al. *Cultural Trauma and Collective Identity.* Berkeley: University of California Press, 2004.

Anderson, Benedict. *Imagined Communities: Reflections on the Origin and Spread of Nationalism.* London: Verso Editions/NLB, 1983.

Annan, Kofi. "Fighting Terrorism on a Global Front." *New York Times,* September 21, 2001. Online: http://www.lexis-nexus.com/.

Aquinas, Thomas St. "The Inaugural Sermons." In *Selected Writings,* edited and translated by Ralph McInerny, 3–17. Penguin Classics. London: Penguin, 1998.

Asad, Talal. *Formations of the Secular: Christianity, Islam, Modernity.* Cultural Memory in the Present. Stanford: Stanford University Press, 2003.

———. *Genealogies of Religion: Discipline and Reasons for Power in Christianity and Islam.* Baltimore: The Johns Hopkins University Press, 1993.

Associated Press. "Business Leaders Driven by Patriotism, Desire to Bolster Capital-ism." September 13, 2001. Online: http://www.lexis-nexus.com/.

———. "Nagin Updates Hurricane-Displaced Residents." November 7, 2005. Online: http://www.lexis-nexus.com/.

———. "New Yorkers Return to Work, Fueled by Determination." September 13, 2001. Online: http://www.lexis-nexus.com/.

Augustine. *Confessions.* Translated by Henry Chadwick. Oxford: Oxford University Press, 1991.

Bader-Saye, Scott. *Church and Israel after Christendom: The Politics of Election.* Eugene, OR: Wipf & Stock, 2005.

Barron, James. "Cardinal Egan Leads Prayers for Victims, and Applause for Rescuers." *New York Times,* September 17, 2001. Online: http://www.lexis-nexus.com/.

Barry, Dan. "At Ground Zero, Seeking Shelter from the Storm." *New York Times,* May 12, 2002. Online: http://www.lexis-nexus.com/.

———. "From a World Lost, Ephemeral Notes Bear Witness to the Unspeakable." *New York Times,* September 25, 2001. Online: http://www.lexis-nexus.com/.

Barth, Karl. *Evangelical Theology: An Introduction.* Translated by Grover Foley. Grand Rapids: Eerdmans, 1963.

Beck, Ulrich. *Ecological Enlightenment: Essays on the Politics of the Risk Society*. Translated by Mark A. Ritter, Atlantic Highlands, NJ: Humanities, 1995.

———. *Risk Society: Towards a New Modernity*. Theory, Culture & Society. Newbury Park, CA: Sage, 1992.

Bell, Daniel M., Jr. *Liberation Theology after the End of History: The Refusal to Cease Suffering*. Radical Orthodoxy Series. London: Routledge, 2001.

Bellah, Robert N. "Civil Religion in America." In *Beyond Belief: Essays on Religion in a Post-Traditional World*, 168–92. New York: Harper & Row, 1970.

———. "Finding the Church: Post-Traditional Discipleship." *The Christian Century*, November 14, 1990, 1060–64. Online: http://www.religion-online.org/show-article.asp?title=438/

———. "New-Time Religion. Review of *Varieties of Religion Today*, by Charles Taylor." *Christian Century*, May 22, 2002, 20–26.

———. "The Revolution and the Civil Religion." In *Religion and the American Revolution*, edited by Jerald C. Brauer, 55–73. Philadelphia: Fortress, 1976.

Benjamin, Walter. "Theses on the Philosophy of History." In *Illuminations: Essays and Reflections*, 253–54. New York: Schocken, 1969.

Bergen, Wesley J. *Reading Ritual: Leviticus in Postmodern Culture*. Journal for the Study of the Old Testament. Supplement Series 417. Playing the Texts 9. London: T. & T. Clark, 2005.

Berry, Wendell. *The Unsettling of America: Culture & Agriculture*. San Francisco: Sierra Club Books, 1996.

Bockmuehl, Markus. *Seeing the Word: Refocusing New Testament Study*. Studies in Theological Interpretation. Grand Rapids: Baker Academic, 2006.

Bonhoeffer, Dietrich. *Christ the Center*. Harper's Ministers Paperback Library. San Francisco: Harper & Row, 1978.

———. *Creation and Fall/Temptation: Two Biblical Studies*. 1st Touchstone edition. New York: Simon and Schuster, 1997.

———. "The Way that Leads to Renewal." In *A Testament to Freedom: The Essential Writings of Dietrich Bonhoeffer*, edited by Geffrey B. Kelly and F. Burton Nelson, 230–33. Revised edition. San Francisco: Harper San Francisco, 1995.

———. "What Is a Christian Ethic?" In *A Testament to Freedom*, edited by Geffrey B. Kelly and F. Burton Nelson, 345–51. Revised edition. San Francisco: HarperSanFrancisco, 1995.

Bourdieu, Pierre. *Outline of a Theory of Practice*. Translated by Richard Nice. Cambridge Studies in Social Anthropology 16. New York: Cambridge University Press, 1977.

"Bricks and Mortar." *Oklahoman,* June 15, 1995, Editorial section, 8.

Browitt, Jeff. "Introduction." In *Practising Theory: Pierre Bourdieu and the Field of Cultural Production*, edited by Jeff Browitt and Brian Nelson, 1–15. Monash Romance Studies. Newark, DE: University of Delaware Press, 2004.

Brubaker, Paul. *Ground Zero Spirituality at Trinity Church Wall Street*. New York: Trinity Television, 2002.

Brubaker, Paul, et al. *Ground Zero Spirituality at Saint Paul's Chapel*. New York: Trinity Television, 2002.

Brueggemann, Walter. *Theology of the Old Testament: Testimony, Dispute, Advocacy*. Minneapolis: Fortress, 1997.

———. *David's Truth in Israel's Imagination and Memory*. 2nd edition. Minneapolis: Fortress, 2002.

————. *The Land: Place as Gift, Promise, and Challenge in Biblical Faith.* 2d edition. Overtures to Biblical Theology. Minneapolis: Fortress Press, 2002.

————. *The Prophetic Imagination.* 2d edition. Minneapolis: Fortress, 2001.

Bruni, Frank. "For President, A Mission and a Role in History." *New York Times,* September 22, 2001. Online: http://www.lexis-nexus.com/.

Brus, Brian, and Pat Gilliland. "Istook Wants U.S. Aid for Churches, Plan Would Fund Repairs." *Oklahoman,* June 17, 1995, News section, 1.

Bush, George W. "President's Remarks at National Day of Prayer and Remembrance." Speech delivered at the National Cathedral, Washington DC, September 14, 2001. Online: http://www.whitehouse.gov/news/releases/2001/09/20010914-2.html/.

Cajee, Mas'ood. *The Oklahoma Hate and Harassment Report.* May 9, 1995. Online: http://www.themodernreligion.com/assault/okla-report.html/.

Candler, Peter M., Jr. *Theology, Rhetoric, and Manuduction, or Reading Scripture Together on the Path to God.* Grand Rapids:. Eerdmans, 2006.

————. "Tolkien or Nietzsche: Philology and Nihilism." Online: http://www .theologyphilosophycentre.co.uk/papers/~Candler_TolkeinNietzsche.doc

Carle, Robert D., and Louis A. DeCaro Jr., editors. *Signs of Hope in the City: Ministries of Community Renewal.* Valley Forge, PA: Judson, 1997.

Carnes, Tony. "Religions in the City: An Overview." In *New York Glory: Religions in the City,* edited by Tony Carnes and Anna Karpathakis, 3–25. New York: New York University Press, 2001.

Carr, Keva. "To: My City." *Rethinking Schools Online* 21 (Fall 2006) n.p. Online: http://www.rethinkingschools.org/archive/21_01/city211.shtml/.

Carroll, James. "Church, State, and Katrina." *Boston Globe,* September 12, 2005, Op-Ed section, A15.

Casanova, José. *Public Religions in the Modern World.* Chicago: University of Chicago Press, 1994.

Cashin, Sheryll. "Katrina: The American Dilemma Redux." In *After the Storm: Black Intellectuals Explore the Meaning of Hurricane Katrina,* edited by David Dante Troutt, 28–37. New York: New Press, 2006.

Casteel, Chris. "State Gets Reassurance on Bomb Aid, Clinton, Gingrich Air Funding Hope." *Oklahoman,* June 22, 1995, News section, 1.

Castoriadis, Cornelius. *The Imaginary Institution of Society.* Translated by Kathleen Blamey. Cambridge: MIT Press, 1987.

Cavanaugh, William T. "Killing for the Telephone Company: Why the Nation-State is Not the Keeper of the Common Good." *Modern Theology* 20 (2004) 243–74.

————. "Sacrifice and the Social Imagination in Early Modern Europe." *Journal of Medieval and Early Modern Studies* 31 (2002) 585–605.

————. *Theopolitical Imagination: Discovering the Eucharist as a Political Act in an Age of Global Consumerism.* London: T. & T. Clark, 2002.

Certeau, Michel de. *The Practice of Everyday Life.* Berkeley: University of California Press, 1984.

Chen, David W. "Flag to Carry Sentiments from Ground Zero to Afghanistan." *New York Times,* November 26, 2001. Online: http://www.lexis-nexus.com/.

Clarke, Lee. *Mission Improbable: Using Fantasy Documents to Tame Disasters.* Chicago: University of Chicago Press, 1999.

Clinton, Bill. "A Time for Healing." Speech delivered on National Prayer Day Oklahoma City, OK, April 23, 1995. Online: http://clinton1.nara.gov/White_House/EOP/OP/html/okla.html/.

Colangelo, Lisa L. "Rudy Finds Plenty to Be Thankful For." *New York Daily News,* November 23, 2001. Online: http://www.lexis-nexus.com/.

Colford, Paul, D. "Hands Off 9/11 Cross." *New York Daily News,* April 12, 2006, Metro News section. Online: www.nydailynews.com/news/local/story/408093p-345464c .html.

Collins, Randall. "On the Micro-Foundations of Macro-Sociology." *American Journal of Sociology* 86 (1981) 984–1014.

———. *Interaction Ritual Chains.* Princeton Studies in Cultural Sociology. Princeton, NJ: Princeton University Press, 2005.

———. "Sociological Theory, Disaster Research, and War." In *Social Structure and Disaster,* edited by Gary A. Kreps, 365–85. Newark, DE: University of Delaware Press, 1989.

———. "Remains Thought to Be from Columbia Crew." Cable News Network, February 1, 2003. Online: http://www.cnn.com/2003/TECH/space/02/01/shuttle .columbia/.

Cox, Harvey. *The Secular City: Secularization and Urbanization in Theological Perspective.* Revised edition. New York: Macmillan, 1966.

Cox Miller, Patricia. "Visceral Seeing: The Holy Body in Late Ancient Christianity." *Journal of Early Christian Studies* 12 (2004) 391–411.

Daly, Michael. "His Words Still Heal Us." *New York Daily News,* September 16, 2001, News section, 18.

Derrida, Jacques. *Derrida.* DVD directed by Kirby Dick and Amy Ziering Kofman. New York: Zeitgeist Films, 2003.

Dewan, Shaila K. "Among the Poor, Sympathy for the Families of Sept. 11." *New York Times,* December 24, 2001. Online: http://www.lexis-nexus.com/.

Dewey, John. *Human Nature and Conduct.* Mineola, NY: Dover, 2002.

DiRenzo, Gordon. *Human Social Behavior: Concepts and Principles of Sociology.* Orlando, FL: Harcourt School Publishers, 1990.

Dombrowsky, Wolf. "Again and Again: Is a Disaster What We call a 'Disaster'?" In *What Is a Disaster? Perspectives on a Question,* edited by E. L. Quarantelli, 19–30. London: Routledge, 1998.

———. "The Social Dimensions of Warning and the Transition from Folk Wisdom to Laymanship." In *Prediction and Perception of Natural Hazards,* edited by Jaromír Ne[insert circumflex over first e]emec, et al., 241–62. Dordrecht: Kluwer Academic, 1993.

Doss, Erika. "Death, Art, and Memory in the Public Sphere: The Visual and Material Culture of Grief in Contemporary America." *Mortality* 7 (2002) 63–82.

Douglas, Mary. *How Institutions Think.* The Frank W. Abrams Lectures. Syracuse: Syracuse University Press, 1996.

Dowell, Sharon. "Red Cross, Salvation Army Workers Praised." *Oklahoman,* May 7, 1995, News section, 17.

Drabek, Thomas E. "Alternative Patterns of Decision-Making in Emergent Disaster Response Networks." *International Journal of Mass Emergency and Disaster* 1 (1983) 277–305.

———. *Emergency Management: Strategies for Maintaining Organizational Integrity.* New York: Springer-Verlag, 1990.

Dwyer, Jim, and Kevin Flynn. *102 Minutes: The Untold Story of the Fight to Survive Inside the Twin Towers.* New York: Times Books, 2005.

Dynes, Russell R. "The Dialogue between Rousseau and Voltaire on the Lisbon Earthquake: The Emergence of a Social Science View." *International Journal of Mass Emergency and Disaster* 18 (2000) 97–115.

———. "Noah and Disaster Planning: The Cultural Significance of the Flood Story." *Journal of Contingencies and Crisis Management* 11 (2003) 170–77.

———. "The Structure of Disaster Research: Its Policy and Disciplinary Implications." *International Journal of Mass Emergency and Disaster* 12 (1994) 5–23.

Eisenach, Eldon J. *The Next Religious Establishment: National Identity and Political Theology in Post-Protestant America.* American Intellectual Culture. Lanham, MD: Rowman and Littlefield, 2000.

El-Gobashy, Tamer. "Funeral Fulfills a Promise." *New York Daily News*, December 18, 2001. Online: http://www.lexis-nexus.com/.

———. "Tears, Cheers for Fireman Who Had a Heart of Gold." *New York Daily News*, November 27, 2001. Online: http://www.lexis-nexus.com/.

Engels, Mary, Bill Farrell, et al. "Hundreds Bid Farewell to Three of the Bravest." *Daily News*, November 7, 2001. Online: http://www.lexis-nexus.com/.

Erwin, Hank. "Alabama Legislator: Katrina Was God's Wrath on Sinful Coast." Associated Press, September 28, 2005.

Estabrook, Carl B. "Ritual, Space, and Authority in Seventeenth-Century English Cathedral Cities." *Journal of Interdisciplinary History* 32 (2002) 593–620.

Etzioni, Amitai and Jared Bloom, editors. *We Are What We Celebrate: Understanding Holidays and Rituals.* New York: New York University Press, 2004.

Evans, John H. "Public Vocabularies of Religious Belief: Explicit and Implicit Religious Discourse in the American Public Sphere." In *The Blackwell Companion to the Sociology of Culture*, edited by Mark D. Jacobs and Nancy Weiss Hanrahan, 474–95. Blackwell Companions to Sociology 12. Malden, MA: Blackwell, 2005.

Eyre, Anne. "In Remembrance: Post-Disaster Rituals and Symbols." *Australian Journal of Emergency Management* 14 (1999) 23–29.

———. "Remembering: Community Commemoration after Disaster." In *The Handbook of Disaster Research*, edited by Havidán Rodríguez et al., 441–55. Handbooks of Sociology and Social Research. New York: Springer, 2007.

Farrell, Bill, et al. "They Lived and Died Together." *New York Daily News*, November 6, 2001. Online: http://www.lexis-nexus.com/.

Fenn, Richard K. *Liturgies and Trials: The Secularization of Religious Language.* New York: Pilgrim, 1982.

———. *Time Exposure: The Personal Experience of Time in Secular Societies.* New York: Oxford University Press, 2001.

———. *Toward a Theory of Secularization.* Storrs, CT: Society for the Scientific Study of Religion, 1978.

Firestone, David. "Sunday of Muted Cheers and Renewed Fears." *New York Times*, October 8, 2001. Online: http://www.lexis-nexus.com/.

Fletcher, Laurel E., et al. "Latino Workers and Human Rights in the Aftermath of Hurri-cane Katrina." *Berkeley Journal of Employment and Labor Law* 28 (2008) 107–62.

Ford, David. *The Shape of Living: Spiritual Directions for Everyday Life.* Grand Rapids: Baker, 2004.

Forliti, Amy. "St. Louis Cathedral Holds Mass; Service First in New Orleans since Katrina Devastated City." *Baton Rouge Advocate*, October 3, 2005, News section, 1-A.

Foucault, Michel. *The Archaeology of Knowledge; and, the Discourse on Language.* New York: Pantheon, 1982.

———. *Security, Territory, Population: Lectures at the Colle*[insert grave accent over first e]*ge de France, 1977–1978.* Edited by Michel Sennelart, Translated by Graham Burchell. Lectures at the Collège de France. Hampshire, UK: Palgrave Macmillan, 2007.

Fowl, Stephen, and L. Gregory Jones. *Reading in Communion.* Eugene, OR: Wipf & Stock, 1998.

Fiorenza, Francis Schüssler. "The Church as a Community of Interpretation: Political Theology between Discourse Ethics and Hermeneutical Reconstruction." In *Habermas, Modernity, and Public Theology*, edited by Don S. Browning and Francis Schüssler Fiorenza, 66–92. New York: Crossroad, 1995.

Gamson, William, and David Meyer. "Framing Political Opportunity." In *Comparative Perspectives on Social Movements*, edited by Doug McAdam, et al., 275–90. Cambridge Studies in Comparative Politics. Cambridge: Cambridge University Press, 1996.

Gearty, Robert, et al. "Tearful Pay Last Respects." *New York Times*, September 23, 2001. Online: http://www.lexis-nexus.com/.

Gellner, Ernest. *Nations and Nationalism.* 2d edition. New Perspectives on the Past. Malden, MA: Blackwell, 2006.

Gest, Emily and Owen Moritz. "'Heaven Has a Heck of a Fire Department Now.'" *New York Daily News.* October 9, 2001. Online: http://www.lexis-nexus.com/.

Gilliland, Pat. "Chaplains Reunite, Reflect on Bombing." *Oklahoman*, July 9, 1995, News section, 20.

———. "Churches Not Eligible for U.S. Repair Funds." *Oklahoman*, June 11, 1995, News section, 1.

———. "Pastor Knows Damage Figure Too Low." *Oklahoman*, June 14, 1995, News section, 23.

———. "Reconciliation Program Set At Bomb Site." *Oklahoman*, June 30, 1995, News section, 14.

Girard, René. *I See Satain Fall Like Ligtening.* Translated with a foreword by James G. Williams. Leominster, UK: Gracewing, 2001.

Giuliani, Rudolph. "Giuliani Talks of City's Spirit, and a Grand Monument to Those Who Died." *New York Times*, December 28, 2001. Online: http://www.lexis-nexus.com/.

Glaser, Barney G., and Anselm Strauss. *Discovery of Grounded Theory: Strategies for Qualitative Research.* Observations. Chicago: Aldine, 1967.

Goodstein, Laurie. "As Attacks' Impact Recedes, A Return to Religion as Usual." *New York Times*, November 26, 2001. Online: http://www.lexis-nexus.com/.

———. "Falwell's Finger-Pointing Inappropriate, Bush Says." *New York Times*, September 15, 2001. Online: http://www.lexis-nexus.com/.

Gordon, Jane. "Parish Pulls Together to Mourn Its Own." *New York Times*, September 30, 2001. Online: http://www.lexis-nexus.com/.

Gorringe, Timothy. *A Theology of the Built Environment: Empowerment.* Cambridge: Cambridge University Press, 2002.

Green, Thomas F. *Voices: The Educational Formation of Conscience.* Notre Dame: University of Notre Dame Press, 1999.

Gupta, Akhil. "Blurred Boundaries: The Discourse of Corruption, the Culture of Politics, and the Imagined State." *American Ethnologist* 22 (1995) 375–402.

Gusfield, Joseph R. *Symbolic Crusade: Status Politics and the American Temperance Movement.* Urbana: University of Illinois Press, 1962.

Gyan, Joe, Jr. "Nagin: 'I'm Rowing Alone'; Frustrated Mayor Says Helping City Will Help Louisiana." *Baton Rouge Advocate*, October 14, 2005, News section, 1-A.

Habermas, Jürgen. *Reason and the Rationalization of Society.* Vol. 1 of *The Theory of Communicative Action.* Translated by Thomas McCarthy. Boston: Beacon, 1992.

———. *The Structural Transformation of the Public Sphere: An Inquiry into Bourgeois Society.* Translated by Thomas Burger with the assistance of Frederick Lawrence. Studies in Contemporary German Social Thought. Cambridge: MIT Press, 1989.

Halbwachs, Maurice. *On Collective Memory.* Edited, translated, with an introduction by Lewis A. Coser. The Heritage of Sociology. Chicago: University of Chicago Press, 1992.

Harris, Sam. *The End of Faith: Religion, Terror, and the Future of Reason.* New York: Norton, 2004.

Haas, Robin, and Owen Moritz. "Church Ruined, but Not Faith." *New York Times,* September 24, 2001. Online: http://www.lexis-nexus.com/.

Hamm, Mark S. *Apocalypse in Oklahoma: Waco and Ruby Ridge Revenged.* Boston: Northeastern University Press, 1997.

Hayes, Carleton Joseph Huntley. *Nationalism: A Religion.* New York: Macmillan, 1960.

Heisler, Bob. "20,000 Join Hands, Hearts at Stadium." *New York Daily News* September 24, 2001. Online: http://www.lexis-nexus.com/.

———. "Memorial at Stadium Joins All Faiths." *New York Daily News.* September 24, 2001. Online: http://www.lexis-nexus.com/.

Henaff, Marcel. "Religious Ethics, Gift Exchange and Capitalism." *European Journal of Sociology* 44 (2003) 293–324.

Henneberger, Melinda. "Cardinal, at Rome Synod, Reflects on New York and Sanctity." *New York Times*, October 11, 2001. Online: http://www.lexis-nexus.com/.

———. "Social Justice and Terror Offer Bishops Tough Issue." *New York Times*, October 28, 2001. Online: http://www.lexis-nexus.com/.

Herbert, Bob. "In America; The Right Answer." *New York Times,* September 20, 2001. Online: http://www.lexis-nexus.com/.

Hewitt, Kenneth. "Excluded Perspectives in the Social Construction of Disaster." *International Journal of Mass Emergencies and Disasters* 13 (1995) 317–39.

Hinton, Carla. "Bomb Survivor to Offer Voice in Music Tribute." *Oklahoman,* November 17, 1995, News section, 10.

"History and Mission." Oklahoma City National Memorial Official Web Site. Online: http://www.oklahomacitynationalmemorial.org/secondary.php?section=5&catid=114&id=155

Hobsbawm, Eric. "Introduction: Inventing Traditions." In *The Invention of Tradition*, edited by Eric Hobsbawm and Terence Ranger, 1–14. Past and Present Publications. Cambridge: Cambridge University Press, 1993.

Hovey, Craig. *To Share in the Body: A Theology of Martyrdom for Today's Church.* Grand Rapids: Brazos, 2008.

Huebner, Chris K. *A Precarious Peace: Yoderian Explorations on Theology, Knowledge, and Identity.* Scottdale, PA: Herald, 2006.

In Memory, in Faith, in Hope: The Archdiocesan September 11 Memorial Brochure. New York: Greek Orthodox Archdiocese of America, 2002.

Jackson, Richard. *Writing the War on Terrorism: Language, Politics, and Counter-Terrorism.* New Approaches to Conflict Analysis. New York: Manchester University Press, 2005.

Jacobs, Andrew. "Delivering the Gospel to Ground Zero's Streets." *New York Times,* October 18, 2001. Online: http://www.lexis-nexus.com/.

———. "In Morning Sky, Seamless Exit for Twin Beams." *New York Times,* April 15, 2002. Online: http://www.lexis-nexus.com/.

Jewett, Robert, and John Shelton Lawrence. *Captain America and the Crusade against Evil: The Dilemma of Zealous Nationalism.* Grand Rapids: Eerdmans, 2003.

Johnson, Norris. "Panic and the Breakdown of Social Order: Popular Myth, Social Theory, Empirical Evidence." *Sociological Focus* 20 (1987) 171–83,

Johnson, Norris, et al. "Microstructure and Panic: The Impact of Social Bonds on Individual Action in Collective Flight from the Beverly Hills Supper Club Fire." In *Disasters, Collective Behavior and Social Organization,* edited R. R. Dynes and K. Tierney, 168–89. Newark, DE: University of Delaware Press, 1994.

Jones, L. Gregory. *Embodying Forgiveness: A Theological Analysis.* Grand Rapids: Eerdmans, 1995.

Jordan, Lara Jakes. "Former FEMA Director Blames Others in Hurricane Response Failures." Associated Press, September 27, 2005. Online: http://agonist.org/story/2005/9/27/111253/362

Jorgensen-Earp, Cheryl R. "Public Memory and Private Grief: The Construction of Shrines at the Sites of Public Tragedy." *Quarterly Journal of Speech* 84 (1999) 150–70.

Kendra, James M., and Tricia Wachtendorf. "Elements of Resilience after the World Trade Center Disaster: Reconstituting New York City's Emergency Operations Center." *Disasters* 27 (2003) 37–53.

———. "The Evacuation of Lower Manhattan by Water Transport on September 11: An Unplanned 'Success.'" *The Joint Commission Journal on Quality and Safety* 29 (2003) 316–18.

Kierkegaard, Søren. "Early Journal Entries." In *The Essential Kierkegaard,* edited by Howard V. Hong and Edna H. Hong, 3–12. Princeton: Princeton University Press, 2000.

———. "The Lily in the Field and the Bird of the Air." In *The Essential Kierkegaard,* edited by Howard V. Hong and Edna H. Hong, 333–38. Princeton: Princeton University Press, 2000.

———. *Practice in Christianity.* Edited and translated with introduction and notes by Howard V. Hong and Edna H. Hong. Kierkegaard's Writings 20. Princeton: Princeton University Press, 1991.

———. "Two Discourses at the Communion on Fridays." In *The Essential Kierkegaard,* edited and translated by Howard V. Hong and Edna H. Hong, 385–92. Princeton, NJ: Princeton University Press, 2000. 391.

————. *Works of Love: Some Christian Reflections in the Form of Discourses*. Translated and edited by Howard V. Hong and Edna H. Hong. New York: Harper & Row, 1964.

Klaff, Vivian Z. "The Religious Demography of New York City." In *New York Glory: Religions in the City*, edited by Tony Carnes and Anna Karpathakis, 26–40. New York: New York University Press, 2001.

Klapp, Orrin Edgar. *Symbolic Leaders: Public Dramas and Public Men*. New York: Minerva, 1968.

Kosmin, Barry A., and Egon Mayer. *The American Religious Identification Survey*, 2001. New York: The Graduate Center of the City University of New York, 2001. Online: http://gc.cuny.edu/faculty/research_briefs/aris.pdf/.

Kosmin, Barry A., and Seymour P. Lachman. *One Nation Under God: Religion in Contemporary American Society*. New York: Harmony, 1993.

Kreps, Gary A. "The Organization of Disaster Response: Some Fundamental Theoretical Issues." In *Disasters: Theory and Research*, edited by E. L. Quarantelli, 64–71. Sage Studies in International Sociology 13. London: Sage, 1978.

Kreps, Gary A., and Thomas Drabek. "Disasters as Nonroutine Social Problems." *International Journal of Mass Emergencies and Disasters* 14 (1996) 129–53.

Kunzelman, Michael. "On Gulf Coast, faith-based goups pick up government's slack." AP, February 15, 2006. No Pages. Online: http://www.socialpolicyandreligion.org/news/article_print.cfm?id=3882.

Lackmeyer, Steve. "Terror Changes Lives of Initial Responders." *Oklahoman*, May 29, 1995, News section, 19.

Lane, Christel. *The Rites of Rulers: Ritual in Industrial Society: The Soviet Case*. Cambridge: Cambridge University Press, 1981.

LaPlante, John, and Gerard Shields. "Nagin: N. O. Should Get Most Aid Dedicated to Hurricane Recovery." *Baton Rouge Advocate*, September 16, 2005, News, 1-B, 2-B.

Lee, Orville. "Race after the Cultural Turn." In *The Blackwell Companion to the Sociology of Culture*, edited by Mark D. Jacobs and Nancy Weiss Hanrahan, 232–49. Blackwell Companions to Sociology 12. Malden, MA: Blackwell, 2005.

Leonard, Bill. "The Southern Crossroads: Religion and Demography." In *Religion and Public Life in the Southern Crossroads: The Showdown States*, edited by William Lindsey and Mark Silk, 27–53. Religion by Region 5. Walnut Creek, CA: AltaMira, 2005.

Levering, Matthew. *Ezra & Nehemiah*. Brazos Theological Commentary on the Bible. Grand Rapids: Brazos, 2007.

Lindbeck, George A. *The Nature of Doctrine: Religion and Theology in a Postliberal Age*. Louisville: Westminster John Knox, 1984.

Tierney, Kathleen J., et al. *Facing the Unexpected: Disaster Preparedness and Response in the United States*. Washington DC: Joseph Henry, 2001.

Linenthal, Edward T. *The Unfinished Bombing: Oklahoma City in American Memory*. New York: Oxford University Press, 2001.

Lockwood-O'Donovan, Joan. "A Timely Conversation with *The Desire of the Nations* on Civil Society, Nation, and State." In *Royal Priesthood?: The Use of the Bible Ethically and Politically: A Dialogue with Oliver O'Donovan*, edited by Craig Bartholomew, et al., 377–84. Scripture and Hermeneutics Series 3. Grand Rapids: Zondervan, 2002.

Lofland, John. "Interactionist Imagery and Analytic Interruptus." In *Human Nature and Collective Behavior: Essays in Honor of Herbert Blumer*, edited by Tomatsu Shibutani, 39–45. New Brunswick, NJ: Transaction, 1973.

Lofland, John, and Lyn H. Lofland. *Analyzing Social Settings: A Guide to Qualitative Observation and Analysis*. 3d edition. Belmont, CA: Wadsworth, 1995.

"Lost: Space Shuttle Columbia." Online: http://www.cnn.com/SPECIALS/2003/shuttle/.

Luhmann, Niklas. *Risk: A Sociological Theory*. Translated by Rhodes Barrett. New York: Aldine de Gruyter, 1993.

Maeder, Jay. "All Over City, Healing Sought through Prayer." *New York Times*, September 17, 2001. Online: http://www.lexis-nexus.com/.

Machiavelli, Niccolo. *The Prince, and Selected Discourses*. Translated with an introduction by Daniel Donno. Bantam Classics. New York: Bantam 1984.

MacIntyre, Alasdair. *Dependent Rational Animals: Why Human Beings Need the Virtues*. The Paul Carus Lecture Series. Chicago: Open Court, 1999.

Marsden, George M. *Understanding Fundamentalism and Evangelicalism*. Grand Rapids: Eerdmans, 1991.

Martin, Stacy. "Historical Society Worries about Explosion Damage." *Oklahoman*, May 7,1995, Business and Real Estate section, 1

Marvin, Carolyn, and David Ingle. *Blood Sacrifice and the Nation: Totem Rituals and the American Flag*. Cambridge Cultural Social Studies. Cambridge: Cambridge University Press, 1999.

McAdam, Doug. "Conceptual Origins, Current Problems, Future Directions." In *Comparative Perspectives on Social Movements*, edited by Doug McAdam et al., 23–40. Cambridge Studies in Comparative Politics. Cambridge: Cambridge University Press, 1996.

McFadden, Robert D. "In a Stadium of Heroes, Prayers for the Fallen and Solace for Those Left Behind." *New York Times*, September 24, 2001. Online: http://www.lexis-nexus.com/.

McReynolds, J. E. "Post-Bomb Murmurs: Enough's Enough." *Oklahoman*, June 25,1995, Editorial section, 10.

Meacham, Jon. *American Gospel: God, the Founding Fathers, and the Making of a Nation*. New York: Random House, 2006.

Milbank, John. "Socialism by Grace." In *Being Reconciled: Ontology and Pardon*, 162–87. Radical Orthodoxy Series. London: Routledge, 2003.

———. *Theology and Social Theory: Beyond Secular Reason*. 2d edition. Oxford: Blackwell, 2006.

———. *The Word Made Strange: Theology, Language, Culture*. Cambridge, MA: Blackwell, 1997.

Mileti, Dennis, with the contributions of the Participants in the Assessment of Research and Applications on Natural Hazards. *Disasters by Design: A Reassessment of Natural Hazards in the United States*. Natural Hazards and Disasters. Washington DC: Joseph Henry, 1999.

Money, Jack. "Expert Urges Rescue of Historic Buildings, Sites Bomb Toll Put at $13.7 Million." *Oklahoman,* June 5, 1995, News section, 1.

Murphy, Dean E. "A Nation Challenged: Farewells; Rites for Victims Resonate across Metro-politan Area." *New York Times*, September 30, 2001. Online: http://query.nytimes.com/gst/fullpage.html?res=9B03E7D9143DF933A0575AC0A9679C8B63.

Myers, Ched. *Binding the Strong Man: A Political Reading of Mark's Story of Jesus.* Maryknoll, NY: Orbis, 1988.

Neal, Arthur. *National Trauma and Collective Memory: Major Events in the American Century.* Armonk, NY: Sharpe, 1998.

Neocleous, Mark. *Imagining the State.* Maidenhead, UK: Open University Press, 2003.

Neiman, Susan. *Evil in Modern Thought: An Alternative History of Philosophy.* Princeton: Princeton University Press. 2002.

New York and New Jersey Port Authority. Ground-Zero Fence Panels. Text copied February 2006.

Nicholls, David. *God and Government in an "Age of Reason."* London: Routledge, 1995.

Niebhur, Gustav. "At Houses of Worship, Feelings Are Shared and Comfort Is Sought in Greater Numbers." *New York Times,* September 17, 2001. Online: http://www.lexis-nexus.com/.

———. "Excerpts from Sermons across the Nation." *New York Times,* September 17, 2001. Online: http://www.lexis-nexus.com/.

———. "Falwell Apologizes for Saying an Angry God Allowed Attacks." *New York Times,* September 18, 2001. Online: http://www.lexis-nexus.com/.

Nigg, Joanne. "Social Action and Social Order in Disaster Research." In *Social Structure and Disaster,* edited by Gary A. Kreps, 389-93. Newark, DE: University of Delaware Press, 1989.

Nolan, Bruce. "Pastors Pray for Spiritual Rebirth—Many say Katrina Was God's Judgment." *New Orleans Times-Picayune,* February 18, 2006, D1.

Noll, Mark A. *The Scandal of the Evangelical Mind.* Grand Rapids: Eerdmans,1994.

Nossiter, Adam. "New Start for Familiar Face: Clarence Ray Nagin." *New York Times,* May 22, 2006. Online: http://www.nytimes.com/2006/05/22/us/22nagin.html/.

O'Donovan, Oliver. *Resurrection and Moral Order: AN Outline for Evangelical Ethics.* Grand Rapids: Eerdmans, 1986.

Oklahoma Department of Civil Emergency Management. *After Action Report: Alfred P. Murrah Federal Building Bombing: 19 April 1995.* Oklahoma City: Oklahoma Department of Civil Emergency Management,1996.

Oklahoma Department of Corrections. "Execution Statistics." Online: http://www.doc.state.ok.us/offenders/deathrow.htm.

Oliver-Smith, Anthony. "The Brotherhood of Pain: Theoretical and Applied Perspectives on Post-Disaster Solidarity." In *The Angry Earth,* edited by Anthony Oliver-Smith and Susannah M. Hoffman, 156–72. New York: Routledge, 1999.

O'Sullivan, John. "Muslims in U.S. Should Proclaim Loyalty." *Chicago Sun-Times,* October 24, 2001. Online: http://www.lexis-nexus.com/.

Patte, Daniel. *What Is Structural Exegesis?* Guides to Biblical Scholarship: New Testament Series. Philadelphia: Fortress, 1976.

Perez-Rivas, Manuel. "Bush Vows to Rid the World of 'Evil-Doers.'" September 16, 2001. Online: http://archives.cnn.com/2001/US/09/16/gen.bush.terrorism/.

Perry, John. "Leaders See Effort Enduring." *Oklahoman,* June 2, 1995, Community III section, 1.

———. "Task Force Makes Initial Tribute Plans." *Oklahoman,* July 27, 1995, News section, 12.

Pickstock, Catherine. "Liturgy and Modernity." *Telos* 113 (1998) 19–40.

Pinches, Charles. "Stout, Hauerwas, and the Body of America." *Political Theology* 8 (2007) 9–31.

Pleck, Elizabeth H. "Who Are We and Where Do We Come From? Rituals, Families, and Identities." In W*e Are What We Celebrate: Understanding Holidays and Rituals*, edited by Amitai Etzioni and Jared Bloom, 43–60. New York: New York University Press, 2005.

Plumberg, Diane. "Workers Pay Respects at Ruins—Applause, Tears Mix at Ceremony." *Oklahoman*, May 6, 1995, News section, 1.

Poggi, Gianfranco. *The Development of the Modern State: A Sociological Introduction.* Stanford: Stanford University Press, 1978.

Polletta, Francesca. "Culture Is Not in Your Head." In *Rethinking Social Movements: Structure, Meaning, and Emotion,* edited by Jeff Goodwin and James M. Jasper, 97–110. People, Passions, and Power. Lanham, MD: Rowman and Littlefield, 2004.

Porfiriev, Boris N. "Issues in the Definition and Delineation of Disasters and Disaster Areas." In *What Is a Disaster? Perspectives on a Question,* edited by E. L. Quarantelli, 56–72. London: Routledge, 1998.

Post, R. L. Grimes, et al., editors. *Disaster Ritual: Explorations of an Emerging Ritual Repertoire.* Liturgia Condenda 15. Leuven, Belgium: Peeters, 2003.

Prayer Card at Heartland Chapel. "A Prayer for America." Collected December 2005 at site.

Prescott, Theodore. "We See Jesus?" Artist of the Month. Special issue, "Art, Faith, Mystery," *Image: A Journal of the Arts and Religion* 10 (1995) 68.

Procter, David E. "Victorian Days: Performing Community through Local Festival." In *We Are What We Celebrate: Understanding Holidays and Rituals,* edited by Amitai Etzioni and Jared Bloom, 131–49. New York: New York University Press, 2005.

Protevi, John. "Thomas Confuses Two Aspects of Katrina." Readers' Views. *Baton Rouge Advocate*, October 14, 2005, News section, Metro edition, 10-B; S.

Prothero, Stephen. *American Jesus: How the Son of God Became a National Icon.* New York: Farrar, Strauss, Giroux, 2003.

Quarantelli, E. L. "The Behavior of Panic Participants." *Sociology and Social Research* 41 (1957) 187–94.

———. "The Disaster Recovery Process: What We Know and Do Not Know from Research." Disaster Research Center: Preliminary Paper #286. Online: http://dspace.udel.edu:8080/dspace/handle/19716/309/.

Redmond, Sean, and Su Holmes. *Stardom and Celebrity: A Reader.* Thousand Oaks, CA: Sage, 2007.

Robbins, M. C., and J. M. Nolan. "A Measure of Dichotomous Category Bias in Free Listing Tasks" *Cultural Anthropology Methods Journal* 9 (1997) 8–12.

Rogers, Eugene, Jr. *After the Spirit: A Constructive Pneumatology from Resources Outside the West.* Radical Traditions. Grand Rapids: Eerdmans, 2005.

Rosenberg, Merri. "Faith, Tested and Abiding." *New York Times*, November 18, 2001. Online: http://www.lexis-nexus.com/.

Rubin, Herbert J., and Irene S. Rubin. *Qualitative Interviewing: The Art of Hearing Data.* Thousand Oaks, CA: Sage, 1995.

Ryan, G., and H. R. Bernard. "Data Management and Analysis Methods." In *Handbook of Qualitative Research,* edited by Norman Denzin and Yvonne Lincoln, 769–802. 2d edition. Thousand Oaks, CA: Sage, 2000.

Sack, Kevin. "Apocalyptic Theology Revitalized by Attacks." *New York Times*, November 23, 2001. Online: http://www.lexis-nexis.com/.

Santos, Gabriel. Focus-group interview of Participants *C3* and *C4*. Digital recording. Oklahoma City, OK.

———. Focus-group interview of Participants *J3, J4,* and *J5*. Digital recording. New York, NY. February 26, 2006.

———. Interview of Participant *A2*. Transcript. Oklahoma City, OK. December 10, 2005.

———. Interview of Participant *A3*. Transcript. Oklahoma City, OK. December 8, 2005.

———. Interview of Participant *B1*. Digital recording. Oklahoma City, OK. December 8, 2005.

———. Interview of Participant *B2*. Digital recording. Oklahoma City, OK. January 18, 2006.

———. Interview of Participant *B3*. Digital recording. Oklahoma City, OK. December 8, 2005.

———. Interview of Participant *C1*. Digital recording. Oklahoma City, OK. January 25, 2006.

December 10, 2005.

———. Interview of Participant *F1*. Digital recording. New York, NY. February 27, 2006.

———. Interview of Participant *G1*. Transcript. New York, NY. March 5, 2006.

———. Interview of Participant *H1*. Transcript. New York, NY. March 3, 2006.

———. Interview of Participant *H2*. Transcript. New York, NY. February 25, 2006.

———. Interview of Participant *H3*. Transcript. New York, NY. February 24, 2006.

———. Interview of Participant *L1*. Digital recording. New Orleans, LA. January 9, 2008.

———. Interview of Participant *L2*. Digital recording. New Orleans, LA. January 8, 2008.

———. Interview of Participant *L3*. Transcript. New Orleans, LA. January 8, 2008.

———. Interview of Participant *M1*. Digital recording. New Orleans, LA. January 8, 2008.

———. Interview of Participant *M2*. Digital recording. New Orleans, LA. January 10, 2008.

———. First Interview of Participant *M4*. Digital recording. New Orleans, LA. January 7, 2008.

———. Second Interview of Participant *M4*. Transcript. New Orleans, LA. January 10, 2008.

———. Interview of Participant *N1*. Transcript. Richmond, VA. January 25, 2008.

———. Interview of Participant *O1*. Digital recording. New Orleans, LA. January 13, 2008.

———. Interview of Participant *P1*. Digital recording. New Orleans, LA. January 9, 2008.

Santos, Gabriel, and Richard Buck. Interview of Respondent 6. Electronic transcript. Edison, NJ. November 14, 2004.

Schmemann, Alexander. *Of Water and the Spirit: A Liturgical Study of Baptism*. Crestwood, NY: St. Vladimir's Seminary Press, 1974.

Scott, James C. *Seeing Like a State: How Certain Schemes to Improve the Human Condition Have Failed.* Yale Agrarian Studies. The Yale ISPS Series. New Haven: Yale University Press, 1998.

Sewell, William H., Jr. "A Theory of Structure: Duality, Agency, and Transformation" *American Journal of Sociology* 98 (1992) 1–29.

Shelby, Joyce, and Brian Kates. "'God Called for Heroes to Rise Above Terror.'" *New York Daily News*, October 7, 2001. Online: http://www.lexis-nexus.com/.

Shilling, Chris. *The Body and Social Theory.* 2d edition. Theory, Culture & Society. London: Sage, 2003.

———. *Changing Bodies: Habit, Crisis, and Creativity.* Thousand Oaks, CA: Sage, 2008.

"A Shout-Out for Churches." *Baton Rouge Advocate*, October 10, 2005. Online: http://www.lexis-nexus.com/.

Smith, J. J., and Stephen Borate. "Salience Counts and So Does Accuracy: Correcting and Updating a Measure for Free-List-Item Salience." *Journal of Linguistic Anthropology* 7 (1998) 208–9.

Smith, Oran P. *The Rise of Baptist Republicanism.* New York: New York University Press, 1997.

Sothern, Billy, with photographs by Nikki Page. *Down in New Orleans: Reflections from a Drowned City.* Berkeley: University of California Press, 2007.

Spielman, Fran. "'Our Family Is Suffering.'" *Chicago Sun-Times*, October 13, 2001. Online: http://www.lexis-nexus.com/.

Stallings, Robert. "Disasters as Social Problems? A Dissenting View" *International Journal of Mass Emergencies and Disasters* 9 (1991) 90–95.

———. "Disaster and the Theory of Social Order." In *What Is a Disaster? Perspectives on a Question*, edited by E. L. Quarantelli, 127–45. London: Routledge, 1998.

———. *Promoting Risk: Constructing the Earthquake Threat.* New York: Aldine de Gruyter, 1995.

Steinberg, Ted. *Acts of God: The Unnatural History of Natural Disaster in America.* New York: Oxford University Press, 2002

———. "Disasters and Deregulation." *Chronicle of Higher Education* 46 (2006) 62.

Steinberger, Peter J. *The Idea of the State.* Contemporary Political Theory. Cambridge: Cambridge University Press, 2004.

Steinhauer, Jennifer. "Giuliani Reports Sharp Increase in the Number of Those Listed as Missing." *New York Times*, September 21, 2001. Online: http://www.lexis-nexus.com/.

———. "Giuliani Takes Charge, and City Sees Him as the Essential Man." *New York Times*, September 14, 2001. Online: http://www.lexis-nexus.com/.

Tanner, Kathryn. *Theories of Culture: A New Agenda for Theology.* Guides to Theological Inquiry. Minneapolis: Fortress, 2002.

Taussig, Michael. *The Nervous System.* New York: Routledge, 1992.

Taylor, Charles. *Modern Social Imaginaries.* Public Planet Books. Durham, NC: Duke University Press, 2004.

Taylor, William. "Storms to Heavily Influence Jewish High Holy Days; B. R. Churches Open Buildings to Displaced Rabbis, Congregations." *Baton Rouge Advocate*, October 1, 2005, Church section, 1-F

Till, Karen E. *The New Berlin: Memory, Politics, Place.* Minneapolis: University of Minnesota Press, 2005.

Tilly, Charles. *Stories, Identities, and Political Change*. Lanham, MD: Rowman and Littlefield, 2002.

Trinity Design Group. "Out of the Dust: A Year of Ministry at Ground Zero . . .The Timeline." Shown as part of the exhibition "Out of the Dust: A Year of Ministry at Ground Zero" at St. Paul's Chapel, New York City.

Troutt, David Dante. "Many Thousands Gone, Again." In *After the Storm: Black Intellectuals Explore the Meaning of Hurricane* Katrina, edited by David Dante Troutt, 13–20. New York: New Press, 2006.

Turner, Bryan S. *The Body and Society: Explorations in Social Theory*, 2008.

Turner, Ralph H. "Integrative Beliefs in Group Crises." *Journal of Conflict Resolution* 16 (1972) 25–40.

Turner, Victor. *The Forest of Symbols: Aspects of Ndembu Ritual*. Ithaca, NY: Cornell University Press, 1967.

Unger, Roberto Mangabeira. *Law in Modern Society: Toward a Criticism of Social Theory*. New York: Free Press, 1976.

United States Bureau of the Census. *State and County Quick Facts: New York City*, 2003. Online: http://quickfacts.census.gov/qfd/states/36/3651000.html/.

United States Court of Appeals, Tenth Circuit. *Donald A. Fleming et al. v. Jefferson City School District*. No. 01-1512 (2002). Online: http://ca10.washburnlaw.edu/cases/2002/06/01-1512.htm/.

United States. Department of Housing and Urban Development. Office of Community Planning and Development. *Oklahoma City, OK Consolidated Plan for* 1995. Executive Summary. Online: http://www.hud.gov/library/bookshelf12/plan/ok/okcityok.html/.

Van den Hoonard, Will C. *Working with Sensitizing Concepts: Analytical Field Research*. Qualitative Research Methods 41. Thousand Oaks, CA: Sage, 1997.

Vanier, Jean. *Befriending the Stranger*. Grand Rapids: Eerdmans, 2005.

Wakin, Daniel J. "At Edge of Ground Zero, Gospel and Giving." *New York Times*, December 1, 2001. Online: http://www.lexis-nexus.com/.

———. "Attacks Spur a Surge of Interest in Religion: As Attendance at Services Rises, Clerics Hope for a General Moral Uplift." *New York Times*, September 30, 2001. Online: http://www.lexis-nexus.com/.

Waldman, Amy. "Changed Lives: Religious Leader Takes His Calling to Ground Zero." *New York Times*, September 20, 2001. Online: http://www.lexis-nexus.com/.

———. "Grief is Lessened by Sharing and Solace from Strangers." *New York Times*, September 14, 2001. Online: http://www.lexis-nexus.com/.

Waldstreicher, David. *In the Midst of Perpetual Fetes: The Making of American Nationalism*. Chapel Hill: University of North Carolina Press, 1997.

Wannenwetsch, Bernd. "The Political Worship of the Church. A Critical and Empowering Practice," *Modern Theology* 12 (1996) 269–99.

———. "'Ruled by the Spirit': Hans Ulrich's Understanding of Political Existence." *Studies in Christian Ethics* 20 (2007) 257–72.

Ward, Graham. *Cultural Transformation and Religious Practice*. Cambridge: Cambridge University Press, 2005.

Warner, R. Stephen. "The Place of the Congregation in the American Religious Configuration." In *New Perspectives in the Study of Congregations*, 54–99. Vol. 2 of *American Congregations*. Edited by James P. Wind and James W. Lewis. Chicago: University of Chicago Press, 1994.

"Weary Nation Turns to God." *Oklahoman,* May 5, 1995, News section, 7.

Webb, Gary R., et al. "Bringing Culture Back In: Exploring the Cultural Dimensions of Disaster." *International Journal of Mass Emergencies and Disasters* 18 (2000) 5–19.

Weber, Max. *The Protestant Ethic and the Spirit of Capitalism.* Mineola, NY: Dover, 2003.

Weil, Jennifer. "Ferrer Has Faith in Clergy Office." *New York Daily News,* December 18, 2001. Online: http://www.lexis-nexus.com/.

Weil, Simone. *Waiting for God.* Translated by Emma Craufurd. New York: Harper & Row, 1973.

White, John Valery. "The Persistence of Race Politics." In *After the Storm: Black Intellectuals Explore the Meaning of Hurricane Katrina,* edited by David Dante Troutt, 41–62. New York: New Press, 2006.

Whitmire, Tim. "Nagin Says Mayors Must Urge Feds to Ramp Up Disaster Response." Associated Press, December 9, 2005.

Wilkerson, Isabel. "Scattered in a Storm's Wake and Caught in a Clash of Cultures." *New York Times,* October 9, 2005, National Desk; special section, "In a Strange Land: From New Orleans to Sallisaw," 1. Online: http://www.nytimes.com/2005/10/09/national/nationalspecial/09Refugee.html?_r=1&scp=2&sq=Wilkerson,%20Isabel&st=cse&oref=slogin/.

Williams, Joe. "Reflect on Reasons U.S. Is Hated, Egan Urges Americans." *New York Daily News,* October 2, 2001. Online: http://www.lexis-nexus.com/.

Williams, Robin M. *American Society: A Sociological Interpretation.* 2d revised edition. New York: Knopf, 1960.

Wills, David W. *Christianity in the United States: A Historical Survey and Interpretation.* Notre Dame: University of Notre Dame Press, 2005.

Wilson, Bryan. *Religion in Sociological Perspective.* Oxford: Oxford University Press. 1982.

Wirzba, Norman. *Living the Sabbath: Discovering the Rhythms of Rest and Delight.* The Christian Practice of Everyday Life. Grand Rapids: Brazos, 2006.

Wittgenstein, Ludwig. *Philosophical Investigations.* 2nd edition. Edited by Rush Rhees et al. Translated by G. E. M. Anscombe. Oxford: Blackwell, 1958.

Wolfe, Alan. *The Transformation of American Religion: How We Actually Live Our Faith.* New York: Free Press, 2003.

Woodhead, Linda, and Paul Heelas. "Religions of Difference." In *Religion in Modern Times: An Interpretive Anthology,* edited by Linda Woodhead and Paul Heelas, 27–33. Religion and Modernity. Malden, MA: Blackwell, 2000.

Wright, Nicholas T. *The Last Word: Beyond the Bible Wars to a New Understanding of the Authority of Scripture.* San Francisco: HarperSanFrancisco, 2005.

———. *Jesus and the Victory of God.* Christian Origins and the Question of God 2. Minneapolis: Fortress, 1997.

———. *The New Testament and the People of God.* Christian Origins and the Question of God 1. Minneapolis: Fortress, 1996.

Wright, Stuart A. *Patriots, Politics, and the Oklahoma City Bombing.* Cambridge Studies in Contentious Politics. Cambridge: Cambridge University Press, 2007.

Wuthnow, Robert. *American Mythos: Why Our Best Efforts to Be A Better Nation Fall Short.* Princeton: Princeton University Press, 2006.

————. "Democratic Renewal and Cultural Inertia: Why Our Best Efforts Fall Short." *Sociological Forum* 20 (2005) 343–67.

————. *Meaning and Moral Order: Explorations in Cultural Analysis.* Berkeley: University of California Press, 1987.

————. *Producing the Sacred: An Essay on Public Religion.* Public Expressions of Religion in America. Urbana: University of Illinois Press, 1994.

————. *Rediscovering the Sacred: Perspectives on Religion in American Society.* Grand Rapids: Eerdmans, 1992.

Yoder, John Howard. *The Priestly Kingdom: Social Ethics as Gospel.* Notre Dame: University of Notre Dame Press, 1985.

Young, Frances M. *Brokenness and Blessing: Towards a Biblical Spirituality.* Grand Rapids: Baker Academic, 2007.

www.ingramcontent.com/pod-product-compliance
Lightning Source LLC
Chambersburg PA
CBHW030837300326
41935CB00037B/438